In Our Own Words

In Our Own Words

Writings From Women's Lives

SECOND EDITION

Mary Crawford
University of Connecticut

Rhoda Unger
Brandeis University

Boston   Burr Ridge, IL   Dubuque, IA   Madison, WI   New York   San Francisco   St. Louis
Bangkok   Bogotá   Caracas   Lisbon   London   Madrid
Mexico City   Milan   New Delhi   Seoul   Singapore   Sydney   Taipei   Toronto

McGraw-Hill Higher Education

A Division of The **McGraw-Hill** Companies

IN OUR OWN WORDS: WRITINGS FROM WOMEN'S LIVES
SECOND EDITION

Published by McGraw-Hill, an imprint of The McGraw-Hill Companies, Inc., 1221 Avenue of the Americas, New York, NY 10020. Copyright © 2001, 1997 by The McGraw-Hill Companies, Inc. All rights reserved. No part of this publication may be reproduced or distributed in any form or by any means, or stored in a database or retrieval system, without the prior written consent of The McGraw-Hill Companies, Inc., including, but not limited to, in any network or other electronic storage or transmission, or broadcast for distance learning.

Some ancillaries, including electronic and print components, may not be available to customers outside the United States.

This book is printed on acid-free paper.

1 2 3 4 5 6 7 8 9 0 QPF/QPF 0 9 8 7 6 5 4 3 2 1 0

ISBN 0-07-237693-7

Vice president and editor-in-chief: *Thalia Dorwick*
Editorial director: *Jane E. Vaicunas*
Sponsoring editor: *Beth Kaufman*
Developmental editor: *Theresa Wise*
Marketing manager: *Daniel M. Loch*
Project manager: *Sheila M. Frank*
Production supervisor: *Enboge Chong*
Freelance design coordinator: *Michelle M. Meerdink*
Designer: *Joshua Van Drake*
Compositor: *Carlisle Communications, Ltd.*
Typeface: *10/12 Palatino*
Printer: *Quebecor Printing Book Group/Fairfield, PA*

The credits section for this book begins on page 322 and is considered an extension of the copyright page.

Library of Congress Cataloging-in-Publication Data
In our own words : writings from women's lives / [selected by] Mary Crawford,
Rhoda Unger.—2nd ed.
   p.   cm.
   ISBN 0-07-237693-7
   1. Women—United States. 2. Sex role—United States. 3. Women—Psychology.
4. Feminist psychology. I. Crawford, Mary (Mary E.) II. Unger, Rhoda Kesler.
HQ1421 .I5   2001
305.4'0973—dc21
                                                              00-056861
                                                              CIP

www.mhhe.com

For Our Mothers and Their Stories

About the Editors

MARY CRAWFORD is Professor of Psychology and Director of the Women's Studies Program at the University of Connecticut. She has taught the psychology of women and gender for twenty-five years, most of that time at West Chester University of Pennsylvania, where she earned the Trustees' Achievement Award for lifetime professional accomplishment. She has also held the Jane W. Irwin Chair in Women's Studies at Hamilton College, served as Distinguished Visiting Teacher-Scholar at the College of New Jersey, and directed the graduate program in women's studies at the University of South Carolina. Professor Crawford received her Ph.D. in experimental psychology from the University of Delaware. She is a consulting editor of *Psychology of Women Quarterly*, an associate editor of *Feminism and Psychology*, and a Fellow of both the American Psychological Society and the American Psychological Association. Mary Crawford has spoken and written about women's issues for audiences as diverse as the British Psychological Society, *Ms.* Magazine, and the Oprah Winfrey show. Works she has authored or edited include *Gender and Thought: Psychological Perspectives* (1989); *Talking Difference: On Gender and Language* (1995); *Gender Differences in Human Cognition* (1997); *In Our Own Words* (1997); *Coming Into Her Own: Education Successes in Girls and Women* (1999); and a special double issue of *Psychology of Women Quarterly* (1999) on innovative methods for feminist research.

RHODA UNGER is Professor Emerita of Psychology at Montclair State University and Resident Scholar in Women's Studies at Brandeis University. She received her Ph.D. in experimental psychology from Harvard University. Professor Unger was the first recipient of the Carolyn Wood Sherif Award from the Division on the Psychology of Women of the American Psychological Association. She is also the recipient of two distinguished publication awards and a distinguished career award from the Association for Women in Psychology. She has been the president of the Division of the Psychology of Women and, more recently, president of the Society for the Psychological Study of Social Issues. She has lectured extensively in the United States and abroad as a Fulbright scholar in Israel, a distinguished lecturer at the University of British Columbia, and as a visiting fellow of the British Psychological Society. She is currently the book review editor of the international journal *Feminism and Psychology* and is editing a handbook on psychology and gender. Professor Unger is the author or editor of seven previous books, including *Resisting Gender: Twenty-five Years of Feminist Psychology; Representations: Social Constructions of Gender; Women, Gender, and Social Psychology;* and *Female and Male*.

Contents

Part Three
MAKING MEANING 147

Part Four
MAKING A LIVING: WOMEN, WORK, AND ACHIEVEMENT 217

Part Five
MAKING A DIFFERENCE 271

Preface

Put a group of women together, and what do they do? They talk to each other, telling stories of their own and others' troubles, foibles, victories, revelations, and changes. Researchers have documented that women's friendships are organized around talk, and much of that talk involves stories about each other's lives. It's not surprising then that in my twenty-five years of teaching I have noticed that when students first begin to learn about the psychology of women and gender, they make sense of it by looking for stories that capture the realities of living in a gendered world. They want to learn about people, and they want to hear the individual voices of girls and women. They seek narrative, unique accounts that capture shared experiences. By listening to the viewpoints of others, students interpret and make meaning of their own experiences.

Students want models of resistance and rebellion, and evidence of social change for the better, to balance the depressing information on prejudice and discrimination that is part of most courses on women and gender. To be sure, statistics about violence against women, the wage gap, and other social issues provide important documentation of sexism, and experimental studies of attributions and stereotypes reveal the workings of gender under the laboratory lens. But such research may also lead to feelings of helplessness. Indeed, we do still live in a sexist world. But that is only part of the picture.

Another limitation of course materials on women and gender is that psychological research historically has oversampled white people, middle-class people, college students, and males. For women and people of color of all ages and social classes, finding those who are like oneself represented in the theories and empirical research of psychology has not been easy.

Filling these gaps intuitively, students often seek out women's stories on their own. Many teachers have noticed that courses in the psychology of women and gender stimulate students to seek out the voices and words of women. And they want to share what they find with other students and with their teacher. By the end of the second week of class, the contributions start coming in. A student shares a "Cathy" cartoon strip. Another brings in a biography of Margaret Mead.

A third offers her copy of a feminist detective novel, and a fourth her favorite Marge Piercy poem. They want to know what their classmates and teacher think of these counternarratives, these idiosyncratic visions of women's lives.

In this collection, we attempt to meet students' needs for women's stories. The women who have written these essays differ in age, sexual orientation, social class, race/ethnicity, sensibility, and opinion. In choosing new readings, we have been mindful of the need to teach critical thinking about women and gender. When students read the accounts in this collection, their ability to think critically about psychological knowledge grows. Seeing an old issue from a new perspective is perhaps one of the great moments in learning, a moment that can be brought about through the unique stories of the diverse women in this anthology.

We offer *In Our Own Words*, then, to share with a new generation our belief that psychology is about very real, very human issues; to demonstrate concretely that women are a diverse group with many divergent viewpoints and experiences; and to help students learn to think critically about psychological research and women's lives. To that end, we have drawn on the richness and diversity of women's own voices as they tell about their lives.

New to This Edition

The selections for the first edition were chosen after extensive classroom testing and evaluation. When it came time to prepare a new edition, we again relied on the judgments of students and teachers who had used the book in their courses over a period of several years, as well as our own experiences with using *In Our Own Words* in the classroom. Most of the selections were "hits": student and teacher favorites. However, it became clear that some of the works had dated, and that there was a need for more ethnic and cultural diversity as well as for more voices of activism and optimism. This new and greatly improved edition now includes

- 15 **new** writings and 26 student and teacher favorites
- More ethnic, diverse, and multicultural voices throughout
- A new section, *Making a Difference*, featuring activist voices that show the past impact and future potential of the global women's movement

Several years' experience teaching from the first edition of *In Our Own Words* led to another major change: more built-in aids for teachers. Like the first edition, this one groups articles into topical sections, with a thought-provoking introduction linking the articles within each section. New to this edition is an individual introduction to each of the 41 writings. These brief but cogent introductions set the articles in context, providing background information on the authors and the issues. Most important, each essay's introduction ends with three or more questions to guide the student's reading.

Organization of This Book

The selections in this book are grouped into five sections that reflect our perspective on gender as a social construction. Part I, *Making Our Voices Heard*, recounts the experiences of women who have faced discrimination on the basis of class, gender, or ethnicity. Part II, *The Making of a Woman: Bodies, Power, and Society,* explores women's understanding of the cultural meanings of the female body. In Part III, *Making Meaning,* women create their own reconstructions of meanings on issues as varied as sexuality and the SAT. Part IV, *Making A Living: Women, Work, and Achievement,* provides the accounts of diverse women in the work force. Finally, Part V, *Making A Difference,* illustrates the power of women's social activism.

Each part is introduced by a short essay that shapes an approach to critical reading of the individual selections, inviting the student reader to engage in dialogue with each author, to compare the divergent viewpoints of the various authors, and to think critically about the implications of their views. A brief *Afterword* invites reflection on how the differences in women's lives are shaped by social class, sexual orientation, race/ethnicity, and age cohort.

Using This Book

In selecting and grouping the narratives for *In Our Own Words,* our goal was to provide a varied collection centered around the main conceptual issues usually addressed in courses on women and gender. Therefore, we chose the five general themes described above, rather than tying the topics to any particular textbook's organization. The collection can stand on its own or be used as a flexible adjunct to any current textbook on women and gender. In writing our own text (*Women and Gender: A Feminist Psychology,* 3rd edition, 2000), we tried to give voice to the experiences and thoughts of individual women as well as to synthesize feminist research. We use *In Our Own Words* in conjunction with our text, and we hope that other instructors who have adopted *Women and Gender* will find *In Our Own Words* a valuable and engaging addition to their syllabus. We also expect that it will find a place in introductory women's studies, introductory psychology, sociology of gender, and counseling, personality, developmental and multicultural psychology courses.

Because the readings and section introductions are quite short, each section can be assigned as a unit. A section of readings might be used to complement or to replace a textbook chapter. Alternatively, selections can be assigned individually or in groupings different from ours. Most can be read in conjunction with several of the topics commonly addressed in courses on women and gender. Because each selection has its own introduction that sets its authors and issues in context, each can be assigned as the basis for a reaction paper or class discussion. This is an anthology of wonderfully unique voices; the organization we have imposed is, in a sense, arbitrary. Each author's voice can stand on its own.

Thanks are due to many users of the first edition who provided constructive comments and suggestions for fine-tuning the new edition. Thorough and very helpful reviews of the first edition were provided by Joyce Carbonell—Florida State University, Susan Franzblau—Fayetteville State University, Susan Hippensteele—University of Hawaii, Cheryl Ann Sexton—Kalamazoo College, and Melissa Schuman Zarin—Hunter College of the City University of New York. We also thank our editors at McGraw-Hill, Beth Kaufman and Terri Wise, for their skill, their dedication to publishing books about women and gender, and most of all, for their patience with us.

Because most of the responsibility for this edition of *In Our Own Words* was mine, I have some personal acknowledgments to make. I would like to thank my partner Roger Chaffin, for his generous support, unfailing love, and willingness to do half the housework even when he's busy writing his own books. Finally, thanks to the students who, over the years, have told me their stories, asked for my own, and eagerly devoured the accounts of women's lives I've assigned them to read. I trust that a new generation of students will find favorites of their own here.

Mary Crawford

PART ONE

Making Our Voices Heard

Just a few generations ago, white, privileged men were the only people thought to be capable of creating knowledge and governing society. For women, making one's voice heard has meant resisting core beliefs of western culture that do not accord us full intellect and agency. These beliefs have been expressed in societal forces that tell women that we are not clever enough, not motivated enough, and simply not good enough—or that if we are, we shouldn't be. Women have faced sex discrimination in access to education, in hiring and promotion, and in judgments about our work. The cumulative effect is a powerful message that women should forget about our dreams of achievement and stay in the place assigned to us.

Women have always resisted staying "in their place." Yet the young women in each new generation might believe themselves to be alone in their struggle because they do not know about the strong women who came before them. Although the issues affecting women today are different from those of our mothers and grandmothers, each of us still is faced with the task of

achieving our full potential, and we all need to find the courage to take ourselves seriously.

In this group of readings you will learn about eight women—three psychologists, a mathematician, a historian and poet, a writer, an attorney, and a social worker—who found ways to make a contribution to society despite obstacles. We chose the stories that appear here because we believe that hearing our foremothers' stories can help women find their own voices. That each of them took different paths and used different tactics reflects their specific situations. As you read their stories, you may want to think about how their social class, their ethnicity, and their era shaped their choices.

We first move back in time to Mary Whiton Calkins, a pioneering woman psychologist. Calkins's story is given voice by Laurel Furumoto, who did her graduate studies in psychology at Harvard just as Calkins had done some eighty years earlier. The saying "Anonymous was a woman" is a feminist truism. Laurel Furumoto says that as a graduate student she learned little about her predecessor's achievements.

Mary Whiton Calkins invented the paired associate technique, developed an influential theory of the self, was president of both the American Psychological Association and the American Philosophical Association, and published prolifically throughout her long career. Were her life and work discussed in any of your psychology textbooks?

Emmy Noether is a woman from a prototypically "male" field, mathematics. Noether's story is told by Mary Crawford, who stumbled on her existence while researching an article on women scientists. Crawford then went to Bryn Mawr College, where Noether spent the last years of her life, and found materials for her story hidden away in the archives. Noether, like Mary Calkins, struggled to gain access to a field in which the power structure was exclusively male. Albert Einstein called Noether a genius, yet many of her colleagues seemed more concerned with her appearance than her mind. Think about what the life of a female genius in mathematics might be like today.

In our third story, like the first two, the heroine is given voice by another woman. Rosario Ceballo describes herself as a woman of color brought up in a working-class immigrant family. She wrote her case study of Mary, an African American social worker, as part of a graduate class in the psychology of women. It is easy to see how Ceballo would have been drawn to Mary, whose strength and resilience helped her overcome racial and economic oppression. Despite her disadvantages, Mary sought out role models, obtained financial support, and developed a distinguished career helping others through social work. Her story takes place in the context of both the Civil Rights movement and the women's movement. However, she reacted to these two social movements differently. Though each woman is shaped by the era she lives in, individuals can differ greatly in the meaning they find in social events.

When Rhoda Unger and I (M. C.) decided to write our own stories as part of this collection, we agreed it would not be easy. Even though, as psychologists, we specialize in human behavior, we were not used to writing about our own lives.

We decided that each of us should write her own account without consulting with the other.

When we traded "first drafts," we were astonished at the similarities in our stories. We have been friends for years; our first extended professional contact was in 1988, when Rhoda spoke at a conference I organized, and we started work together on our textbook *Women and Gender* in 1989. We had talked about some similarities in our personal histories: that each of us was the first in her family to go to college, for example, and that each of us had switched from experimental to social psychology along the way. But neither of us had ever expressed to the other just how lonely we were as aspiring young students, how "different" we felt, or how difficult it was to combine marriage, motherhood, and our work. Each of us describes various roadblocks we encountered, as well as some sources of encouragement and support along the way.

Like Unger and Crawford, Noemi Alindogan-Medina entered adulthood just as the women's movement was beginning to affect her society. Her story illustrates some of the effects of global feminism. Alindogan-Medina is a Filipina history professor who writes about how her contact with feminist ideas through her career as a teacher had great impact on her personal and professional life. Indeed, she came to rewrite her own history as she looked back on her childhood and saw sexism where before she had thought her upbringing had been relatively gender-neutral. She became aware not only of sex discrimination, but of class and color biases in Philippine society. Alindogan-Medina became an activist for women's studies education and in the process has found voice as a poet as well.

Dorothy Allison, in "A Question of Class," powerfully reminds us that social class prejudice and discrimination are issues in U.S. society, too. Allison grew up poor in South Carolina, her people denigrated as "white trash." Born "queer in a world that hates queers" and "poor into a world that despises the poor," and coping with the effects of incest and physical abuse, Allison describes how she developed a deep habit of hiding her history and her self from others. It was only when she began to write that she faced up to the necessity of telling the truth about herself. Her story is a testimony to the difficulty of claiming an identity in the context of prejudice based on class, gender, race, and sexual orientation— what she calls "the cauldron of hatred."

While Dorothy Allison's ethnic and class background are denigrated by mainstream society, Phoebe Eng comes from a group that is sometimes held up as the "Model Minority": Asian Americans. Eng is a former corporate attorney who is now a full-time social activist on behalf of Asian American women. Here, she writes about how the norms of her family background in the Chinese immigrant community clash with the norms of corporate culture. Faced with the "fork in the road" of deciding whether to behave more like an Asian woman or an American woman, how can one decide which is best? And what are the consequences of each choice? Eng reconciles the two through her own experience of learning to voice her rage.

After you have read all of these stories, you might want to look back over them for common themes. Even though these eight women differ in many ways, they have in common a struggle to make their voices heard. How does gender interact with social class, ethnicity, and other systems of discrimination? What were some of the ways that each woman was denied credit and recognition for her work? Do these means of erasing women's achievements still occur? What were the sources of strength that enabled each woman to counter the negative influences in her environment?

The stories of these eight women span a period of more than a hundred years, from the 1890s to the present. During this time, women's access to educational and professional resources has changed a great deal. Today, women are no longer denied degrees from prestigious universities, and they are more visible as researchers, attorneys, scientists, and writers. Many students think that gender equality now exists, and that all a woman needs to succeed is intelligence and motivation. Clearly, all of the women in these stories were talented, smart, and motivated. Yet there are untold stories, too. Many women with similar strengths were not able to succeed and write their stories for others to read. Are women still in danger of having our full humanity denied? Can our potential to contribute to society now be achieved, no matter what our social class or color?

Laurel Furumoto

Mary Whiton Calkins (1863–1930) Fourteenth President of the American Psychological Association

Mary Whiton Calkins was a pioneering woman psychologist who published a great deal of important research throughout her long career, but who wrote little about her own life. Her story is given voice by Laurel Furumoto, a feminist psychologist who does research on the "lost women" in psychology's past. In Calkins's day, psychology was a new field of study; its power structure (and that of higher education in general) was exclusively male.

As You Read, Ask Yourself . . .

How did influential men both help and hinder Mary Calkins?

Do you think it would be necessary today for a young woman to seek out one of the "great men" of the field for mentoring and professional advancement?

How did Calkins's social class and family background shape her experience? Look for both opportunities and constraints.

When I was a graduate student in the Department of Psychology at Harvard University, I learned two things from my adviser about Mary Whiton Calkins. One was that, contrary to popular belief, she, rather than Georg Müller and Alphons Pilzecker, was the inventor of the paired-associate technique. The other was that she declined to accept a Radcliffe Ph.D. on the grounds that she had done all of her graduate work at Harvard. This second fact seemed to amuse my adviser a great deal, whereas it simply puzzled me. I could not understand why it was so important where her work had been done. Now, almost fifteen years later, I have come to appreciate the principle involved.

Calkins did postgraduate work at Harvard in the 1890s under William James, Josiah Royce, and Hugo Münsterberg. She took seminars with Royce and James and conducted experimental work in Münsterberg's laboratory, the results of which formed the basis of a doctoral dissertation on association which she presented to the Department of Philosophy. She was given an oral examination by the members of this department who subsequently communicated to the president and fellows of Harvard College that she had completed all the requirements for the Ph.D. However, she was not granted the degree; the presumptive basis for this decision being that Harvard does not grant degrees to women.

Several years later, after Radcliffe College had been founded, plans were made to offer a Radcliffe Ph.D. to Calkins and three other women who had undertaken graduate studies at Harvard but were denied the Ph.D. because of their sex.[1] In the spring of 1902, after approval by Harvard and Radcliffe, Dean Agnes Irwin of Radcliffe wrote to Calkins offering her the degree. The following is part of Calkins's reply:

> I hope that I may make quite clear to you my reasons for declining to accept the honor of the Radcliffe doctor's degree. I sincerely admire the scholarship of the three women to whom it is to be given and I should be very glad to be classed with them. I furthermore think it highly probable that the Radcliffe degree will be regarded, generally, as the practical equivalent of the Harvard degree. And, finally I should be glad to hold the Ph.D. degree, for I occasionally find the lack of it an inconvenience, and now that the Radcliffe Ph.D. is offered, I doubt whether the Harvard degree will ever be open to women.
>
> On the other hand, I still believe that the best ideals of education would be better served if Radcliffe College refused to confer the doctor's degree. You will be quick to see that, holding this conviction, I cannot rightly take the easier course of accepting the degree.[2]

The contents of this letter, coupled with Calkins's firmly held belief that there were no inherent sex differences in qualities of mind, lead me to believe that she refused the degree on the principle that the Harvard Ph.D. should be awarded for graduate work done at Harvard and that the sex of the recipient was irrelevant; that is, she believed that Harvard should not discriminate against women in granting degrees.

Aside from an autobiographical chapter,[3] most of which she devoted to a discussion of her system of self-psychology, there has been very little published about the life of Mary Whiton Calkins, fourteenth president of the American Psychological Association. One of the aims of the present article is to describe briefly her family background, career, and contributions to psychology. A corollary aim is to give a chronicle of Calkins's graduate education because of the insights into American psychology in the 1890s which it provides, as well as the way in which it illustrates the difficulties encountered by a woman pursuing graduate work in psychology during that era.

Mary Whiton Calkins was born in 1863, the eldest of five children in the family of Charlotte and Wolcott Calkins. The family was extremely close-knit, and the most salient and persuasive theme in Calkins's life was her steadfast devotion to her family. In 1880 the family—father, mother, two daughters, and three sons—moved from Buffalo, New York, where Calkins had spent her childhood, to Newton, Massachusetts. Here her father, a Congregational clergyman, assumed the ministry of a new church and built a house which remained Calkins's home for the rest of her life.

Both her parents traced their lineage back to the early settlers in this country. Her father's family, of Welsh origin, first arrived here in 1638, and her mother was of triple Mayflower descent.[4] Wolcott Calkins was characterized by his youngest son, Grosvenor, in the following way: "Father's strongest characteristics [were] . . . complete . . . confidence in his ability to deal personally with almost any mechanical or construction project and a resolute determination to carry through his projects in the face of any obstacles."[5]

7

LAUREL FURUMOTO
Mary Whiton Calkins
(1863–1930)
Fourteenth President
of the American
Psychological
Association

These traits of "confidence" and "resolute determination" were also apparent in Wolcott Calkins's ideas about education. He felt that much time was lost in ordinary schooling and alternately pushed his children ahead in school at certain points and removed them at others in order to have them tutored or to take them to Europe where they learned foreign languages by being boarded out with French and German families. He firmly believed that prolonged and constant exposure was the only way to acquire a foreign language. That he acted on this belief is indicated by his son Grosvenor: "In order to give her an early knowledge of German, no other language was used in the home for five or six years following my sister Mary's birth."[6] As a consequence of his educational program, all the Calkins children entered college with advanced standing, graduated at the usual age after attending for only three years, and could read and speak fluently both French and German.

Unfortunately, there is less detailed information available about Calkins's mother, Charlotte. The image that emerges is of a patient, sensitive, intelligent, and physically very frail, but resolute, woman who was devoted to her family. It is also clear that the relationship between Calkins and her mother was remarkably warm, close, and enduring.

Calkins's middle brother, Raymond, noted in his journal that his sister's departure for Smith College in the fall of 1882 was the first break in the family circle.[7] Another, unexpected and tragic, soon followed when Calkins's sixteen-year-old sister, Maude, became seriously ill during that same fall, and after months of suffering, died in the spring of 1883. Presumably because of her grief and a reluctance to leave her family at this time, Calkins remained at home the following academic year studying and taking private lessons in Greek. She reentered Smith in the fall of 1884 with senior standing and graduated with the class of 1885 having concentrated in classics and philosophy. The following year she remained at home tutoring her brothers and studying on her own.

In May 1886, the entire family set out on a journey to Europe, traveling first in England and then France. Wolcott Calkins returned to his pastoral duties in Massachusetts in the fall while the rest of the family went to Germany and set up winter quarters in Leipzig. Here Mary Calkins became acquainted with an instructor from Vassar College who invited Calkins to accompany her on a trip to Greece. The two left in early winter, traveled through Italy, and then proceeded to Greece. During their several months in Greece, Calkins took the opportunity to study modern Greek.

After sixteen months in Europe, the family returned home. Calkins took a position at Wellesley College, a recently founded liberal arts college for women, where she taught Greek for the next three years. Referring to her time in Italy and Greece, her brother Raymond commented in his journal, "She was then preparing to teach Greek to private pupils, if a college position did not offer. But as a result of father's interview with Miss Freeman, then President at Wellesley, an appointment as Instructor in Greek there was offered and accepted. She entered upon that work as soon as we returned home."[8]

Soon after Calkins began teaching at Wellesley, she happened to borrow a volume on the history of Greece from a professor in the philosophy department. When she went to the professor's quarters to get the book, Calkins noticed her collection of philosophy books and confided to the professor "her deep interest in that subject and her ardent desire for an opportunity to continue her study of it."[9]

Two unrelated factors combined to provide Calkins the opportunity to fulfill her desire. One of these was the explicitly acknowledged aim of the fledgling institution to keep abreast of the latest developments in the liberal arts and sciences. Therefore, in the late 1880s, about a decade after the founding of Wilhelm Wundt's laboratory and just as the first crop of American psychological laboratories was beginning to spring up, Wellesley College began to feel the need to represent the new experimental psychology, complete with laboratory, in its curriculum. As was generally true in that period, the instruction in psychology was to be carried on within the philosophy department.

The second circumstance that could make a promising young teacher in the Greek department a candidate for founding a laboratory of psychology was the scarcity of academically qualified women. The recruiting policy of one of Wellesley College's early presidents has been summarized as follows: "Find the right person; preparation can be discussed later."[10] It was in this spirit that the professor to whom Calkins had expressed her interest in philosophy recommended to the president of the college that she consider Calkins for the proposed psychology position. Early in 1890, the president agreed to recommend Calkins for the position on the condition that she first prepare herself by studying psychology for a year.

Accepting this proposition, Calkins considered where she might undertake a year of study. Her correspondence from this period indicates that she sought advice from a number of people. She wrote to one of her former instructors at Smith College asking him whether he would advise her to study abroad and, if so, with whom. Or, she inquired, whether he thought she should work in this country "with Dr. Ladd of New Haven, or with Professor James of Harvard, or with Dr. Hall at Worcester."[11] The instructor replied that he would recommend that she study in Germany if women were allowed the same privileges as men. The same sentiment was expressed by another of her former instructors, who wrote, "Germany is a good place to study . . . [but] . . . whether you could have the privilege of attending lectures or obtaining private instruction in psychology and philosophy in any of the German universities outside of Zurich, I do not know."[12]

Another letter to Calkins regarding study in Göttingen had a distinctly discouraging tone: "A common friend of ours, Miss Molly Knox, has asked me to give you my opinion about a woman's chances of study at the University of Göttingen. I wish I might encourage you; but past experience has proved to me the utter uselessness of trying to enlighten the authorities, at least, in our generation."[13]

Calkins also must have considered going to Michigan to study with John Dewey. A letter Dewey wrote to Calkins in May 1890 outlined the offerings in psychology and philosophy at the University of Michigan and indicated that he hoped to meet with her to discuss things in more detail during a trip to the Boston area that summer.[14]

A Smith classmate of Calkins, Anna A. Cutler, was doing graduate work in psychology at Yale with G. T. Ladd. In a letter to Calkins dated May 1890, Cutler wrote:

> He [Ladd] knows of no reason why you could not take courses 2, 3, 4, & 8 with himself, if you chose. 6 & 7 are undergraduate courses likely to be crowded by men. He would have to ask advice before admitting any women to the Physiolog.[ical] Psychol.[ogy]. I think he would be glad to arrange some way by which you could get that course if possible. . . . He would be very glad to have a côterie of women as students under him, and as he said yesterday "I am glad to put myself out to help any earnest woman especially one who is going to teach."[15]

After Cutler had consulted further with Ladd, she wrote again to Calkins with additional information:

> He said among other things that the Physiolog.[ical] Psychol.[ogy] course next year is to be taken by a very few men, and that you would be allowed to attend as a guest (that being an undergraduate course you could open your mouth only after decree of the Faculty & Corporation. The P.[ost] G.[raduate] courses you can take as full a part in as you choose. We were invited to read papers this year).[16]

Calkins did not take advantage of the opportunity to study at Yale under Ladd's direction or at Michigan with Dewey. Perhaps it was because she was reluctant to leave her family, or because neither institution had a psychological laboratory. In one of her letters Cutler mentioned the lack of a "regular psycholog.[ical] laboratory" at Yale,[17] and Dewey revealed in his letter that he did not know how much laboratory work there might be in connection with the course in physiological psychology because there was "no regular psychophysical laboratory."[18]

It was important to Calkins that she spend part of her year studying physiological psychology, at that time roughly synonymous with the new experimental psychology. It is also quite probable that she thought it important to undertake her work in physiological psychology in an institution with a psychological laboratory. If so, in the United States in 1890, she would have been limited to less than a dozen institutions. Harvard was among the handful of those with a psychological laboratory, and it was also within commuting distance of her family home.

In late spring of 1890, it was to Harvard that Calkins turned seeking permission to enter Philosophy 20a and b in the academic year 1890–1891. Philosophy 20a was a seminar in physiological psychology taught by William James; Philosophy 20b, a seminar on Hegel, was taught by Josiah Royce. Both James and Royce were eager to welcome Calkins into their seminars, but President Charles Eliot refused to give them permission to do so because official policy prohibited the admission of women to Harvard courses.

In a letter to Calkins expressing his regret over the enforcement of this policy, James inquired, "Can't you get to Worcester almost as easily as to Cambridge? Stanley Hall's Psychological department ought to be the best in the world."[19]

LAUREL FURUMOTO
Mary Whiton Calkins
(1863–1930)
Fourteenth President
of the American
Psychological
Association

Calkins heeded James's advice about seeking instruction in Hall's department, but she did not give up on Harvard. Nor did James immediately give up on Eliot. At the end of May he wrote to Calkins:

> I have been attacking the President again on the subject you know of. He tells me that the overseers are so sensitive on the subject that he dares take no liberties. He received such a "tremendous wigging" from them a few years ago for winking at just this thing, that he is forced now to be strict. . . . I think that in justice to him you should know these facts.[20]

James's desire to be fair to Eliot did not prevent him from expressing his feelings about Calkins being "kept out. . . . Enough to make dynamiters of you and all women."[21]

It was not to dynamite but to a petition that Calkins turned next in a renewed attempt to get permission to enter James's and Royce's seminars. In July 1890, Calkins's father submitted a petition to the Corporation of Harvard University, supported by a letter from the president of Wellesley College, requesting that his daughter be allowed to take courses with James and Royce. The phrasing of the petition minimized the coeducational aspect and was framed in terms of one institution (Wellesley College) asking a favor from another institution (Harvard University), this favor being "postgraduate and professional instruction for one who is already a member of a college faculty."[22] On 1 October 1890, Harvard voted to permit Calkins to attend Philosophy 20a and b during that year. It was specifically noted in the Harvard Corporation records that in accepting this "privilege" she would not become a student of the university entitled to registration.[23]

Two days after the decision, James wrote to Calkins welcoming her into his seminar:

> My students 4 in number seem of divergent tendencies and I don't know just what will come of the course. Having published my two rather fat tomes, I shan't lecture, but the thing will probably resolve itself into advice and possibly some experimentation. Our evening meetings have been provisionally fixed for Thursdays at 7:15. Will you please come if you can next Thursday at seven so as to have a little talk in advance, or rather come at 1/2 past six and take tea.[24]

Thus began Calkins's graduate career in psychology at Harvard. She attended James's seminar which turned into a tête-à-tête as the other members dropped away early in the term leaving only her and James at either side of a library fire with his "two rather fat tomes." Calkins recalled, "The *Principles of Psychology* was warm from the press; and my absorbed study of those brilliant, erudite, and provocative volumes, as interpreted by their writer, was my introduction to psychology."[25]

In addition to attending James's and Royce's seminars during her year of preparation in psychology, Calkins also arranged to do some work as a private school pupil with E. C. Sanford at Clark University. She undertook some dream research with him, the results of which he reported at the first annual meeting of the American Psychological Association in 1892.[26]

In the fall of 1891, Calkins returned to Wellesley College as an instructor in psychology and taught a new offering in the Department of Philosophy: psychology approached from the physiological standpoint. The college catalog for the year 1891–1892 included a description of the new psychological laboratory:

LAUREL FURUMOTO
Mary Whiton Calkins
(1863–1930)
Fourteenth President
of the American
Psychological
Association

> Students in Physiological Psychology have the use of models and plates of the brain; dissecting instruments, a pressure balance, a color wheel, a perimeter, a Wheatstone stereoscope, apparatus for experiments in simultaneous contrast, reaction-times apparatus, a stopwatch, and other simple appliances. Required experiments are chiefly in sensation, space perception, and reaction-times, sensational and intellectual.[27]

The report of the president of the college for that year indicated that fifty-four students had elected the new physiological psychology course. It also noted that Calkins had expressed "her indebtedness to Dr. Sanford of Clark University for invaluable counsel, and for personal superintendence of the construction of part of the apparatus" for the new psychological laboratory.[28]

During this undoubtedly strenuous year of teaching and setting up a laboratory, Calkins also actively sought a place where she could undertake further study in psychology. Letters from Sanford, Royce, and James, all written in February 1892, offered her advice in this matter. The contents of the letters suggest that she was considering, among other possibilities, studying under Frank Angell at Cornell and Hugo Münsterberg at Freiburg.

Sanford wrote:

> Assuming . . . that you are going to study next year, should it be Cornell or Europe? I say Europe. Why? Because . . . a European Ph[.]D[.] will do you more good I believe than an American one, I don't think that my J.[ohns]H.[opki]N.[s] Ph[.]D[.] is quite so impressive to the average person in authority as a Leipzig one would be. . . . Also I saw when at Harvard the other day a picture of Münsterberg and his seminary—among the rest a lady! I infer that she was a student, and think there is ground for the inference . . . . They are beginning to wake up over there, the more shame to John Hopkins and Clark—an ineffable shame that you can't get a fellowship in your own country in institutions given to advanced work.[29]

Royce, on the other hand, advised her to take her next year at Cornell if she could get a fellowship. He urged her not to postpone further study too long, issuing the following caution: "One who teaches too steadily before reaching the studious maturity which one's ideals had planned, becomes too easily content with one's limitations."[30]

From James came a plea to delay as long as possible the decision of where to undertake further study. He affirmed that Münsterberg had had a woman student the previous year and advised Calkins to wait a bit longer before making a decision with the reassurance that more information would soon become available about the relative advantages of the various schools.[31] At the end of April 1892, a letter from James to Calkins announced that Münsterberg would be coming to Harvard the following academic year.[32]

Another petition was submitted to Harvard, this time by Calkins in her own behalf, and was approved on 9 January 1893. Calkins was advised that she would be welcome to attend the instruction of Professor Münsterberg in his laboratory as his guest but not as a registered student of the university.[33] Calkins recalled her plans to study with Münsterberg as follows: "In the very fall of 1892, when I had planned to ask admission to his Freiburg Laboratory, he came instead to Harvard; and for parts of three years I worked under his inspiring direction in the old Psychology Laboratory of Dane Hall."[34] During 1893 and the first half of 1894, Calkins taught at Wellesley College and worked in Münsterberg's laboratory. In the academic year 1894–1895, she went on leave from the college to devote herself full time to the work at Harvard.

From 1892 on, Calkins was a steady contributor to the psychological literature. In that year she published her first paper on association, which grew out of the seminar she took with James.[35] Also in 1892, there appeared a description of the new course in experimental psychology at Wellesley College.[36] In 1893, her work with Sanford on dreams[37] and research on mental forms[38] done in the Wellesley laboratory were reported. The first of a series of papers communicating minor studies undertaken in the Wellesley laboratory appeared in 1894.[39] Also published in that year was the first of a series of reports on work she had done in Münsterberg's laboratory: experiments on association using the paired-associate technique which she had invented.[40]

In October 1894, Münsterberg wrote to the president and fellows of Harvard College inquiring if there were a chance that Calkins might be admitted as a candidate for the Ph.D. The following is an excerpt from his letter:

> With regard to her ability, I may say that she is the strongest student of all who have worked in the laboratory in these three years. Her publications and her work here do not let any doubt to me that she is superior also to all candidates of the philosophical Ph.D. during the last years. More than that: she is surely one of the strongest professors of psychology in this country. . . . the Harvard Ph.D. attached to the name of Mary W. Calkins would mean not only a well deserved honor for her, but above all an honor for the philosophical department of Harvard University.[41]

The Harvard Corporation records for 29 October 1894 note that Münsterberg's request was considered and refused.[42]

In the spring of 1895, Calkins presented her thesis—"An Experimental Research on the Association of Ideas"—to the Department of Philosophy at Harvard. The thesis was approved by the members of the department, and after conducting an informal and unauthorized Ph.D. examination of the candidate, her examiners forwarded a communication to the president and fellows of Harvard College. It read in part: "At the examination, held May 28, 1895, before Professors Palmer, James, Royce, Münsterberg, Harris, and Dr. Santayana it was unanimously voted that Miss Calkins satisfied all the customary requirements for the degree."[43] The communication was duly noted in the Harvard Corporation records for 10 June 1895.[44]

Her graduate studies successfully accomplished, except for the lack of a degree, Calkins returned to Wellesley College in the autumn of 1895 as Associate Professor of Psychology and Philosophy. Over the next five years there appeared in the psychological literature a steady stream of studies from the Wellesley College psychological laboratory communicated by Calkins.[45]

One of these reports is of more than usual interest because it appears to have touched off the first controversy over sex differences in cognitive processes in the psychological literature.[46] In 1891, Joseph Jastrow reported the results of a study he had conducted with female and male college students in his psychology class at the University of Wisconsin. He instructed his students to write out 100 words as rapidly as possible, and he then analyzed the lists thus produced. Among his conclusions were the following: ". . . the feminine traits revealed by this study are an attention to the immediate surroundings, to the finished product, to the ornamental, the individual, and the concrete; while the masculine preference is for the more remote, the constructive, the useful, the general, and the abstract."[47]

An attempted replication of Jastrow's study by one of Calkins's students produced results interpreted as contradictory to his. Following the publication of this study, there was a heated exchange between Calkins[48] and Jastrow[49] with Jastrow criticizing the replication for its inexactness and Calkins commenting on the impossibility of making valid distinctions between masculine and feminine intellect when one cannot eliminate the effect of the environment.

During this period Calkins also published two more papers reporting the results of her work on association in Münsterberg's laboratory, including the work that would have been her doctoral thesis.[50] In 1900 there appeared the first of a series of papers in which she developed her ideas about psychology as a science of self,[51] and the following year her first book, *An Introduction to Psychology*,[52] was published. . . .

Calkins published prolifically in both psychology and philosophy; four books and well over a hundred papers are divided fairly evenly between the two disciplines. Her work in psychology tends to cluster in the first half of her career, while her concern with philosophy was a continuing thread that became increasingly prominent after the last of her experimentally based work was published in 1900. This shift in emphasis is reflected in her election to the presidencies of the American Psychological Association in 1905 and the American Philosophical Association in 1918.

It is generally acknowledged that Calkins's philosophical thinking, in the idealist tradition, was strongly influenced by her teacher Josiah Royce. She was a proponent of personalism, "that philosophy which makes personality the ultimate reality in the universe."[60] It is worth noting that all of her work in philosophy as well as psychology came to center around the importance of self.

In 1929, after a teaching career spanning forty-two years, Calkins retired from Wellesley College. It was said that she planned to devote her time to writing and enjoying the companionship of her mother, but less than one year later she was dead, the victim of an inoperable cancer. She left behind a prodigious amount of published work in psychology and philosophy and a carefully thought out system of self-psychology. Aside from the presidency of APA, the eminence that Calkins achieved as a psychologist can be judged by the fact that when in 1903 a list of fifty leading psychologists in the United States was arranged in order of distinction, Calkins ranked twelfth on the list.[61] She had been the recipient of many academic and professional honors, but one which she believed she had rightly earned—the Harvard Ph.D.—perpetually eluded her grasp.

LAUREL FURUMOTO
Mary Whiton Calkins
(1863–1930)
Fourteenth President
of the American
Psychological
Association

More than three decades after Münsterberg and the other members of her thesis committee had failed in their efforts to persuade Harvard to grant Calkins the Ph.D., a group of her colleagues renewed the effort. In 1927, Christian A. Ruckmick, a psychologist at the University of Iowa who had become acquainted with Calkins when he was teaching for a short time in the department at Wellesley, sent a letter to President Abbot Lowell of Harvard containing a petition on behalf of Calkins signed by a number of psychologists and philosophers who were Harvard graduates.[62]

The petition outlined Calkins's career at Harvard and commented on "her subsequent achievements as a constructive psychologist and philosopher of outstanding international reputation." It concluded by recommending that Harvard grant her the degree of doctor of philosophy and was signed by a group of thirteen Harvard graduates, many of whom were professors of psychology at prestigious institutions. Among the names on the list were R. S. Woodworth, R. M. Yerkes, and E. L. Thorndike. Less than two weeks after Ruckmick had mailed the petition to Harvard, Lowell's secretary sent him a reply indicating that the recommendation had been considered, and it was decided "that there was no adequate reason" for granting Calkins the degree.[63]

Although this belated attempt to secure the Harvard Ph.D. for Calkins had failed, the attempt itself was an impressive tribute to her reputation as a scholar. The petition with its list of signatures, many of acknowledged leaders in the field of psychology, must have provided some consolation to Calkins. For, unquestionably, to be the inspiration for a testimonial of this kind is a far rarer and more remarkable honor than to be the recipient of a Harvard Ph.D.

Notes

1. Minutes of the meeting of the Radcliffe Academic Board, 10 April 1902. Radcliffe College Archives, Cambridge, Mass.
2. Calkins to Irwin, 30 May 1902, Radcliffe College Archives.
3. Mary W. Calkins, in *History of Psychology in Autobiography*, ed. C. Murchison (Worcester, Mass.: Clark University Press, 1930), 1: 31–62.
4. Raymond Calkins, "Mary Whiton Calkins," in *In Memoriam: Mary Whiton Calkins (1863–1930)* (Boston: Merrymount Press, 1931), pp. 1–19.
5. Grosvenor Calkins, "Notes from Father's Log."
6. Ibid.
7. Raymond Calkins, "Volume 1 (1869–1890)."
8. Ibid.
9. R. Calkins, "Mary Whiton Calkins," p. 7.
10. Ibid., p. 8.
11. Calkins to Charles Edward Garman, 22 February 1890, Amherst College Archives, Amherst, Mass.
12. H. N. Gardiner to Calkins, 1 May 1890.
13. M. L. Perrin to Calkins, 12 July 1890.
14. Dewey to Calkins, 28 May 1890.
15. Cutler to Calkins, 28 May 1890.
16. Cutler to Calkins, 5 June 1890.
17. Cutler to Calkins, 28 May 1890.
18. Dewey to Calkins, 28 May 1890.

15

LAUREL FURUMOTO
Mary Whiton Calkins
(1863–1930)
Fourteenth President
of the American
Psychological
Association

19. James to Calkins, 24 May 1890.
20. James to Calkins, 29 May 1890.
21. James to Calkins, 30 July 1890.
22. Wolcott Calkins, Petition to the Corporation of Harvard University, 1 July 1890, Harvard University Archives, Cambridge, Mass.
23. Corporation Records, 1 October 1890, Harvard University Archives.
24. James to Calkins, 3 October 1890.
25. Calkins, *History of Psychology in Autobiography,* p. 31.
26. Michael M. Sokal, "APA's First Publication: Proceedings of the American Psychological Association, 1892–1893," *American Psychologist* 28 (1973): 277–292.
27. "Calendar of Wellesley College (1891–1892)," Wellesley College Archives, Wellesley, Mass.
28. Helen A. Shafer, "President's Report," (1892), Wellesley College Archives.
29. Sanford to Calkins, 16 February 1892.
30. Royce to Calkins, 17 February 1892.
31. James to Calkins, 14 February 1892.
32. James to Calkins, 29 April 1892.
33. Eliot to Calkins, 9 January 1893.
34. Calkins, *History of Psychology in Autobiography,* p. 33.
35. Mary W. Calkins, "A Suggested Classification of Cases of Association," *Philosophical Review* 1 (1892): 389–402.
36. Mary W. Calkins, "Experimental Psychology at Wellesley College," *American Journal of Psychology* 5 (1892): 260–271.
37. Mary W. Calkins, "Statistics of Dreams," *American Journal of Psychology* 5 (1893): 311–343.
38. Mary W. Calkins, "A Statistical Study of Pseudo-chromesthesia and Mental Forms," *American Journal of Psychology* 5 (1893): 439–464.
39. Mary W. Calkins, "Wellesley College Psychological Studies," *Educational Review* 8 (1894): 269–286.
40. Mary W. Calkins, "Association I." *Psychological Review* 1 (1894): 476–483.
41. Münsterberg to President and Fellows of Harvard College. 23 October 1894, Harvard University Archives.
42. Corporation Records, 29 October 1894, Harvard University Archives.
43. Royce, Palmer, James, Santayana, Münsterberg, and Harris to President and Fellows of Harvard College, 29 May 1895, Harvard University Archives.
44. Corporation Records, 10 June 1895, Harvard University Archives.
45. Mary W. Calkins, "Minor Studies from the Psychological Laboratory of Wellesley College," *American Journal of Psychology* 7 (1895): 86–107; idem, "Wellesley College Psychological Studies," *Pedogogical Seminary* 3 (1895): 319–341; idem, "Wellesley College Psychological Studies," *Psychological Review* 2 (1895): 363–367; idem, "Minor Studies from the Psychological Laboratory of Wellesley College," *American Journal of Psychology* 7 (1896): 405–411; idem, "Short Studies in Memory and Association from the Wellesley Laboratory," *Psychological Review* 5 (1898): 451–462; idem, "Wellesley College Psychological Studies," ibid. 7 (1900): 580–591.
46. Calkins, "Wellesley College Psychological Studies," *Psychological Review,* 1895.
47. Joseph Jastrow, "A Study in Mental Statistics," *New Review* 5 (1891): 559–568.
48. Mary W. Calkins, "Community of Ideas of Men and Women," *Psychological Review* 3 (1896): 426–430.
49. Joseph Jastrow, "Community of Ideas of Men and Women," *Psychological Review* 3 (1896): 68–71.
50. Mary W. Calkins, "Association: An Essay Analytic and Experimental," *Psychological Review Monograph Supplement Number 2* (1896): 1–56; idem, "Association II," *Psychological Review* 3 (1896): 32–49.

51. Mary W. Calkins, "Psychology as Science of Selves," *Philosophical Review* 9 (1900): 490–501.

52. Mary W. Calkins, *An Introduction to Psychology* (New York: Macmillan, 1901).

. . .

60. E. S. Brightman, "Mary Whiton Calkins: Her Place in Philosophy," in *In Memoriam*, p. 45.

61. James McKeen Cattell and Jacques Cattell, eds. *American Men of Science: A Biographical Directory*, 5th ed. (New York: Science Press, 1933).

62. Ruckmick to Lowell, 4 June 1927.

63. F. W. Hunnewell to Ruckmick, 16 June 1927.

The author wishes to thank the family of Mary W. Calkins for their generosity in making available to her letters, journals, and scrapbooks which provided much of the documentation for this paper. She also wishes to thank Elizabeth S. Goodman, State University College, Fredonia, N.Y., for helpful comments on an earlier draft of this paper. The assistance of the Amherst College Archives, the Boston Public Library, the Harvard University Archives, the Radcliffe College Archives, the Smith College Archives, and the Wellesley College Archives in providing background information and documentation is gratefully acknowledged. Permission from Alexander R. James is also gratefully acknowledged to reprint portions of the letters of William James.

Mary Crawford

Emmy Noether:
She Did Einstein's Math

Emmy Noether made very important contributions to mathematics. Albert Einstein called her a genius. Yet most people have never heard of her. Mary Crawford found materials for her story in the archives of a small women's college, and recreates what it may have been like for Noether as a woman in a society where university teaching and intellectual life were clearly marked "For Men Only." Today, careers and professions involving mathematics, such as engineering and computer science, remain highly gender-imbalanced, with far more men than women.

As You Read, Ask Yourself . . .

How did Emmy Noether's family background provide her with a head start in mathematics?

How was Noether dependent on the good will of influential men?

Why did Noether leave her native Germany for the United States, and how did her life change as a result?

Imagine a female mathematics genius born in, say, 1990. How might her experiences be both similar to and different from Emmy Noether's?

It was 1915. For years young mathematicians around the world had been hearing the same advice from their mentors: "Pack your suitcase and take yourself to Göttingen."

I like to think of her arriving at the Göttingen train station in Germany, wearing stout shoes and a sturdy serge dress with a token bit of lace at the collar, carrying a worn satchel. A rare intelligence and singleness of purpose shone in the eyes behind her little round spectacles. Though the men who would be her colleagues sometimes dwelt more on her appearance than her skills—one described her as an energetic and very nearsighted washerwoman—she knew they needed her knowledge in their work on the general theory of relativity. Emmy Noether was determined to seize her chance.

Emmy had absorbed mathematics all her life, growing up in a swirl of discussions on algebraic functions. Her father Max was professor of mathematics at the University of Erlangen when she was born in 1882, and his close friend and colleague Paul Gordan, whom Emmy knew from early childhood as "uncle," then mentor, supervised her doctoral dissertation. Gordan's interest was in formal algebraic processes; Noether's thesis, "On Complete Systems of Invariants for Ternary Biquadratic Forms," was very much the product of his influence. The famous mathematician Hermann Weyl, her colleague, called it an "awe-inspiring piece of work"; she would later move so far beyond it that she'd dismiss it as "a jungle of formulas."

Gordan's algebra provided the initial discipline that honed her genius. In her twenties she had already published half a dozen papers and occasionally substituted for her father at lectures. By the time she moved to Göttingen she was ready to take a place beside David Hilbert and Felix Klein, two of the great mathematicians of the era who welcomed and eagerly began to work with her.

Noether's forte was invariant theory. An algebraic equation is said to be *transformed* when every x in it is replaced by y-2. A geometric figure in a plane can be transformed, too, for example, by stretching it. But some aspects of an equation or a geometric shape remain unchanged during transformation—and these *invariants* can provide extremely significant information.

Despite its name, relativity is really a theory of invariants. It is concerned largely with how physical processes such as motion will appear to observers located at different places and traveling at various speeds in various directions. Some things will look different—in the classic example, if you are sitting in the dining car of a train, the vase of flowers on your table appears to be immobile in front of you; to a worker along the tracks it flashes by. Some things will look the same to different observers, however, and it is the discussion of these particular invariants that begins the subject of relativity.

Einstein had already created his grand plan for the theory of relativity, but it had yet to be laid out in concrete mathematical form. Hilbert and Klein were interested in mathematical realizations of Einstein's ideas. Noether's skills and knowledge were crucial to progress in the area because Einstein had initially underestimated the complexity of the mathematics that would be required to express the fundamental laws of physics.

Hermann Weyl describes Göttingen University as "a great center for the passionate scientific life." Unfortunately, this was exceeded by the professors' passion for retaining an all-male faculty. Hilbert's efforts to obtain a post for Noether were met with implacable resistance, more from Göttingen's philosophers and historians than from its mathematicians. In *Hilbert* (Springer-Verlag, 1970), author Constance Reid describes his struggle:

> They argued formally: "How can it be allowed that a woman become a Privatdozent [lecturer]? She can then become a member of the University Senate. Is it permitted that a woman enter the Senate?" They argued informally: "What will our soldiers think when they return to the University and find that they are expected to learn at the feet of a woman?"

Hilbert declared in a faculty meeting: "I do not see that the sex of the candidate is an argument against her admission as Privatdozent. After all, we are a university, not a bathhouse." But his indignation was to no avail. Emmy Noether's lectures were simply announced under Hilbert's name.

I imagine her striking off on one of her "mathematical walks" through the narrow streets of Göttingen. Wild gesticulations punctuate her analysis of some abstruse point. Students cluster, chicks to her mother hen. She loves these students, pokes into their personal lives, steers them to the most fruitful research questions. As she plumps along, she tosses off ideas that will become a dissertation for this student, a seminal paper for that one, the start of a new research area and lasting fame for another. The faculty calls the recipients of this intellectual generosity "the Noether boys"; they are her family.

Perhaps it was her own upbringing in a loving, stable, and cultured family that formed her genuine goodheartedness. Weyl remembers her as "warm like a loaf of bread . . . a broad, comforting, vital warmth." All who knew her remember her essential kindness and generosity of spirit.

Still, her students cannot have had an easy time in class. Even her friend Weyl admits that her lectures were a bit erratic and enormously demanding. The problem lay in her phenomenal imagination and her habit of puzzling out brand-new solutions to problems in mid-lecture. One student remembers the day she was to teach a standard proof of a classical theorem. Just before class she brainstormed a unique proof based entirely on concepts and axioms rather than on calculations. Of course the proof wasn't entirely thought out, but the intrepid Noether planned to develop it "on her feet" as she lectured. After entering one blind alley after another (and thoroughly confusing her students), Noether, overcome with rage at the intractability of the problem, threw her chalk to the floor, stamped on it, shouted, "There, I'm forced to do it the way I don't want to!" and then calmly and flawlessly taught the traditional proof.

She was at her best only when she was free to move beyond traditional themes and present her own work in progress. Sometimes she lectured on the same topic semester after semester, probing into unsolved problems more deeply each time. To the students who could give themselves entirely to Noether's paths of thought, she was "an inspired teacher."

Noether worked for six years without pay or formal status before being appointed *Nichtbeamteter ausserordentlicher Professor,* a position whose importance is inversely related to the length of its title. It means, roughly, a "non-tenured irregular faculty member." She was also given a contract to teach abstract algebra, with an extremely modest stipend.

Emmy Noether's work, like much of modern mathematics, deals with abstractions of abstractions and is not easily reduced to everyday language. She was 38 years old when her first ground-breaking work, a paper on differential operators, was published in 1920. It marked the beginning of her development of conceptual axiomatics as a powerful research tool. The goal of the axiomatic method is to clarify an area of study by splitting problems into smaller parts and stripping them of inessential features to reveal their basic underlying logic. The art lies in being able to perceive the most fruitful ways of partitioning the problems.

Noether's strengths as a mathematician lay in her ability to think in abstractions, rather than resort to concrete examples, and to visualize remote connections. She strove to simplify, purify, and unify areas of theory. Weyl was awed by her "mighty imagination." Einstein agreed, writing: "In the realm of algebra, in which the most gifted mathematicians have been busy for centuries, she discovered methods which have proved of enormous importance in the development of the present-day younger generation of mathematicians." Noether, he stated, was a "creative mathematical genius."

Noether held her modest place in the official hierarchy at Göttingen for 11 years. In 1930 her friend Hermann Weyl joined the faculty and tried to win a promotion for her: "I was ashamed to occupy such a preferred position beside her whom I knew to be my superior as a mathematician in many respects." His efforts failed. "Tradition, prejudice, external considerations weighted the balance against her scientific merits and scientific greatness, by that time denied by no one. She was without doubt the strongest center of mathematical activity at Göttingen, considering both the fertility of her scientific research program and her influence upon a large circle of pupils." Yet even her editing of Germany's scholarly journal of mathematics went officially unacknowledged.

The Göttingen school, once described as a perpetual international congress of mathematicians, was utterly destroyed by the Nazi takeover of 1933. Emmy Noether—liberal, pacifist, Jewish, woman professor—hadn't a hope of staying on, though Weyl, Hilbert, and others flooded the Ministry of Education with testimonials on her behalf. Weyl vividly recalls that "her courage, her frankness, her unconcern about her own fate . . . were in the midst of all the hatred and meanness, despair, and sorrow surrounding us, a moral solace." Finally, she left for Bryn Mawr College in the United States. And Weyl joined Einstein at the Institute for Advanced Study in Princeton, where the two welcomed Noether's visits and guest lectures.

Emmy Noether had her huge desk shipped to Bryn Mawr from Germany and settled into a joyous life of work with women students and friends. "Our lives were intertwined, like a family," says former student Grace Shover Quinn of Noether, her four graduate students, and Anna Wheeler (head of the mathematics department). "I remember many cups of tea at Emmy's apartment," says Quinn, "and of course the mathematical walks. Those walks were the bane of our lives—Emmy was rotund, with thick glasses, rather unconventional-looking, and spoke loudly and in a strange mix of English and German." Completely absorbed in a mathematical point, she would stop suddenly in mid-street, leaving her students to nudge her to the curb.

Her satisfaction with her new life was evident even to those outside the little circle. A colleague recalls: "Work was only the core of her relation to students. She looked on the world with direct friendliness and unfeigned interest, and she wanted them to do the same. Mathematical meetings at the University of Pennsylvania, at Princeton, at New York, began to watch for the little group, slowly growing, which always brought something of the freshness and buoyance of its leader."

For the first time in her life, Emmy Noether began to receive the respect and recognition due her. She was 53, and, according to Weyl, at the summit of her creative power. "Her far-reaching imagination and her technical abilities . . . had come to a perfect balance; she had eagerly set to work on new problems." No one was prepared for her sudden death on April 14, 1935, of complications following surgery.

Weyl's eulogy, delivered at Bryn Mawr shortly after her death, is a moving remembrance of her personality as well as her work. Yet, like many of his colleagues, he still seemed unable to reconcile himself to the reality of "woman" and "mathematician" in the same body. Acknowledging her evident genius, he was forced to deny her "femininity":

> It was only too easy for those who met her for the first time, or had no feeling for her creative power, to consider her queer and to make fun at her expense. She was heavy of build and loud of voice, and it was often not easy for one to get the floor in competition with her. . . . In everyday life she was most unassuming and utterly unselfish: she had a kind and friendly nature. Nevertheless she enjoyed the recognition paid her; she could answer with a bashful smile like a young girl to whom one had whispered a compliment. No one could contest that the Graces had stood by her cradle; but if we in Göttingen often chaffingly referred to her as "der Noether" [with the masculine article], it was also done with a respectful recognition of her power as a creative thinker who seemed to have broken . . . the barrier of sex.

But Weyl remains puzzled: what sort of woman was she? "Essential aspects of human life remained undeveloped in her, among them, I suppose, the erotic . . . the strongest source of emotions, raptures, desires, and sorrows, and conflicts."

I wonder about the inner life of Emmy Noether. We know nothing of her "emotions and conflicts." Even her letters are about mathematics, with only a phrase or two of personal news appended. But judging from the memories of her colleagues, she survived as woman and scholar through her generosity of spirit. Meanness, discrimination, and misogyny completely escaped her notice. As Weyl says, "she did not believe in evil—indeed it never entered her mind that it could play a role among men." From Noether we have no angry words, only the abstract beauty of her work.

Rosario Ceballo

A Word and a Kindness: The Journey of a Black Social Worker

In this story, a young student gets a chance to learn from an elder whose life has spanned most of the twentieth century. Rosario Ceballo describes how she first met Mary at a political rally and was impressed by the older woman's energy and activism. Later, as part of a graduate class in the psychology of women, she interviewed Mary and wrote the oral history of her life that is summarized here.

Mary, born in the segregated South, endured many hardships including poverty, emotional neglect, and the early loss of her mother. Moreover, she was affected by institutionalized racism, classism, and sexism. Yet she achieved a successful career in social work. Ceballo focuses not on Mary's disadvantages but on her strength and resiliency in resisting oppression, and their sources in her community.

As You Read, Ask Yourself . . .

What relationships did Mary seek out for role models, financial support, and mentoring?

How was she affected by the demands of women's traditional role as caretaker, and how did she sidestep that role later on?

What did Mary contribute to and gain from the Civil Rights movement and the women's movement? Why do you think she reacted to these two social movements differently?

How did gender, race, and social class interact in Mary's development?

Mary, my friend's great-aunt, is an elderly African-American woman I first met at a college graduation in 1986. I was taking pictures of a rally for South African divestment when Mary was pointed out to me. I was struck by the ease with which she settled in among the crowd of college students. Most of the other parents and family members of graduating students watched the event from a safe, neutral distance. But Mary joined the rally, chanting with determination and raising her fist to the air. I was immediately drawn by the spark for life I saw in her.

23

ROSARIO CEBALLO
A Word and a
Kindness: The
Journey of a Black
Social Worker

In the years that followed, I had several opportunities to get to know Mary better. I was delighted when she allowed me to do an oral history of her life for my graduate school class on the psychology of women. I interviewed Mary over a span of three days during winter 1992, when she was seventy-six. We talked in the living room of her home in Oxford, North Carolina, and she allowed me to tape record most of our conversations. I have sought Mary's approval on everything I have written about her life, and she has therefore read and commented on all drafts of this chapter.

Mary was the youngest of nine children born in the Jim Crow South in 1915. She was only three years old when she experienced the traumatic loss of her mother, who died of TB. Three of Mary's older siblings also died around this time, and as a result, Mary grew up as the only female child in a family with her father and five older brothers. Mary's father, William, remained committed to raising all of his children himself with only periodic help from relatives. Although he initially hired people to look after the children, he later relied on his sons to look after Mary. The result, as Mary remembered, is that she was often left alone for much of the day. "They [her brothers] had to take care of me. But I remember that they would go off during the day and leave me in the house by myself. And they wouldn't come back until it was time for Dad to get home. Then they'd show up. I don't think I ever told on them."

Mary described her father as a quiet, undemonstrative, distant man, somewhat inept at managing the household of children he had been left with. Although he did not receive a formal grammar school education, he was taught enough in a neighbor's home to pass the entrance exam to Shaw University in Raleigh, North Carolina. After college, he "read law," apprenticing with a white lawyer for seven years. Upon passing the bar, William moved his family from Oxford to Durham, North Carolina, where Mary was born. As a young child, Mary spent several summers back in Oxford, where she stayed with relatives from both her father's and her mother's family. In 1926 when Mary was 10 years old, William moved the family to Washington, D.C. Mary then lived in other people's homes or in apartments where she, her father, and an older brother shared one rented room. "You see, we lived in rooms. We never established a home or anything. We had a room in somebody's house. That was the way we grew up."

While in the eleventh grade, Mary developed rheumatic fever, and her education was consequently interrupted by a series of hospitalizations. As a complication of this early illness, Mary was afflicted by a reactive arthritis, a form of ankylosing spondylitis, in her right hip. This condition was treated surgically, but Mary has slightly dragged one foot ever since. Despite these medical difficulties, Mary graduated on schedule with her high school class in 1934. She spent the next four years caring for the house and children of her oldest brother, Bob, whose first wife had passed away. She cooked, cleaned, did the laundry, and provided child care. Mary remembers those Depression years as particularly bleak and dreary. Her experiences during those years likely influenced the steadfast determination with which she later sought her independence. At age twenty-three, Mary gathered the determination and financial resources to enroll in Howard University. By 1948, she had received a master's degree from the Smith College School for Social Work and launched a successful career in the field of social work.

Mary's life story is marked by an ongoing struggle to cope with personal misfortunes and institutionalized systems of racism and sexism. In this chapter, I will explore how Mary's sense of identity emerged from interwoven layers of membership in different social groups and incorporated her transition in social class status. I will underscore Mary's use of relationships and surrogate family systems as a source of resilience. Finally, I will outline and examine the development of Mary's awareness of systems of racial oppression, beginning with her virtual lack of contact with white people as a child, extending to her pioneering efforts as the only black social worker in all-white social service agencies, and culminating with her participation in the civil rights movement as a fifty-one-year old, single black woman. I will also address how Mary's involvement in the struggle for civil rights influenced her reactions to the women's movement.

IDENTITY: RACE, CLASS, AND GENDER

Black feminist scholars have recently emphasized the need to explore interconnections between gender, race, and social class when investigating black women's identities and experiences with oppression. In addressing Mary's identity, I therefore wish to heed Patricia Hill Collins's (1990) advice of not starting "with gender and then adding in other variables such as age, sexual orientation, race, social class, and religion, [but rather thinking] of these systems as part of an interlocking matrix of relationships" (p. 20). Indeed, as an adolescent Mary struggled with understanding just this kind of complicated matrix in her own identity.

Mary straddled the painful and complicated boundary of simultaneously belonging to an educationally privileged group of blacks while living under conditions of economic hardship. Academic achievement was a greatly esteemed and prominent value in Mary's family, and Mary excelled in all of her scholastic pursuits. Yet despite her father's legal career, Mary's family always lived under conditions of economic hardship. "It was a very, very peculiar kind of situation," Mary explained. "My dad, he was a good lawyer . . . but he never made money." William never became a prominent, financially well established attorney, in part because of his inability to participate in the social networks of the black middle class. He was a loner who did not care for the social obligations that accompany business life. For example, he attended church regularly, but never used the opportunities offered by the church's social network to foster a business clientele.

The tenuous interconnections between Mary's membership in different social groups marked several painful life experiences. For instance, Mary described the incompatibility of her educational privilege and lower socioeconomic status when she lived in the status-conscious black community of Washington, D.C. She described herself as a "little ragged kid who never had any decent anything. And here I sat in this school with these fancy D.C. folks' kids. When I had to go into another grade, you had to say what your daddy did. And I had to put on this thing that my daddy was a lawyer, and here I was looking like a Rag-a-muffin."

25

*ROSARIO CEBALLO
A Word and a
Kindness: The
Journey of a Black
Social Worker*

Moreover, the socially segregated climate of the black community in Washington, D.C., was not solely based on economic and occupational status. Discrimination pervaded all institutions, including the school system, where it was based on personal attributes such as hair type and skin color. Mary recalled a particularly illustrative school experience with great detail.

> I remember one time, I sat next to Charlotte. Her father was a doctor. She was very pretty, and very fair, and so on. She and I got along fine. A new teacher came and the first thing she did was rearrange the class and put all of the kids, the socialites, in front. And all of us, the rest of us had to go in the back. This is absolutely true, I am not lying. This was based on color and clout. Color and status . . . Yes, I was the blackest, and the poorest [in that class that went on to Dunbar high school].

Thus, Mary's sense of identity developed in recognition of her complex membership in different social categories of race, gender, and social class. Her sense of herself as an adolescent incorporated the ambiguous nature of her family's social class—a father who worked as a lawyer, but maintained a working-class lifestyle, her privileged academic orientation, her experiences as the only female child in a family of men, and the "blackness" of her hair and skin color. By the same token, Mary experienced the interlocking force of several oppressive systems. She simultaneously encountered classism due to her family's limited resources, racism based on the color of her skin, and sexism due to her gender. Mary's burden in navigating race-, class-, and gender-based oppressions was not like carrying separate and distinct weights, for as Elizabeth Spelman (1988) explained, "How one form of oppression is experienced is influenced by and influences how another form is experienced" (p. 123). It becomes clear then that the form of discrimination Mary experienced in school was linked to her gender (by the feminine attributes valued in black girls) as well as her lower socioeconomic standing.

RELATIONSHIPS AND FAMILIES

A significant source of Mary's resilient functioning lies in her ability to foster and then make use of relationships and surrogate family systems. Her father was unable to create a cohesive family unit following his wife's death, and Mary quickly learned that she would have to rely on a foundation of relationships with people outside of her immediate family to gain strength and nurturance. Mary's relational coping strategy is consistent with the psychological literature on "resilient children" who function adaptively in the face of severe and enduring strain. Stable relationships with adults buffer these children from a host of adverse life circumstances (Rutter, 1979; Werner and Smith, 1982).

Mary sought and found early positive role models among the extended family she visited in Oxford, North Carolina, during her childhood summers. For example, she frequently found a way of escaping the church revivals, attended mostly by the older people in the community, and visiting with the younger relatives, her maternal aunts. These aunts were young black teachers in their teens and early twenties who became important role models for Mary.

She recalled that during her last summer in Oxford, "Sally was nineteen. That [teaching] was her first job, and I thought that was so wonderful, that she was going to be a teacher at nineteen! . . . Lena, Beecher, and Sally. They were all teachers."

Further, Mary was able to use a network of relationships to facilitate her own emotional growth and introspection during a difficult time in her life. After graduating from high school, she was hospitalized again for several long periods. During these hospitalizations, she was in a body cast for several months at a time. She believes the time spent in the hospital cured her of her "dependency needs." I knew all of the residents," she explained, "and everybody in the hospital knew me by then. I got a lot of attention, a lot of strokes. . . . I think I cured my dependency problem. . . . I mean I had all these needs that hadn't really been met. All the feelings I had about not being well taken care of somehow were satisfied during this period."

Although the story of Mary's unconventional route to college is poignantly heartwarming, it also illustrates how her life was powerfully shaped by the ties she established with others and how her professional beliefs incorporated an understanding of the primary role relationships may occupy in one's life.

> Let me tell you about how I happened to go to school. I came down here [Oxford, North Carolina] that summer, and Beecher [a maternal aunt] always somehow, was kind of special. I was special to her. She said to me, "We should have kept you after your mother died. If we had kept you, you would be finishing college this year." And it was true. If I'd stayed, I would have gone to college. So I went back to Washington, I told my brother, Buster, that I wanted to go to school. And he said, "okay," and he said that "it was way late, but I'll help you." And I went to Howard and applied, and they accepted me, and he paid my tuition all through. He was working at the post office. He sent me through school.

I said, "And that all came about . . ." and Mary finished, "because of what Beecher said. And you never know. This is one of the things in the helping profession. This is one of the things I've learned. You never know the effect you're going to have on people. You never know. Just a word, or a kindness, or something can mean a lot to a person in life. The whole pattern of my life was set from just this one comment that she made."

Mary found a significant mentor and role model at Howard University, where she majored in sociology. E. Franklin Frazier chaired the Department of Sociology at that time, and Mary, who proved herself to be conscientious and dedicated, became one of his favorite students. The importance of familial ties and relationships had a profound influence on the professional goals Mary pursued after Howard. During an earlier hospitalization, Mary became friends with Catherine, her doctor's daughter. Catherine was a young black woman who was finishing her studies at the New York School of Social Work. Mary's motivation to become a social worker evolved out of this friendship. Upon graduating from college in 1943, she enrolled in Howard's two-year certificate program in social work and did her first clinical placement in a family agency. In view of her search and desire for supportive family connections, "it seems natural in terms of working, you work in a family agency. . . . The first job I had was in a family agency. Basically, my whole professional experience was with families."

Mary identifies her search for close, familial relationships as a salient theme resonating throughout her life story. "Throughout all of this, lack of family, lack of stability, I gravitate to situations where I'm in a family." In 1945 there was a small group of black professionals living in Milwaukee, Wisconsin, where Mary accepted her first job. This small professional group provided a supportive network for incoming members like Mary. Mary lived with one of these professional black families for ten years until she moved to accept a prominent position in a Philadelphia agency. To this day, they remain a surrogate family for her.

This family cushioned Mary's transition in social class status. Her socioeconomic position changed greatly as she became a securely established member of the black professional class in Milwaukee. Like her father, Mary spurned a socially elite lifestyle. However, her new family modeled positive attributes among middle-class blacks that Mary could accept. "This black group that I was in was not based just on social things. It was based on professional things, civic responsibility . . . That, I could accept."

27

ROSARIO CEBALLO
*A Word and a
Kindness: The
Journey of a Black
Social Worker*

DEVELOPING RACIAL AWARENESS

As Mary found ways to overcome the impediments that life placed before her, her awareness regarding systems of racial oppression developed in a remarkable fashion. Having come of age in the Jim Crow South, Mary's childhood was virtually devoid of any contact with white people. Black families who were financially more secure, like Mary's, could avoid interacting with whites to a great extent. Her parent's relatives owned their own land in the rural county surrounding Oxford, North Carolina. Because their primary source of income was farming, they did not have to work closely with white people in Oxford's city proper. The adults would take vegetables and butter to Oxford to sell to white people, but "that's the only contact they had [with them]. . . . They didn't work for them. They weren't maids or cooks for them." The amount of contact Mary had with white people was also influenced by her gender. For example, Mary's brother, William, Jr., was allowed to earn money by delivering newspapers to the white students at Duke University in Durham, North Carolina. In these instances, her family's financial circumstances and her gender shielded Mary from experiencing the subservient roles blacks occupied in their interactions with whites.

Not only did Mary have few physical interactions with white people, but the extent to which white people entered her daily thoughts and consciousness was negligible. I asked Mary, "What did you think about white people? What were you told about white people? How did your father feel about white people?" Mary explained, "He [her father] didn't talk about them. Certainly didn't talk about the racial part of it. You know, it was very interesting in the South. Because you just avoided everything. Your parents, they didn't tell you anything. They didn't talk about it." It was not until Mary was nine years old and spent a year in Boston living with her older brother George and his wife, Isabella, that she interacted with white children on a regular basis. In Boston she played and went to school with both black and white children.

As a child, Mary's understanding of racism did not emerge from a context of white-black relationships, but rather from experiences with the internalized racism exhibited by black people among themselves. Mary experienced discrimination in school at the hands of her black teachers who valued wealthy, well-dressed, light-skinned black children above the rest. When I asked Mary what she thought about the discrimination she had experienced at school, she replied, "We thought that the teachers were prejudiced. You just accepted it. It was just the way things are. I don't remember having really strong feelings about it one way or another. . . . I don't think I thought anything, except that it wasn't right. . . . That's just the way it was done. It wasn't anything you questioned." At this point, Mary did not have the life experiences to understand the hideous connections between society's racism and the ways in which black people came to despise their own culture. Mary resigned herself to accepting discrimination as part of the way the world worked.

Through her late twenties, Mary's awareness of racism continued to lie dormant. With a social work certificate in hand, she accepted her first job at a family agency that sought a black social worker to work with its black clientele. Mary remained the agency's only black social worker for several years. Although as a therapist, Mary saw only black clients, the clients of the white therapists were always white. Despite this practice, the social work profession in general avoided cultural issues in theoretical philosophy and clinical practice. The prevailing attitudes seemed to coalesce around a doctrine of unadulterated color blindness.

Mary learned to embrace this color-blind philosophy that asserted that race and culture do not enter into the clinical equation. At the time, she did not think that cultural factors influenced her professional work. She remembered not believing that race and culture "made any difference at all." After acquiring a master's degree in social work, Mary returned to work at the same Milwaukee agency where the policy of assigning therapists to clients of the same race had been abolished. Mary wondered how white clients would respond to working with a black therapist, but she did not discuss her concerns with anyone. "I think what happened in our day is that we didn't handle it," she explained. "It was really always covert. It was never really out in the open and on the table, unless some client came in and said, 'I will not work with a _____,' and then changes had to be made. But if it ever happened, then that was the only time it was discussed."

The denial of the presence and importance of racial issues applied not only to her views about clinical practice but also to her conceptualization of society at large.

> I think we [black women] kidded ourselves. I think we sort of bought into this total picture, treated ourselves as if we were totally like the white community, and that's absolutely not true. . . . Maybe it was not until the agitation from the civil rights [movement], where we began to take a look. You really had been kidding yourself. It's different. Society is different. Blacks have had a different experience. The black experience is different. . . . You really do live in a segregated society. No matter what you think, how you change your hair, where you live, how much money you make, as far as you go.

ROSARIO CEBALLO
*A Word and a
Kindness: The
Journey of a Black
Social Worker*

Mary's participation in the civil rights movement marks a dramatic and striking departure from her earlier ideas about the role of race and culture in our society. A new and deeper awareness coupled with a national movement of protest sparked Mary's desire to resist racial oppression. Her involvement in the movement sprang from a well of rising and unsuppressible anger.

> The whole anger, the whole thing just sort of caved in at me. . . . As far as my working relationships, they were good, and I didn't have serious problems. But suddenly, socially, the many feelings that I had harbored throughout my life about being black and how I was treated and how blacks were treated just sort of caved in on me. And I just had to get out and get involved.

The events that created a movement in Selma, Alabama, drew Mary back to the South to join the struggle for civil rights. Alabama's proportion of blacks on the voter registration rolls was one of the lowest in the nation. Student Non-Violent Coordinating Committee (SNCC) workers in Alabama made voter registration a top priority in 1963, and the Southern Christian Leadership Conference (SCLC) began a similar campaign in 1965. In Selma, Sheriff Jim Clark's repeated use of force against blacks attempting to register received national media coverage. Coverage of the obstacles faced by blacks trying to vote continued with Martin Luther King, Jr.,'s arrest, a march to the courthouse by over one hundred black school teachers, and the arrest of over a thousand people, including five hundred protesting school children (Carson, 1981; Garrow, 1978; Williams, 1987).

The shooting of Jimmie Lee Jackson, a twenty-six-year-old black man, during a nighttime march stimulated renewed protest and SCLC's announcement of a fifty-mile march across the Edmund Pettus Bridge in Selma, along Route 80 to the Montgomery capitol. On Sunday, March 7, 1965, Alabama state troopers met 2000 marchers on the Edmund Pettus Bridge. Tear gas was fired onto the marchers as policemen on horseback charged into the crowds. The day was dubbed "Bloody Sunday." King announced that the march would begin again as planned two days later. Hundreds of people from all over the country went to Selma for this march (Carson, 1981; Garrow, 1978; Williams, 1987).

Following King's announcement of another march attempt, Mary spontaneously bought a plane ticket to Selma. "I really called the airport, got a reservation, and just took off without too much thought about anything. I just wanted to be on that bridge, across the bridge, that was important to me." The rage that inspired Mary to buy a plane ticket on the spur of the moment marked the beginning of her activities in the civil rights movement. Mary's heightened awareness of her anger at racial injustice released a sense of rage and urgency and a strenuous desire to change society. "I had all these feelings in me, and I never recognized them or had not permitted myself to recognize them. And suddenly I'm angry . . . [and have] the anger and the energy to begin to do something about it, to fight, and to declare some of it." The Justice Department strongly urged King to call off the march. But before turning the march around, King led 1500 people across the bridge to face a line of state troopers on March 9, 1965. After the "Turnaround Tuesday" march, Mary returned to work, but she was not deterred by King's decision to abort that march. (It was not until March 21, 1965, that thousands of people set out on the march that would ultimately reach the Montgomery capitol with 25,000 people as Congress debated the Voting Rights Act.)

The following summer, Mary decided to go on a trip to Jackson, Mississippi, sponsored by a group called "Wednesdays in Mississippi," a subgroup of the National Council of Negro Women established in 1964 (Fitzgerald, 1985). This group consisted of black and white women who worked closely with SNCC's freedom schools, held conferences to discuss the problems blacks were facing in Mississippi, and developed programs to address these concerns. Afterward, Mary decided to join SCLC and spend the rest of her summer vacation participating in civil rights activities in the South. "The idea was to spend the whole vacation in the South. I don't know what I thought I was doing. I guess I thought I was being helpful, but I think that basically it was just an expression of my own anger at all of it."

During her vacation, Mary worked in Jackson, Mississippi; Atlanta, Georgia; Greensboro, Eutaw, Selma, and Birmingham, Alabama. Her memories about this time eagerly rushed forward, her words spilling over each other with enthusiasm. She remembered staying in King's house and being "the only old person there. The rest of them were young people. There were kids from all over the country in this house." She was stunned and outraged by the severity of the poverty she saw among the blacks whom she encouraged to vote and attend church rallies. She also recalled several frightening encounters with state troopers in which she knew her life was in danger.

Many black women have described a process of self-affirmation as a result of their involvement in the civil rights movement. For example, Bernice Reagon explained it as having "a sense of power, in a place where you didn't feel you had any power . . . a sense of confronting things that terrified you . . . [leading to] a change in my concept of myself and how I stood" (Cluster, 1979, p. 29). Similarly, Mary's experiences in the movement gave her insight into the strength and force of her own potential and abilities as a black woman. In this context, she explained her determination in the midst of extreme danger. "At this point I was so angry that I didn't care. I was scared that I might get killed, but I was determined. . . . In other words, you gotta fight it. Unless you get there and fight it, you gotta be willing to die or else nothing will ever happen. That was the way I was feeling." Standing for a principle that she believed in completely and resolutely and accepting the consequences of her actions yielded a powerfully self-affirming and liberating force on Mary's sense of identity.

Mary's desire and expectations for social change were also fulfilled during this time. "This was change," she explained. "This was definitely change. When blacks were staying in the [white] motel in Jackson, Mississippi, and when blacks were registered, and when I was standing on the sidelines seeing voters register in a small, rural community of Alabama, that was change!" Mary's sense of herself and of society was transformed by the movement's quest to end the legacy of slavery, segregation, and other racial injustices. She is immensely proud of having played an active role at a time and a place where history was made.

Mary's emerging awareness of her anger and her participation in the struggle for civil rights may appear somewhat sudden, but they are understandable if viewed in the larger context of the time. Mary had previously accepted society's systems of institutionalized racism because there were no practical alternatives, not because she found these systems and their values to be morally justifiable. The civil rights movement opened a door for the possibility of concrete change. It provided an alternative, a vehicle for channeling the accumulation of lifelong anger and the hope that change could happen. Belief in the possibility of change tipped the odds in favor of participation and action. Moreover, the impetus to act was reinforced by the belief that implementing change could not be left up to the federal courts. Black people had to assert control over their own destiny and unequivocally demand their basic human rights. The key issue then, as Mary sees it, is captured in a phrase from a song that she often heard during the movement: "The only thing that we did wrong was to let this go on so long."

It seems surprising that Mary felt her activities in the civil rights movement did not affect her professional work in a family agency. She identified her involvement in the movement as being of an extremely personal nature that did not permeate other areas of her life and career. "It was really personal. It didn't have to do with my working experience." When she returned to Philadelphia, it was "business as usual." Nothing had changed "in terms of my job and profession." She did not even share her experiences with co-workers. Stewart and Healy (1989) posited that the impact of historical events on women's individual development is dependent upon a woman's age and life stage. Perhaps Mary's experiences in the civil rights movement were not immediately integrated into her professional work because they occurred when Mary was an older adult with firmly established life patterns and commitments.

FEMINISM AND THE WOMEN'S MOVEMENT

I wondered if Mary's heightened awareness of racial oppression influenced her reaction to the women's movement. In contrast to her involvement with the civil rights movement, Mary's sense of connection to the women's movement is very faint. She acknowledged the similarities between the women's movement and the goals of blacks during the civil rights movement, but personally her heart was only drawn to one of these agendas. Her identification with the struggle of black people runs deeper than her association with the experiences of women as a whole.

Feminist scholars have offered a multitude of theories to explain black women's limited involvement in the women's movement. Hooks (1981) argued that as a result of their participation in the civil rights movement, black women came to value "race as the only relevant label of identification" (p. 1). She went on to explain, "When the women's movement raised the issue of sexist oppression, we argued that sexism was insignificant in light of the harsher, more brutal reality of racism. We were afraid to acknowledge that sexism could be just as oppressive as racism. We clung to the hope that liberation from racial oppression would be all that was necessary for us to be free" (p. 1). Historical accounts have also documented that black female leaders of the civil rights movement were generally united in their belief that sexism was of secondary importance to the discrimination and oppression faced by blacks (Giddings, 1984; Standley, 1990).

31

ROSARIO CEBALLO
A Word and a
Kindness: The
Journey of a Black
Social Worker

Indeed, black women had many reasons to be suspicious of the women's movement, which quickly concentrated on the concerns of white, middle-class women. However, as Giddings (1984) remarked, "Not only were the problems of the White suburban housewife (who may have had black domestic help) irrelevant to black women, they were also alien to them" (p. 299). This situation was aggravated by the fact that white women continued to compare their status within society to that of blacks. In addition, black women in the civil rights movement did not experience the same degree and form of sexism that white women did. Black women were not, for example, entirely shut out of leadership circles, as the experiences of women like Diane Nash, Ruby Doris [Smith] Robinson, and Ella Baker attest (Giddings, 1984). Black women were also suspicious of the women's movement because its rise coincided with the decline of the civil rights movement, and black women were keenly aware of the fact that it was not only white men but also white women who perpetuate racism (Giddings, 1984; Fitzgerald, 1985). Several explanations may therefore account for the tenuousness of Mary's connections to the women's movement.

Although it is true that Mary's sense of connection to the women's movement remains weak, her endorsement of feminism is steadfast. To claim that black women felt no ties to women's rights and other issues raised in the women's movement is far too simplistic, especially following their experiences in the civil rights movement. Black women were consistently in the forefront of the civil rights struggle; they carried the momentum and provided the stamina for the movement's progress. Black women did not "reject feminism itself but only the bourgeois white feminism that was at the heart of the women's movement" (Fitzgerald, 1985, p. 5) at that time. Mary showed no hesitancy in identifying herself as a feminist. "I consider myself a feminist because I believe in women's rights, but it isn't the feminism that I think whites are talking about, because my stronger feelings are about the racial thing."

To a great extent, many areas of Mary's life are characterized by feminist goals and values. As a young woman, Mary was guided by a burning desire to establish her independence and acquire a professional career. In her master's thesis at Smith, she directly addressed gender issues in professional relationships. She studied the working relationship between psychiatrists (the majority of whom were male) and the predominantly female social workers who made up an enormously undervalued segment of hospitals' mental health teams. Mary never acquired the traditional female roles of wife and mother. Moreover, she never felt an imperative to be married. "I never had the feeling that I had to be married. My feeling is that it would have to be somebody that I would want." She firmly declared a lack of regret about her life decisions and identified ways in which feminism has shaped her thinking. For example, she explained that "the new feminism has absolved me from much anxiety about the single state."

CONCLUSION

Mary's life is marked by her strong-willed determination to overcome the personal and societal obstacles that fall along her path. The obstacles have been numerous and significant: the early death of her mother, her family's limited fi-

33

ROSARIO CEBALLO
A Word and a
Kindness: The
Journey of a Black
Social Worker

nancial resources, discrimination in the Jim Crow South, the absence of family unity, and a series of health problems and hospitalizations. Mary did not simply persevere and cope with these obstacles, she resisted their limitations and excelled beyond the boundaries they imposed on her. She attained exceptional academic, professional, and personal success. However, black female experiences should not, as Hooks (1981) cautions, be romanticized into the stereotypical image of the "strong" black woman. Strength alone does not allow us to circumvent the forces of systemic oppression, but Mary and other women like her have given me courage and inspiration for continued struggle. As a woman of color who was raised in a working-class, immigrant family and as someone starting a career in psychology, I am strongly drawn to Mary and the ways in which she has lived her life despite the many obstacles in her path.

Academics in many fields, including psychology, have traditionally framed the study of black families on a deficit model. The use of white, middle-class families as a standard and basis for comparison draws out and highlights areas of deficiency and neglect among blacks in the United States. Mary is not privileged by her race, gender, or original social class position. She is neither white nor middle class, and she was not raised within the bonds of a cohesive nuclear family. Yet it would be a grave mistake to characterize Mary's life as deficient when her life and accomplishments are in fact remarkable in their richness. Approaching Mary's life with a focus on strengths and resiliency offers one road toward understanding how people located in the margins of society struggle with, resist, and in many ways, surmount oppression.

Appreciating the complexity and significance of intersecting social locations in Mary's life experiences also requires a sufficiently broad feminist perspective. A focus relying solely on gender as an analytical technique would conceal rather than illuminate our understanding. For instance, Mary did not resonate to the feminism she felt white women were addressing in the 1960s. She instead sought a balance between her feminist allegiance and those loyalties based on race and culture. To have narrowly zoomed in on a single historical moment in Mary's life would have provided a static picture. Instead, I have tried to document how the degree and nature of her feminist and racial awareness varied and changed throughout her life course as they do for all of us.

References

CARSON, C. (1981). *In struggle: SNCC and the black awakening of the 1960s.* Cambridge, MA: Harvard University Press.

CLUSTER, D. (1979). *They should have served that cup of coffee.* Boston: South End Press.

COLLINS, P. H. (1990). Women's studies: Reform or transformation? *Sojourner: The Women's Forum, 10,* 18–20.

FITZGERALD, T. A. (1985). *The national council of Negro women and the feminist movement 1935–1975.* Washington, DC: Georgetown University Press.

GARROW, D. J. (1978). *Protest at Selma: Martin Luther King, Jr., and the voting rights act of 1965.* New Haven: Yale University Press.

GIDDINGS, P. (1984). *When and where I enter: The impact of black women on race and sex in America.* New York: Bantam Books.

HOOKS, B. (1981). *Ain't I a woman: Black women and feminism.* Boston: South End Press.

RUTTER, M. (1979). Protective factors in children's responses to stress and disadvantage. In M. W. Kent & J. E. Rolf (Eds.), *Primary prevention of psychopathology: Vol. 3.* Social competence in children (pp. 49–74). Hanover, NH: University Press of New England.

SPELMAN, E. V. (1988). *Inessential woman: Problems of exclusion in feminist thought.* Boston: Beacon Press.

STANDLEY, A. (1990). Women in the civil rights movement. Trailblazers and torchbearers, 1941–1965. In V. L. Crawford, J. A. Rouse, & M. Walker (Eds.), *Black Women in United States History* (pp. 1–11). New York: Carlson.

STEWART, A. J., & HEALY, J. M. (1989). Linking individual development and social changes. *American Psychologist, 44,* 30–42.

WERNER, E. E., & SMITH, R. S. (1982). *Vulnerable but invincible: A study of resilient children.* New York: McGraw-Hill.

WILLIAMS, J. (1987). *Eyes on the prize: America's civil rights years 1954–1965.* New York: Penguin Books.

Mary Crawford

Claiming the Right to Know: A Personal History

Girls who grew up in the United States shortly after the Second World War had few female models of achievement. It was an era of tremendous social pressure for (white middle-class) women to find purpose in their lives only through marriage and motherhood. In this story of a journey from obedient Catholic daughter to feminist activist and psychologist, Mary Crawford writes about the personal and societal influences on her career path.

As You Read, Ask Yourself . . .

How did personal and social structural factors interact in creating roadblocks for women of Crawford's generation?

Where did Crawford find role models?

Do you think Crawford has been successful in reconciling her identities as a feminist and a psychologist? Why might this be difficult?

When I was growing up, there seemed to be no women out in the world. Maybe I got an overdose of patriarchy at an early age. First of all, it was the 1950s, and the women I knew were all full-time homemakers. Aside from Aunt Tacy Jane, a cashier in a supermarket, and Aunt Ruth, a seamstress, none of them had a dime of her own in her pocket.

My father was an Air Force sergeant. I grew up on and around military bases. When my family went to church on Sunday, the priest stood with his back to the congregation and chanted the Mass in Latin in homage to a trinity of male gods. Even the servers at Mass were always boys.

Okay, I found a few straws to grasp. At the age of five, I became a big fan of Dale Evans. Never mind that she was second-in-command to Roy Rogers—she had her own horse, a lasso, and a gun! I cajoled a cowgirl outfit from my parents and spent hours fantasizing giving orders from atop my palomino. In third grade, my class read "Trees," by Joyce Kilmer. I loved this poem ("I think that I shall never see / A poem lovely as a tree . . ."), and I thought how wonderful it must be to write something in a book for children to read. I wanted to be Joyce Kilmer, woman writer. Unfortunately, I later discovered that Kilmer was a man.

Moving on, I discovered Nancy Drew, the answer to my brother's Hardy Boys mysteries. Nancy was way cool, with her roadster, her smarts, and her boyfriend. In high school, I stumbled on Margaret Mead. Her *Coming of Age in Samoa* dazzled me. From it I began to learn how people are shaped by culture, and—equally important—that a woman could be smart and tough enough to go off by herself and discover something new about the world. And I heard about Golda Meir, Prime Minister of the new state of Israel. In fact, Meir provided me with one of my first moments of feminist awakening. Confronted with a suggestion in parliament to reduce crime and sexual assault by restricting the hours women could travel in public, Meir replied that it would be better to restrict the men, who were committing the crimes.

The parental guidance I remember was composed of "don'ts," from "Don't talk back," to "Don't get pregnant before you're married." Education was seen as a way up the ladder of social class for boys, not girls. Of course, a girl could always try to become an honorary male by studying hard and going on to college—but a "bookworm" was likely to end up an "old maid." In high school, I developed an advanced case of cynicism, making sarcastic remarks about stupid housewives, grubby little kids, and dumb husbands, and declaring dramatically, I Will Never Marry. The bookworm wanted to be prepared in case nobody ever asked!

My SAT scores were the best in the class. The boy with the next-best scores went on to Harvard; I went to a nearby branch of a state college. Did I perceive this as an injustice? Absolutely not. I felt wildly lucky to be going to college at all. I was the first person in my family to do so, and I did not appreciate the fine nuances involved in comparing Harvard and State Teachers' College. I just got out of town as fast as I could.

I wish I had known while I was growing up about all the other women who have struggled to find their place in the world. Though I write about it lightly now, I can easily remember the doubts, the lack of confidence, the uncertainty and confusion I experienced. Who was I; what could I become? I was afraid and shy much of the time. I was chronically ambivalent, dreaming of being a writer or a scientist yet doubting whether I was smart enough to do much of anything. Most of all, I just felt lonely.

I graduated from college with a degree in music education, not because I had any great talents in this direction, but because teaching music was considered a tolerable deviance for women. I did like music, and I wanted to lead a high school chorus or symphonic band. The only jobs I was offered were part-time elementary music teaching. A few years of listening to third-graders play scales on their little plastic recorders was more than enough of that.

I discovered psychology later, as a returning student in my late twenties. It was then that I came to appreciate the power of making knowledge—in, of all places, "stat class." I loved learning how to design a study to find out something new about the world. It was hard, to be sure—correlations, regressions, t tests, analyses of variance, interactions, sampling distributions—but I loved the power of it. It felt like I was learning the passwords to a secret society. I would become one of the chosen few, the Scientists. It never occurred to me to question why there were so few women in my classes or textbooks, or why "women's issues" were never the topic of research. I had found what I was good at doing, and I would become an honorary man.

Not that there weren't reminders of my marginality as I proceeded to become an experimental psychologist:

- I am a graduate student at my first professional conference. Of course, there are ten times as many men there as women. On an elevator, I see a man whose presentation I had attended earlier in the day. It was about tonic immobility, a reaction that can be seen in birds and some other animals, in which they go limp and "play dead" when they are attacked. Turning to the man, I remark that I enjoyed his presentation. He launches into a routine about how the technique works with women, too: just grab 'em by the neck and they go limp and stop resisting. He continues his extended rape joke until the elevator doors open.

- I am about to collect the data for my Ph.D. dissertation when the faculty member in charge of the animal laboratory decides that certain grad students (me) should not have access to animal subjects, which are to be reserved for faculty and selected grad students (his). I protest in vain. Then I find that half the animals are being discarded. Nobody wants the female rats, it seems; all of the researchers think that their hormonal cycles will mess up the data. I snag the female rats and run my dissertation study (they do not mess up the data).

- I start my first job, team-teaching Introductory Psychology with my husband, also a brand-new Ph.D. We decide that we will debate issues in class, so that students can learn critical thinking. I'll start off as the leader with my husband as respondent, and later in the semester we will switch. We think we are doing just great. Then the dean's wife tells me that a student has described our class to her as "the one where the woman talks and the man corrects her when she's getting it wrong."

- I move on to a larger university. When I sign the contract as an assistant professor, it specifies exactly how many articles per year I must publish and what journals they must be in. Later, I find that no male hired by the department, before or after, has ever had such a contract. It is assumed that the men will know where and when to publish their research, and that rigid rules would stifle their creativity. With the help of a female department chair, I got a contract like the men's.

- The year I apply for promotion to full professor, five women and fifteen men apply. One-third of the men, and none of the women, get promoted. With the other women, I file a complaint. Two years later, the university settles in our favor.

In 1975, I started to get involved in Women's Studies by teaching a mini-course in Psychology of Women. The discovery that there was no research on women in the field that claimed to be "the science of human behavior" was galvanizing. I began to realize that psychology, my intellectual home, had serious flaws, and that the problem extended to all knowledge. Although I did not read her words until much later, I had come to the same realization as the poet Adrienne Rich: what I learned in college and graduate school was

> how *men* have perceived and organized their experience, their history, their ideas of social relationships, good and evil, sickness and health, etc. When you read or hear about "great issues," "major texts," "the mainstream of Western thought," you are learning about what men, above all white men, in their male subjectivity, have decided is important (1979:232).

At this time, the women's movement was growing, and I got involved in various kinds of political and social activism. Meanwhile, my experimental work was starting to get published and noticed. Rather than bringing me satisfaction, my dual identities as activist and psychologist seemed at odds with each other. More and more, my research seemed like a series of intellectual puzzles that had no connection to the rest of my life. In the laboratory, I studied abstract theories of conditioning, accepting the assumption that the principles were similar for rats and humans. In the "real world," I perceived injustice everywhere and sought to understand the reasons for it. I became aware of sexual harassment, wife battering, media stereotyping, and other kinds of sexism that were just then being named by the women's movement. Also, trying to build a marriage between equal partners and bring up my children in nonsexist ways made me much more aware of social pressures to conform to traditional gender roles. (For another chapter in this story, see "Two Jobs, Three Kids, and Her 2000-Mile Commute," in Part V.) I began to ask myself why I was doing a kind of psychology that had so little to say about the real problems of women. I turned to social psychology and the study of women/gender to make my personal and professional life congruent and to begin using my skills as a psychologist on behalf of social change.

Finding my second intellectual home in the psychology of women has expanded my thinking and also has given me a new vantage point for looking at psychology. From women's studies, I have learned that laboratory research using experimental and statistical techniques is not the only route to knowledge. I have learned how radically a research agenda can change when you start to ask, "Where are the women?" Each question about women and their lives leads to another, more daring question, which leads to developing new methods for finding answers, until you have followed a path that leaves most of psychology behind.

I still value my early work and training in psychology. From it, I learned how to go about scientific inquiry systematically and responsibly. However, my beliefs about what are the important questions in psychology, and the best ways to go about answering them, have changed. So I stand both within and outside the "mainstream" of psychology, enjoying the contradictions of feeling both marginal and at the center.

When I hear that in a survey of APA members, Division 35 (Psychology of Women) was ranked 33rd out of 40 in importance, I feel marginal. Conversely, women now earn more than half the Ph.D.s in psychology—the days of professional conferences with ten times as many men as women are over. Women's studies, with programs in more than 600 universities around the country, is not going to fade away. Division 35 and the Association for Women in Psychology provide a home that women have never had before in psychology's history. In being part of these changes, I believe that I am at the center of a revolution. Shifting from margin to center and back gives a unique double vantage point. Articulating this "double vision" is, I think, one of the most important contributions of feminist psychology.

It is not easy for me to write about my own struggles to get an education and to be treated fairly in my profession. Part of the training a psychologist receives is to learn how to conceal oneself, the better to speak as an expert on other people. And even now there is a part of me that believes that the loneliness and difficulties I have experienced must have been partly my fault. Living a prosperous and contented life today, it would be easier to forget how hard it has been to get here. From women's studies I have learned, though, that if I am to take my students seriously, I must be honest with myself and them. There is always a new generation of young women trying to claim their right to an education, and they need to hear from those who have gone before. Knowledge is power.

Reference

RICH, A. (1979). Claiming an education. In *On lies, secrets and silences: Selected prose 1966–1978* (pp. 231–235). New York: Norton.

Making a Feminist: A Personal History

Rhoda Unger describes what it was like to become a psychologist forty years ago, when women were an almost-invisible minority and sexism abounded in personal interactions and institutional policies. As might be expected, deep loneliness and feelings of marginality were a price paid by women of Unger's generation, even those talented and fortunate enough to attend Ivy League colleges, as she did. However, Unger achieved individual success, publishing many influential books and articles, and has also worked together with others to improve women's status in psychology.

As You Read, Ask Yourself . . .

How does Rhoda Unger view marginality as both a disadvantage and a source of strength?

Which of the sexist incidents and practices she describes would be rare today, and which might still occur?

What were some sources of encouragement and support for Unger and the other women entering psychology in the 1960s?

How did women's organizations within psychology make a difference?

I never planned to study women or gender. Most of the women in my generation did not. There were no courses, no journals, and little history. Most of us had forgotten that there had ever been a first wave of feminism in the 1920s, and, if we remembered, we considered it to be irrelevant to our lives and work.

Looking back, it is hard to remember how lonely I felt in most academic/professional contexts. I started college in 1956, graduate school in 1960, and my professional career (my first full-time position) in 1966. There are figures about the percentage of women who participated in the American Psychological Association's annual conventions during these years—10.8 percent in 1956 and 13.9 percent in 1966. But I am not sure these numbers convey the isolation of women psychologists within the university environment and, especially, when we ventured into the "outside world" of professional meetings.

During conferences women were invisible except as potential sexual partners. Invitations for dinner at these meetings (even when one paid for oneself) seemed to be taken as invitations for sexual trysts afterwards. Although we were visible as potential sexual partners, we were completely invisible as professional colleagues. In 1966 I went to a meeting with my husband (who is not a psychologist) just after getting married. I was on the job market at the time. We became involved in a number of conversations in which senior men asked my husband what I did (I was right there at the time!). He was even offered a position at a prestigious university because he was a good listener for the distinguished professor who was holding forth at the time. Needless to say, when he indicated that he was not professionally qualified, the position was not offered to me.

Most of the feminist psychologists who were professionally active during this period have their own "war stories." But most of us were socialized to believe that personal history was irrelevant for us as objective social scientists. Some, like myself, have internalized that belief, and it is only recently that I have begun to reveal myself in my scholarly papers. I am still very uncomfortable in doing so.

Nevertheless, the first personal comments I ever made in a professional context (in 1985) seem quite revealing:

> Rhoda Kesler Unger regards herself as having been marginal throughout her professional career. She was the only woman in her year in the Experimental Psychology program at Harvard from which she received her Ph.D. She is a Professor of Psychology at Montclair State College and an active researcher in a primarily teaching institution. She is a feminist married to her first and only husband, with whom she is rearing two teen-aged daughters. . . . She believes that marginality explains her scholarly concerns as well as expanding their perspective. (In O'Leary, Unger, & Wallston, 1985, p. xii.)

Actually, my perceptions of marginality date from earlier in my life. Like many other feminist academics of my acquaintance, I am from a working-class background. I was the first member of my family to go to college. Graduate school was not even part of our awareness. The elementary school system that I attended could be characterized as "inner city" even then. And I was a bookish "ugly duckling" who was beloved by my teachers but ignored by my peers.

My experiences during my elementary and high school years had led me to believe that hard work paid off. When I performed very well academically at Brooklyn College, I saw no reason to believe that I could not do as well in a Ph.D. program. In some ways my marginalization had sheltered me from the sexism of the 1950s. Because there was no one in my family with whom to compare myself in terms of class mobility, I ignored gender constraints as well. Harvard was quite an awakening in this regard!

I have since learned from male classmates that they perceived the years of graduate school as dehumanizing too, but at the time, they did not confide this. The style at Harvard was "academic macho," which meant pretending that one neither studied nor worried and passed examinations through innate brilliance. The male faculty (of course, there was not a single female to be found) took on the most promising (and arrogant) male graduate students as apprentices. However, they did not want female apprentices because they believed that women could not achieve professional "stardom." Women were to be tracked into teaching positions. In my second year of graduate school, they did not offer me the usual research assistantships that my surviving male classmates received. Instead, they found me a teaching assistantship at MIT, where a graduate program in psychology was being started and they did not have enough graduate students of their own to teach undergraduate sections. The male graduate students, however, were taught to write grant proposals, conduct research, and give professional presentations.

The faculty at Harvard did not seem to believe that training women for their doctorates involved any responsibility for them afterward. As I found out accidentally later on, letters of recommendation could contain potential bombshells. For example, one faculty member from whom I had received "*A's*" wrote that I was argumentative (I had once criticized his changing his name to what I perceived as a less Jewish one, and I was outspoken in his seminars), and another stated that I was "ambitious" (I was, but "highly motivated" might have been a less loaded term). These letters resulted in a "stress interview" for a postdoctoral position in which I was asked whether I got along with other women (which seems ironic now) instead of what kind of research I was interested in. I must have given the "right answers," because I did get the position.

Of course, I was left to find my own job after receiving my Ph.D. The field was still expanding then, so teaching positions were not hard to find. Positions at elite research institutions (comparable to those that almost all my male classmates obtained) were not available for women in experimental psychology. The percentage of women in this subdiscipline at the time was less than 10 percent. Most of the women could be found in teaching institutions or as research associates at large universities where their husbands were employed. I found myself a position at a teaching institution.

My political views were not particularly popular at this university, where I was one of the first two young women hired by the psychology department. My personal style was also rather "hippie" at the time. For example, I had long straight hair down to my waist (I did wear it up for classes). One of the senior women in the department was unhappy with my style, which she thought would lead the students to not respect me. She requested that I cut my hair before she would let me teach graduate courses. I was still politically naive and somewhat arrogant (I thought my professional credentials were more important than my appearance), so I laughed, told the story to others, and did not cut my hair. I also did not get tenure.

I would not suggest that there was a direct connection between hairstyle and tenure. However, my experience is indicative of the dilemmas encountered by at least one young female faculty member during a period when the "rules" were changing. There were a lot of double binds around. For example, I thought I could combine a career and children—rare among earlier generations of women academics (who were sometimes penalized professionally if they even married). I tried to time my pregnancies to coincide with academic vacations. Unfortunately, I miscalculated on my first pregnancy and was informed that insurance regulations would not permit me to teach at the institution during late pregnancy. My graduate seminar met at my home for a few weeks—much to the displeasure of higher authorities.

Moreover, no one during my graduate training had ever pointed out to me how difficult it would be to maintain a career in physiological psychology and have any semblance of a normal family life. The facts that animals had to be fed every day or that brain operations could not be interrupted for family emergencies were not seen as relevant when the researchers were male. The practical problems that I encountered trying to do such research combined with the increasing irrelevance I found in studies of the caudate nucleus in rats (on which I had done my Ph.D. dissertation) moved me to reconsider my research goals.

During this time I had become involved in developing curricular materials for a course in the psychology of women. When I did not receive tenure in 1972, I moved to Montclair State University, where I have remained. When I interviewed at Montclair, I was much more aware of potential political problems in decisions about promotion and tenure than I had been six years earlier. During the hiring interview, I announced that I was in the process of shifting fields from physiological to social psychology and that I was interested in developing a course on the psychology of women for the institution. There was much ignorance about the area, but not too much hostility, and I was hired. Some of the questions asked were amusing and, in hindsight, predictable. They included: "Don't we cover the area in human sexuality?" "Will we have a comparable class in the psychology of men?" "Is there enough material for such a course?" And, "Who will teach this course if you do not?" The answer to the latter question was a chorus from all the other women in the room. Obviously, Montclair was a much more comfortable academic environment for me than my previous institution had been.

While I was beginning my career and having children (two daughters, one born in 1968 and one in 1970), other women were entering psychology and also encountering sexism on both personal and professional levels. Book titles were unabashedly sexist, positions were advertised for men only, and if women were interviewed for positions, they were routinely asked about their marital and childbearing plans.

The Association for Women in Psychology (AWP) began from informal conversations at meetings of graduate students and younger academic women who, like myself, had been influenced by popular feminists. It was an enormous relief to share experiences with other women who were having difficulty getting positions, were underemployed, and, somewhat later, were encountering difficulties obtaining tenure. We also shared stories about the difficulties of finding mentors, juggling roles, sexual harassment, and the alienation we felt from being in a virtually all-male environment.

We had long, emotional conversations about current problems and future plans. Our friendships transcended geography and subdisciplinary affiliation. They served as the nucleus for more formal networks as women in psychology became increasingly politically organized.

Involvement with feminist organizations within psychology helped to give legitimacy to research on women. We were able, for example, to develop journals such as the *Psychology of Women Quarterly* and *Sex Roles*. Our goals, as first stated, were not, however, particularly activist in nature. Instead, the organizers of APA's Division on the Psychology of Women stressed the scientific value of scholarship on women.

Today it is important to me to be *both* a scholar and an activist. This was not always true. I cannot say that I was a feminist from the earliest point of my professional life. It took me a while to identify the fundamental sexism of psychology and in academia as a whole. Until graduate school the meritocratic system seemed to have worked for me. I blamed my growing sense of alienation from psychology on my own inadequacies as a person and as a researcher.

I became a feminist through writing my first textbook (published in 1975). As I read more and more sources needed to write this text, I recognized that my own experiences of injustice were shared by others and were grounded in structural processes rather than personal inadequacies.

The book was driven by passion. We wanted to demonstrate that psychological research could illuminate the way sexual inequality was produced and maintained and to show that such inequality had no basis in fact. We believed in the power of science to effect social change.

The writing of a feminist textbook twenty years after the first one is more of a political act. Mary Crawford and I want to move psychology beyond its narrow concern with laboratory research. At the same time, we wish to use such research to examine women and gender. This forces us to use the scholarly base of traditional psychology while attempting to deconstruct that tradition. I have not lost hope that we can do both.

Many of you reading this story are probably surprised by the notion that I continue to view myself as an "outsider." This is partly a consequence of my early history, but it is also attributable to some deeply held beliefs that I share with other social activists. I have found that many influential feminists have a contradictory view of themselves and the world. They recognize that authority is not synonymous with truth, that people are not always rational, and that chance is important in human affairs. Conversely, they also possess a deep conviction that their actions can change reality. This contradictory view is what gives them the wisdom to understand social injustices and the energy to challenge them. My own ability to balance contradictory behaviors such as involvement in both traditional scholarship and movements for social change is nourished by my identification with marginality. It is my hope that I will always retain such an identification.

Reference

O'LEARY, V. E., UNGER, R. K., & WALLSTON, B. S. (Eds.) (1985). *Women, gender, and social psychology.* Hillsdale, N.J.: Erlbaum.

Noemi Alindogan-Medina

Women's Studies:
A Struggle for a Better Life

Noemi Alindogan-Medina is a professor of history at Philippine Normal University. She has published articles and poems on women and is a leader in women's studies and women's issues in the Philippines. Here, she writes about how she came to understand the need for women's studies, how she found her own voice as a poet through connecting with other women, and her work in developing women's studies programs in her country.

As You Read, Ask Yourself . . .

How did Noemi Alindogan-Medina first become aware that the personal experiences of women are politically and socially significant?

How were the roles and status of men and boys different from those of women and girls when Alindogan-Medina was growing up, and how did this affect her path to a college education?

How did discrimination by social class and skin color interact with gender discrimination in Alindogan-Medina's community?

How did she turn personal insights into political activism?

THE AWAKENING

How did I ever get into women's studies? What was it that hit me so hard, so deep in my heart, roused my consciousness, and made me see things beyond pleasant domesticities? What motivated me to join the women's movement in the Philippines? These questions come to mind when I seek to recall how I became a feminist.

Women's studies and feminism—I was a stranger to both until 1987, when I was sent as a representative of the Philippine Normal College to attend a national consultation on women and education sponsored by the National Commission on Women in Quezon City. I went with great reluctance because its first day happened to be the day of our college commencement exercises, at which

President Corazon Aquino was the guest of honor, and I did not want to miss the chance of seeing her in person. Not surprisingly, I reported at the venue of the seminar with little enthusiasm and no curiosity.

The seminar was attended by more than a hundred women teachers and administrators from all over the country. After the introduction and the keynote speech, the participants were divided into small groups, and each participant was asked to reflect upon and share with others a situation in her life that had placed her in a disadvantageous position as a female teacher. I wondered what the facilitators were up to, involving us in such a futile exercise. As far as I knew, women, especially those in education, were neither disadvantaged nor oppressed. I knew Filipinas were considered the most liberated among Asian women and that there were no visible signs of oppression among us. The small-group discussion ended without any contribution from me. For one thing, I was by nature too reserved to discuss personal matters, especially with people I had just met. Also, I preferred to keep things to myself, rather than talk about people who had oppressed me in any way.

Things turned out unexpectedly, however, during the plenary session that afternoon. It was like seeing for myself how much the house needed cleaning, and I couldn't deny the glaring reality that indeed things were not in their proper place. Much dirt had been swept under that beautifully designed carpet for too long a time, and I needed to do something about it at once. In other words, I fully agreed with the presentation made to show how education and media reinforce one another to bring about oppression in different forms among Filipino women. I began to see how we were being projected in films and television as well as in the educational system—in its curriculum, textbooks, and audio-visual materials and in our teaching processes, policies, and administrative practices, which collectively influenced the thought and behavior of students, teachers in particular, and the family and society in general. The nature and extent of the gender issue in education and its relation to the larger society were made clear to us. It was only after more than twenty years in the teaching profession that I became aware of the hidden implications that teachers have unconsciously enforced and perpetuated through generations. This had indeed caused enough damage and I felt that we had to do something to rectify the errors of the past. Now we have to make students aware of how certain laws, some aspects of our history and culture, as well as our educational system have stunted the growth and progress of women and curtailed the full development of our talents, potentialities, and capabilities. With this realization, I committed myself to integrating feminist concepts in my social science courses and to gradually introducing women's issues in the curriculum. I felt that my efforts could have a multiplier effect as some of our college students would become teachers who could also introduce such concepts to their pupils.

Before the break on the last day of the seminar, we were given pieces of paper on which we had to write down the insights we had gained from the activities and our evaluation of the seminar. When I wrote down my thoughts, what came out were statements in poetic form which were well received when I read them before the assembly. The chair of the convenor's group of that seminar reacted by quoting again what feminism aspires to: "a more caring society that gives not only to men but also to women, both bread and roses, poetry and power." Some participants called me a poet and one of them asked for a copy and my permission to have the poem published in their magazine. I was overwhelmed not only by the recognition given me but by my own discovery of a talent of which I was not fully aware. Still unbelieving that I could really write poetry, I tried writing again when I got home. Two poems emerged during the night, which I immediately delivered to the office of the National Commission on Women. Six months later, one of the poems came out in *Ani,* the literary journal of the Cultural Center of the Philippines; the other was published in the *Philippine Journal of Education.* This gave me more self-confidence and encouraged me to write more poems on women.

GROWING UP

It is said that someone has to plant the seed; that if the seed is buried in fertile and moist soil it will grow into a plant. Others will come and help take care of that plant so that it will grow fast and bear flowers and fruit, from which new seeds can be taken for others to plant again. This, in a way, is how I see myself in my growth and development as a feminist. That first seminar on women was followed by similar seminars sponsored by women's groups. Invitations came and, every time, I would beg our dean of instruction to designate me to attend the seminar. Considering my previous lack of interest, my present eagerness must have surprised her.

The second seminar that I attended was on women and development in the teaching of the social sciences and the humanities. . . . It was there that I learned more about women's studies and how women's issues and concerns can be integrated in teaching certain courses in the social sciences.

The third seminar was . . . a national teacher-training workshop in May 1988.

On the first day we talked about the definition of women's studies, which places women's own experiences at the center of the process that establishes women's reality. This was followed by the sharing of personal experiences in small groups, in which we discovered how disadvantaged we were as women. Now that I fully understood that experiences shared by group members form the basis of analyzing women's oppression, I was no longer hesitant to open up and share even those thoughts that I had kept to myself for a long, long time. It was still a difficult thing to do, to dig into my innermost thoughts and deepest feelings about people whom I have loved but whom I now saw as the cause of my oppression. It was doubly difficult to break away from the deeply embedded belief which said we should love and respect our parents as we owe our life and whatever we have now to them, and this love and respect can best be manifested by keeping to ourselves our bitter memories of them.

I grew up in Resurreccion, a small barrio along the sea, under the municipality of San Fernando, a town on Ticao Island, roughly 128.9 square miles in area, in the province of Masbate, Philippines. I was the third child, but the second daughter, in the family. Our eldest sister was taken by our grandmother to live with her in another town, so I became my mother's helping hand, so to speak, as two brothers immediately followed after me and four other children came thereafter.

I was in fourth grade in elementary school when my mother gave birth to another baby girl. I can still remember how I used to wash the diapers and baby dresses at lunch break before going to school, while my brothers just played around. I was the one who cooked our food for breakfast and for supper. Often I would fetch water from an open well about a hundred yards away and gather firewood under the coconut trees before I could start cooking. The boys were nowhere to be found.

After a year, my father went into the fishing business while my mother opened a small grocery store. Early in the morning, when my father's fishermen returned from overnight fishing, my mother would assist him in gathering the catch from every boat that came ashore. At such times my mother would ask me to look after the store as well as my baby sister. She preferred that I should tend the store in her absence rather than my playful brothers. There were times when the catch was plentiful and I would help sell the fish in the village. All this was routine work for me during out-of-school hours.

Weekends were scheduled for washing and ironing the week's clothes. As it was more difficult to wash by the deep well, the women in the village preferred to walk a kilometer along a dirt road to the knee-deep stream. With some women neighbors, my mother and I would start very early in the morning on foot, the big bundles of dirty clothes on our heads. We would wash them the whole morning, then spread them out on the grass to dry. We ate our packed lunch at noon and, if we finished early enough, I also had fun swimming with friends in the cool, fresh water of the stream. After gathering the dried clothes we would walk homeward with the big bundles on our heads.

On Sundays, while the women were again busy ironing clothes, the men would usually have some relaxation. Some of them would preen their game-cocks or play cards. Others would drink *tuba* or cheap bottled liquor while exchanging stories of adventures during their youth. Most often the drinking session would end only when they felt groggy; their legs wobbly as they went home. No wife would dare remind her husband to stop drinking and go home, as that would be a sign of being controlled by a mere woman and would start a quarrel in public. Once the husband reached home, it would be the duty of the wife to attend to his needs and make him feel better and superior.

Among his pastimes, my father preferred drinking *tuba,* although he would do it only occasionally. Whenever he joined such a group, my mother and all of us children would be very nervous at home, as if we were waiting for the arrival of a strong typhoon. We knew what would happen, as it had happened often in the past. Usually, the moment he got home my father would start talking in a loud voice. My mother would be very careful in her responses. Sometimes she preferred to keep quiet while giving him a warm sponge bath. Even then, Father would shout and bang things about with his fists, something which made us tremble under our blankets. We would come out of hiding only when he finally started snoring. Next morning, everybody, including the neighbors, would pretend that nothing out of the ordinary had taken place. But they talked about it in whispers, for if the subject of their conversation found out, he would remember it the next time he got drunk.

Almost the same things were going on in other homes as well. Women and children could do nothing but suffer in silence, even when they were physically hurt. In some cases where a wife was battered, the old folks openly talked about it, but usually placed the blame on the wife for not knowing her husband's true nature and for not giving in to someone who was "not in his proper senses." It is from the old folks that I learned what is expected of a "good wife": that it is the duty of a wife to serve her husband, to give in to his wishes, even his whims, and to attend to his needs; to preserve his name and dignity, and therefore to be loyal to him in thought, word, and deed; to sacrifice everything for the family and accept thankfully whatever kind of husband God has given her. To rebel against these strictures was to question God's will.

As a mother, the woman should therefore train her daughters to do household chores so as to prepare them to be good wives. The daughters should also be reared in docility and passivity, reared to sacrifice so as to carry the whole burden that God had placed on them. Such "words of wisdom" strongly influenced the thoughts and behavior of the girls and women in the community and were transmitted from generation to generation. These old folks had been influenced by their Spanish parents or grandparents and by the teachings of the Spanish priests who had stayed on the island for many years. In fact, my parents have traces of Spanish-Mexican blood in their veins.

These norms, however, did not find acceptance in my young mind, and I swore to myself that I would rather not get married to a man from our locality, as every man there seemed to be doing the same dreadful things. I did not want to relive the experiences that my mother and other women in our village were going through. I also promised myself that never would I allow my future children to live in such a place or to go through the same experiences that had been so traumatic for me.

And so I went on with my studies until I graduated with the highest honors from grade six in 1957. In high school, however, I did not make it to the top, although I remained a good student. I knew I would not be able to keep it up as I did not have much time to compete with those students who lived closer to the school, which was four kilometers away from our home. Most often I walked to school and back, as there was only one minibus in the entire island. My older brother was allowed to study in another high school in Masbate Island, where there were board and lodging facilities. That was not possible for me as my parents would not want me to stay elsewhere.

After graduation, I was eagerly waiting to be sent to Manila for my college education when my father decided that I should stay at home as it would be useless for me to study further. He believed, as other fathers did, that women do not need a college education as they only get married and have children. My brother was allowed to leave for Manila because he was a man and, when he married, he would be the breadwinner of the family. I begged my mother to intercede on my behalf but her ominous silence meant that we could not do anything but follow my father's decision. We did not even have the nerve to question the wisdom of his decisions or to prove him wrong as he had the final say in everything. For a whole year I led a virtually useless life at home, doing the usual household chores.

Luckily, a visiting aunt from Manila convinced my father to let me go with her so that I could take a college degree. My father was apprehensive of what city life might do to a young woman, but my aunt promised to take charge of me. Taking his silence as a sign of assent, my aunt began asking me what course I wished to take. I answered "journalism." Suddenly, my father told my aunt to forget about it, as he would rather see me without a college education than working with men late at night as a journalist. He believed that journalism was a man's profession. When I settled for an education course and promised to study hard, to disregard any distractions, and to come back to our barrio to teach, my father finally agreed to let me go. Indeed, I took up elementary education even though I did not like it then. True to my promise, I went back to teach in our barrio school. Every paycheck that I received was immediately turned over to my parents. Then, after two years, I married and left our island for good.

It can be said that, for a husband, I intentionally chose a man from a far-off place. Marriage for me was, in a certain sense, an escape from the autocratic ways of my father and from the stifling lifestyle in our community. Looking back on my married life today, I can say that it was not really a complete escape from the claws of oppression. In the first place, my husband is also a product of a community which has its own idiosyncracies evident in the values and beliefs of its people. At the same time, he is an army officer who faithfully follows the saying that a soldier is married to the service 99 percent, and to his wife only 1 percent, even if he loves her very much.

No, I had not planned to marry a man in the military. I was in my last year in college and he was then a law school graduate when I accepted his love. I was already teaching on our island when he wrote to say that he had entered military service and was assigned to Mindanao. After two years he came to our island to propose marriage. Learning that he was an army lieutenant, my parents and friends warned me that I may not be able to cope with the demands and pressures of army life. They also thought I was a worrier and that I might not last long with a man whose life could be in constant danger. As I had already made a commitment, my father gave his consent on the condition that I take along my younger sister and see her through high school.

After our military wedding in Manila and honeymoon in Baguio City, my husband took me to Taal, Batangas, to meet his family and relatives. Although he had warned me about his sister, it still hurt when I heard her say to a friend: "My brother should have married Nancy, who is much fairer. Besides, how much is a teacher's salary? I can earn that amount in one day with my business." I was thankful to get away to Davao City in Mindanao where my husband was posted.

In Davao, we lived in a rented cottage in a thinly populated town about two kilometers away from the army camp and fourteen kilometers away from the heart of the city. As there was much work to be done, my husband told me that the wife of one of his soldiers would help me with the laundry. She came with two others, but once the introductions were over, they talked among themselves in Cebuano, which I happened to understand. Just like my sister-in-law, they too noticed my complexion and were greatly disappointed. As if, to be an officer's wife, it is essential to have fair skin. After that first visit not one of them came back. I learned that they worked for an officer's wife whose skin was "like an American's." We stayed in Davao City for three years, after which we transferred to Camp Aguinaldo, Quezon City. With two small children to take care of, I still managed to get a teaching job in an elementary school in Manila. I also enrolled for a master's degree at the Philippine Normal College, where I was taken in as a faculty member after graduation.

ASSESSMENT

My experiences and my exposure to feminism raise many questions in my mind. Looking back, I cannot help wondering what my life would have been like had I not gone to college. In a wider sense, what happens to daughters who are not sent to college? If they look for jobs, where do they work? Do they become domestic labor, victims of discrimination? Do they get less pay for doing the same job as a man? The last to be hired and the first to be fired, do they suffer sexual abuse and harassment on the job? If they ever get married, what are their chances of having an understanding husband, a man who would be responsible and worthy of raising children who can be useful citizens of the country?

If we dig deeper into my case—and it could well be the case of many other young women from a similar background—there are still a number of questions that need to be answered. For instance, why are daughters not given preference for a college education? Even if daughters are allowed to go to college, where are they sent? Do they have the freedom to make their own choice of a career or vocation, to make their own decision as to what they want to do with their lives? How many opportunities are denied to daughters whose lives are controlled by their fathers and whose mothers cannot do anything to defend their daughters' aspirations? How does culture typecast women? The same culture that makes fathers the sole decision makers of the family? How does a highly patriarchal setup affect the daughter's performance when she has to face the world by herself?

In my case, as I have realized only recently, I cannot overcome my fear and inhibitions in expressing my thoughts and feelings, ideas and opinions in the presence of someone who is an authority on the subject. Why can I not be assertive enough in pursuing a certain goal? Why do I always think that I cannot make it because I am weak, because I am only a woman? How many chances of early success did I let go of because of my cowardice, my inability to speak out? What held me back? Why am I like this?

Why do some women think that the wife of a military officer should be fair complexioned and look like a half-breed to be considered beautiful? What kind of orientation and education did these women get out of the system?

The next live-in seminar workshop that I attended was quite different in the sense that the participants came mostly from the grassroots level. There were only two of us who were teachers; the rest were health workers, church workers, women from poor urban communities, farmers, peasants, fisherfolk, and factory workers. This was my first exposure to women from such a wide variety of backgrounds. It turned out to be one of my most rewarding experiences. It was here that I realized that these women—all without college degrees and only elementary or high school graduates—could speak authoritatively on the realities of life, the hardships and difficulties that life offers to us women, who give and nurture life. They called for change not for our own sake anymore but for the generations to come, perhaps because as women and as mothers we have more concern for the future.

Before the three-day workshop was over, I came to know more about women from the grassroots, their thoughts and aspirations, their dreams and wishes, which they were actively striving to fulfill. And I could not help but compare them with the women of the same level in our island. The island women seem to entrust their lives and futures to the men of the family for whatever it brings them and their children. They are inexorably tied down by old customs and traditions to the roles they must perform. They might constitute a vital force in shaping the future of an ideal barrio or town on our island or elsewhere but, without empowerment, are unable to do so. Having grown up on that island and having retained my roots there, it bothers me to no end that the island women should suffer in this way. I keep thinking about what I can do to empower the women in our town so that they, too, can determine the direction their lives should take.

My new experiences reinforced my conviction that there is indeed a great need for change in the role and status of women in the country, and this can be systematically introduced through education. It may be a long and arduous process, and the results may not be readily manifest, but I feel something must be done right away. I have to do my share in this collective endeavor.

Another seminar I attended was the 1990 National Conference and Festival on Women, spearheaded by the Women's Resource and Research Center (WRRC) and supported by the Institute of Women's Studies, the Women's Desk of the Cultural Center of the Philippines, the Association of Philippine Medical Colleges Foundation, and the Women's Desk of the Philippine Council for Development. It was held in February 1990 at the Manila Film Center. This was the biggest workshop I have ever attended as almost eight hundred representatives of different sectors from all over the country converged for the national consultation, with the theme "Women's Power in Us: Reflecting on Philippine Feminism." This time I was also invited to be one of the resource persons for the education sector and I shared with the group how I, along with some colleagues in the college, joined the call for feminism.

I also joined group discussions on various topics, and one of them was on the militarization of women. One resource person shared her experiences about what some soldiers did to her when she was suspected of working for the rebels in their area. She narrated the dangers encountered living in a place where a military operation was going on. During the open forum I could not help but react to her story in my attempt to make it clear that women, whoever and wherever they are, are the real sufferers of military operations, which are obviously conducted by men in uniform.

I shared with the group my experiences during the coup attempts that were made before daybreak, and each time we were always caught unprepared. Before we could even confirm its veracity, all the gates of Camp Aguinaldo would be closed, making it very difficult for us to evacuate to a safer place. Our cottage inside Camp Aguinaldo is quite close to EDSA, across Camp Crame. This area was considered a war zone during the EDSA Revolution in 1987 and the August 1988 and December 1989 coup attempts. This was where the real action took place, but in all these uprisings nobody seemed to give attention to the safety of the families living inside the camp. With all attention concentrated on the enemy forces, the lives of military dependants were virtually forgotten.

To leave the camp on our own was risky and impossible. We couldn't do anything but lie flat on the floor or seek cover under tables every time war planes or helicopters flew over. It was like being caught in a crossfire, and we didn't know where to go. It was indeed a traumatic experience since I was alone with my children all the time. Even during a lull we hesitated to get out of the house as uniformed men were all around, and it was not easy to identify the rebels.

We have to consider the root causes of all these happenings. Why are Filipinos fighting each other? Why do some of them become rebels? Who suffers the most as a result of their action? In the case of soldiers or a husband who died during encounters, who is left behind to take over the family responsibilities? Who is left behind to suffer humiliation when the husband-turned-rebel is killed or imprisoned? Who is left behind to explain to the children why their father behaved the way he did?

THE FLOWERING

Back in college, I started sharing the insights I gained from my experiences with six colleagues who also happened to have participated in similar seminars and workshops conducted by other women's groups. Together we formed an organization of college women and called it URDUJA. Urduja was a Filipina who held a prestigious position in her tribe during the precolonial period. She was a beautiful and intelligent princess who was also a brave warrior and freedom fighter. Her name, therefore, represented a cherished ideal for the women in this country.

The newly formed group then identified their objectives: to develop awareness of women's issues and concerns among faculty members and students; to identify specific content areas where women's studies could be introduced or integrated; to develop strategies and techniques for introducing, integrating, and teaching women's issues and concerns in different subject areas; to improve one's level of consciousness through sharing knowledge and information from seminars and readings on women's studies; and to collect, collate, and reproduce instructional materials for women's studies.

From then on, the core group continued to meet whenever necessary to discuss ways and means of carrying out our set goals. As we did not have the funds to support our needs, we decided to coordinate with existing organizations at the college to cosponsor the following activities:

- A panel discussion on women's studies with three resource speakers from WRRC, Lucia Pavia-Ticzon, Josefa Francisco, and Lorna Israel. They talked on women's issues, why there is a need for women's studies and for integrating women's studies in the curriculum, as well as how women's studies can bring about change in a person's life. The discussion was well attended by faculty members and college students, most of whom probably learned something new about themselves, as was evident from their reactions. This activity was cosponsored by the Philippine Association of University Women—PNC chapter.

- A panel discussion, "Women's Rights: A Step towards Relevant Education," was held 10 February 1990, with the PNC Graduate Assembly as cosponsor. The guest panelists were Aurora Javate-de Dios, Aida Maranan, and Lyn Lee. The audience, numbering more than two hundred graduate students from different specializations, learned much from the topics discussed. There were plenty of questions asked even after the discussion was over, as some students still made follow-up inquiries while the guests were having a snack at a nearby canteen.

- A lecture forum on women in history and religion, which had Sr Kristia Bacani of St Scholastica's College as guest speaker. This was cosponsored by the undergraduate Freshmen Assembly and was attended by more than five hundred college students. Many questions were raised by the students on the role of women as chronicled in the Bible, especially those which were being given different interpretations by their priests in homilies in the church.

- A symposium on sexual violence and rape, which had the Social Science Club as a cosponsor and ten members of WRRC and Women's Crisis Center as resource persons. Again, this was attended by more than five hundred college students who showed much interest in the topics discussed. They were also given a demonstration on how to defend oneself in case of sexual harassment.

- A seminar on the psychology of Filipino women overseas workers (Japayuki, domestic helpers, and mail-order brides), which was cosponsored by the Pambansang Samahan sa Siko-lohiyang Pilipino. Aurora Javate-de Dios presented the life of Filipino women in Japan who work as dancers, commonly known as Japayuki. Gina Alunan-Melgar and Vina Bugayong, of the Kanlungan Center for Migrant Workers, talked about Filipinas as brides for sale in Europe. I presented the results of a study I had made of domestic helpers in the Middle East. This activity was also attended by faculty members and students of other colleges and universities.

All these activities were intended to raise the level of consciousness of faculty members and students on the status of Filipino women. At the same time, they were meant to test the water, so to speak, for us to know how open and receptive our administrators are to this area. After the first two activities, URDUJA came up with a proposal to offer an introductory course on women's studies for the summer of 1990. Luckily, this was approved by both the Dean of the School of Social Sciences and the Vice President for Academic Affairs. Although the announcement came out quite late, twenty graduate students enrolled in the course which I was handling. . . .

Between 1990 and 1991, six other faculty members joined URDUJA. With this development, I requested WRRC to conduct an orientation session with the twelve of us, especially as we had many questions wc wanted to ask. There was also the need to understand fully the theoretical framework of women's studies. Two other similar sessions followed when we decided to come up with a course outline on women in history, which we wanted to propose as an alternative to a Spanish course.

Sr. Mary John Mananzan, who chairs the Inter-Institutional Consortium, also contributes a great deal to the effort. She conducts a Gender Fair Education Seminar-Workshop at least twice a year for members of the consortium, of which Philippine Normal College, now a university, is a member. So far, eight members of URDUJA have attended these seminars and workshops, which deepened their understanding of and commitment to the cause of women.

In consonance with our goals and objectives, members of URDUJA try as much as possible to integrate women's issues and concerns into the different subject areas taught at the college. We watch out for possible entry points through which women's issues can be discussed. Given the right techniques and strategies, we feel the lessons can bring about a change in the level of consciousness of the students. After a year, we saw the growing enthusiasm of the students for joining us in the organization. This brought about the birth of the students' organization which we call the Kabataang Urduja. The organization was formally introduced to the academic community on 19 July 1991 in the presence of our college administrators. On 3 August 1991 we conducted the first seminar-workshop for the members of Kabataang Urduja, with the support and assistance of Lucia Pavia-Ticzon and two other members of WRRC. This was attended by 118 of the initial 135 members of this new students' organization.

The members of URDUJA have also increased to twenty-one faculty members representing the following departments: history, social sciences, psychology, education, value education, child study, mathematics, natural sciences, language, and literature, as well as the Research Center and the Students' Affairs Office.

As agreed upon, a number of us are recording our respective experiences in integrating women's issues and concerns into the different subject areas. Our goal is to come up with instructional materials from these journals, or diaries, that we are striving to maintain. This should help guide other teachers who would want to venture into the same area.

On a more personal note, my involvement in seminars and workshops on women inspired me to write poems, which have been compiled in book form called *Ugat,* or Roots, published by WRRC. I have tried out most of these poems with my students and have found that they are effective as consciousness-raising activities in and out of the classroom. Most of them can also be used in introductory lessons in women's studies or as springboards to introduce women's issues into different subject areas.

I am also at present working on my dissertation on women in the military. This entails a lot of hard work, time, and patience but I am slowly pushing my way through in spite of my jobs at home and in college. I believe I can make some contribution in raising the status of women in the military. The result of my study could perhaps form a basis for revising some obsolete policies that are discriminatory to women.

Another area we are trying to explore is that of research. Some of us teach a course called Research Designs. In my two classes, for instance, I have encouraged my students to come up with studies on women for their mini-theses which form the main requirement for this course. The following topics have been chosen by the students, and their research efforts were presented for oral defense: women in media, women as breadwinners, single parenthood, women in the integrated national police, domestic helpers, Japayuki, women behind bars, and life histories of women of three generations (grandmother, mother, and daughter). For supplementary reading the students made use of the reading materials collected by URDUJA members for their office and library. Yes, URDUJA now has an office, given to us by the Dean of the School of Social Sciences, perhaps in recognition of our efforts. Our modest library is also a realization of one of our prime objectives: to collect, collate, and reproduce instructional materials for women's studies. The inclusion of our organization in the Directory of WRRC has helped us greatly in collecting materials from various sources. From time to time we receive magazines, and even books, sent by other women's groups, locally and from other countries.

THE FUTURE LIES BEFORE US

Once we start work on women's studies, we cannot merely limit our energies to a certain area. We cannot simply concentrate on curricular and materials development without paying attention to the possible result of this: the growing need for students to organize themselves and to find answers to the many questions that spring up through these consciousness-raising activities. The process of seeking the answers leads students to conduct research on women's issues.

For our part, we would not have been able to handle these demands and the challenges that come along the way without the support and cooperation of friends in the movement. As the overall coordinator of URDUJA, I have gathered much strength and encouragement from Lucia Pavia-Ticzon, Josefa Francisco, and the staff of WRRC, from Sr. Mary John Mananzan and the Interinstitutional Consortium, and from friends like Aurora Javate de Dios who support our activities. In all this I see the importance of women's solidarity in the attainment of a common goal: to make life worth living for half of the country's population.

So what made me get into women's studies? As I see it now, it is my very life which is, in itself, a spectrum of experiences that I once recalled with bitterness and resentment. Such experiences were caused by people around me who had lived, thought, and believed that the essence of life and virtue lay in abiding by the rules of a patriarchal society. Their lives were dictated by norms set by people who had been colonized both in mind and body. They based the roles of men and women on schoolbooks and rules perpetuated by the old folks who, in their unlettered wisdom, told the young to obey these rules, so as to be accepted members of the community.

What made me get into women's studies, then, was the realization that something has to change in the way things are, that women should act together and resolutely evolve a better life not only for a few but for all women in all sectors of society. It was the awareness of the necessity for sharing and learning from one another; for examining minutely the factors that chain us and control our hearts, minds, and bodies within the walls of an invisible cage; and for coming out with a concrete effort to free ourselves from our fetters so that we may explore all possibilities of discovering and utilizing our talents, strengths, and resources. Only in this way may we become worthy trustees of the riches of our country. Truly, women must work together to bring about "a more caring society that will give not only to men but also to women, both bread and roses, poetry and power."

Freedom For All

I lived with eyes closed in an invisible cage
Like any other girl of my time and age
Blindly I acted the roles traditions dictate
Women are slaves to men, and thus nurture hate.

Household chores have sapped me of initiatives
Restrained me from exploring possibilities
Circumscribing my world and my perspectives
To discover my talents and potentialities.

As I face the world and life's stern reality
I felt the effects of piled-up insecurity
Inferiority, inhibitions gnawing at me
Getting out of my cage was a difficulty.

I bolted out of my cage: yet long did I know
The claws of oppression followed me through;
Church and school only emboldened the forces
That chained me to mere pleasant domesticities.

Now with my eyes open I desire and strive
To cut off the chains so I can stay alive:
I have discovered my true worth in life
No more a slave of traditions, and less strife.

Let me be free as a bird, not controlled like a kite
Let me soar through the sky with my own wings and might
And let this be so for all women in cages of distress
Let us all feel freedom, equality, happiness!

A Question of Class

Dorothy Allison, author of the acclaimed novel Bastard Out of Carolina, *writes here about the greatest, yet least recognized, dividing line in American society: social class. As a lesbian feminist who comes from an impoverished working-class family, she insists that these multiple identities must be claimed. Allison describes how she learned to hide and run away from her family background and her history of sexual and physical abuse. As a writer, however, she learned to give voice to the contradictions of her multiple identities.*

As You Read, Ask Yourself . . .

How does Dorothy Allison explain her attempts to present a false self to friends and lovers?

How did her family's move from South Carolina to Florida present an opportunity for personal redefinition?

How is class bias expressed within the women's movement and how might it be changed?

What strengths has Allison derived from her background and how are they evident in her writing?

The first time I heard, "They're different than us, don't value human life the way we do," I was in high school in Central Florida. The man speaking was an army recruiter talking to a bunch of boys, telling them what the army was really like, what they could expect overseas. A cold angry feeling swept over me. I had heard the word *they* pronounced in that same callous tone before. *They,* those people over there, those people who are not us, they die so easily, kill each other so casually. They are different. *We,* I thought. *Me.*

When I was six or eight back in Greenville, South Carolina, I had heard that same matter-of-fact tone of dismissal applied to me. "Don't you play with her. I don't want you talking to them." Me and my family, we had always been *they.* Who am I? I wondered, listening to that recruiter. Who are my people? We die so easily, disappear so completely—we/they, the poor and the queer. I pressed my bony white trash fists to my stubborn lesbian mouth. The rage was a good feeling, stronger and purer than the shame that followed it, the fear and the sudden urge to run and hide, to deny, to pretend I did not know who I was and what the world would do to me.

My people were not remarkable. We were ordinary, but even so we were mythical. We were the *they* everyone talks about—the ungrateful poor. I grew up trying to run away from the fate that destroyed so many of the people I loved, and having learned the habit of hiding, I found I had also learned to hide from myself. I did not know who I was, only that I did not want to be *they*, the ones who are destroyed or dismissed to make the "real" people, the important people, feel safer. By the time I understood that I was queer, that habit of hiding was deeply set in me, so deeply that it was not a choice but an instinct. Hide, hide to survive, I thought, knowing that if I told the truth about my life, my family, my sexual desire, my history, I would move over into that unknown territory, the land of they, would never have the chance to name my own life, to understand it or claim it.

Why are you so afraid? my lovers and friends have asked me the many times I have suddenly seemed a stranger, someone who would not speak to them, would not do the things they believed I should do, simple things like applying for a job, or a grant, or some award they were sure I could acquire easily. Entitlement, I have told them, is a matter of feeling like we rather than they. You think you have a right to things, a place in the world, and it is so intrinsically a part of you that you cannot imagine people like me, people who seem to live in your world, who don't have it. I have explained what I know over and over, in every way I can, but I have never been able to make clear the degree of my fear, the extent to which I feel myself denied: not only that I am queer in a world that hates queers, but that I was born poor into a world that despises the poor. The need to make my world believable to people who have never experienced it is part of why I write fiction. I know that some things must be felt to be understood, that despair, for example, can never be adequately analyzed; it must be lived. But if I can write a story that so draws the reader in that she imagines herself like my characters, feels their sense of fear and uncertainty, their hopes and terrors, then I have come closer to knowing myself as real, important as the very people I have always watched with awe.

I have known I was a lesbian since I was a teenager, and I have spent a good twenty years making peace with the effects of incest and physical abuse. But what may be the central fact of my life is that I was born in 1949 in Greenville, South Carolina, the bastard daughter of a white woman from a desperately poor family, a girl who had left the seventh grade the year before, worked as a waitress, and was just a month past fifteen when she had me. That fact, the inescapable impact of being born in a condition of poverty that this society finds shameful, contemptible, and somehow deserved, has had dominion over me to such an extent that I have spent my life trying to overcome or deny it. I have learned with great difficulty that the vast majority of people believe that poverty is a voluntary condition.

I have loved my family so stubbornly that every impulse to hold them in contempt has sparked in me a countersurge of pride—complicated and undercut by an urge to fit us into the acceptable myths and theories of both mainstream society and a lesbian-feminist reinterpretation. The choice becomes Steven Spielberg movies or Erskine Caldwell novels, the one valorizing and the other caricaturing, or the patriarchy as villain, trivializing the choices the men and women of my family have made. I have had to fight broad generalizations from every theoretical viewpoint.

Traditional feminist theory has had a limited understanding of class differences and of how sexuality and self are shaped by both desire and denial. The ideology implies that we are all sisters who should only turn our anger and suspicion on the world outside the lesbian community. It is easy to say that the patriarchy did it, that poverty and social contempt are products of the world of the fathers, and often I felt a need to collapse my sexual history into what I was willing to share of my class background, to pretend that my life both as a lesbian and as a working-class escapee was constructed by the patriarchy. Or conversely, to ignore how much my life was shaped by growing up poor and talk only about what incest did to my identity as a woman and as a lesbian. The difficulty is that I can't ascribe everything that has been problematic about my life simply and easily to the patriarchy, or to incest, or even to the invisible and much-denied class structure of our society.

In my lesbian-feminist collective we had long conversations about the mind/body split, the way we compartmentalize our lives to survive. For years I thought that that concept referred to the way I had separated my activist life from the passionate secret life in which I acted on my sexual desires. I was convinced that the fracture was fairly simple, that it would be healed when there was time and clarity to do so—at about the same point when I might begin to understand sex. I never imagined that it was not a split but a splintering, and I passed whole portions of my life—days, months, years—in pure directed progress, getting up every morning and setting to work, working so hard and so continually that I avoided examining in any way what I knew about my life. Busywork became a trance state. I ignored who I really was and how I became that person, continued in that daily progress, became an automaton who was what she did.

I tried to become one with the lesbian-feminist community so as to feel real and valuable. I did not know that I was hiding, blending in for safety just as I had done in high school, in college. I did not recognize the impulse to forget. I believed that all those things I did not talk about, or even let myself think too much about, were not important, that none of them defined me. I had constructed a life, an identity in which I took pride, an alternative lesbian family in which I felt safe, and I did not realize that the fundamental me had almost disappeared.

It is surprising how easy it was to live that life. Everyone and everything cooperated with the process. Everything in our culture—books, television, movies, school, fashion—is presented as if it is being seen by one pair of eyes, shaped by one set of hands, heard by one pair of ears. Even if you know you are not part of that imaginary creature—if you like country music not symphonies, read books cynically, listen to the news unbelievingly, are lesbian not heterosexual, and surround yourself with your own small deviant community—you are still shaped by that hegemony, or your resistance to it. The only way I found to resist that homogenized view of the world was to make myself part of something larger than myself. As a feminist and a radical lesbian organizer, and later as a sex radical (which eventually became the term, along with pro-sex feminist, for those who were not anti-pornography but anti-censorship, those of us arguing for sexual diversity), the need to belong, to feel safe, was just as important for me as for any heterosexual, nonpolitical citizen, and sometimes even more important because the rest of my life was so embattled.

The first time I read the Jewish lesbian Irena Klepfisz's poems,* I experienced a frisson of recognition. It was not that my people had been "burned off the map" or murdered as hers had. No, we had been encouraged to destroy ourselves, made invisible because we did not fit the myths of the noble poor generated by the middle class. Even now, past forty and stubbornly proud of my family, I feel the draw of that mythology, that romanticized, edited version of the poor. I find myself looking back and wondering what was real, what was true. Within my family, so much was lied about, joked about, denied, or told with deliberate indirection, an undercurrent of humiliation or a brief pursed grimace that belied everything that had been said. What was real? The poverty depicted in books and movies was romantic, a backdrop for the story of how it was escaped.

The poverty portrayed by left-wing intellectuals was just as romantic, a platform for assailing the upper and middle classes, and from their perspective, the working-class hero was invariably male, righteously indignant, and inhumanly noble. The reality of self-hatred and violence was either absent or caricatured. The poverty I knew was dreary, deadening, shameful, the women powerful in ways not generally seen as heroic by the world outside the family.

My family's lives were not on television, not in books, not even comic books. There was a myth of the poor in this country, but it did not include us, no matter how hard I tried to squeeze us in. There was an idea of the good poor—hardworking, ragged but clean, and intrinsically honorable. I understood that we were the bad poor: men who drank and couldn't keep a job; women, invariably pregnant before marriage, who quickly became worn, fat, and old from working too many hours and bearing too many children; and children with runny noses, watery eyes, and the wrong attitudes. My cousins quit school, stole cars, used drugs, and took dead-end jobs pumping gas or waiting tables. We were not noble, not grateful, not even hopeful. We knew ourselves despised. My family was ashamed of being poor, of feeling hopeless. What was there to work for, to save money for, to fight for or struggle against? We had generations before us to teach us that nothing ever changed, and that those who did try to escape failed.

My mama had eleven brothers and sisters, of whom I can name only six. No one is left alive to tell me the names of the others. It was my grandmother who told me about my real daddy, a shiftless pretty man who was supposed to have

---

A Few Words in the Mother Tongue: Poems, Selected and New (Eighth Mountain Press: Portland, Oregon, 1990)

married, had six children, and sold cut-rate life insurance to poor Black people. My mama married when I was a year old, but her husband died just after my little sister was born a year later.

When I was five, Mama married the man she lived with until she died. Within the first year of their marriage Mama miscarried, and while we waited out in the hospital parking lot, my stepfather molested me for the first time, something he continued to do until I was past thirteen. When I was eight or so, Mama took us away to a motel after my stepfather beat me so badly it caused a family scandal, but we returned after two weeks. Mama told me that she really had no choice: she could not support us alone. When I was eleven I told one of my cousins that my stepfather was molesting me. Mama packed up my sisters and me and took us away for a few days, but again, my stepfather swore he would stop, and again we went back after a few weeks. I stopped talking for a while, and I have only vague memories of the next two years.

My stepfather worked as a route salesman, my mama as a waitress, laundry worker, cook, or fruit packer. I could never understand, since they both worked so hard and such long hours, how we never had enough money, but it was also true of my mama's brothers and sisters who worked hard in the mills or the furnace industry. In fact, my parents did better than anyone else in the family. But eventually my stepfather was fired and we hit bottom—nightmarish months of marshals at the door, repossessed furniture, and rubber checks. My parents worked out a scheme so that it appeared my stepfather had abandoned us, but instead he went down to Florida, got a new job, and rented us a house. He returned with a U-Haul trailer in the dead of night, packed us up, and moved us south.

The night we left South Carolina for Florida, my mama leaned over the backseat of her old Pontiac and promised us girls, "It'll be better there." I don't know if we believed her, but I remember crossing Georgia in the early morning, watching the red clay hills and swaying grey blankets of moss recede through the back window. I kept looking at the trailer behind us, ridiculously small to contain everything we owned. Mama had packed nothing that wasn't fully paid off, which meant she had only two things of worth: her washing and sewing machines, both of them tied securely to the trailer walls. Throughout the trip I fantasized an accident that would burst that trailer, scattering old clothes and cracked dishes on the tarmac.

I was only thirteen. I wanted us to start over completely, to begin again as new people with nothing of the past left over. I wanted to run away from who we had been seen to be, who we had been. That desire is one I have seen in other members of my family. It is the first thing I think of when trouble comes—the geographic solution. Change your name, leave town, disappear, make yourself over. What hides behind that impulse is the conviction that the life you have lived, the person you are, is valueless, better off abandoned, that running away is easier than trying to change things, that change itself is not possible. Sometimes I think it is this conviction—more seductive than alcohol or violence, more subtle than sexual hatred or gender injustice—that has dominated my life and made real change so painful and difficult.

Moving to Central Florida did not fix our lives. It did not stop my stepfather's violence, heal my shame, or make my mother happy. Once there, our lives became controlled by my mother's illness and medical bills. She had a hysterectomy when I was about eight and endured a series of hospitalizations for ulcers and a chronic back problem. Through most of my adolescence she superstitiously refused to allow anyone to mention the word *cancer*. When she was not sick, Mama and my stepfather went on working, struggling to pay off what seemed an insurmountable load of debts.

By the time I was fourteen, my sisters and I had found ways to discourage most of our stepfather's sexual advances. We were not close, but we united against him. Our efforts were helped along when he was referred to a psychotherapist after he lost his temper at work, and was prescribed drugs that made him sullen but less violent. We were growing up quickly, my sisters moving toward dropping out of school while I got good grades and took every scholarship exam I could find. I was the first person in my family to graduate from high school, and the fact that I went on to college was nothing short of astonishing.

We all imagine our lives are normal, and I did not know my life was not everyone's. It was in Central Florida that I began to realize just how different we were. The people we met there had not been shaped by the rigid class structure that dominated the South Carolina Piedmont. The first time I looked around my junior high classroom and realized I did not know who those people were—not only as individuals but as categories, who their people were and how they saw themselves—I also realized that they did not know me. In Greenville, everyone knew my family, knew we were trash, and that meant we were supposed to be poor, supposed to have grim low-paid jobs, have babies in our teens, and never finish school. But Central Florida in the 1960s was full of runaways and immigrants, and our mostly white working-class suburban school sorted us out not by income and family background but by intelligence and aptitude tests. Suddenly I was boosted into the college-bound track, and while there was plenty of contempt for my inept social skills, pitiful wardrobe, and slow drawling accent, there was also something I had never experienced before: a protective anonymity, and a kind of grudging respect and curiosity about who I might become. Because they did not see poverty and hopelessness as a foregone conclusion for my life, I could begin to imagine other futures for myself.

In that new country, we were unknown. The myth of the poor settled over us and glamorized us. I saw it in the eyes of my teachers, the Lion's Club representative who paid for my new glasses, and the lady from the Junior League who told me about the scholarship I had won. Better, far better, to be one of the mythical poor than to be part of the *they* I had known before. I also experienced a new level of fear, a fear of losing what had never before been imaginable. Don't let me lose this chance, I prayed, and lived in terror that I might suddenly be seen again as what I knew myself to be.

As an adolescent I thought that my family's escape from South Carolina played like a bad movie. We fled the way runaway serfs might have done, with the sheriff who would have arrested my stepfather the imagined border guard. I am certain that if we had remained in South Carolina, I would have been trapped by my family's heritage of poverty, jail, and illegitimate children—that even being smart, stubborn, and a lesbian would have made no difference.

My grandmother died when I was twenty, and after Mama went home for the funeral, I had a series of dreams in which we still lived up in Greenville, just down the road from where Granny died. In the dreams I had two children and only one eye, lived in a trailer, and worked at the textile mill. Most of my time was taken up with deciding when I would finally kill my children and myself. The dreams were so vivid, I became convinced they were about the life I was meant to have had, and I began to work even harder to put as much distance as I could between my family and me. I copied the dress, mannerisms, attitudes, and ambitions of the girls I met in college, changing or hiding my own tastes, interests, and desires. I kept my lesbianism a secret, forming a relationship with an effeminate male friend that served to shelter and disguise us both. I explained to friends that I went home so rarely because my stepfather and I fought too much for me to be comfortable in his house. But that was only part of the reason I avoided home, the easiest reason. The truth was that I feared the person I might become in my mama's house, the woman of my dreams—hateful, violent, and hopeless.

It is hard to explain how deliberately and thoroughly I ran away from my own life. I did not forget where I came from, but I gritted my teeth and hid it. When I could not get enough scholarship money to pay for graduate school, I spent a year of rage working as a salad girl, substitute teacher, and maid. I finally managed to find a job by agreeing to take any city assignment where the Social Security Administration needed a clerk. Once I had a job and my own place far away from anyone in my family, I became sexually and politically active, joining the Women's Center support staff and falling in love with a series of middle-class women who thought my accent and stories thoroughly charming. The stories I told about my family, about South Carolina, about being poor itself, were all lies, carefully edited to seem droll or funny. I knew damn well that no one would want to hear the truth about poverty, the hopelessness and fear, the feeling that nothing I did would ever make any difference and the raging resentment that burned beneath my jokes. Even when my lovers and I formed an alternative lesbian family, sharing what we could of our resources, I kept the truth about my background and who I knew myself to be a carefully obscured mystery. I worked as hard as I could to make myself a new person, an emotionally healthy radical lesbian activist, and I believed completely that by remaking myself I was helping to remake the world.

For a decade, I did not go home for more than a few days at a time.

When in the 1980s I ran into the concept of feminist sexuality, I genuinely did not know what it meant. Though I was, and am, a feminist, and committed to claiming the right to act on my sexual desires without tailoring my lust to a sex-fearing society, demands that I explain or justify my sexual fantasies have left me at a loss. How does anyone explain sexual need?

The Sex Wars are over, I've been told, and it always makes me want to ask who won. But my sense of humor may be a little obscure to women who have never felt threatened by the way most lesbians use and mean the words *pervert* and *queer*. I use the word queer to mean more than lesbian. Since I first used it in 1980 I have always meant it to imply that I am not only a lesbian but a trans-gressive lesbian—femme, masochistic, as sexually aggressive as the women I seek out, and as pornographic in my imagination and sexual activities as the heterosexual hegemony has ever believed.

My aunt Dot used to joke, "There are two or three things I know for sure, but never the same things and I'm never as sure as I'd like." What I know for sure is that class, gender, sexual preference, and prejudice—racial, ethnic, and religious—form an intricate lattice that restricts and shapes our lives, and that resistance to hatred is not a simple act. Claiming your identity in the cauldron of hatred and resistance to hatred is infinitely complicated, and worse, almost unexplainable.

I know that I have been hated as a lesbian both by "society" and by the intimate world of my extended family, but I have also been hated or held in contempt (which is in some ways more debilitating and slippery than hatred) by lesbians for behavior and sexual practices shaped in large part by class. My sexual identity is intimately constructed by my class and regional background, and much of the hatred directed at my sexual preferences is class hatred—however much people, feminists in particular, like to pretend this is not a factor. The kind of woman I am attracted to is invariably the kind of woman who embarrasses respectably middle-class, politically aware lesbian feminists. My sexual ideal is butch, exhibitionistic, physically aggressive, smarter than she wants you to know, and proud of being called a pervert. Most often she is working class, with an aura of danger and an ironic sense of humor. There is a lot of contemporary lip service paid to sexual tolerance, but the fact that my sexuality is constructed within, and by, a butch/femme and leather fetishism is widely viewed with distaste or outright hatred.

For most of my life I have been presumed to be misguided, damaged by incest and childhood physical abuse, or deliberately indulging in hateful and retrograde sexual practices out of a selfish concentration on my own sexual satisfaction. I have been expected to abandon my desires, to become the normalized woman who flirts with fetishization, who plays with gender roles and treats the historical categories of deviant desire with humor or gentle contempt but never takes any of it so seriously as to claim a sexual identity based on these categories. It was hard enough for me to shake off demands when they were made by straight society. It was appalling when I found the same demands made by other lesbians.

One of the strengths I derive from my class background is that I am accustomed to contempt. I know that I have no chance of becoming what my detractors expect of me, and I believe that even the attempt to please them will only further engage their contempt, and my own self-contempt as well. Nonetheless, the relationship between the life I have lived and the way that life is seen by strangers has constantly invited a kind of self-mythologizing fantasy. It has always been tempting for me to play off of the stereotypes and misconceptions of mainstream culture, rather than describe a difficult and sometimes painful reality.

I am trying to understand how we internalize the myths of our society even as we resist them. I have felt a powerful temptation to write about my family as a kind of morality tale, with us as the heroes and middle and upper classes as the villains. It would be within the romantic myth, for example, to pretend that we were the kind of noble Southern whites portrayed in the movies, mill workers for generations until driven out by alcoholism and a family propensity for rebellion and union talk. But that would be a lie. The truth is that no one in my family ever joined a union.

Taken to its limits, the myth of the poor would make my family over into union organizers or people broken by the failure of the unions. As far as my family was concerned union organizers, like preachers, were of a different class, suspect and hated however much they might be admired for what they were supposed to be trying to achieve. Nominally Southern Baptist, no one in my family actually paid much attention to preachers, and only little children went to Sunday school. Serious belief in anything—any political ideology, any religious system, or any theory of life's meaning and purpose—was seen as unrealistic. It was an attitude that bothered me a lot when I started reading the socially conscious novels I found in the paperback racks when I was eleven or so. I particularly loved Sinclair Lewis's novels and wanted to imagine my own family as part of the working man's struggle.

"We were not joiners," my aunt Dot told me with a grin when I asked her about the union. My cousin Butch laughed at that, told me the union charged dues, and said, "Hell, we can't even be persuaded to toss money in the collection plate. An't gonna give it to no union man." It shamed me that the only thing my family wholeheartedly believed in was luck and the waywardness of fate. They held the dogged conviction that the admirable and wise thing to do was keep a sense of humor, never whine or cower, and trust that luck might someday turn as good as it had been bad—and with just as much reason. Becoming a political activist with an almost religious fervor was the thing I did that most outraged my family and the Southern working-class community they were part of.

Similarly, it was not my sexuality, my lesbianism, that my family saw as most rebellious; for most of my life, no one but my mama took my sexual preference very seriously. It was the way I thought about work, ambition, and self-respect. They were waitresses, laundry workers, counter girls. I was the one who went to work as a maid, something I never told any of them. They would have been angry if they had known. Work was just work for them, necessary. You did what you had to do to survive. They did not so much believe in taking pride in doing your job as in stubbornly enduring hard work and hard times. At the same time, they held that there were some forms of work, including maid's work, that were only for Black people, not white, and while I did not share that belief, I knew how intrinsic it was to the way my family saw the world. Sometimes I felt as if I straddled cultures and belonged on neither side. I would grind my teeth at what I knew was my family's unquestioning racism while continuing to respect their pragmatic endurance. But more and more as I grew older, what I felt was a deep estrangement from their view of the world, and gradually a sense of shame that would have been completely incomprehensible to them.

"Long as there's lunch counters, you can always find work," I was told by my mother and my aunts. Then they'd add, "I can get me a little extra with a smile." It was obvious there was supposed to be nothing shameful about it, that needy smile across a lunch counter, that rueful grin when you didn't have rent, or the half-provocative, half-pleading way my mama could cajole the man at the store to give her a little credit. But I hated it, hated the need for it and the shame that would follow every time I did it myself. It was begging, as far as I was concerned, a quasi-prostitution that I despised even while I continued to rely on it. After all, I needed the money.

"Just use that smile," my girl cousins used to joke, and I hated what I knew they meant. After college, when I began to support myself and study feminist theory, I became more contemptuous rather than more understanding of the women in my family. I told myself that prostitution is a skilled profession and my cousins were never more than amateurs. There was a certain truth in this, though like all cruel judgments rendered from the outside, it ignored the conditions that made it true. The women in my family, my mother included, had sugar daddies, not johns, men who slipped them money because they needed it so badly. From their point of view they were nice to those men because the men were nice to them, and it was never so direct or crass an arrangement that they would set a price on their favors. Nor would they have described what they did as prostitution. Nothing made them angrier than the suggestion that the men who helped them out did it just for their favors. They worked for a living, they swore, but this was different.

I always wondered if my mother hated her sugar daddy, or if not him then her need for what he offered her, but it did not seem to me in memory that she had. He was an old man, half-crippled, hesitant and needy, and he treated my mama with enormous consideration and, yes, respect. The relationship between them was painful, and since she and my stepfather could not earn enough to support the family, Mama could not refuse her sugar daddy's money. At the same time the man made no assumptions about that money buying anything Mama was not already offering. The truth was, I think, that she genuinely liked him, and only partly because he treated her so well.

Even now, I am not sure whether there was a sexual exchange between them. Mama was a pretty woman, and she was kind to him, a kindness he obviously did not get from anyone else in his life. Moreover, he took extreme care not to cause her any problems with my stepfather. As a teenager, with a teenager's contempt for moral failings and sexual complexity of any kind, I had been convinced that Mama's relationship with that old man was contemptible. Also, that I would never do such a thing. But the first time a lover of mine gave me money and I took it, everything in my head shifted. The amount was not much to her, but it was a lot to me and I needed it. While I could not refuse it, I hated myself for taking it and I hated her for giving it. Worse, she had much less grace about my need than my mama's sugar daddy had displayed toward her. All that bitter contempt I felt for my needy cousins and aunts raged through me and burned out the love. I ended the relationship quickly, unable to forgive myself for selling what I believed should only be offered freely—not sex but love itself.

When the women in my family talked about how hard they worked, the men would spit to the side and shake their heads. Men took real jobs—harsh, dangerous, physically daunting work. They went to jail, not just the cold-eyed, careless boys who scared me with their brutal hands, but their gentler, softer brothers. It was another family thing, what people expected of my mama's people, mine. "His daddy's that one was sent off to jail in Georgia, and his uncle's another. Like as not, he's just the same," you'd hear people say of boys so young they still had their milk teeth. We were always driving down to the county farm to see somebody, some uncle, cousin, or nameless male relation. Shaven-headed, sullen, and stunned, they wept on Mama's shoulder or begged my aunts to help. "I didn't do nothing, Mama," they'd say, and it might have been true, but if even we didn't believe them, who would? No one told the truth, not even about how their lives were destroyed.

One of my favorite cousins went to jail when I was eight years old, for breaking into pay phones with another boy. The other boy was returned to the custody of his parents. My cousin was sent to the boys' facility at the county farm. After three months, my mama took us down there to visit, carrying a big basket of fried chicken, cold cornbread, and potato salad. Along with a hundred others we sat out on the lawn with my cousin and watched him eat like he hadn't had a full meal in the whole three months. I stared at his near-bald head and his ears marked with fine blue scars from the carelessly handled razor. People were laughing, music was playing, and a tall, lazy, uniformed man walked past us chewing on toothpicks and watching us all closely. My cousin kept his head down, his face hard with hatred, only looking back at the guard when he turned away.

"Sons-a-bitches," he whispered, and my mama shushed him. We all sat still when the guard turned back to us. There was a long moment of quiet, and then that man let his face relax into a big wide grin.

"Uh-huh," he said. That was all he said. Then he turned and walked away. None of us spoke. None of us ate. He went back inside soon after, and we left. When we got back to the car, my mama sat there for a while crying quietly. The next week my cousin was reported for fighting and had his stay extended by six months.

My cousin was fifteen. He never went back to school, and after jail he couldn't join the army. When he finally did come home we never talked, never had to. I knew without asking that the guard had had his little revenge, knew too that my cousin would break into another phone booth as soon as he could, but do it sober and not get caught. I knew without asking the source of his rage, the way he felt about clean, well-dressed, contemptuous people who looked at him like his life wasn't as important as a dog's. I knew because I felt it too. That guard had looked at me and Mama with the same expression he used on my cousin. We were trash. We were the ones they built the county farm to house and break. The boy who was sent home was the son of a deacon in the church, the man who managed the hardware store.

As much as I hated that man, and his boy, there was a way in which I also hated my cousin. He should have known better, I told myself, should have known the risk he ran. He should have been more careful. As I grew older and started living on my own, it was a litany I used against myself even more angrily than I used it against my cousin. I knew who I was, knew that the most important thing I had to do was protect myself and hide my despised identity, blend into the myth of both the good poor and the reasonable lesbian. When I became a feminist activist, that litany went on reverberating in my head, but by then it had become a groundnote, something so deep and omnipresent I no longer heard it, even when everything I did was set to its cadence.

By 1975 I was earning a meager living as a photographer's assistant in Tallahassee, Florida. But the real work of my life was my lesbian-feminist activism, the work I did with the local women's center and the committee to found a women's studies program at Florida State University. Part of my role, as I saw it, was to be a kind of evangelical lesbian feminist, and to help develop a political analysis of this woman-hating society. I did not talk about class, except to give lip service to how we all needed to think about it, the same way I thought we all needed to think about racism. I was a determined person, living in a lesbian collective—all of us young and white and serious—studying each new book that purported to address feminist issues, driven by what I saw as a need to revolutionize the world.

Years later it's difficult to convey just how reasonable my life seemed to me at that time. I was not flippant, not consciously condescending, not casual about how tough a struggle remaking social relations would be, but like so many women of my generation, I believed absolutely that I could make a difference with my life, and I was willing to give my life for the chance to make that difference. I expected hard times, long slow periods of self-sacrifice and grinding work, expected to be hated and attacked in public, to have to set aside personal desire, lovers, and family in order to be part of something greater and more important than my individual concerns. At the same time, I was working ferociously to take my desires, my sexuality, my needs as a woman and a lesbian more seriously. I believed I was making the personal political revolution with my life every moment, whether I was scrubbing the floor of the childcare center, setting up a new budget for the women's lecture series at the university, editing the local feminist magazine, or starting a women's bookstore. That I was constantly exhausted and had no health insurance, did hours of dreary unpaid work and still sneaked out of the collective to date butch women my housemates thought retrograde and sexist never interfered with my sense of total commitment to the feminist revolution. I was not living in a closet: I had compartmentalized my own mind to such an extent that I never questioned why I did what I did. And I never admitted what lay behind all my feminist convictions—a class-constructed distrust of change, a secret fear that someday I would be found out for who I really was, found out and thrown out. If I had not been raised to give my life away, would I have made such an effective, self-sacrificing revolutionary?

The narrowly focused concentration of a revolutionary shifted only when I began to write again. The idea of writing stories seemed frivolous when there was so much work to be done, but everything changed when I found myself confronting emotions and ideas that could not be explained away or postponed until after the revolution. The way it happened was simple and unexpected. One week I was asked to speak to two completely different groups: an Episcopalian Sunday school class and a juvenile detention center. The Episcopalians were all white, well-dressed, highly articulate, nominally polite, and obsessed with getting me to tell them (without their having to ask directly) just what it was that two women did together in bed. The delinquents were all women, 80 percent Black and Hispanic, wearing green uniform dresses or blue jeans and workshirts, profane, rude, fearless, witty, and just as determined to get me to talk about what it was that two women did together in bed.

I tried to have fun with the Episcopalians, teasing them about their fears and insecurities, and being as bluntly honest as I could about my sexual practices. The Sunday school teacher, a man who had assured me of his liberal inclinations, kept blushing and stammering as the questions about my growing up and coming out became more detailed. I stepped out into the sunshine when the meeting was over, angry at the contemptuous attitude implied by all their questioning, and though I did not know why, so deeply depressed I couldn't even cry.

The delinquents were another story. Shameless, they had me blushing within the first few minutes, yelling out questions that were part curiosity and partly a way of boasting about what they already knew. "You butch or femme?" "You ever fuck boys?" "You ever want to?" "You want to have children?" "What's your girlfriend like?" I finally broke up when one very tall, confident girl leaned way over and called out, "Hey, girlfriend! I'm getting out of here next weekend. What you doing that night?" I laughed so hard I almost choked. I laughed until we were all howling and giggling together. Even getting frisked as I left didn't ruin my mood. I was still grinning when I climbed into the waterbed with my lover that night, grinning right up to the moment when she wrapped her arms around me and I burst into tears.

That night I understood, suddenly, everything that had happened to my cousins and me, understood it from a wholly new and agonizing perspective, one that made clear how brutal I had been to both my family and myself. I grasped all over again how we had been robbed and dismissed, and why I had worked so hard not to think about it. I had learned as a child that what could not be changed had to go unspoken, and worse, that those who cannot change their own lives have every reason to be ashamed of that fact and to hide it. I had accepted that shame and believed in it, but why? What had I or my cousins done to deserve the contempt directed at us? Why had I always believed us contemptible by nature? I wanted to talk to someone about all the things I was thinking that night, but I could not. Among the women I knew there was no one who would have understood what I was thinking, no other working-class woman in the women's collective where I was living. I began to suspect that we shared no common language to speak those bitter truths.

In the days that followed I found myself remembering that afternoon long ago at the county farm, that feeling of being the animal in the zoo, the thing looked at and laughed at and used by the real people who watched us. For all his liberal convictions, that Sunday school teacher had looked at me with the eyes of my cousin's long-ago guard. I felt thrown back into my childhood, into all the fears I had tried to escape. Once again I felt myself at the mercy of the important people who knew how to dress and talk, and would always be given the benefit of the doubt, while my family and I would not.

I experienced an outrage so old I could not have traced all the ways it shaped my life. I realized again that some are given no quarter, no chance, that all their courage, humor, and love for each other is just a joke to the ones who make the rules, and I hated the rule-makers. Finally, I recognized that part of my grief came from the fact that I no longer knew who I was or where I belonged. I had run away from my family, refused to go home to visit, and tried in every way to make myself a new person. How could I be working class with a college degree? As a lesbian activist? I thought about the guards at the detention center. They had not stared at me with the same picture-window emptiness they turned on the girls who came to hear me, girls who were closer to the life I had been meant to live than I could bear to examine. The contempt in their eyes was contempt for me as a lesbian, different and the same, but still contempt.

While I raged, my girlfriend held me and comforted me and tried to get me to explain what was hurting me so bad, but I could not. She had told me so often about her awkward relationship with her own family, the father who ran his own business and still sent her checks every other month. She knew almost nothing about my family, only the jokes and careful stories I had given her. I felt so alone and at risk lying in her arms that I could not have explained anything at all. I thought about those girls in the detention center and the stories they told in brutal shorthand about their sisters, brothers, cousins, and lovers. I thought about their one-note references to those they had lost, never mentioning the loss of their own hopes, their own futures, the bent and painful shape of their lives when they would finally get free. Cried-out and dry-eyed, I lay watching my sleeping girlfriend and thinking about what I had not been able to say to her. After a few hours I got up and made some notes for a poem I wanted to write, a bare, painful litany of loss shaped as a conversation between two women, one who cannot understand the other, and one who cannot tell all she knows.

It took me a long time to take that poem from a raw lyric of outrage and grief to a piece of fiction that explained to me something I had never let myself see up close before—the whole process of running away, of closing up inside yourself, of hiding. It has taken me most of my life to understand that, to see how and why those of us who are born poor and different are so driven to give ourselves away or lose ourselves, but most of all, simply to disappear as the people we really are. By the time that poem became the story "River of Names,"* I had made the decision to reverse that process: to claim my family, my true history, and to tell the truth not only about who I was but about the temptation to lie.

By the time I taught myself the basics of storytelling on the page, I knew there was only one story that would haunt me until I understood how to tell it— the complicated, painful story of how my mama had, and had not, saved me as a girl. Writing *Bastard Out of Carolina*** became, ultimately, the way to claim my family's pride and tragedy, and the embattled sexuality I had fashioned on a base of violence and abuse.

The compartmentalized life I had created burst open in the late 1970s after I began to write what I really thought about my family. I lost patience with my fear of what the women I worked with, mostly lesbians, thought of who I slept with and what we did together. When schisms developed within my community; when I was no longer able to hide within the regular dyke network; when I could not continue to justify my life by constant political activism or distract myself by sleeping around; when my sexual promiscuity, butch/femme orientation, and exploration of sadomasochistic sex became part of what was driving me out of my community of choice—I went home again. I went home to my mother and my sisters, to visit, talk, argue, and begin to understand.

Trash (Firebrand Books: Ithaca, New York, 1988)
**Dutton: New York, 1992

Once home I saw that as far as my family was concerned, lesbians were lesbians whether they wore suitcoats or leather jackets. Moreover, in all that time when I had not made peace with myself, my family had managed to make a kind of peace with me. My girlfriends were treated like slightly odd versions of my sisters' husbands, while I was simply the daughter who had always been difficult but was still a part of their lives. The result was that I started trying to confront what had made me unable really to talk to my sisters for so many years. I discovered that they no longer knew who I was either, and it took time and lots of listening to each other to rediscover my sense of family, and my love for them.

It is only as the child of my class and my unique family background that I have been able to put together what is for me a meaningful politics, to regain a sense of why I believe in activism, why self-revelation is so important for lesbians. There is no all-purpose feminist analysis that explains the complicated ways our sexuality and core identity are shaped, the way we see ourselves as parts of both our birth families and the extended family of friends and lovers we invariably create within the lesbian community. For me, the bottom line has simply become the need to resist that omnipresent fear, that urge to hide and disappear, to disguise my life, my desires, and the truth about how little any of us understand—even as we try to make the world a more just and human place. Most of all, I have tried to understand the politics of *they*, why human beings fear and stigmatize the different while secretly dreading that they might be one of the different themselves. Class, race, sexuality, gender—and all the other categories by which we categorize and dismiss each other—need to be excavated from the inside.

The horror of class stratification, racism, and prejudice is that some people begin to believe that the security of their families and communities depends on the oppression of others, that for some to have good lives there must be others whose lives are truncated and brutal. It is a belief that dominates this culture. It is what makes the poor whites of the South so determinedly racist and the middle class so contemptuous of the poor. It is a myth that allows some to imagine that they build their lives on the ruin of others, a secret core of shame for the middle class, a goad and a spur to the marginal working class, and cause enough for the homeless and poor to feel no constraints on hatred or violence. The power of the myth is made even more apparent when we examine how, within the lesbian and feminist communities where we have addressed considerable attention to the politics of marginalization, there is still so much exclusion and fear, so many of us who do not feel safe.

I grew up poor, hated, the victim of physical, emotional, and sexual violence, and I know that suffering does not ennoble. It destroys. To resist destruction, self-hatred, or lifelong hopelessness, we have to throw off the conditioning of being despised, the fear of becoming the *they* that is talked about so dismissively, to refuse lying myths and easy moralities, to see ourselves as human, flawed, and extraordinary. All of us—extraordinary.

She Learns to Shout

Phoebe Eng is a former corporate attorney and a past publisher of A. Magazine, *an influential national magazine for Asian Americans. She is now a full-time social activist who has advised the U.S. Department of Justice, the Ford Foundation, the Urban League, and various media groups, corporations, and universities on issues of diversity and multiculturalism. In this excerpt from her book* Warrior Lessons, *Eng tells a story from her own life to show how stereotypes of the docile Asian woman and the norms for good behavior in her own Chinese American community led her to tolerate harassment and verbal abuse at work. Despite the social pressures toward conformity and passivity, however, Phoebe Eng learned to voice her anger and demand respect.*

As You Read, Ask Yourself . . .

What were the expectations for feminine polite behavior in Eng's family?

What roles did gender, race, and status play in setting up and maintaining the "snake pit" atmosphere in the law office where Eng was employed?

Eng describes a critical "fork in the road" for many Asian American women. What is that fork and why is it so critical to the development of self and identity?

He was just having a bad day. A three-hundred-million-dollar real estate deal, the Japanese buyout of the Regal Empress Hotel, was his biggest in years, and it was falling through before his eyes. And so Robert's mood was bound to be bad. With his reputation, partnership status, and the seventeen thousand dollars he required each month to maintain his quality of life and his kids' tuition payments at Trinity, who could blame him for his behavior? After all, being a partner in one of New York's top international law firms was a tough and tense way to make a living. Every partner, even the nicest of them, falls into tense moments like that. It was part of the job. I felt sure that when I became a partner in a few years time and some big deal began to spin out of control, I'd have my bad moments, too.

I was always finding excuses like this for Robert, my boss. I had to make myself feel better somehow. I had to justify why the hell I was staying in that snake pit, slaving away like some church mouse, unnoticed, and unappreciated. When it came right down to it, I really hated this job.

It was the holiday season, and I knew that, like last year, I would be spending Christmas Day at the office, reviewing documents I didn't care about and spell-checking merger agreements, while the firm's partners and our clients would be skiing in Aspen or Mont Blanc with their families, as, in the great scheme of things, I felt they ought to be. And by some strange reasoning process, I had also accepted that I was also where *I* ought to be, sacrificing my precious holiday time with family and friends by paying my flesh-equity dues for a crack at becoming a partner one day.

In retrospect, I now realize that Robert was just a bad boss and that none of his antics should have been taken personally. But at the time, all I knew was that I was the young lawyer he was using instead to be his very highly paid secretary. His form of training was to dig his red pen into my drafts, berating me for missing my commas, saying that I was not careful enough, always looking for errors in meaningless minutiae. If I drafted a cover letter for him that read, "Please find enclosed. . ." he would slash it out like Zorro and write, "Enclosed please find. . ." Maybe small tyrannies gave him pleasure. He was, in short, a troubled soul who felt power in controlling tiny things, and here I was stuck in pencil-pushing hell with him.

Unfortunately for me, Robert also had a volatile temper. When in the wrong mood, Robert would insult and verbally annihilate those he felt he could terrorize, including neophyte associates, like me. I lived in a constant state of fear of him. I learned to tiptoe around his office, put his tiny proofreading projects at the top of my priority list, forsaking the legal work of other partners that would have taught me more. Somehow, I thought that if I ingratiated myself, Robert would stop insulting me.

Needless to say, it hardly ever worked.

Robert was having a bad day, for sure. So when I heard him screaming and stomping through the halls, my heart started beating fast as my survival adrenaline kicked in.

Robert barged into my office. Bingo, I had hit the jackpot.

"What the hell did I tell you to do last week?" Robert looked crazed. He obviously wasn't looking for an answer, just a little of my blood. He slammed a one-page document onto my desk and told me that it should have been three-hole punched and that the signature should have been signed in blue.

"What are you doing at this firm? What are you, STUPID? Why can't you just do what I asked for JUST ONCE? CAN'T YOU UNDERSTAND ENGLISH? READ MY LIPS," he enunciated. "A CHILD COULD DO THIS!" He slammed my desk with his fist and my pile of papers flew to the ground.

Is it clear yet that Robert had a bit of a temper problem?

He was screaming into my face. I could hear other associates kick their doors shut to block out their own stress and wage their own passive but audible protest against his absurd tantrum.

"WE DON'T PAY YOU PEOPLE ALL THAT MONEY FOR NOTHING! Fix this document RIGHT NOW. IN FRONT OF ME. I WANT TO SEE YOU DO IT."

Running through my mind were the biting insults I wanted to hurl back if I could only open my mouth and stop shaking. *Bing!* There went my Guilt-Over-Salary button. ("Yes, indeed, Robert, I know I'm overpaid, especially since all I'm asked to do is type and proofread!" I thought.) *Bong!* There went the I-Can't-Stand-Being-Ordered-Around-Especially-by-Older-Presumptuous-Men button. ("I wish I could give you a swift kick in the balls right now, Robert, but somehow right now I can't seem to move," I thought.) *Bing bong!* There went the Why-Me? buzzer, as my face grew hot and a lump started forming in my throat. And "Can't you understand English?" What was *that* supposed to mean? Like a well-trained sadist, Robert was hitting all my buttons. And like a well-trained victim, I could only sit there shocked, saying nothing.

"You know, Robert, I think you are a *bit* out of control." I tried to fake a smile to be polite. It was one of my typical reactions, coming from a combination of charm-school teaching from my gracious Chinese mother and my gut fear of being fired. Both of them had taught me well that "Save the job" was the bottom line. A quick strategy assessment: Yes, well, maybe everything would turn out fine if I just nodded and spoke in a calm, sweet voice. Maybe I could appeal to Robert's sense of reason.

I must really have been living in la-la land.

Robert was treating me this way because experience told him that he'd get away with it. Even if I *was* a lawyer who had passed the bar exam with flying colors. Even if I was just as smart as my fellow associates, even if I could spot a loophole as quickly as any of them. And even as the other partners told me that I had a shining future with the firm. Why did Robert assume that I would gladly do this drudge work?

As Robert slammed and cursed at me, I felt something snap inside. I suddenly realized how tired I was of lowering my voice and taking two steps back so that Robert could feel more comfortable, more in charge, less threatened. I was tired of laughing off his tantrums as the silly ravings of a neurotic boss. He was being offensive, no matter where his words were coming from. And I suddenly understood how much energy it took to stifle myself all the time. These thoughts swirled in my head, free associations that were finally clicking into place.

Now this maniac was still yelling in my face, ranting on now about how I would thank him later for teaching me a lesson.

That was the cue I was waiting for. I, the little church mouse, began to roar.

"Robert," I interrupted. I cleared my throat to stop my heart from falling out of my mouth. "Don't you *ever* talk to me like that." My shaking voice had slipped back into my throat midsentence, but I swallowed and forced myself to go on. "In fact, I never want to hear you talk to *anyone* like that in front of me. You are embarrassing yourself."

Robert looked at me stunned, and pounded his fist on the wall.

"GODDAMMIT, YOU WANT TO ARGUE WITH ME? WHY CAN'T YOU JUST DO WHAT I TOLD YOU TO DO! JUST LISTEN TO ME AND DO WHAT I SAY!" His six-foot-two frame towered over me, the sitting church mouse, and he pounded my desk so hard that I jumped up at the impact.

This was it, I told myself. Trust the moment, Phoebe, and go with what you feel for once. If you're going to lose your job, you had better go out fighting. I hit cruise control.

I finally let go with the anger that had been gnawing at me ever since I had set foot in that law firm and its wacky, illogical processes. And as I yelled back at Robert, my words found a natural, poetic flow, finally liberated from the stiff clip of legalese. They expressed the natural thoughts of a confused associate who was only trying to find some core, some anchor of meaning and dignity in an otherwise tortured situation. Still, to eke out each word required me to transcend the present and its dire consequences:

"THAT'S IT, ROBERT. I'm taking this straight to the management committee. I HAVE HAD IT WITH YOUR BULLSHIT." My voice shook, and steadied itself only when I forced it louder. As a reflex, he stepped back as if I had pushed him.

In my mind, all I could picture was my mother's face, horrified and ashamed at my outburst:

Aiyo! Good Chinese girls don't curse in public, Ah-Phee. It's not very attractive. Very shameful. Keep quiet, Ah-Phee! He will go away if you just ignore him.

It was too late to invoke Chinese common sense. It had come time for a good old American fist-in-the-face battle. So I drew in a deep breath and delivered the sledgehammer.

"NOW GET OUT OF MY OFFICE!"

Who was this woman talking? It couldn't have been me. I could almost hear the whiplike crack of my words as they slapped against his face.

As his volume level rose in response, so did mine, so that the two of us, shouting over each other, lost all communication. But connection wasn't what I was looking for then. I had no need for that. I just needed to shout. Without realizing it, my voice had become resolute, indignant, *loud.*

In the halls, they were listening. The soothing computer tap of secretaries typing and the murmur of business deals being made had suddenly and disturbingly stopped. That silence gave me the time I needed to finally realize that this was serious. I was telling off my assigning partner for all to hear. For a brief moment, my first since becoming a lawyer, I felt myself rising to my own call. And I was probably going to be fired within the next few minutes.

Robert snatched away his one-page document and stomped off.

And in the silent aftershock of the next few seconds, I started to hyperventilate, as if the truth of my words and the power of my own voice was too much to handle. Those vocal cords hadn't been stretched like that since God knows when. What had I done? It took no time for the faces to emerge from the offices.

"You showed him."

"You were brave. I never could have done that."

Where were all these people before? None of them, not even my office mates, my comrades-in-arms only a few minutes ago, had offered to help or intervene. Was everyone really that fearful? Did they think that I deserved to be berated? Was I wrong to have kicked up a retaliatory fuss? More sympathetic attorneys came in.

"It wasn't you; it was his deal falling through."

"An asshole, isn't he?"

But I had already entered a hyper-heaving stage when I realized that, despite my verbal pyrotechnics, I was hurting from Robert's stabbing remarks. Like a homing missile, they struck their target of a self-doubtful place deep inside. Maybe I wasn't good enough. Maybe Robert was right. I had no right to work here.

I relaxed my strongman guard for only a millisecond, and immediately collapsed into tears of disbelief. I gulped and gasped uncontrollably like a drowning victim in trauma, but refusing to die. Someone handed me a tissue. How very humiliating, I thought. How utterly. . . *uncorporate* and *distasteful* to reveal emotion.

Embarrassed by my weakness, I excused myself and headed straight to the ladies' room. It's the one place where women attorneys and secretaries have been known to hide themselves in fits of frustration and tears when confronted with the identical kind of situation. I stayed there within the safety of calming beige walls for what seemed like an awfully long time.

I told you, Ah-Phee. You should have just shut your big mouth. Haven't you learned yet? Don't be so American loud! It will just hurt you in the end. Can't you just understand that silence can be your strength?

I imagined my mother's disappointment and the way she'd shake her head. Once again, I thought, her homespun advice was so completely useless in my world.

TURNING POINTS

There are times in our lives when we are faced with a fork in the road that presents us with two distinct choices. These can be moments of opportunity, when the choice that we make will impact who we will be, what we will achieve, and how we find what is meaningful to us.

In my conversations with hundreds of Asian American women, I found that many of us will have in common at least one fork in the road. The election to claim and outwardly express rage will be one of our pivotal life choices. That rage might emanate from family pressures and expectations for us to be dutiful daughters. It might be the rage of having to deal with false stereotypes and biases of an outside world that keep us from realizing our full potential. It may be the rage of having to put up with those who disempower us by disrespectful behavior. If we choose to recognize it, explore it, and channel it constructively, that rage can lead to a new sense of power. Deny it, and we are thrown back into situations that continue to wear us down.

While my run-in with Robert may seem like an ordinary confrontation with a maladjusted boss, it wasn't so for me. The outburst with Robert signified a fork in the road. At that point I was no longer willing to endure the path of a painful situation in order to fulfill my family's expectations or my sense of honor as a gracious Chinese daughter or as the first lawyer in the Eng family. Not on these terms. Not when Robert's tirades called my self-esteem into question on a daily basis. For me, it was a defining moment when I recognized that, in fact, I *was* being treated and perceived differently, and that it was going to be hard, damn hard, to be taken seriously as a fighter, as an equal on a professional level, but that I was willing to do what was required. It was the first time, after almost thirty years and some of the best education money could buy, that I finally understood that life was nothing like what school or my parents had prepared me for. I thought that good performance, good grades, and efficient turnaround would get me what I wanted, as they always had in the past. *I now understood and accepted the reality that unless I started using my voice to stick up for myself, no one would be doing it for me.*

When called to the table to explain his behavior, Robert was at an uncharacteristic loss for words. He had no justifiable alibis, and I won the moral victory. The partners that supported me gave me pep talks in the months that followed. They cared about keeping me, they said, because I showed promise as a fighter.

In their book *Female Rage,* Mary Valentis and Anne Devane write that rage can be used to empower women's lives. But upbringing and social codes can make it difficult to allow that rage to create change in the situations around us. Valentis and Devane talk about a "geisha" complex, not necessarily limited to Asian women, but named for the icon of submission that we all know so well. According to Valentis and Devane, the "geisha" as an archetype is a woman who is "constantly pleasing others and putting herself in second place. Unable to separate her thoughts and feelings from other people's, she lacks self-confidence and boundaries and is prone to tolerate abuse. Her aim is to maintain the status quo at any cost." In her hostile dependencies, her anger remains unexpressed. Instead it is unconsciously captured in her body before it escapes. The result, the authors write, may be chronic fatigue, a locked jaw, panic disorders, or irrational fears, such as agoraphobia. The rage of the "geisha" is like a powder keg. Once ignited, it explodes with a shocking boom, in a rash response that may not be a reaction to the immediate situation, but is instead the result of the long-term suppression of anger.

How much of the geisha was in me? As much as I thought of myself as strong, resilient, and outspoken, I felt that every word of that definition fit my own actions to a tee.

I chose to unleash my anger on Robert that day, but it could have been anybody. So much of my life had spun out of control at that point. I was confused about my career choice, pursued to please my parents. I knew that I didn't enjoy the practice of corporate law. When I returned home drained to the bone near midnight on a regular basis, I was greeted by the cold shoulder of the man with whom I'd been living, who felt that I should have been home to greet him with dinner. Then on weekends, I would visit my family only to listen to my mother tell me why I shouldn't be living with a man from Italy because he was just using me and had no intentions of marrying me. Squeezed to the hilt at work, ignored at home, and disapproved of by family, it was no wonder that I blew my fuse one day when the world stopped making sense.

It seems that sudden explosions of anger have been part of Asian culture throughout its modern history. In fact, the outburst of wild rage called "running amok" is derived from a Malay word, *amoq,* which originally meant "engaging furiously in battle." In a 1990 study described by Aurora Tiu and Julian Seneriches, this behavior was documented among Filipino women who felt that they had been shamed or had experienced an act of disrespect, much in the same way that I had. According to Tiu and Seneriches, angry outbursts are common in cultures that impose heavy restrictions on aggressive behavior and stress concepts of honor, hierarchy, deference, and etiquette. Their cases describe women who had experienced a series of belittlements and a sense of being undeservedly disregarded. They suppressed their anger until they could no longer keep it in. And then they hit the roof.

Because the tendency to express anger or to engage in conflict is frowned upon as either unattractive behavior for women, or dishonorable and shameful behavior because we are Asian, we have found subtler forms of playing out our anger. Instead of lashing out, we may avoid confrontation by getting back at people through gossip. We might use sarcasm or imagine elaborate revenges. We might grind our teeth, use alcohol, or bury ourselves in work. "I write my anger down on paper, and usually I don't show it to anyone—it is just for me to vent frustration," one Vietnamese American woman, an executive director of a large national organization shared. "Or I'll close the door and scream alone just to release it." "I cry in my car, because it's the only private space and time I have," was the solution for one of the young women I spoke with. Yet if we are able to reframe rage as a positive experience, to connect it back to the situations that caused the rage in the first place, we can use it as a powerful tool rather than as a source of anxiety. *Anger tells us and those around us where our innate boundaries are, what we instinctively feel is tolerable or intolerable, and can signal when those limits have been trespassed. Most important, what causes us to rage most wildly is also what we fear the most.* Anger is a built-in alarm system. As is only sensible with alarms, it makes sense to acknowledge and respond.

PART TWO

The Making of a Woman: Bodies, Power, and Society

An oft-repeated feminist message is that in our society (as well as many others) a woman's value is defined by the attractiveness of her body. We hope these readings will bring you new insights. Women's relationships to their bodies are indeed complicated by social pressures, but by no means are women merely passive victims of social forces. The eleven women who speak here about the limitations and the pleasures of the body reveal that even while they are being judged by others on their shape and size, women are voicing their own ideas about their physical embodiment.

Our writers are a culturally diverse group, and the differences in their experiences show that what becomes an issue or a problem about a woman's body depends on the cultural and social context. Skin color, for example, has different meanings within different social groups. Judith Ortiz Cofer writes that how her color is perceived when she is in her native Puerto Rico, where she is considered "white," is quite different from how it is perceived in the United States, where she is "brown."

Being different in appearance can lead to self-rejection. Nellie Wong's poem tells of her desire, as a young Chinese American girl, to have white skin like the blonde girls she envied. "Ann Rex" (a pseudonym) writes of her recurrent struggle with bulimia in an effort to live up to an image of "perfect body, brains, and bravado." And Eugenia Kaw interviews Asian American women who choose to "westernize" their eyes through cosmetic surgery in order to look more like the white majority. A different solution to fitting in is articulated by Christy Haubegger when she says, "I'm not fat, I'm Latina." Within Latina culture, women who might be judged overweight by white standards are considered curvy, sexy, and "bien cuidada"—well cared for.

Because women are judged so greatly on appearance, those who do not or cannot conform are often stigmatized. Nancy Datan, a feminist psychologist who is well aware of the stigma of looking different, speaks eloquently of the messages given to women who have breast cancer and of her own struggles to redefine her relationship with her body after breast cancer surgery.

Ynestra King's disability is not life-threatening like Datan's, but it too provides her with a unique vantage point: she is defined as able-bodied when seated and disabled when she is moving around. In some ways, her experiences of "passing" are similar to the experiences of individuals of color who look white. She can see very clearly how she is stigmatized only when her disability is noticed.

Clearly, there is a need for more positive, affirming views of women's bodies. Where can we find these different visions? Ursula K. Le Guin demonstrates a more positive view of women's bodies by considering menopause as a rite of passage. It involves not just loss (the end of fertility) but entry into "white-crowned" old age. A "crone" is an archetypal figure representing female wisdom. Think about whether you have known any "crones" and what lessons they might have taught.

We close this section with the smart and sassy voices of two third-wave feminists. For many young women who identify as feminists, taking charge of their own sexuality and sexual expression is an important value. However, women's sexual agency still must be expressed in the context of patriarchal constraints. Jayne Air confronts this issue directly by urging young women to appropriate the word *cunt* as a celebration of their own sexuality. Cunt is taboo, she writes, and taboo things are powerful. Just as people say admiringly of a man that he "has balls," she advocates using cunt to describe a woman who is bold and ready to take charge. In recent years, women have reappropriated the words *girl* and *bitch*; is *cunt* going too far?

Celina Hex sings the pleasures of the vibrator. Though boys learn at an early age to masturbate for pleasure, many girls do not. Hex asks why women should be denied the pleasure of orgasm and argues that using a vibrator makes it easier and more fun. Indeed, she says, she could no sooner do without her vibrator than her answering machine. She asks an important question about women's sexuality: how can we become more comfortable about claiming the right to sexual pleasure?

After you have read this diverse and challenging group of stories, think about the following questions: What does beauty (or its perceived lack) mean to individual women from ethnically diverse groups? Who has the power to determine standards of attractiveness? What happens to women who violate these standards? What are some ways that women express their power and control over their bodies? How can women claim both pleasure and power from their bodies?

As a final question, think about the relationship between women's ways of resisting domination and the many varieties of feminism. Is any one approach the best?

Judith Ortiz Cofer

The Story of My Body

Migration is the story of my body.

—Victor Hernandez Cruz

Born in Puerto Rico and brought up both there and in the United States, Judith Ortiz Cofer is bicultural, which probably fostered her ability to see that appearance is a social construction. Is she short or tall? fair-skinned or dark? pretty or not? The answer, she realizes, depends on where she is and who is doing the judging. Her story forces us to think about the relative nature of attractiveness. It shows, too, how painful it can be for an adolescent girl to be evaluated on color and ethnicity.

As You Read, Ask Yourself . . .

Under what circumstances was Judith Ortiz Cofer's skin color defined as light or dark? Under what circumstances was she defined as short or tall?

Was Ortiz Cofer free to construct her own definitions of her physical body?

As a teenage girl, which was more important to her—being judged pretty or intelligent? Which view of herself did she internalize as a permanent part of her adult identity?

1. SKIN

I was born a white girl in Puerto Rico, but became a brown girl when I came to live in the United States. My Puerto Rican relatives called me tall; at the American school, some of my rougher classmates called me "skinny-bones" and "the shrimp," because I was the smallest member of my classes all through grammar school until high school, when the midget Gladys was given the honorary post of front-row center for class pictures and scorekeeper, bench warmer in P.E. I reached my full stature of five feet even in sixth grade.

I started out life as a pretty baby and learned to be a pretty girl from a pretty mother. Then at ten years of age I suffered one of the worst cases of chicken pox I have ever heard of. My entire body, including the inside of my ears and in between my toes, was covered with pustules that, in a fit of panic at my appearance, I scratched off of my face, leaving permanent scars. A cruel school nurse told me I would always have them—tiny cuts that looked as if a mad cat had plunged its claws deep into my skin. I grew my hair long and hid behind it for the first years of my adolescence. This was when I learned to be invisible.

2. COLOR

In the animal world it indicates danger: The most colorful creatures are often the most poisonous. Color is also a way to attract and seduce a mate. In the human world color triggers many more complex and often deadly reactions. As a Puerto Rican girl born of "white" parents, I spent the first years of my life hearing people refer to me as *blanca,* white. My mother insisted that I protect myself from the intense island sun because I was more prone to sunburn than some of my darker, *triqeno* playmates. People were always commenting within my hearing about how my black hair contrasted so nicely with my "pale" skin. I did not think of the color of my skin consciously, except when I heard the adults talking about complexion. It seems to me that the subject is much more common in the conversation of mixed-race peoples than in mainstream U.S. society, where it is a touchy and sometimes even embarrassing topic to discuss, except in a political context. In Puerto Rico I heard many conversations about skin color. A pregnant woman could say "I hope my baby doesn't turn out *prieto* (slang for dark or black) like my husband's grandmother, although she was a good-looking *negra* in her time." I am a combination of both, being olive-skinned—lighter than my mother yet darker than my fair-skinned father. In America, I am a person of color, obviously a Latina. On the island I have been called everything from a *paloma blanca,* after the song (by a black suitor), to *la gringa.*

My first experience of color prejudice occurred in a supermarket in Paterson, New Jersey. It was Christmastime and I was eight or nine years old. There was a display of toys in the store where I went two or three times a day to buy things for my mother who never made lists but sent for milk, cigarettes, a can of this or that, as she remembered from hour to hour. I enjoyed being trusted with money and walking half a city block to the new, modern grocery store. It was owned by three good-looking Italian brothers. I liked the younger one with the crew-cut blond hair. The two older ones watched me and the other Puerto Rican kids as if they thought we were going to steal something. The oldest one would sometimes even try to hurry me with my purchases, although part of my pleasure in these expeditions came from looking at everything in the well-stocked aisles. I was also teaching myself to read English by sounding out the labels in packages: L&M cigarettes, Borden's homogenized milk, Red Devil potted ham, Nestlé's chocolate mix, Quaker oats, and Bustelo coffee, Wonder bread, Colgate toothpaste, Ivory soap, and Goya (makers of products used in Puerto Rican dishes) everything—these are some of the brand names that taught me nouns.

Several times this man had come up to me wearing his bloodstained butcher's apron and, towering over me, had asked in a harsh voice whether there was something he could help me find. On the way out I would glance at the younger brother who ran one of the registers and he would often smile and wink at me.

It was the mean brother who first referred to me as "colored." It was a few days before Christmas and my parents had already told my brother and me that since we were in *los estados* now, we would get our presents on December twenty-fifth instead of *Los Reyes, Three Kings Day,* when gifts are exchanged in Puerto Rico. We were to give them a wish list that they would take to Santa Claus, who apparently lived in the Macy's store downtown—at least that's where we had caught a glimpse of him when we went shopping. Since my parents were timid about entering the fancy store, we did not approach the huge man in the red suit. I was not interested in sitting on a stranger's lap anyway. But I did covet Susie, the talking schoolteacher doll that was displayed in the center aisle of the Italian brothers' supermarket. She talked when you pulled a string on her back. Susie had a limited repertoire of three sentences: I think she could say: "Hello, I'm Susie Schoolteacher; two plus two is four," and one other thing I cannot remember. The day the older brother chased me away, I was reaching to touch Susie's blond curls. I had been told many times, as most children have, not to touch anything in a store that I was not buying. But I had been looking at Susie for weeks. In my mind, she was my doll. After all, I had put her on my Christmas wish list. The moment is frozen in my mind as if there were a photograph of it on file. It was not a turning point, a disaster, or an earthshaking revelation. It was simply the first time I considered—if naively—the meaning of skin color in human relations.

I reached to touch Susie's hair. It seems to me that I had to get on tiptoe since the toys were stacked on a table and she sat like a princess on top of the fancy box she came in. Then I heard the booming "Hey, kid, what do you think you're doing!" spoken very loudly from the meat counter. I felt caught although I knew I was not doing anything criminal. I remember not looking at the man, but standing there feeling humiliated because I knew everyone in the store must have heard him yell at me. I felt him approach and when I knew he was behind me, I turned around to face the bloody butcher's apron. His large chest was at my eye level. He blocked my way. I started to run out of the place, but even as I reached the door I heard him shout after me: "Don't come in here unless you gonna buy something. You PR kids put your dirty hands on stuff. You always look dirty. But maybe dirty brown is your natural color." I heard him laugh and someone else too in the back. Outside in the sunlight I looked at my hands. My nails needed a little cleaning as they always did since I liked to paint with watercolors, but I took a bath every night. I thought the man was dirtier than I was in his stained apron. He was also always sweaty—it showed in big yellow circles under his shirt sleeves. I sat on the front steps of the apartment building where we lived and looked closely at my hands, which showed the only skin I could see, since it was bitter cold and I was wearing my quilted play coat, dungarees, and a knitted navy cap of my father's. I was not pink like my friend Charlene and her sister Kathy who had blue eyes and light-brown hair. My skin is the color of the coffee my grandmother made, which was half milk, *leche con café* rather than *café con leche*. My mother is the opposite mix. She has a lot of café in her color. I could not understand how my skin looked like dirt to the supermarket man.

I went in and washed my hands thoroughly with soap and hot water, and, borrowing my mother's nail file, I cleaned the crusted watercolors from underneath my nails. I was pleased with the results. My skin was the same color as before, but I knew I was clean. Clean enough to run my fingers through Susie's fine gold hair when she came home to me.

3. SIZE

My mother is barely four feet eleven inches in height, which is average for women in her family. When I grew to five feet by age twelve, she was amazed and began to use the word tall to describe me, as in: "Since you are tall, this dress will look good on you." As with the color of my skin, I didn't consciously think about my height or size until other people made an issue of it. It is around the preadolescent years that in America the games children play for fun become fierce competitions where everyone is out to "prove" they are better than others. It was in the playground and sports fields that my size-related problems began. No matter how familiar the story is, every child who is the last chosen for a team knows the torment of waiting to be called up. At the Paterson, New Jersey, public schools that I attended, the volleyball or softball game was the metaphor for the battlefield of life to the inner city kids—the black kids vs. the Puerto Rican kids, the whites vs. the blacks vs. the Puerto Rican kids; and I was 4F, skinny, short, bespectacled, and apparently impervious to the blood thirst that drove many of my classmates to play ball as if their lives depended on it. Perhaps they did. I would rather be reading a book than sweating, grunting, and running the risk of pain and injury. I simply did not see the point in competitive sports. My main form of exercise then was walking to the library, many city blocks away from my barrio.

Still, I wanted to be wanted. I wanted to be chosen for the teams. Physical education was compulsory, a class where you were actually given a grade. On my mainly all-A report card, the C for compassion I always received from the P.E. teachers shamed me the same as a bad grade in a real class. Invariably, my father would say: "How can you make a low grade *for playing games*?" He did not understand. Even if I had managed to make a hit (it never happened), or get the ball over that ridiculously high net, I already had a reputation as a "shrimp," a hopeless nonathlete. It was an area where the girls who didn't like me for one reason or another—mainly because I did better than they on academic subjects—could lord it over me; the playing field was the place where even the smallest girl could make me feel powerless and inferior. I instinctively understood the politics even then; how the *not* choosing me until the teacher forced one of the team captains to call my name was a coup of sorts—there you little show-off, tomorrow you can beat us in spelling and geography, but this afternoon you are the loser. Or perhaps those were only my own bitter thoughts as I sat or stood in the sidelines while the big girls were grabbed like fish and I, the little brown tadpole, was ignored until Teacher looked over in my general direction and shouted, "Call Ortiz," or worse, "Somebody's got to take her."

No wonder I read Wonder Woman comics and had Legion of Super Heroes daydreams. Although I wanted to think of myself as "intellectual," my body was demanding that I notice it. I saw the little swelling around my once-flat nipples; the fine hairs growing in secret places; but my knees were still bigger than my thighs and I always wore long or half-sleeve blouses to hide my bony upper arms. I wanted flesh on my bones—a thick layer of it. I saw a new product advertised on TV. Wate-On. They showed skinny men and women before and after taking the stuff, and it was a transformation like the 97-pound weakling turned into Charles Atlas ads that I saw on the back cover of my comic books. The Wate-On was very expensive. I tried to explain my need for it in Spanish to my mother, but it didn't translate very well, even to my ears—and she said with a tone of finality, eat more of my good food and you'll get fat—anybody can get fat. Right. Except me. I was going to have to join a circus someday as "Skinny Bones," the woman without flesh.

Wonder Woman was stacked. She had a cleavage framed by the spread wings of a golden eagle and a muscular body that has become fashionable with women only recently. But since I wanted a body that would serve me in P.E., hers was my ideal. The breasts were an indulgence I allowed myself. Perhaps the daydreams of bigger girls were more glamorous, since our ambitions are filtered through our needs, but I wanted first a powerful body. I daydreamed of leaping up above the gray landscape of the city to where the sky was clear and blue, and in anger and self-pity I fantasized about scooping my enemies up by their hair from the playing fields and dumping them on a barren asteroid. I would put the P.E. teachers each on their own rock in space too where they would be the loneliest people in the universe since I knew they had no "inner resources," no imagination, and in outer space, there would be no air for them to fill their deflated volleyballs with. In my mind all P.E. teachers have blended into one large spiky-haired woman with a whistle on a string around her neck and a volleyball under one arm. My Wonder Woman fantasies of revenge were a source of comfort to me in my early career as a shrimp.

I was saved from more years of P.E. torment by the fact that in my sophomore year of high school I transferred to a school where the midget, Gladys, was the focal point of interest for the people who must rank according to size. Because her height was considered a handicap, there was an unspoken rule about mentioning size around Gladys, but of course there was no need to say anything. Gladys knew her place: front-row center in class photographs. I gladly moved to the left or to the right of her, as far as I could without leaving the picture completely.

4. LOOKS

Many photographs were taken of me as a baby by my mother to send to my father who was stationed overseas during the first two years of my life. With the army in Panama when I was born, he later joined the navy and traveled often on tours of duty. I was a healthy, pretty baby. Recently I read that people are drawn to big-eyed round-faced creatures, like puppies, kittens, and certain other mammals and marsupials, koalas for example, and, of course, infants. I was all eyes, since my head and body, even as I grew older, remained thin and small-boned. As a young child I got a lot of attention from my relatives and many other people we met in our barrio. My mother's beauty may have had something to do with how much attention we got from strangers in stores and on the street. I can imagine it. In the pictures I have seen of us together, she is a stunning young woman by Latino standards: long, curly black hair and round curves in a compact frame. From her I learned how to move, smile, and talk like an attractive woman. I remember going into a bodega for our groceries and being given candy by the proprietor as a reward for being *bonita,* pretty.

I can see in the photographs and I also remember that I was dressed in the pretty clothes, the stiff, frilly dresses, with layers of crinolines underneath, the glossy patent leather shoes, and, on special occasions, the skull-hugging little hats and the white gloves that were popular in the late fifties and early sixties. My mother was proud of my looks, although I was a bit too thin. She could dress me up like a doll and take me by the hand to visit relatives, or go to the Spanish mass at the Catholic church, and show me off. How was I to know that she and the others who called me pretty were representatives of an aesthetic that would not apply when I went out into the mainstream world of school?

In my Paterson, New Jersey, public schools there were still quite a few white children, although the demographics of the city were changing rapidly. The original waves of Italian and Irish immigrants, silk-mill workers and laborers in the cloth industries, had been "assimilated." Their children were now the middle-class parents of my peers. Many of them moved their children to the Catholic schools that proliferated enough to have leagues of basketball teams. The names I recall hearing still ring in my ears: Don Bosco High vs. St. Mary's High, St. Joseph's vs. St. John's. Later I too would be transferred to the safer environment of a Catholic school. But I started school at Public School Number 11. I came there from Puerto Rico, thinking myself a pretty girl, and found that the hierarchy for popularity was as follows: pretty white girl, pretty Jewish girl, pretty Puerto Rican girl, pretty black girl. Drop the last two categories; teachers were too busy to have more than one favorite per class, and it was simply understood that if there was a big part in the school play, or any competition where the main qualification was "presentability" (such as escorting a school visitor to or from the principal's office), the classroom's public address speaker would be requesting the pretty and/or nice-looking white boy or girl. By the time I was in the sixth grade, I was sometimes called by the principal to represent my class because I dressed neatly (I knew this from a progress report sent to my mother, which I translated for her), and because all the "presentable" white girls had moved to the Catholic schools (I later surmised this part). But I was still not one of the popular girls with the boys. I remember one incident where I stepped out into the playground in my baggy gym shorts and one Puerto Rican boy said to the other: "What do you think?" The other one answered: "Her face is okay, but look at the toothpick legs." The next best thing to a compliment I got was when my favorite male teacher, while handing out the class pictures, commented that with my long neck and delicate features I resembled the movie star Audrey Hepburn. But the Puerto Rican boys had learned to respond to a fuller figure: long necks and a perfect little nose were not what they looked for in a girl. That is when I decided I was a "brain." I did not settle into the role easily. I was nearly devastated by what the chicken-pox episode had done to my self-image. But I looked into the mirror less often after I was told that I would always have scars on my face, and I hid behind my long black hair and my books.

After the problems at the public school got to the point where even nonconfrontational little me got beaten up several times, my parents enrolled me at St. Joseph's High School. I was then a minority of one among the Italian and Irish kids. But I found several good friends there—other girls who took their studies seriously. We did our homework together and talked about the Jackies. The Jackies were two popular girls, one blonde and the other red-haired, who had women's bodies. Their curves showed even in the blue jumper uniforms with straps that we all wore. The blonde Jackie would often let one of the straps fall off her shoulder, and although she, like all of us, wore a white blouse underneath, all the boys stared at her arm. My friends and I talked about this and practiced letting our straps fall off our shoulders. But it wasn't the same without breasts or hips.

My final two and a half years at high school were spent in Augusta, Georgia, where my parents moved our family in search of a more peaceful environment. There we became part of a little community of our army-connected relatives and friends. School was yet another matter. I was enrolled in a huge school of nearly two thousand students that had just that year been forced to integrate. There were two black girls and there was me. I did extremely well academically. As to my social life, it was, for the most part, uneventful—yet it is in my memory blighted by one incident. In my junior year, I became wildly infatuated with a pretty white boy. I'll call him Ted. Oh, he was pretty: yellow hair that fell over his forehead, a smile to die for, and he was a great dancer. I watched him at Teen Town, the youth center at the base where all the military brats gathered on Saturday nights. My father had retired from the military and we had all our base privileges—one other reason we had moved to Augusta. Ted looked like an angel to me. I worked on him for a year before he asked me out. This meant maneuvering to be within the periphery of his vision at every possible occasion. I took the long way to my classes in school just to pass by his locker, I went to football games that I detested, and I danced (I too was a good dancer) in front of him at Teen Town—this took some fancy footwork since it involved subtly moving my partner toward the right spot on the dance floor. When Ted finally approached me, "A Million to One" was playing on the jukebox, and when he took me into his arms, the odds suddenly turned in my favor. He asked me to go to a school dance the following Saturday. I said yes, breathlessly, I said yes but there were obstacles to surmount at home. My father did not allow me to date casually. I was allowed to go to major events like a prom or a concert with a boy who had been properly screened. There was such a boy in my life, a neighbor who wanted to be a Baptist missionary and was practicing his anthropological skills on my family. If I was desperate to go somewhere and needed a date, I'd resort to Gary. This is the type of religious nut that Gary was: When the school bus did not show up one day, he put his hands over his face and prayed to Christ to get us a way to get to school. Within ten minutes a mother in a station wagon on her way to town stopped to ask why we weren't in school. Gary informed her that the Lord had sent her just in time to get us there for roll call. He assumed that I was impressed. Gary was even good-looking in a bland sort of way, but he kissed me with his lips tightly pressed together. I think Gary probably ended up marrying a native woman from wherever he may have gone to preach the Gospel according to Paul. She probably believes that all white men pray to God for transportation and kiss with their mouths closed. But it was Ted's mouth, his whole beautiful self that concerned me in those days. I knew my father would say no to our date, but I planned to run away from home if necessary. I told my mother how important this date was. I cajoled and pleaded with her from Sunday to Wednesday. She listened to my arguments, and must have heard the note of desperation in my voice. She said very gently to me: "You better be ready for disappointment." I did not ask what she meant. I did not want her fears for me to taint my happiness. I asked her to tell my father about my date. Thursday at breakfast my father looked at me across the table with his eyebrows together. My mother looked at him with her mouth set in a straight line. I looked down at my bowl of cereal. Nobody said anything. Friday I tried on every dress in my closet. Ted would be picking me up at six on Saturday: dinner and then the sock hop at school. Friday night I was in my room doing my nails or something else in preparation for Saturday (I know I groomed myself nonstop all week) when the telephone rang. I ran to get it. It was Ted. His voice sounded funny when he said my name, so funny that I felt compelled to ask: "Is something wrong?" Ted blurted it all out without a preamble. His father had asked who he was going out with. Ted had told him my name. "Ortiz? That's Spanish, isn't it?" the father had asked. Ted had told him yes, then shown him my picture in the yearbook. Ted's father had shaken his head. No. Ted would not be taking me out. Ted's father had known Puerto Ricans in the army. He had lived in New York City while studying architecture and had seen how the *spics* lived. Like rats. Ted repeated his father's words to me as if I should understand *his predicament* when I heard why he was breaking our date. I don't remember what I said before hanging up. I do recall the darkness of my room that sleepless night, and the heaviness of my blanket in which I wrapped myself like a shroud. And I remember my parents' respect for my pain and their gentleness toward me that weekend. My mother did not say "I warned you," and I was grateful for her understanding silence.

In college, I suddenly became an "exotic" woman to the men who had survived the popularity wars in high school, who were now practicing to be worldly: They had to act liberal in their politics, in their lifestyles, and in the women they went out with. I dated heavily for a while, then married young. I had discovered that I needed stability more than social life. I had brains for sure, and some talent in writing. These facts were a constant in my life. My skin color, my size, and my appearance were variables—things that were judged according to my current self-image, the aesthetic values of the times, the places I was in, and the people I met. My studies, later my writing, the respect of people who saw me as an individual person they cared about, these were the criteria for my sense of self-worth that I would concentrate on in my adult life.

Nellie Wong

When I Was Growing Up

Because there is a single ideal of beauty in western culture, based on white norms, women of color in particular might experience conflict and self-rejection around issues of looks and appearance. In this poignant poem, Nellie Wong describes how she longed to be white. Because white girls were portrayed as all-American girls in the media and rewarded with status in high school, she wanted to erase her ethnic heritage.

As You Read, Ask Yourself . . .

How might Nellie Wong's desire to be white have affected her relationships with other girls?

How did it affect her relationships with white and Asian American men?

Which stereotypes of Chinese Americans did Wong attempt to conform to? Which did she reject?

How can women of color develop positive identities in a white-dominated culture?

I know now that once I longed to be white.
How? you ask.
Let me tell you the ways.

> when I was growing up, people told me
> I was dark and I believed my own darkness
> in the mirror, in my soul, my own narrow vision

> > when I was growing up, my sisters
> > with fair skin got praised
> > for their beauty, and in the dark
> > I fell further, crushed between high walls

> when I was growing up, I read magazines
> and saw movies, blonde movie stars, white skin,
> sensuous lips and to be elevated, to become
> a woman, a desirable woman, I began to wear
> imaginary pale skin

when I was growing up, I was proud
of my English, my grammar, my spelling
fitting into the group of smart children
smart Chinese children, fitting in,
belonging, getting in line

when I was growing up and went to high school,
I discovered the rich white girls, a few yellow girls,
their imported cotton dresses, their cashmere sweaters,
their curly hair and I thought that I too should have
what these lucky girls had

when I was growing up, I hungered
for American food, American styles,
coded: white and even to me, a child
born of Chinese parents, being Chinese
was feeling foreign, was limiting,
was unAmerican

when I was growing up and a white man wanted
to take me out, I thought I was special,
an exotic gardenia, anxious to fit
the stereotype of an oriental chick

when I was growing up, I felt ashamed
of some yellow men, their small bones,
their frail bodies, their spitting
on the streets, their coughing,
their lying in sunless rooms,
shooting themselves in the arms

when I was growing up, people would ask
if I were Filipino, Polynesian, Portuguese.
They named all colors except white, the shell
of my soul, but not my dark, rough skin

when I was growing up, I felt
dirty. I thought that god
made white people clean
and no matter how much I bathed,
I could not change. I could not shed
my skin in the gray water

when I was growing up, I swore
I would run away to purple mountains,
houses by the sea with nothing over
my head, with space to breathe,
uncongested with yellow people in an area
called Chinatown, in an area I later learned
was a ghetto, one of many hearts
of Asian America

I know now that once I longed to be white
How many more ways? you ask.
Haven't I told you enough?

Ann Rex

My Left Hand

Warning: This story is not fun to read. One of the most devastating consequences of our increasing societal obsession with weight and appearance is the epidemic of eating disorders among adolescent girls. Here, "Ann Rex" (a pseudonym) writes about her struggle with bulimia. Driven by the desire to be perfect—the most popular girl, with the best-looking boyfriend, the straight A's, and the perfect body—Rex relied on bingeing and purging as a means of weight control. Her account of the process, and the body hatred that drove it, are frank and compelling.

As You Read, Ask Yourself . . .

At what age did Ann Rex start monitoring her body?

What were the physical and social consequences of her bulimia?

What were her sources of support in confronting her problem?

After conquering her eating disorder, how did Rex's body image change?

For as long as I can remember, I have always been obsessed about my weight. I was worried about how my body looked long before I ever picked up an issue of *Cosmo,* long before I realized that models were actually people behind the cool gazes and stretched bodies, long before I realized the difference between skinny mirrors and fat mirrors. As early as the age of ten, even, I monitored my body's growth. I'd place my tiny hand on my upper thigh, my self-appointed barometer of policed weight control, making sure that the width of my thigh did not exceed the width of my outspread hand.

As I blossomed into a full-fledged voluptuous teenager, my obsession seemed to expand exponentially. In high school, I was the leader of my own little rat pack of girls; I was a Heather, an "IT" girl, and so my so-called friends adopted my everything—from my outfits to my mannerisms—in their efforts to be just like me, popular. I always felt like I had to live up to my "image"—a manipulated concoction of perfect body, brains, and bravado—in order to maintain my hierarchical status. To be the "IT" girl my minions had pegged me for, I had to spend a lot of time *being* her, being a troublemaker, being the girl with the most cake, being a touchy and untouchable entity. But I could never just be. And to further aggravate matters, such as my dilemma of quelling my insecurities about my body, my problems, my needs while still being a cool chick, I had no one to turn to when I felt weak, unsure, heavy.

As I got older, the self-inflicted pressure to be this girl increased. My fears manifested themselves in my ravenous appetite. I had a sweet tooth; it began at breakfast with a can of Coke and the potpourri of junk food I shoveled into my mouth just continued from there. When I was seventeen, my father warned me that my butt would balloon into a Goodyear blimp if I kept up the pace of my "diet." Concerned, I immediately cut out carbonated drinks from my daily intake.

In the summer of my eighteenth year, I discovered my left hand. I learned that I could still be this girl—the one with an effervescent personality and a perfect body—and be in control of my weight while still eating everything I wanted. So while the other little rat packers counted calories, I gloated about not getting bloated.

My left hand and I had an unusual first date, and like the first time I fucked, it hurt and I cried. I thought this was going to be easy. I thought I could eat as much as I wanted and get rid of it all and everything would be fine, I'd still be skinny. I didn't expect the tears, I didn't expect the pain, the gagging, the bile. But I was not to be daunted—the challenge of perfecting my skills had been triggered, the goal of having it all loomed on the horizon and I was only going to remain thin if my inept left hand would become a skilled crafts hand. In short, I was hooked by the southpaw.

And so, I turned into a shove-your-fist-in-your-mouth-till-your-knuckles-bleed kind of gal. My life became a constant merry-go-round of overeating (bingeing) and cheating (purging), a free ride of brownies and pasta, an eyes-closed whirlpool of gradually degenerating degrees of self-control. My left hand became my heroine; not an instrument of destruction but of reconstruction. A beacon of hope, of keeping everything under control, of having my cake and purging it if I had to. And so I lived this sort of hazy nether beat-the-scale world for quite some time. I was fueled by my acute desire to remain popular, to have the best-looking boyfriend, to be a straight-A student, to be a perfect daughter, and to keep my perfect body. And as I got older, and *Cosmo* finally did infiltrate my life, this perspective of perfection was based on everyone else's, and yet no one's. It came from an amalgam of body parts I had seen on *The Brady Bunch* (they had great hair) and in magazines and other women's bodies in my life whom I had looked up to and at, who functioned as role models, teachers, what have you, women like my mom—the kind of woman I aspired to be like, to look like too.

At the height of my first (yes, there were two!) bout with bulimia, I was bingeing and purging up to eight times a day. My left hand was adept at getting rid of food without much effort. In and out, I used to say. However, the toll the binge/purge cycle took on my body was another story. By the end of the day I would lie down, fatigue-ridden from the day's events. My eyes were often puffy from involuntary tears, complete with burst capillaries turned into raspberry speckles all around my cheeks and eyes. Not a pretty picture.

When it finally occurred to me that I had a problem I sought therapy. I knew I needed help, but finding the right kind of help proved to be even more devastating than admitting I had a problem. In the end it was actually my brother who came to my aid by basically threatening to tell my parents. And the idea of shattering their image of their perfect daughter was so terrifying to me that I stopped after months of sometimes gentle, sometimes rough brother-sister therapy/intervention. A week before I turned twenty-two, I gave my left hand an extended, overdue vacation.

For the next four years, my body healed itself. My knuckles were no longer red from the constant scraping against my teeth. The back of my throat was no longer irritated all the time, having been scratched to bits by my fingernails. I had energy, I felt great about myself. Things started to "happen." I was out of college; I met the most perfect man in the world who ended up being the most perfect boyfriend for the next few years; I pursued a career. And I had a great body, again.

Unfortunately, I relapsed. After four years, my career was going nowhere, I lost my perfect boyfriend, I didn't like my friends. I began to see lumps and bumps in my thighs, the kind I'd never seen before. In short, all my fears had come back to haunt me, except this time I knew I was fat. By then, models had names, MTV flooded the senses, AIDS prohibited uninhibited sexual behavior. By then I had the awareness I did not have at eighteen; I was painfully aware of how inadequate I had become in my old age. I read . . . magazines and I knew what "willowy" and "lithe" referred to and I knew it wasn't me.

I began to hate my body. *Hate.* I wanted to be like the thin models, except I knew I couldn't be; I was short and I was fat. I hated to see my reflection in the mirror—I felt horror every time I saw yet another piece of me expand or sag. I would not be catching anyone's eye if I remained looking this way, because after all, what else could I offer to a guy who might be fantasizing about some current hot babe/media goddess when, in fact, I was anything but?

And so it began, except this time, it was not an experiment. Every time I looked at my left hand, I knew, I fucking knew that what I was about to do was self-destructive. I knew about destroying the electrolyte balance, and I knew how the acid produced in my belly would rot my teeth. But once I relapsed I could not stop. The familiarity fit my left hand like a glove as the bingeing and purging again became a part of my everyday lifestyle.

All the old habits returned, the feasts, the treats. I began carrying a compact toothbrush, floss, and toothpaste with me at all times. The purging process had its own set of rituals. I would lock myself in the bathroom while the shower loudly ran cold water to muffle the gagging and coughing sounds, so as not to arouse the suspicions of my roommates. And then, once the purge was complete, I would draw a nice lukewarm bath, to soothe my shaking body and rid myself of the accompanying, necessary evils (bile-filled mouth, puffy eyes, racing heartbeat). Then the self-abuse would begin, the utter hatred, the abysmal shame, the unreality of it all. Depression would sweep over me.

I began to believe that therapy was the only way out. I was bulimic. I was addicted to bingeing and purging. I needed help. I was just too emotionally volatile. After almost every purge, I would swear up and down never ever to do it again. Sometimes I would succeed for a day or so, but if I was just slightly upset, the evil bug would come back, over and over again. And this cyclical behavior was not going to stop unless I sought help.

Because this second bout was not like the first time. There was something more pathetic and desperate about this round. This time everything hurt. Not just my body, but my heart and my mind were much more worn out than when I had been bulimic in my teens. The puffiness didn't dissipate as quickly as it once did, the capillaries took longer to repair themselves, and the fatigue was unshakable. I was the worst kind of addict; I lied to everyone, pretending everything was okay, perfect in fact. Three years into the second round, I got the scare of my lifetime.

I had been in the bathroom for over an hour. My knuckles, scarred from never healed scabs, were bleeding, my fingers had turned into pruny prongs, my irritated throat was punctured by my insistent relentless attempt to purge the evening's bacchanalian binge. I could feel the pop pop pop of blood vessels in my face exploding each time I leaned over. My eyes were heaving closed, every pore in my body was gasping for air, and I was panicking, because nothing was coming out. I mean, I had eaten a lot of food and not a damn morsel was coming out, no matter how many fingers I stuck into my mouth. Nothing was working and I was getting worried. The longer the food sat in my stomach the sooner it would get digested and I would get fatter soon if something didn't give.

I didn't know what to do, so I decided to stand up and get some water. However, I was so disoriented, I could barely stand. Instead I lay down on the cold tile bathroom floor for what I thought was a few minutes, but when I finally popped my eyes open, dusk had turned to dawn and panic set in.

Oh god, what had I done? Was I going to die, now? Like this? Possibly from a heart attack and then my roommate would find me, arm drenched in bile, toilet bowl full of halfhearted spew? What would my parents say? She died because she thought she was fat? Oh god oh god oh god. Suddenly I was afraid, not just roller-coaster butterflies in my stomach afraid, no this was a deeper fear. Terror had set in, a pure unadulterated unconditional cold heartless sensation that bled blackness. Ohmigod. I'm not sure how long I sat in the murkiness of my mind's revolt; I had no grasp on myself, my sense of anything. But then, as if someone, maybe me, flicked a switch, it happened: the epiphany. I suddenly did not feel clammy, but happy, this bizarre giddiness that came from this well of knowledge. It was over. I was going to be okay. Just like that.

What? Yeah. I'm not saying cold turkey works for everyone, but I just sat up and I was fine. I had been abusing my body for years, how could I be "just fine"? But, the prophetic gaze into the nadir of my soul reminded me that I could get better. I was still fat, no question, I still felt fat, but if that feeling could be dealt with, then maybe I could accept and learn to love the body that I had. My terror angel had waited to rear its ugly head, always just lurking on the horizon, just waiting for the right moment to go Boo! And when it did, I woke up.

Truth is, I still miss the perfectness of my body; I don't have it anymore. But my idea of perfection has changed; so maybe in a perfect world perfect doesn't really exist. In my world I am okay, and that kind of feeling is just about perfect. The models, well, they still haunt me, but frankly, being 5 feet 11 inches tall thinthinthin and heartachingly beautiful is not a norm, it's an anomaly. Models stand out because they are so different than the rest of us, and different is still cool.

I am different too now, new on the inside. No matter how many times a lover will oooh and ahh over my DD-size breasts, I still wonder how he will react when he sees what they really look like when the bra is off and they hang so gloriously low. Does this mean I'll lop them off so they'll look like someone else's breasts? Nope. It just means I am still insecure about my body but at least now I don't want to punish myself for it. Now I can eat as much as I want with a group of people and not have to be embarrassed about excusing myself from the table at just the right moment. Because now when I go to the bathroom during a meal, it's because I have to pee, and that makes me feel really good.

"Opening" Faces: The Politics of Cosmetic Surgery and Asian American Women

Eugenia Kaw's extensive interviews with Asian American women who have chosen to have cosmetic surgery on their eyes show us how views of beauty are race and class based. Is it better for women of color to try to look more like the white majority if this can bring them advantages in the workplace and in their personal lives? Think about how the emphasis on individual change and conformity versus collective action relates to other kinds of body standards such as weight. What happens to women who cannot or will not conform? But what price is paid by women who strive to meet external standards?

As You Read, Ask Yourself . . .

Do you agree with those who argue that such expensive and uncomfortable surgery is acquiescence to societal oppression? Or do you agree with those women who state that they have made a personal choice to improve an unattractive feature and increase their chances of career advancement?

Ellen, a Chinese American in her forties, informed me she had had her upper eyelids surgically cut and sewed by a plastic surgeon twenty years ago in order to get rid of "the sleepy look," which her naturally "puffy" eyes gave her. She pointed out that the sutures, when they healed, became a crease above the eye which gave the eyes a more "open appearance." She was quick to tell me that her decision to undergo "double-eyelid" surgery was not so much because she was vain or had low self-esteem, but rather because the "undesirability" of her looks before the surgery was an undeniable fact.

During my second interview with Ellen, she showed me photos of herself from before and after her surgery in order to prove her point. When Stacy, her twelve-year-old daughter, arrived home from school, Ellen told me she wanted Stacy to undergo similar surgery in the near future because Stacy has only single eyelids and would look prettier and be more successful in life if she had a fold above each eye. Ellen brought the young girl to where I was sitting and said, "You see, if you look at her you will know what I mean when I say that I had to have surgery done on my eyelids. Look at her eyes. She looks just like me before the surgery." Stacy seemed very shy to show me her face. But I told the girl truthfully that she looked fine and beautiful the way she was. Immediately she grinned at her mother in a mocking, defiant manner, as if I had given her courage, and put her arm up in the manner that bodybuilders do when they display their bulging biceps.

As empowered as Stacy seemed to feel at the moment, I could not help but wonder how many times Ellen had shown her "before" and "after" photos to her young daughter with the remark that "Mommy looks better after the surgery." I also wondered how many times Stacy had been asked by Ellen to consider surgically "opening" her eyes like "Mommy did." And I wondered about the images we see on television and in magazines and their often negative, stereotypical portrayal of "squinty-eyed" Asians (when Asians are featured at all). I could not help but wonder how normal it is to feel that an eye without a crease is undesirable and how much of that feeling is imposed. And I shuddered to think how soon it might be before twelve-year-old Stacy's defenses gave away and she allowed her eyes to be cut.

The permanent alteration of bodies through surgery for aesthetic purposes is not a new phenomenon in the United States. As early as World War I, when reconstructive surgery was performed on disfigured soldiers, plastic surgery methods began to be refined for purely cosmetic purposes (that is, not so much for repairing and restoring but for transforming natural features a person is unhappy with). Within the last decade, however, an increasing number of people have opted for a wide array of cosmetic surgery procedures, from tummy tucks, facelifts, and liposuction to enlargement of chests and calves. By 1988, two million Americans had undergone cosmetic surgery (Wolf 1991:218), and a 69 percent increase had occurred in the number of cosmetic surgery procedures between 1981 and 1990, according to the ASPRS or American Society of Plastic and Reconstructive Surgeons (n.d.).

Included in these numbers are an increasing number of cosmetic surgeries undergone by people like Stacy who are persons of color (American Academy of Cosmetic Surgery press release, 1991). In fact, Asian Americans are more likely than any other ethnic group (white or nonwhite) to pursue cosmetic surgery. ASPRS reports that over thirty-nine thousand of the aesthetic procedures performed by its members in 1990 (or more than 6 percent of all procedures performed that year) were performed on Asian Americans, who make up 3 percent of the U.S. population (Chen 1993:15). Because Asian Americans seek cosmetic surgery from doctors in Asia and from doctors who specialize in fields other than surgery (e.g., ear, nose, and throat specialists and ophthalmologists), the total number of Asian American patients is undoubtedly higher (Chen 1993:16).

The specific procedures requested by different ethnic groups in the United States are missing from the national data, but newspaper reports and medical texts indicate that Caucasians and nonwhites, on the average, seek significantly different types of operations (Chen 1993; Harahap 1982; Kaw 1993; LeFlore 1982; McCurdy 1980; Nakao 1993; Rosenthal 1991). While Caucasians primarily seek to augment breasts and to remove wrinkles and fat through such procedures as facelifts, liposuction, and collagen injection, African Americans more often opt for lip and nasal reduction operations; Asian Americans more often choose to insert an implant on their nasal dorsum for a more prominent nose or undergo double-eyelid surgery whereby parts of their upper eyelids are excised to create a fold above each eye, which makes the eye appear wider.[1]

Though the American media, the medical establishment, and the general public have debated whether such cosmetic changes by nonwhite persons reflect a racist milieu in which racial minorities must deny their racial identity and attempt to look more Caucasian, a resounding no appears to be the overwhelming opinion of people in the United States.[2] Many plastic surgeons have voiced the opinion that racial minorities are becoming more assertive about their right to choose and that they are choosing not to look Caucasian. Doctors say that nonwhite persons' desire for thinner lips, wider eyes, and pointier noses is no more than a wish to enhance their features in order to attain "balance" with all their other features (Kaw 1993; Merrell 1994; Rosenthal 1991).

Much of the media and public opinion also suggests that there is no political significance inherent in the cosmetic changes made by people of color which alter certain conventionally known, phenotypic markers of racial identity. On a recent Phil Donahue show where the racially derogatory nature of blue contact lenses for African American women was contested, both white and nonwhite audience members were almost unanimous that African American women's use of these lenses merely reflected their freedom to choose in the same way that Bo Derek chose to wear corn rows and white people decided to get tans (Bordo 1990). Focusing more specifically on cosmetic surgery, a *People Weekly* magazine article entitled "On the Cutting Edge" (January 27, 1992, p. 3) treats Michael Jackson (whose nose has become narrower and perkier and whose skin has become lighter through the years) as simply one among many Hollywood stars whose extravagant and competitive lifestyle has motivated and allowed them to pursue cosmetic self-enhancement. Clearly, Michael Jackson's physical transformation within the last decade has been more drastic than Barbara Hershey's temporary plumping of her lips to look younger in *Beaches* or Joan Rivers's facelift, yet his reasons for undergoing surgery are not differentiated from those of Caucasian celebrities; the possibility that he may want to cross racial divides through surgery is not an issue in the article.

When critics speculate on the possibility that a person of color is attempting to look white, they often focus their attack on the person and his or her apparent lack of ethnic pride and self-esteem. For instance, a *Newsweek* article, referring to Michael Jackson's recent television interview with Oprah Winfrey, questioned Jackson's emphatic claim that he is proud to be a black American: "Jackson's dermatologist confirmed that the star has vitiligo, a condition that blocks the skin's ability to produce pigment . . . [however,] most vitiligo sufferers darken their light patches with makeup to even the tone. Jackson's makeup solution takes the other tack: less ebony, more ivory" (Fleming and Talbot 1993:57). Such criticisms, sadly, center around Michael Jackson the person instead of delving into his possible feelings of oppression or examining society as a potential source of his motivation to alter his natural features so radically.

In this chapter, based on structured, open-ended interviews with Asian American women like Ellen who have or are thinking about undergoing cosmetic surgery for wider eyes and more heightened noses, I attempt to convey more emphatically the lived social experiences of people of color who seek what

101

EUGENIA KAW
"Opening" Faces: The
Politics of Cosmetic
Surgery and Asian
American Women

appears to be conventionally recognized Caucasian features. Rather than mock their decision to alter their features or treat it lightly as an expression of their freedom to choose an idiosyncratic look, I examine everyday cultural images and social relationships which influence Asian American women to seek cosmetic surgery in the first place. Instead of focusing, as some doctors do (Kaw 1993), on the size and width of the eyelid folds the women request as indicators of the women's desire to look Caucasian, I examine the cultural, social, and historical sources that allow the women in my study to view their eyes in a negative fashion—as "small" and "slanted" eyes reflecting a "dull," "passive" personality, a "closed" mind, and a "lack of spirit" in the person. I explore the reasons these women reject the natural shape of their eyes so radically that they willingly expose themselves to a surgery that is at least an hour long, costs one thousand to three thousand dollars, entails administering local anesthesia and sedation, and carries the following risks: "bleeding and hematoma," "hemorrhage," formation of a "gaping wound," "discoloration," scarring, and "asymmetric lid folds" (Sayoc 1974:162–166).

In our feminist analyses of femininity and beauty we may sometimes find it difficult to account for cosmetic surgery without undermining the thoughts and decisions of women who opt for it (Davis 1991). However, I attempt to show that the decision of the women in my study to undergo cosmetic surgery is often carefully thought out. Such a decision is usually made only after a long period of weighing the psychological pain of feeling inadequate prior to surgery against the possible social advantages a new set of features may bring. Several of the women were aware of complex power structures that construct their bodies as inferior and in need of change, even while they simultaneously reproduced these structures by deciding to undergo surgery (Davis 1991:33).

I argue that as women and as racial minorities, the psychological burden of having to measure up to ideals of beauty in American society falls especially heavy on these Asian American women. As women, they are constantly bombarded with the notion that beauty should be their primary goal (Lakoff and Scherr 1984, Wolf 1991). As racial minorities, they are made to feel inadequate by an Anglo American-dominated cultural milieu that has historically both excluded them and distorted images of them in such a way that they themselves have come to associate those features stereotypically identified with their race (i.e., small, slanty eyes, and a flat nose) with negative personality and mental characteristics.

In a consumption-oriented society such as the United States, it is often tempting to believe that human beings have an infinite variety of needs which technology can endlessly fulfill, and that these needs, emerging spontaneously in time and space, lack any coherent patterns, cultural meanings, or political significance (Bordo 1991; Goldstein 1993; O'Neill 1985:98). However, one cannot regard needs as spontaneous, infinite, harmless, and amorphous without first considering what certain groups feel they lack and without first critically examining the lens with which the larger society has historically viewed this lack. Frances C. MacGregor, who between 1946 and 1959 researched the social and cultural motivations of such white ethnic minorities as Jewish and Italian Americans to seek rhinoplasty, wrote, "The statements of the patients . . . have a certain face validity and explicitness that reflect both the values of our society and the degree to which these are perceived as creating problems for the deviant individual" (MacGregor 1967:129).

Social scientific analyses of ethnic relations should include a study of the body. As evident in my research, racial minorities may internalize a body image produced by the dominant culture's racial ideology and, because of it, begin to loathe, mutilate, and revise parts of their bodies. Bodily adornment and mutilation (the cutting up and altering of essential parts of the body; see Kaw 1993) are symbolic mediums most directly and concretely concerned with the construction of the individual as social actor or cultural subject (Turner 1980). Yet social scientists have only recently focused on the body as a central component of social self-identity (Blacking 1977; Brain 1979; Daly 1978; Lock and Scheper-Hughes 1990; O'Neill 1985; Turner 1980; Sheets-Johnstone 1992). Moreover, social scientists, and sociocultural anthropologists in particular, have not yet explored the ways in which the body is central to the everyday experience of racial identity.

METHOD AND DESCRIPTION OF SUBJECTS

In this article, I present the findings of an ethnographic research project completed in the San Francisco Bay Area. I draw on data from structured interviews with doctors and patients, basic medical statistics, and relevant newspaper and magazine articles. The sampling of informants for this research was not random in the strictly statistical sense since informants were difficult to find. Both medical practitioners and patients treat cases of cosmetic surgery as highly confidential, as I later discuss in more detail. To find a larger, more random sampling of Asian American informants, I posted fliers and placed advertisements in various local newspapers. Ultimately, I was able to conduct structured, open-ended interviews with eleven Asian American women, four of whom were referred to me by the doctors in my study and six by mutual acquaintances: I found one through an advertisement. Nine had had cosmetic surgery of the eye or the nose; one recently considered a double-eyelid operation; one is considering undergoing double-eyelid operation in the next few years. The women in my study live in the San Francisco Bay Area, except for two who reside in the Los Angeles area. Five were operated on by doctors who I also interviewed for my study, while four had their operations in Asia—two in Seoul, Korea, one in Beijing, China, and one in Taipei, Taiwan. Of the eleven women in my study, only two (who received their operations in China and in Taiwan) had not lived in the United States prior to their operations.[3] The ages of the Asian American women in my study range from eighteen to seventy-one; one woman was only fifteen at the time of her operation. Their class backgrounds are similar in that they were all engaged in middle-class, white-collar occupations: there were three university students, one art student, one legal assistant, one clerk, one nutritionist, one teacher, one law student, and two doctors' assistants.

Although I have not interviewed Asian American men who have or are thinking of undergoing cosmetic surgery, I realize that they too undergo double-eyelid and nose bridge operations. Their motivations are, to a large extent, similar to those of the women in my study (Iwata 1991). Often their decision to undergo surgery also follows a long and painful process of feeling marginal in society (Iwata 1991). I did not purposely exclude Asian American male patients from my study; rather, none responded to my requests for interviews.

To understand how plastic surgeons view the cosmetic procedures performed on Asian Americans, five structured, open-ended interviews were conducted with five plastic surgeons, all of whom practice in the Bay Area. I also examined several medical books and plastic surgery journals which date from the 1950s to 1990. And I referenced several news releases and informational packets distributed by such national organizations as the American Society of Plastic and Reconstructive Surgeons, an organization which represents 97 percent of all physicians certified by the American Board of Plastic Surgery.

To examine popular notions of cosmetic surgery, in particular how the phenomenon of Asian American women receiving double-eyelid and nose bridge operations is viewed by the public and the media, I have referenced relevant newspaper and magazine articles.

I obtained national data on cosmetic surgery from various societies for cosmetic surgeons, including the American Society of Plastic and Reconstructive Surgeons. Data on the specific types of surgery sought by different ethnic groups in the United States, including Asian Americans, were missing from the national statistics. At least one public relations coordinator told me that such data is unimportant to plastic surgeons. To compensate for this lack of data, I asked the doctors in my study to provide me with figures from their respective clinics. Most told me they had little data on their cosmetic patients readily available.

COLONIZATION OF ASIAN AMERICAN WOMEN'S SOULS: INTERNALIZATION OF GENDER AND RACIAL STEREOTYPES

Upon first talking with my Asian American women informants, one might conclude that the women were merely seeking to enhance their features for aesthetic reasons and that there is no cultural meaning or political significance in their decision to surgically enlarge their eyes and heighten their noses. As Elena, a twenty-one-year-old Chinese American who underwent double-eyelid surgery three years ago from a doctor in my study, stated: "I underwent my surgery for personal reasons. It's not different from wanting to put makeup on . . . I don't intend to look Anglo-Saxon. I told my doctor, 'I would like my eyes done with definite creases on my eyes, but I don't want a drastic change.'" Almost all the other women similarly stated that their unhappiness with their eyes and nose was individually motivated and that they really did not desire Caucasian features. In fact, one Korean American woman, Nina, age thirty-four, stated she was not satisfied with the results of her surgery from three years ago because her doctor made her eyes "too round" like that of Caucasians. One might deduce from such statements that the women's decision to undergo cosmetic surgery of the eye and nose is harmless and may be even empowering to them, for their surgery provides them with a more permanent solution than makeup for "personal" dissatisfactions they have about their features.

However, an examination of their descriptions of the natural shape of their eyes and nose suggests that their "personal" feelings about their features reflect the larger society's negative valuation and stereotyping of Asian features in general. They all said that "small, slanty" eyes and a "flat" nose suggest, in the Asian person, a personality that is "dull," "unenergetic," "passive," and "unsociable" and a mind that is narrow and "closed." For instance, Elena said, "When I look at other Asians who have no folds and their eyes are slanted and closed, I think of how they would look better more awake." Nellee, a twenty-one-year-old Chinese American, said that she seriously considered surgery for double eyelids in high school so that she could "avoid the stereotype of the 'oriental bookworm' " who is "dull and doesn't know how to have fun." Carol, a thirty-seven-year-old Chinese American who received double eyelids seven years ago, said: "The eyes are the window of your soul . . . [yet] lots of oriental people have the outer corners of their eyes a little down, making them look tired. [The double eyelids] don't make a big difference in the size of our eyes but they give your eyes more spirit." Pam, a Chinese American, age forty-four, who received double-eyelid surgery from another doctor in my study, stated, "Yes, Of course. Bigger eyes look prettier. . . . Lots of Asians' eyes are so small they become little lines when the person laughs, making the person look sleepy." Likewise, Annie, an eighteen-year-old Korean American woman who had an implant placed on her nasal dorsum to build up her nose bridge at age fifteen, said: "I guess I always wanted that sharp look—a look like you are smart. If you have a roundish kind of nose it's like you don't know what's going on. If you have that sharp look, you know, with black eyebrows, a pointy nose, you look more alert. I always thought that was cool." The women were influenced by the larger society's negative valuation of stereotyped Asian features in such a way that they evaluated themselves and Asian women in general with a critical eye. Their judgments were based on a set of standards, stemming from the eighteenth- and nineteenth-century European aesthetic ideal of the proportions in Greek sculpture, which are presumed by a large amount of Americans to be within the grasp of every woman (Goldstein 1993:150, 160).

Unlike many white women who may also seek cosmetic surgery to reduce or make easier the daily task of applying makeup, the Asian American women in my study hoped more specifically to ease the task of creating with makeup the illusion of features they do not have as women who are Asian. Nellee, who has not yet undergone double-eyelid surgery, said that at present she has to apply makeup everyday "to give my eyes an illusion of a crease. When I don't wear make-up I feel my eyes are small." Likewise, Elena said that before her double-eyelid surgery she checked almost every morning in the mirror when she woke up to see if a fold had formed above her right eye to match the more prominent fold above her left eye: "[on certain mornings] it was like any other day when you wake up and don't feel so hot, you know. My eye had no definite folds, because when Asians sleep their folds change in and out—it's not definite." Also, Jo, a twenty-eight-year-old Japanese American who already had natural folds above each eye but wishes to enlarge them through double-eyelid surgery, explained:

I guess I just want to make a bigger eyelid [fold] so that they look bigger and not slanted. I think in Asian eyes it's the inside corner of the fold [she was drawing on my notebook] that goes down too much. . . . Right now I am still self-conscious about leaving the house without any makeup on, because I feel just really ugly without it. I try to curl my eyelashes and put on mascara. I think it makes my eyes look more open. But surgery can permanently change the shape of my eyes. I don't think that a bigger eyelid fold will actually change the slant but I think it will give the perception of having less of it, less of an Asian eye.

105

EUGENIA KAW
"Opening" Faces: The
Politics of Cosmetic
Surgery and Asian
American Women

For the women in my study, their oppression is a double encounter: one under patriarchal definitions of femininity (i.e., that a woman should care about the superficial details of her look), and the other under Caucasian standards of beauty. The constant self-monitoring of their anatomy and their continuous focus on detail exemplify the extent to which they feel they must measure up to society's ideals.

In the United States, where a capitalist work ethic values "freshness," "a quick wit," and assertiveness, many Asian American women are already disadvantaged at birth by virtue of their inherited physical features which society associates with dullness and passivity. In this way, their desire to look more spirited and energetic through the surgical creation of folds above each eye is of a different quality from the motivation of many Anglo Americans seeking facelifts and liposuction for a fresher, more youthful appearance. Signs of aging are not the main reason Asian American cosmetic patients ultimately seek surgery of the eyes and the nose; often they are younger (usually between eighteen and thirty years of age) than the average Caucasian patient (Kaw 1993). Several of the Asian American women in my study who were over thirty years of age at the time of their eyelid operation sought surgery to get rid of extra folds of skin that had developed over their eyes due to age; however, even these women decided to receive double eyelids in the process. When Caucasian patients undergo eyelid surgery, on the other hand, the procedure is almost never to create a double eyelid (for they already possess one); in most cases, it is to remove sagging skin that results from aging. Clearly, Asian American women's negative image of their eyes and nose is not so much a result of their falling short of the youthful, energetic beauty ideal that influences every American as it is a direct product of society's racial stereotyping.

The women in my study described their own features with metaphors of dullness and passivity in keeping with many Western stereotypes of Asians. Stereotypes, by definition, are expedient caricatures of the "other," which serve to set them apart from the "we"; they serve to exclude instead of include, to judge instead of accept (Gilman 1985:15). Asians are rarely portrayed in the American print and electronic media. For instance, Asians (who constitute 3 percent of the U.S. population) account for less than 1 percent of the faces represented in magazine ads, according to a 1991 study titled "Invisible People" conducted by New York City's Department of Consumer Affairs (cited in Chen 1993:26). When portrayed, they are seen in one of two forms, which are not representative of Asians in general; as Eurasian-looking fashion models and movie stars (e.g., Nancy Kwan who played Suzy Wong) who already have double eyelids and pointy noses; and as stereotypically Asian characters such as Charlie Chan, depicted with personalities that are dull, passive, and nonsociable (Dower 1986; Kim 1986; Ramsdell 1983; Tajima 1989). The first group often serves as an ideal toward which Asian American women strive, even when they say they do not want to look Caucasian. The second serves as an image from which they try to escape.

Asian stereotypes, like all kinds of stereotypes, are multiple and have changed throughout the years; nevertheless they have maintained some distinct characteristics. Asians have been portrayed as exotic and erotic (as epitomized by Suzie Wong, or the Japanese temptress in the film *The Berlin Affair*), and especially during the U.S. war in the Pacific during World War II, they were seen as dangerous spies and mad geniuses who were treacherous and stealthy (Dower 1986; Huhr and Kim 1989). However, what remains consistent in the American popular image of Asians is their childishness, narrow-mindedness, and lack of leadership skills. Moreover, these qualities have long been associated with the relatively roundish form of Asian faces, and in particular with the "puffy" smallness of their eyes. Prior to the Japanese attack on Pearl Harbor, for instance, the Japanese were considered incapable of planning successful dive bombing attacks due to their "myopic," "squinty" eyes; during the war in the Pacific, their soldiers were caricatured as having thick horn-rimmed glasses through which they must squint to see their targets (Dower 1986). Today, the myopic squinty-eyed image of the narrow-minded Asian persists in the most recent stereotype of Asians as "model minorities" (as epitomized in the Asian exchange student character in the film *Sixteen Candles*). The term *model minority* was first coined in the 1960s when a more open-door U.S. immigration policy began allowing an unprecedented number of Asian immigrants into the United States, many of whom were the most elite and educated of their own countries (Takaki 1989). Despite its seemingly complimentary nature, *model minority* refers to a person who is hardworking and technically skilled but desperately lacking in creativity, worldliness, and the ability to assimilate into mainstream culture (Huhr and Kim 1989; Takaki 1989). Representations in the media, no matter how subtle, of various social situations can distort and reinforce one's impressions of one's own nature (Goffman 1979).

Witnessing society's association of Asian features with negative personality traits and mental characteristics, many Asian Americans become attracted to the image of Caucasian, or at least Eurasian, features. Several of the women in my study stated that they are influenced by images of fashion models with Western facial types. As Nellee explained: "I used to read a lot of fashion magazines which showed occidental persons how to put makeup on. So I used to think a crease made one's eyes prettier. It exposes your eyelashes more. Right now they all go under the hood of my eyes." Likewise, Jo said she thought half of her discontent regarding her eyes is a self-esteem problem, but she blames the other half on society: "When you look at all the stuff that they portray on TV and in the movies and in Miss America Pageants, the epitome of who is beautiful is that all-American look. It can even include African Americans now but not Asians." According to Jo, she is influenced not only by representations of Asians as passive, dull, and narrow-minded, but also by a lack of representation of Asians in general because society considers them un-American, inassimilable, foreign, and to be excluded.

Similar images of Asians also exist in East and Southeast Asia, and since many Asian Americans are immigrants from Asia, they are likely influenced by these images as well. Multinational corporations in Southeast Asia, for example, consider the female work force biologically suited for the most monotonous industrial labor because they claim the "Oriental girl" is "diligent" and has "nimble fingers" and a "slow-wit" (Ong 1987:151). In addition, American magazines and films have become increasingly available in many parts of Asia since World War II, and Asian popular magazines and electronic media depict models with Western facial types, especially when advertizing Western products. In fact, many of my Asian American woman informants possessed copies of such magazines, available in various Asian stores and in Chinatown. Some informants, like Jane, a twenty-year-old Korean American who underwent double-eyelid surgery at age sixteen and nasal bridge surgery at age eighteen, thumbed through Korean fashion magazines which she stored in her living room to show me photos of the Western and Korean models who she thought looked Caucasian, Eurasian, or had had double-eyelid and nasal bridge surgeries. She said these women had eyes that were too wide and noses that were too tall and straight to be on Asians. Though she was born and raised in the United States, she visits her relatives in Korea often. She explained that the influences the media had on her life in Korea and in the United States were, in some sense, similar: "When you turn on the TV [in Korea] you see people like Madonna and you see MTV and American movies and magazines. In any fashion magazine you don't really see a Korean-type woman; you see Cindy Crawford. My mother was telling me that when she was a kid, the ideal beauty was someone with a totally round, flat face. Kind of small and five feet tall. I guess things began to change in the 50s when Koreans started to have a lot of contact with the West." The environment within which Asian women develop a perspective on the value and meaning of their facial features is most likely not identical in Asia and the United States, where Asian women are a minority, but in Asia one can still be influenced by Western perceptions of Asians.

Some of the women in my study maintained that although racial inequality may exist in many forms, their decision to widen their eyes had little to do with racial inequality; they were attempting to look like other Asians with double eyelids, not like Caucasians. Nina, for example, described a beautiful woman as such: "Her face should not have very slender eyes like Chinese, Korean, or Japanese but not as round as Europeans. Maybe a Filipino, Thai, or other Southeast Asian faces are ideal. Basically I like an Asian's looks. . . . I think Asian eyes [not really slender ones] are sexy and have character." The rest of her description, however, makes it more difficult for one to believe that the Asian eyes she is describing actually belong on an Asian body: "The skin should not be too dark . . . and the frame should be a bit bigger than that of Asians." Southeast Asians, too, seek cosmetic surgery for double eyelids and nose bridges. One doctor showed me "before" and "after" photos of many Thai, Indonesian, and Vietnamese American women, who, he said, came to him for wider, more definite creases so that their eyes, which already have a double-eyelid, would look deeper-set.

In the present global economy, where the movement of people and cultural products is increasingly rapid and frequent and the knowledge of faraway places and trends is expanding, it is possible to imagine that cultural exchange

107

EUGENIA KAW
"Opening" Faces: The
Politics of Cosmetic
Surgery and Asian
American Women

happens in a multiplicity of directions, that often people construct images and practices that appear unconnected to any particular locality or culture (Appadurai 1990). One might perceive Asian American women in my study as constructing aesthetic images of themselves based on neither a Caucasian ideal nor a stereotypical Asian face. The difficulty with such constructions, however, is that they do not help Asian Americans to escape at least one stereotypical notion of Asians in the United States—that they are "foreign" and "exotic." Even when Asians are considered sexy, and attractive in the larger American society, they are usually seen as exotically sexy and attractive (Yang and Ragaz 1993:21). Since their beauty is almost always equated with the exotic and foreign, they are seen as members of an undifferentiated mass of people. Even though the women in my study are attempting to be seen as individuals, they are seen, in some sense, as less distinguishable from each other than white women are. As Lumi, a Japanese former model recently told *A. Magazine: The Asian American Quarterly,* "I've had bookers tell me I'm beautiful, but that they can't use me because I'm 'type.' All the agencies have their one Asian girl, and any more would be redundant" (Chen 1993:21).

The constraints many Asian Americans feel with regard to the shape of their eyes and nose are clearly of a different quality from almost every American's discontent with weight or signs of aging: it is also different from the dissatisfaction many women, white and nonwhite alike, feel about the smallness or largeness of their breasts. Because the features (eyes and nose) Asian Americans are most concerned about are conventional markers of their racial identity, a rejection of these markers entails, in some sense, a devaluation of not only oneself but also other Asian Americans. It requires having to imitate, if not admire, the characteristics of another group more culturally dominant than one's own (i.e., Anglo Americans) in order that one can at least try to distinguish oneself from one's own group. Jane, for instance, explains that looking like a Caucasian is almost essential for socioeconomic success: "Especially if you go into business, or whatever, you kind of have to have a Western facial type and you have to have like their features and stature—you know, be tall and stuff. So you can see that [the surgery] is an investment in your future."

Unlike those who may want to look younger or thinner in order to find a better job or a happier social life, the women in my study must take into consideration not only their own socioeconomic future, but also more immediately that of their offspring, who by virtue of heredity, inevitably share their features. Ellen, for instance, said that "looks are not everything. I want my daughter, Stacy, to know that what's inside is important too. Sometimes you can look beautiful because your nice personality and wisdom inside radiate outward, such as in the way you talk and behave." Still, she has been encouraging twelve-year-old Stacy to have double-eyelid surgery because she thinks "having less sleepy looking eyes would make a better impression on people and help her in the future with getting jobs." Ellen had undergone cosmetic surgery at the age of twenty on the advice of her mother and older sister and feels she has benefited.[4] Indeed, all three women in the study under thirty who have actually undergone cosmetic surgery did so on the advice of their mother and in their mother's presence at the clinic. Elena, in fact, received her double-eyelid surgery as a high school graduation present from her mother, who was concerned for her socioeconomic future.

The mothers, in turn, are influenced not so much by a personal flaw of their own which drives them to mold and perfect their daughters as by a society that values the superficial characteristics of one race over another.

A few of the women's dating and courtship patterns were also affected by their negative feelings toward stereotypically Asian features. Jo, for example, who is married to a Caucasian man, said she has rarely dated Asian men and is not usually attracted to them, partly because they look too much like her: "I really am sorry to say that I am not attracted to Asian men. And it's not to say that I don't find them attractive on the whole. But I did date a Japanese guy once and I felt like I was holding my brother's hand [she laughs nervously]."

109

Eugenia Kaw
"Opening" Faces: The
Politics of Cosmetic
Surgery and Asian
American Women

A MUTILATION OF THE BODY

Although none of the women in my study denied the fact of racial inequality, almost all insisted that the surgical alteration of their eyes and nose was a celebration of their bodies, reflecting their right as women and as minorities to do what they wished with their bodies. Many, such as Jane, also said the surgery was a rite of passage or a routine ceremony, since family members and peers underwent the surgery upon reaching eighteen. Although it is at least possible to perceive cosmetic surgery of the eyes and nose for many Asian Americans as a celebration of the individual and social bodies, as in a rite of passage, this is clearly not so. My research has shown that double-eyelid and nasal bridge procedures performed on Asian Americans do not hold, for either the participants or the larger society, cultural meanings that are benign and spontaneous. Rather, these surgeries are a product of society's racial ideologies, and for many of the women in my study, the surgeries are a calculated means for socioeconomic success. In fact, most describe the surgery as something to "get out of the way" before carrying on with the rest of their lives.

Unlike participants in a rite of passage, these Asian American women share little *communitas* (an important element of rites of passage) with each other or with the larger society. Arnold Van Gennup defined rites of passage as "rites which accompany every change of place, state, social position, and age" (quoted in Turner 1969:94). These rites create an almost egalitarian type of solidarity (communitas) between participants and between the participants and a larger social group. A body modification procedure which is an example of such a rite is the series of public head-scarification rituals for pubescent boys among the Kabre of Togo, West Africa (Brain 1979:178). The final scars they acquire make them full adult members of their group. Their scarification differs considerably from the cosmetic surgery procedures of Asian American women in my study in at least two of its aspects: (1) an egalitarian bond is formed between the participants (between and among those who are doing the scarring and those who are receiving it); and (2) both the event and the resulting feature (i.e., scars) signify the boy's incorporation into a larger social group (i.e., adult men), and therefore, both are unrelentingly made public.

The Asian American women who undergo double-eyelid and nasal bridge surgeries do not usually create bonds with each other or with their plastic surgeons. Their surgery, unlike the scarification rite of the Kabre, is a private event that usually occurs in the presence of the patient, the doctor, and the doctor's assistants only. Moreover, there is little personal connection between doctor and patient. Though a few of the Asian American women in my study were content with their surgery and with their doctors, most describe their experience on the operating table as one of fear and loneliness, and some described their doctors as impersonal, businesslike, and even tending toward profitmaking. Annie, for instance, described the fear she felt being alone with the doctor and his assistants in the operating room, when her mother suddenly left the room because she could not bear to watch:

> They told me to put my thumbs under my hips so I didn't interfere with my hands. I received two anesthesia shots on my nose—this was the only part of the operation that hurt, but it hurt! I closed my eyes. I didn't want to look. I didn't want to see like the knives or anything. I could feel like the snapping of scissors and I was aware when they were putting that thing up my nose. My mom didn't really care. They told her to look at my nose. They were wondering if I wanted it sharper and stuff. She said, "Oh no. I don't want to look" and just ran away. She was sitting outside. I was really pissed.

Elena described her experience of surgery in a similar manner: "I had no time to be nervous. They drugged me with valium, I think. I was awake but drugged, conscious but numb. I remember being on the table. They [doctor and nurses] continued to keep up a conversation. I would wince sometimes because I could feel little pinches. He [the doctor] would say, "Okay, Pumpkin, Sweetheart, it will be over soon.". . . I didn't like it, being called Pumpkin and being touched by a stranger. . . . I wanted to say Shut up! to all three people." Clearly, the event of surgery did not provide an opportunity or the atmosphere for the women in my study to forge meaningful relationships with their doctors.

Asian American women who undergo cosmetic surgery also have a very limited chance of bonding with each other by sharing experiences of the surgery, because unlike participants in a Kabre puberty rite, these women do not usually publicize either their operation or their new features. All informed me that apart from me and their doctors, few people knew about their surgery since at the most they had told three close friends and/or family members about it. As Annie stated, "I don't mind if people found out [that I had a nose operation], but I won't go around telling them." Jane explained: "It's nothing to be ashamed of, not at all, but it's not something you brag about either. . . . To this day my boyfriend doesn't notice I had anything done. That makes me feel pretty good. It's just that you want to look good, but you don't want them [other people] to know how much effort goes into it." In fact, all the women in my study said they wanted a "better" look, but one that was not so drastically different from the original that it looked "unnatural." Even those who underwent revision surgeries to improve on their first operation said they were more at ease and felt more effective in social situations (with boyfriends, classmates, and employers) after their primary operation, mainly because they looked subtly "better," not because they looked too noticeably different from the way they used to look. Thus, it is not public awareness of these women's cosmetic surgery or the resulting features which win them social acceptance. Rather, the successful personal concealment of the operation and of any glaring traces of the operation (e.g., scars or an "unnatural" look) is paramount for acceptance. Clearly, the alteration of their features is not a rite of passage celebrating the incorporation of individual bodies into a larger social body; rather, it is a personal quest by marginal people seeking acceptance in a society where the dominant culture's ideals loom large and are constraining. The extent to which the Asian American women have internalized society's negative valuation of their natural features is best exemplified by the fact that these women feel more self-confident in social interactions as a result of this slight alteration of their eyelids—that is, with one minor alteration in their whole anatomy—which others may not even notice.

MEDICINE AND THE "DISEMBODIMENT" OF THE ASIAN AMERICAN FEMALE CONSUMER

Some sectors of the medical profession fail to recognize that Asian American women's decision to undergo cosmetic surgery of the eyelid and the nose is not so much triggered by a simple materialistic urge to feel better with one more status item that money can buy as much as it is an attempt to heal a specific doubt about oneself which society has unnecessarily brought on. For instance, one doctor in my study stated the following about double-eyelid surgery on Asian American women: "It's like when you wear certain shoes, certain clothes, or put certain makeup on, well—why do you wear those? Why this brand of clothes and not another? . . . You can label these things different ways, but I think that it [the double-eyelid surgery of Asian Americans] is just a desire to look better. You know, it's like driving a brand-new car down the street or having something bought from Nordstrom." By viewing cosmetic surgery and items bought from a department store as equally arbitrary, plastic surgeons, like economists, sometimes assume that the consumer (in this case, the cosmetic surgery client) is disembodied (O'Neill 1985:103). They view her as an abstract, nonhuman subject whose choice of items is not mediated by any historical circumstances, symbolic meaning, or political significance.

With "advances" in science and technology and the proliferation of media images, the number of different selves one can become appears arbitrary and infinite to many Americans, including the women in my study. Thus, many of them argue, as do some plastic surgeons (see Kaw 1993), that the variation in the width of the crease requested by Asian Americans (from six to ten millimeters) is indicative of a whole range of personal and idiosyncratic styles in double-eyelid operations. The idea is that the women are not conforming to any standard, that they are molding their own standards of beauty. However, they ignore that a primary goal in all double-eyelid operations, regardless of how high or how far across the eyelid the crease is cut, is to have a more open appearance of the eye, and the trend in all cases is to create a fold where there was none. These operations are an instance of the paradoxical "production of variety within standardization" in American consumer culture (Goldstein 1993:152). Thus, there is a double bind in undergoing a double-eyelid operation. On the one hand, the women are rebelling against the notion that one must be content with the physical features one is born with, that one cannot be creative in molding one's own idea of what is beautiful. On the other hand, they are conforming to Caucasian standards of beauty.

The women in the study seem to have an almost unconditional faith that science and technology will help them feel satisfied with their sense of self. And the plastic surgery industry, with its scientific advances and seemingly objective stance, makes double-eyelid surgery appear routine, necessary, and for the most part, harmless (Kaw 1993). The women in my study had read advertisements of cosmetic surgery clinics, many of them catering to their specific "needs." In my interviews with Nellee, who had once thought about having double-eyelid surgery, and Jo, who is thinking about it for the near future, I did not have to tell them that the operation entailed creating a crease on the upper eyelid through incision and sutures. They told me. Jo, for instance, said, "I know the technology and it's quite easy, so I am not really afraid of it messing up."

CONCLUSION: PROBLEM OF RESISTANCE IN A CULTURE BASED ON ENDLESS SELF-FASHIONING

My research has shown that Asian American women's decision to undergo cosmetic surgery for wider eyes and more prominent noses is very much influenced by society's racial stereotyping of Asian features. Many of the women in my study are aware of the racial stereotypes from which they suffer. However, all have internalized these negative images of themselves and of other Asians, and they judge the Asian body, including their own, with the critical eye of the oppressor. Moreover, almost all share the attitude of certain sectors of the media and medicine in regard to whether undergoing a surgical operation is, in the end, harmful or helpful to themselves and other Asian Americans; they say it is yet another exercise of their freedom of choice.

The American value of individualism has influenced many of the women to believe that the specific width and shape they choose for their eyelid folds and nose bridges indicate that they are molding their own standards of beauty. Many said they wanted a "natural" look that would be uniquely "in balance" with the rest of their features. However, even those such as Jane, who openly expressed the idea that she is conforming to a Western standard of beauty, emphasized that she is not oppressed but rather empowered by her surgical transformation: "Everything is conforming as I see it. It's just a matter of recognizing it. . . . Other people—well, they are also conforming to something else. Nothing anybody has ever done is original. And it's very unlikely that people would go out and be dressed in any way if they hadn't seen it somewhere. So I don't think it's valid to put a value judgment on [the type of surgery I did]. I'm definitely for self-improvement. So if you don't like a certain part of your body, there's no reason not to change it."

The constraints Asian American women in my study feel every day with regard to their natural features are a direct result of unequal race relationships in the United States. These women's apparent lack of concern for their racial oppression is symptomatic of a certain postmodern culture arising in the United States which has the effect of hiding structural inequalities from public view (Bordo 1990). In its attempt to celebrate differences and to shun overgeneralizations and totalizing discourses that apparently efface diversity among people in modern life, this postmodern culture actually obscures differences; that is, by viewing differences as all equally arbitrary, it effaces from public consciousness historically determined differences in power between groups of people. Thus, blue contact lenses for African American women, and double eyelids and nose bridges for Asian women are both seen as forms of empowerment and indistinguishable in form and function from perms for white women, corn rows on Bo Derek, and tans on Caucasians. All cosmetic changes are seen in the same way—as having no cultural meaning and no political significance. In this process, what is trivialized and obscured is the difficult and often frustrated struggle with which subordinate groups must assert their difference as something to be proud of in the face of dominant ideologies (Bordo 1990:666).

With the proliferation of scientific and technological industries, the many selves one can become appear infinite and random. Like the many transformations of the persona of Madonna throughout her career or the metamorphosis of Michael Jackson's face during his "Black and White" video, the alteration of bodies through plastic surgery has become for the American public simply another means of self-expression and self-determination. As Ellen said, "You can be born Chinese. But if you want to look like a more desirable one, and if surgery is available like it is now, then why not do it?" She said that instead of having to undergo the arduous task of placing thin strips of transparent plastic tape over the eyelids to create a temporary crease (a procedure which, she said, many Asians unhappy with single eyelids used to do), Asians now have the option to permanently transform the shape of their eyes.

Thus, instead of becoming a battleground for social and cultural resistance, the body has become a playground (Bordo 1990:667). Like Michael Jackson's lyrics in the song "Man in the Mirror" ("If you want to make the world a better place, then take a look at yourself and make a change"; Jackson 1987), it is ambiguous whether political change and social improvement are best orchestrated through changing society or through an "act of creative interpretation" (Bordo 1990) of the superficial details of one's appearance. The problem and dilemma of resistance in U.S. society are best epitomized in this excerpt of my interview with Jo, the twenty-eight-year-old law student who is thinking of having double-eyelid surgery:

> Jo: In my undergraduate college, every Pearl Harbor Day I got these phone calls and people would say, "Happy Pearl Harbor Day," and they made noises like bombs and I'd find little toy soldiers at my dorm door. Back then, I kind of took it as a joke. But now, I think it was more malicious. . . . [So] I think the surgery is a lot more superficial. Affecting how society feels about a certain race is a lot more beneficial. And it goes a lot deeper and lasts a lot longer.
>
> INTERVIEWER: Looking into the future, do you think you will do both?
>
> Jo: Yeah [nervous laughter]. I do. I do.

Jo recognizes that undergoing double-eyelid surgery, that is, confirming the undesirability of Asian eyes, is in contradiction to the work she would like to do as a teacher and legal practitioner. However, she said she cannot easily destroy the negative feelings she already possesses about the natural shape of her eyes.

IMPLICATIONS: ASIAN AMERICANS AND THE AMERICAN DREAM

The psychological burden of having constantly to measure up has been often overlooked in the image of Asian Americans as model minorities, as people who have achieved the American dream. The model minority myth assumes not only that all Asian Americans are financially well-to-do, but also that those Asian Americans who are from relatively well-to-do, non-working-class backgrounds (like many of the women in my study) are free from the everyday constraints of painful racial stereotypes (see Takaki 1989; Hurh and Kim 1989). As my research has shown, the cutting up of Asian Americans' faces through plastic surgery is a concrete example of how, in modern life, Asian Americans, like other people of color, can be influenced by the dominant culture to loathe themselves in such a manner as to begin mutilating and revising parts of their body.

Currently, the eyes and nose are those parts of the anatomy which Asian Americans most typically cut and alter since procedures for these are relatively simple with the available technology. However, a few of the women in my study said that if they could, they would also want to increase their stature, and in particular, to lengthen their legs; a few also suggested that when safer implants were found, they wanted to augment their breasts; still others wanted more prominent brow bridges and jawlines. On the one hand, it appears that through technology women can potentially carve an endless array of new body types, breaking the bounds of racial categories. On the other hand, these desired body types are constructed in the context of the dominant culture's beauty ideals. The search for the ideal body may have a tremendous impact, in terms of racial discrimination, on patterns of artificial genetic selection, such as occurs at sperm banks, egg donation centers, and in the everyday ritual of courtship. . . .

Notes

1. I have not yet found descriptions, in medical texts and newspaper articles, of the types of cosmetic surgery specifically requested by Latinos. However, one newspaper article (Ellison 1990) reports that an increasing number of Mexicans are purchasing a device by which they can attain a more Nordic and Anglo-Saxon "upturned" nose. It requires inserting plastic hooks in the nostrils.

2. The shapes of the eye and nose of Asians are not meant in this chapter to be interpreted as categories which define a group of people called Asians. Categories of racial groups are arbitrarily defined by society. Likewise, the physical traits people in a racial group are recognized by are arbitrary (see Molnar 1983).

   Also, I use the term *Asian American* to name collectively the women in this study who have undergone or are thinking about undergoing cosmetic surgery. Although I recognize their ethnic, generational, and geographical diversity, people of Asian ancestry in the United States share similar experiences in that they are subject to many of the same racial stereotypes (see Hurh and Kim 1989; Takaki 1989).

3. Cosmetic surgery for double eyelids, nasal tip refinement, and nose bridges are not limited to Asians in the United States. Asians in East and Southeast Asia have requested such surgeries since the early 1950s, when U.S. military forces began long-term occupations of such countries as Korea and the Philippines. Some American

doctors (such as Millard) were asked by Asians in these countries to perform the surgeries. See Harahap 1982; Kristof 1991; Millard 1964; Sayoc 1954.

4. Ellen's mother, however, did not receive double-eyelid or nose bridge surgery. It appears that the trend of actually undergoing such surgeries began with Asian women who are now about forty to fifty years of age. Jane and Annie, sisters in their early twenties, said that though their mother who is about fifty had these surgeries, their grandmother did not. They also said that their grandmother encouraged them to have the operation, as did their mother.

None of the women in my study mentioned their father or other males in their household or social networks as verbally encouraging them to have the surgeries. However, many said they felt their resulting features would or did help them in their relationships with men, especially boyfriends (Asians and non-Asians alike). We did not discuss in detail their father's reaction to their surgery, but those who mentioned their father's reaction summed it up mainly as indifference.

115

*EUGENIA KAW
"Opening" Faces: The
Politics of Cosmetic
Surgery and Asian
American Women*

References

American Society of Plastic and Reconstructive Surgeons (ASPRS). N.d. "Estimated Number of Cosmetic Surgery Procedures Performed by ASPRS Members in 1990." Pamphlet.

APPADURAI, ARJUN. 1990. "Disjuncture and Difference in the Global Cultural Economy." *Public Culture* 2(2): 1–24.

BLACKING, JOHN. 1977. *The Anthropology of the Body.* London: Academic Press.

BORDO, SUSAN. 1990. "Material Girl: The Effacements of Postmodern Culture." *Michigan Quarterly Review* 29:635–676.

BRAIN, ROBERT. 1979. *The Decorated Body.* New York: Harper and Row.

CHEN, JOANNE. 1993. "Before and After: For Asian Americans, the Issues Underlying Cosmetic Surgery Are Not Just Skin Deep." *A. Magazine: The Asian American Quarterly* 2(1): 15–18, 26–27.

DALY, MARY. 1978. *Gyn/ecology: The Metaethics of Radical Feminism.* Boston: Beacon Press.

DAVIS, KATHY. 1991. "Remaking the She-Devil: A Critical Look at Feminist Approaches to Beauty." *Hypatia* 6(2): 21–43.

DOWER, JOHN. 1986. *War without Mercy: Race and Power in the Pacific War.* New York: Pantheon.

ELLISON, KATHERINE. 1990. "Mexico Puts on a Foreign Face." *San Jose Mercury News*, December 16, p. 14a.

FLEMING, CHARLES, AND MARY TALBOT. 1993. "The Two Faces of Michael Jackson." *Newsweek*, February 22, p. 57.

GILMAN, SANDER L. 1985. *Difference and Pathology: Stereotypes of Sexuality, Race and Madness.* Ithaca, N.Y.: Cornell University Press.

GOFFMAN, ERVING. 1979. *Gender Advertisement.* Cambridge: Harvard University Press.

GOLDSTEIN, JUDITH. 1993. "The Female Aesthetic Community." *Poetics Today* 14(1): 143–163.

HARAHAP, MARWALI. 1982. "Oriental Cosmetic Blepharoplasty." In *Cosmetic Surgery for Non-white Patients*, ed. Harold Pierce, pp. 79–97. New York: Grune and Stratton.

HURH, WON MOO, AND KWANG CHUNG KIM. 1989. "The 'Success' Image of Asian Americans: Validity, and Its Practical and Theoretical Implications." *Ethnic and Racial Studies* 12(4):512–537.

IWATA, EDWARD. 1991. "Race without Face." *San Francisco Image Magazine*, May, pp. 51–55.

JACKSON, MICHAEL. 1987. "Man in the Mirror." On *Bad.* Epic Records, New York.

KAW, EUGENIA. 1993. "Medicalization of Racial Features: Asian American Women and Cosmetic Surgery." *Medical Anthropology Quarterly* 7(1):74–89.

KIM, ELAINE. 1986. "Asian-Americans and American Popular Culture." In *Dictionary of Asian-American History,* ed. Hyung-Chan Kim. New York: Greenwood Press.

KRISTOF, NICHOLAS. 1991. "More Chinese Look 'West.' " *San Francisco Examiner and Chronicle,* July 7.

LAKOFF, ROBIN T., AND RAQUEL L. SCHERR. 1984. *Face Value: The Politics of Beauty.* Boston: Routledge and Kegan.

LEFLORE, IVENS C. 1982. "Face Lift, Chin Augmentation and Cosmetic Rhinoplasty in Blacks." In *Cosmetic Surgery in Non-White Patients,* ed. Harold Pierce. New York: Grune and Stratton.

LOCK, MARGARET, AND NANCY SCHEPER-HUGHES. 1990. "A Critical-Interpretive Approach in Medical Anthropology: Rituals and Routines of Discipline and Dissent." In *Medical Anthropology: Contemporary Theory and Method,* ed. Thomas Johnson and Carolyn Sargent, pp. 47–72. New York: Praeger.

MCCURDY, JOHN A. 1990. *Cosmetic Surgery of the Asian Face.* New York: Thieme Medical Publishers.

MACGREGOR, FRANCES C. 1967. "Social and Cultural Components in the Motivations of Persons Seeking Plastic Surgery of the Nose." *Journal of Health and Social Behavior* 8(2):125–135.

MERRELL, KATHY H. 1994. "Saving Faces." *Allure,* January, pp. 66–68.

MILLARD, RALPH, JR. 1964. "The Original Eyelid and Its Revision." *American Journal of Ophthalmology* 57:546–649.

MOLNAR, STEPHEN. 1983. *Human Variation: Races, Types, and Ethnic Groups.* Englewood Cliffs, N.J.: Prentice-Hall.

NAKAO, ANNIE. 1993. "Faces of Beauty: Light Is Still Right." *San Francisco Examiner and Chronicle,* April 11, p. D-4.

O'NEILL, JOHN. 1985. *Five Bodies.* Ithaca, N.Y.: Cornell University Press.

ONG, AIHWA. 1987. *Spirits of Resistance and Capitalist Discipline: Factory Women in Malaysia.* Albany: State University of New York Press.

RAMSDELL, DANIEL. 1983. "Asia Askew: U.S. Best-sellers on Asia, 1931–1980." *Bulletin of Concerned Asian Scholars* 15(4):2–25.

ROSENTHAL, ELISABETH. 1991. "Ethnic Ideals: Rethinking Plastic Surgery." *New York Times,* September 25, p. B7.

SAYOC, B. T. 1954. "Plastic Construction of the Superior Palpebral Fold." *American Journal of Ophthalmology* 38:556–559.

———. 1974. "Surgery of the Oriental Eyelid." *Clinics in Plastic Surgery* 1(1):157–171.

SHEETS-JOHNSTONE, MAXINE, ed. 1992. *Giving the Body Its Due.* Albany: State University of New York Press.

TAJIMA, RENEE E. 1989. "Lotus Blossoms Don't Bleed: Images of Asian Women." In *Making Waves: An Anthology of Writings by and about Asian American Women,* ed. Diane Yeh-Mei Wong, pp. 308–317. Boston: Beacon Press.

TAKAKI, RONALD. 1989. *Strangers from a Different Shore.* Boston: Little, Brown.

TURNER, TERENCE. 1980. "The Social Skin." In *Not Work Alone,* ed. J. Cherfas and R. Lewin, pp. 112–114. London: Temple Smith.

TURNER, VICTOR. 1969. *The Ritual Process: Structure and Anti-Structure.* Chicago: Aldine.

WOLF, NAOMI. 1991. *The Beauty Myth: How Images of Beauty Are Used against Women.* New York: William Morrow.

YANG, JEFF, AND ANGELO RAGAZ. 1993. "The Beauty Machine." *A. Magazine: The Asian American Quarterly* 2(1):20–21.

Christy Haubegger

I'm Not Fat, I'm Latina

Fat is a relative term. Stroll through any art museum and you will see that the women painted by artists from Reubens to Renoir as icons of female beauty are, by today's standards, victims of serious cellulite. Standards for women's weight differ not only across time but across cultures and ethnic groups as well. Christy Haubegger writes that the thin ideal of white culture looks dried-up and neglected in Latino culture, where the ideal is the bien cuidada, *the well-cared-for, curvy woman.*

As You Read, Ask Yourself . . .

What influences caused Christy Haubegger to evaluate herself in terms of the white ideal?

What was the turning point for her in acceptance of her own size and shape?

How can women of color create a community of acceptance for diverse beauty ideals?

I recently read a newspaper article that reported that nearly 40 percent of Hispanic and African-American women are overweight. At least I'm in good company. Because according to even the most generous height and weight charts at the doctor's office, I'm a good 25 pounds overweight. And I'm still looking for the panty-hose chart that has me on it (according to Hanes, I don't exist). But I'm happy to report that in the Latino community, my community, I fit right in.

Latinas in this country live in two worlds. People who don't know us may think we're fat. At home, we're called *bien cuidadas* (well cared for).

I love to go dancing at Cesar's Latin Palace here in the Mission District of San Francisco. At this hot all-night salsa club, it's the curvier bodies like mine that turn heads. I'm the one on the dance floor all night while some of my thinner friends spend more time waiting along the walls. Come to think of it, I wouldn't trade my body for any of theirs.

But I didn't always feel this way. I remember being in high school and noticing that none of the magazines showed models in bathing suits with bodies like mine. Handsome movie heroes were never hoping to find a chubby damsel in distress. The fact that I had plenty of attention from Latino boys wasn't enough. Real self-esteem cannot come from male attention alone.

My turning point came a few years later. When I was in college, I made a trip to Mexico, and I brought back much more than sterling-silver bargains and colorful blankets.

I remember hiking through the awesome ruins of the Maya and the Aztecs, civilizations that created pyramids as large as the ones in Egypt. I loved walking through temple doorways whose clearance was only two inches above my head, and I realized that I must be a direct descendant of those ancient priestesses for whom those doorways had originally been built.

For the first time in my life, I was in a place where people like me were the beautiful ones. And I began to accept, and even like, the body that I have.

I know that medical experts say that Latinas are twice as likely as the rest of the population to be overweight. And yes, I know about the health problems that often accompany severe weight problems. But most of us are not in the danger zone; we're just bien cuidadas. Even the researchers who found that nearly 40 percent of us are overweight noted that there is a greater "cultural acceptance" of being overweight within Hispanic communities. But the article also commented on the cultural-acceptance factor as if it were something unfortunate, because it keeps Hispanic women from becoming healthier. I'm not so convinced that we're the ones with the problem.

If the medical experts were to try and get to the root of this so-called problem, they would probably find that it's part genetics, part enchiladas. Whether we're Cuban-American, Mexican-American, Puerto Rican or Dominican, food is a central part of Hispanic culture. While our food varies from fried plaintains to tamales, what doesn't change is its role in our lives. You feed people you care for, and so if you're well cared for, *bien cuidada,* you have been fed well.

I remember when I used to be envious of a Latina friend of mine who had always been on the skinny side. When I confided this to her a while ago, she laughed. It turns out that when she was growing up, she had always wanted to look more like me. She had trouble getting dates with Latinos in high school, the same boys that I dated. When she was little, the other kids in the neighborhood had even given her a cruel nickname: *la seca,* "the dry one." I'm glad I never had any of those problems.

Our community has always been accepting of us well-cared-for women. So why don't we feel beautiful? You only have to flip through a magazine or watch a movie to realize that beautiful for most of this country still means tall, blond and underfed. But now we know it's the magazines that are wrong. I, for one, am going to do what I can to make sure that *mis hijas,* my daughters, won't feel the way I did.

Illness and Imagery: Feminist Cognition, Socialization, and Gender Identity

Nancy Datan has visited a place where no woman wants to go: the breast cancer ward. She writes, not about the illness itself, but about the expectations for women who have survived it. Does a woman's feminine identity depend on having intact breasts? Datan's answer is an emphatic no. But how does she then reconcile the social imperative to conceal all evidence of her surgery through breast prostheses and reconstruction?

Datan's eloquent personal account of how she reacted to advice on "restoring her femininity" after mastectomy highlights some double binds for women.

As You Read, Ask Yourself . . .

Does flouting rules about one's appearance represent a failure of socialization?

Are private consciousness and public display related?

Is denial of physical impairment psychologically healthy or destructive?

What does it mean to define oneself as a victim or a survivor?

In 1980, the feminist poet Audre Lorde wrote in *The Cancer Journals:* "May these words serve as encouragement for other women to speak and to act out of our experiences with cancer and with other threats of death, for silence has never brought us anything of worth" (1980a, p. 10). With her encouragement, today I will explore a web of taboos and silences that surround breast cancer, a disease that affects so many of us that we can all expect a friend, if not ourselves, to experience it. Breast cancer currently affects one of every eleven women and is expected to affect one out of ten in the near future. Of those, some will inevitably be feminists. I am one of them.

It is a central tenet of feminism that women's invisible, private wounds often reflect social and political injustices. It is a commitment central to feminism to share burdens. And it is an axiom of feminism that the personal is political. It is in that spirit that I ask you to come with me in imagination where I hope nobody will ever go in fact, to a hospital bed on the morning after a mastectomy, where I found new expression for a recent theme of the *The Journal of Social Issues,* "Social Issues and Personal Life: The Search for Connections" (Clayton & Crosby, 1986).

Studies of women with breast cancer typically focus on women's responses to the disease. This chapter is a naturalistic ethnography which explores a stimulus designed to shape women's responses: the Reach to Recovery material presented to women after surgery. Crisis demands coping: Reach to Recovery is an effort to shape coping responses.

In its own words, "Reach to Recovery is one woman reaching out to share and support another in time of need. . . . Reach to Recovery works through carefully selected and trained volunteers who have fully adjusted to their surgery. . . . The volunteer visitor brings a kit containing a temporary breast form, manuals of information and appropriate literature for husbands, children, other loved ones, and friends. The visitor can provide information on types of permanent prostheses and lists of where they are available locally. . . . Reach to Recovery can provide information to women interested in breast reconstruction" (American Cancer Society, 1982b). Thus the first message of Reach to Recovery is that one's body has been mutilated and that steps must be taken to remedy its deficiency.

My Reach to Recovery volunteer brought a kit with exercise equipment, cosmetic disguise, and a collection of reading material, all for me to keep; and three samples of breast prostheses for me to examine. The exercise equipment consisted of a small rubber ball attached to a length of elastic cord and a length of nylon rope knotted at each end with two wooden tongue depressors to be inserted into the knots. The cosmetic disguise was a small pink nylon-covered, dacron-filled pillow, which proved more useful and safer for throwing exercises than the rubber ball intended for that purpose, which rebounded on its elastic cord painfully into my chest when I threw it.

Substitute breasts of various sorts outweighed everything else in the Reach to Recovery visitor's kit; a corresponding weight was found in the reading material. A crude quantitative analysis of the Reach to Recovery reading material offers a preview of the emphasis on the prosthetic.

One-page pamphlets or form letters:

- What is Reach to Recovery?
- After Mastectomy: The Woman on Her Own
- "An Ounce of Prevention:" Suggestions for Hand & Arm Care
- How to examine your breasts
- A letter to husbands
- A letter to daughters
- A letter to sons

And, at greater length:

- Exercises after Mastectomy: Patient Guide (8 pages)
- Helpful Hints and How To's (8 pages)
- After Mastectomy: A Patient Guide (10 pages)
- Prostheses List 1984–1986 (14 pages)
- Breast Reconstruction Following Mastectomy (20 pages)

Buried in this material is the fact that a mastectomy may bring disability and even occasionally death as a consequence of damage to lymphatic circulation, which may produce permanent arm swelling. Of a total of 67 pages of information, only one page addresses this issue. Surgery limits arm motion: exercises that promote recovery and help prevent arm swelling take up an additional eight pages. Thus only about 10% of this material is actually addressed to health considerations. What then is the nature of the "recovery" to which one is supposed to reach?

121

*NANCY DATAN
Illness and Imagery:
Feminist Cognition,
Socialization, and
Gender Identity*

The principal focus of this material, the exclusive focus of three of the five multipage pamphlets, of 42 of a total of 67 pages of information, is on strategies for temporary or permanent substitutes for the missing breast. Thus on quantitative grounds alone, the woman who has just had a mastectomy is overwhelmed by the message that her body is now defective and that her first priority will be to seek an artificial, cosmetic remedy. Her kit provides her with an emergency solution—the small pink pillow that can be pinned into her clothing even before her bandages are removed. It is illusory comfort, like the promise of ice cream after a tonsillectomy to a child who wakes up to discover a throat too sore to swallow. But throats do heal, so the illusion and the consequent disillusion are short-lived. Reach to Recovery offers a woman a lifetime of disguise. What this kit does not provide is room to accept the loss of a breast, the wound, and the scar that healing will bring.

I came to surgery with a very different view of mastectomy, which I owe to Audre Lorde, whom I first discovered in April 1980, when *Savvy* carried her article "After Breast Cancer: I am a Warrior, not a Victim." She described her rejection of the physical pretense in the cosmetic emphasis of Reach to Recovery in words that transcended the experience she had just had and I never anticipated:

> Implying to a woman that, with the skillful application of a lambswool puff or an implantation of silicone gel, she can be the same as before surgery prevents her from dealing with herself as real, physically and emotionally. . . . We are expected to mourn the loss of a breast in secret, as if it were a guilty crime . . . [but] When Moshe Dayan stands before Parliament with an eye patch over his empty eye socket . . . he is viewed as a warrior with an honorable wound. . . . Well, we are warriors also. I have been to war, and so has every woman with breast cancer, the female scourge of our time. . . . "Nobody will know the difference," said the Reach to Recovery volunteer, with her lambswool puff. But it is that very difference which I wish to affirm, because I have lived it, and survived it and grown stronger through it. I wish to share that strength with other women. (1980b, pp. 68–69)

In 1980 it seemed so simple. Even in 1986 it did not seem so complex: Audre Lorde had spoken first and assured me a voice for my autonomy and my grief. As she did, I mourned my breast. It was the first breast to develop erotic feelings, the first breast to fill with milk, the first breast my firstborn child suckled, and the last breast my last child suckled. That breast carried a special aura into middle age: one summer afternoon our small red dog shepherded me into a hike with a leap and nip exquisitely and precisely placed at the very tip of my nipple. I also remembered the last time that breast was part of my body in lovemaking, just a handful of hours before surgery. As Audre Lorde had done, I intended to grieve, and to go on, with gratitude to her for going before me and making it easier.

I had rejoiced in Audre Lorde's rejection of a prosthesis and shared her horror at the reprimand her surgeon's nurse issued:

"We really like you to wear [a prosthesis] when you come in. Otherwise it's bad for the morale of the office."

I could scarcely believe my ears [wrote Lorde]. Every woman there had either had a mastectomy, or might have a mastectomy. Every woman there could have used the reassurance that having one breast did not mean life was over, nor did it mean she was condemned to using a placebo in order to feel good about herself and the way she looked. . . . I refuse to have my scars hidden or trivialized behind a puff of lambswool or silicone gel (1980b, p. 69).

If the need for defiance was regrettable, it was not incomprehensible: ground rules for public appearance occupy fashion pages in the daily newspaper. To flout them is to defy culture, and Lorde was clearly, intentionally doing precisely that. I looked forward to joining her in revolution. But it had not occurred to me until I found myself in a hospital bed with a lapful of Reach to Recovery material that it would be war 24 hours a day. A mastectomy, it seems, ushers in a lifetime of round-the-clock disguise: so I discovered after I found that I underestimated the power of a nonconscious ideology. Breast cancer is not a cosmetic disease, but it is embedded in a larger social and political context in which the cosmetic industry is itself a social and political phenomenon. Thus, if one rejects the a priori assumption that a missing breast demands an all-out coverup, one finds oneself at war with the very material that is meant to promote healing. This discussion follows the course of a naturalistic ethnography which I undertook involuntarily in my hospital bed, reading the Reach to Recovery material with the vulnerability that comes after surgery and the educated cynicism that comes from years of feminist analysis.

In 1964, driving down Jaffa Road in Jerusalem, pregnant with my second child, my breasts swelling and my brassiere confining, I reached under my shirt in the middle of traffic, unhooked it, removed it, and never expected to think about brassieres again. But on December 3, 1986, as a conscientious patient intending to learn all I could about mastectomy and the healing process following surgery, I read every word of the Reach to Recovery material, and the first lesson I learned was that I was expected to resume wearing a brassiere as part of my recovery: "Reach to Recovery suggests and encourages each woman to wear the bra in which she is most comfortable. When your doctor says you are ready, you should be fitted with the breast substitute—prosthesis—suited to you," instructs the cover page of the *Prostheses List, 1984–1986* (American Cancer Society, 1984).

That imperative is twofold if one has not worn a brassiere for 22 years: not only should you be fitted with a substitute breast—Audre Lorde had prepared me for that—but you should wear a brassiere. And nothing prepared me for that. If, for whatever reason—political principle or personal comfort—one has discarded a brassiere, both freedom and comfort come to an end with breast cancer: research has shown that discomfort in wearing a prosthesis is a commonly reported physical complaint following mastectomy (Meyerowitz, Chaiken, & Clark, 1988). Yet this instruction—no mention of the discomfort—is the message a woman gets on the first morning after surgery.

The invasion of the brassiere was just the beginning. The booklet *Helpful Hints and How To's* assured me that leisure and sleep bras "provide a solution for the woman who feels she needs to wear a breast form in bed. Women who do not want to wear a bra and form to bed, but still want contour on the side of the surgery might want to make a form similar to the temporary form in the Reach to Recovery kit and attach it inside the bodice of their sleepwear garment. Nylon netting can be gathered in a round shape and with some experimentation can also be attached inside a loose garment to simulate the contour of the natural unsupported breast" (American Cancer Society, 1982a, pp. 1–2).

It is not enough to deceive the public; not even enough to deceive one's mate—I assumed that "the woman who feels she needs to wear a breast form in bed" does not sleep alone. *Helpful Hints and How To's* encourages the woman who has had a mastectomy to deceive herself. A reader of Audre Lorde's *The Cancer Journals* (1980a) might assume that "making your own form" refers to the construction of a dressmaker's form adapted to one's altered body. But no: "form" takes on new meaning after breast cancer and is used as a presumably innocuous substitute for "substitute breast." The reader is warned that such a "form," if not weighted properly, will cause that side of the brassiere to ride up on the body (p. 5). The Reach to Recovery solution: "use the pocket of the temporary Reach to Recovery form as a pattern and fill it with birdseed, rice, barley, small plastic beads . . . drapery weights, fishing sinkers, gunshot or BB's" (p. 1).

My first reaction to this suggestion was the cognitive equivalent of wound shock. Surely this represented a merger of Frederick's of Hollywood, Ace Hardware, and the American Cancer Society. Yes, one possible first response to this suggestion is to assume that it is a bad joke and to fight off the assault on one's intelligence with better jokes.

But when the initial shock wears off, the imagination does not have to work very hard to call up the confining sensation of a brassiere, the discomfort compounded by one side riding up over wounded or scarred flesh, and the remedy proposed by Reach to Recovery and published with the seal of the American Cancer Society: a pouch of birdseed or gunshot, lying against the body where there was once the first touch of a boy's hand or a baby's mouth—or even a small dog's teeth. In 1980, I agreed immediately with Audre Lorde when she declared: "For not even the most skillful prosthesis in the world could undo that reality, or feel the way my breast had felt, and either I would love my body one-breasted now, or remain forever alien to myself" (1980a, p. 44). It seemed to me then, and still does, that hers was the most elemental of protests: do not add insult to injury. I had no way of guessing how outrageous these insults could be.

The pièce de resistance, most extensive and handsomest of the material put into my hands the day after surgery, is a 20-page pamphlet, nearly one-third of the total number of pages in my kit, on breast reconstruction, urging that the most effective treatment for breast surgery is more surgery. I thought I was prepared for this as well: breast reconstruction had been mentioned by every doctor I had seen from the time I was first told that I had cancer. Since no surgeon could restore the flesh that had swollen first with desire and then with milk, it seemed pointless to me until I inquired about the procedure itself. A mastectomy, I was told, is comparatively simply surgery—45 minutes or so. A reconstruction is more complex—it may involve several operations, the removal of muscle from the back to be inserted into the chest wall, and the subsequent insertion of a silicone implant. When I asked my oncologist why any woman would subject herself to that, he explained that it would avoid the inconvenience of a prosthesis that might slip out of place. Surely if one rejected the first premise, that would be that.

But I was wrong again. The war on cancer patients is being fought with as much or more determination as the war on cancer. The booklet on breast reconstruction goes beyond the helpful hints and how-to's which keep one's bra from riding up and "allow" one to wear one's favorite clothes. It redefines one's sexual identity at the very moment that identity is most vulnerable. This booklet is written in question and answer format. It should be required reading as part of training in questionnaire construction and restricted to graduate students. Instead, it is distributed to women on the morning after surgery.

Question: "Should every woman have a breast reconstruction after mastectomy?" Answer: "Every woman should know that breast reconstruction is possible and make her own decision. Some women seem to be able to adapt psychologically to the post-mastectomy physiological change. Others who opt for breast reconstruction are usually the strongly motivated patients who are willing to undergo an additional operation" (pp. 5–6). As someone with a high need for achievement, I read this material with the best of intentions, hoping to make the most of my experience. I graduated from college with honors, had managed other life transitions with some distinction, and meant to do the same with cancer. I had always considered myself to be strongly motivated. And so, as students of cognitive dissonance will understand, I turned to the title page to find out who the responsible reference group was, so that I could dissociate myself from it and retain my claim to strong motivation.

Like everything else about the cosmetic approach to breast cancer, that seemed easy enough at first. Unlike every other item in my kit, this was not the work of Reach to Recovery, but of the American Society of Plastic and Reconstructive Surgeons, Incorporated. Like the birdseed breast, it seemed at first to be a bad joke. But if one is trying to make sense of a new experience, one seizes upon whatever is offered; in an understimulating hospital room, one reads whatever is available; and, although knowledge of the distorting effects of questions and answers skewed in the direction of presumed social desirability, like any other knowledge, provides some power, on the first day after surgery one is simply not powerful enough to dismiss casually such statements as the following:

> If you are like most women, your breasts have great psychological significance
> to you and you will feel more feminine and more secure socially and sexually
> with a reconstructed breast following mastectomy for cancer. (p. 6)

In other words, your sisterhood or your scar: if your breast has mattered to you, and mine certainly had, you are told that you will want the benefit of "surgical advances [which] have provided plastic and reconstructive surgeons with techniques to create the appearance of breasts" (p. 4). If not, Aristotelian logic leads the reader to believe, you are not like most women. And if so, you have cancer, you are groggy from surgery, and you are all alone.

Here I distinguish between the 20,000 women who undergo breast reconstruction every year, according to this booklet, and the authors of the booklet. Two Reach to Recovery volunteers came to my bedside, the first, like me a runner, as part of her scheduled round and the second, like me a cross-country skier, at my surgeon's request. The first had run a 10K and the second had skied the Korte-loppet after surgery; that bonded us. Both had had "implants," as they termed them; that divided us. Which took priority, our commonalities or our differences?

Virginia O'Leary offers a model for the reconciliation of our differences in her Division 35 presidential remarks, "Musings on the Promise (and Pain) of Feminism" (1987). She notes: "The very intensity of involvement that makes women's connections with women so rewarding has the potential to evoke pain as well. . . . Trashing someone usually involves impugning her (feminist) motives." Since I have identified myself with feminist Audre Lorde and have agreed that the cosmetic response to breast cancer leads to self-alienation, does it follow that I am forced to deny the feminism implicit in my visitors' athletic efforts, or for that matter in their volunteer participation in a program of women helping women? Indeed not. If a hospital room is no place for a crash course in Total Womanhood, neither is it the place for retroactive consciousness raising. Breast cancer is a trauma; if a woman feels she is entitled to four silicone breasts after a mastectomy, I applaud her originality, and, as O'Leary does, I urge tolerance of the diversity of interpersonal styles, in sickness as well as in health. It is precisely the question of tolerance for diversity which was the issue in my hospital room.

In the spirit of tolerance for diversity, I considered breast reconstruction. In the words of its advocates, the American Society of Plastic and Reconstructive Surgeons, Incorporated, a breast reconstruction

> will not only provide greater physical self-confidence, but will also enable you to wear a wide range of clothing. After reconstruction, you need not worry about "slipping" or displacement of the prosthesis which may occur with external devices. (p. 7)

However, it is acknowledged that even modern surgery will not bring you everything:

> The reconstructed breast will look reasonably normal when covered with an undergarment but will show scarring and subtle imperfections when you are nude (p. 9). . . . Breast reconstruction cannot restore normal sensation to a breast after mastectomy (p. 14). . . . Most women say it may take a while to get used to the reconstructed breast . . . there may be some tenderness and discomfort when you [sleep on your stomach] . . . when people hug you they may not be able to distinguish any difference in the feel of the breasts. In some cases, however, the contraction of your body tissues around the implant may cause the reconstructed breast to feel firmer than your other breast. (p. 15)

Furthermore,

> Complications can occur. . . . If an infection or heavy bleeding occurs around a breast implant, it sometimes has to be removed but it can usually be replaced after a period of several months. If the implant shifts to an undesirable location or feels hard due to the contraction of the tissue, an additional surgical procedure may be required to release it. (p. 9)

Finally,

> A small number of recurrences [of cancer] occur on the chest wall itself and breast reconstruction might delay but would not prevent detection of these. (p. 14)

125

Nancy Datan
Illness and Imagery:
Feminist Cognition,
Socialization, and
Gender Identity

Thus, in the words of a pamphlet intended to promote the process, breast reconstruction makes it easy to wear clothes, but not to go naked. The public self is affirmed, but it is at the expense of discomfort to the private self, who wants to hug or to sleep on her stomach. The surgery carries a risk of complications and further surgery and might delay detection of a recurrence of the cancer—and this procedure, it is claimed, provides "greater physical self-confidence" (p. 7).

My quarrel is not with the women who choose this procedure but with the surgeons who assert that physical self-confidence will be enhanced by this painful, potentially dangerous invasion of the body. It is one option. Another option is to live, as Audre Lorde inspired me to do, without any thought of disguise: this enables one to hug, to find erotic nerves reawakening even before the mastectomy incision is fully healed, and to sleep on one's stomach, all components of my physical self-confidence.

Now the time has come to get out of the hospital bed and to resume my identity as a feminist social scientist. What if this experience is not merely an illness, but a naturalistic experiment designed by Rhoda Unger as a test of my epistemology? In that case it is not my body which is in need of reconstruction—it is reality.

I begin by disputing a 1983 volume of *The Journal of Social Issues* (Janoff-Bulman & Frieze, 1983) which takes as its theme "Reactions to Victimization," among whom are numbered cancer victims. I read those words without a pause in 1983, not even the briefest of pauses to consider that Audre Lorde's 1980 article, which I remembered nearly verbatim, had been entitled, "After Breast Cancer: I am a Warrior, not a Victim." However, the word "victim" becomes far more salient when it refers to oneself. And, after a while, it becomes offensive. One is "stricken," "afflicted," maybe even "victimized" by cancer at first. But months later? Years? Have I earned tenure as a victim?

The term victim suggests passive acceptance, when responding adequately to cancer demands continuous active coping. Consider the distinction Bruno Bettelheim makes of the Holocaust: its victims are those who were buried; those who go on are survivors. Circumstances victimize; the individual coping response is part of the struggle for survival. Bettelheim states:

> [Holocaust] survivors are not alone in that they must learn to integrate an experience which, when not integrated, is either completely overwhelming, or forces one to deny in self-defense what it means to one personally in the present. . . . Engaging in denial and repression in order to save oneself the difficult task of integrating an experience into one's personality is of course by no means restricted to [Holocaust] survivors. . . . Survivors have every right to choose their very own way of trying to cope. The experience of being a concentration camp prisoner is so abominable, the trauma so horrendous, that one must respect every survivor's privilege to try to master it as best they know and can. . . . But to have come face to face with such mass murder, to have come so close to being one of its victims, is a relatively unique, psychologically and morally most difficult, experience. It follows that the survivor's new integration will be more difficult—and, one may hope, also more meaningful—than that of [those] spared subjection to an extreme experience (1979, pp. 24, 33, 34)

Denial or integration, the polarities of response to the Holocaust described by Bettelheim, parallel those found in Reach to Recovery and in Audre Lorde's response: oblivion or awareness. Oblivion is a form of death of the self. Yet awareness in an oblivious world is agony, as Wisconsin naturalist Aldo Leopold observed:

127

NANCY DATAN
Illness and Imagery:
Feminist Cognition,
Socialization, and
Gender Identity

> One of the penalties of an ecological education is that one lives alone in a world of wounds. Much of the damage inflicted on land is quite invisible to laypersons. Ecologists must either harden their shell and make believe that the consequences of science are none of their business, or be the doctor who sees the marks of death in a community that believes itself well and does not want to be told otherwise. (1953, p. 165)

Substitute feminism for ecology and we see a spectrum of social ills which feminism has rendered visible. The woman who has been raped or might be, the mother seeking child care, or the woman seeking an abortion, all face issues that once were defined as personal and private and now are seen as public and political. Breast cancer too can be seen as more than a singular affliction, as feminists consider rape to be not an isolated personal trauma but an expression of a larger social context in which male sexuality, the patriarchal family, and aggression against women are blended. Similarly, breast cancer is not a solitary ordeal but an illness of the community, to which the community responds with an expression of communal values, which may certainly include repudiation, denial, and isolation.

These communal values are highlighted by issues in gender identity specific to particular illnesses (Meyerowitz et al., 1988). As journalist Martha Weinman Lear observes:

> To be American, male, in one's fifties, a compulsive worker—as who of them is not—worried about cholesterol and unpaid bills, working under stress and watching old friends succumb, one by one, to that crisis of the heart . . . I do not suppose women can fully understand that fear. Not that particular one. We agonize instead over cancer; we take as a personal threat the lump in every friend's breast. (1980, p. 11)

Many researchers (Meyerowitz et al., 1988; Rosen and Bibring, 1968) have noted that heart attacks strike at masculine values: aggression, achievement, striving, and sexuality come to have new meanings. Rosen and Bibring (1968) suggest that heart attacks in young men accelerate issues of aging and dependency, since the immediate treatment demands enforced passivity. Breast cancer strikes at the core of femininity: as Rossi observes, "in contemporary Western societies the breast has become an erotic symbol," rather than a functional component of reproduction (1986, p. 120).

Recovery from a heart attack is measured by renewed participation in activities: for example, some survivors of heart attacks go on to run marathons. No such physical triumphs are celebrated by recovery from breast cancer, which is measured by the restoration of appearance. To put it another way, the implied identities regained by men and women recovering from these gender-specific illnesses are that of the midlife jock and the would-be perpetual cheerleader. Last year I ran my first marathon, at the age of 45. As Audre Lorde wrote after her Reach to Recovery volunteer had visited her: "I ached to talk to women about the experience I had just been through, and about what might be to come, and how were they doing it and how had they done it. But I needed to talk with women who shared at least some of my major concerns and beliefs and visions, who shared at least some of my language" (1980a, p. 42). I have never been a cheerleader, and I could not see trying out for the part with falsies. I want to run another marathon, and nothing at all in Reach to Recovery tells me about my prospects as a distance runner.

I propose that Reach to Recovery is, however inadvertently, an example of what sociologist Irving Rosow (1974) terms the socialization to old age, which he views as socialization to a normless, devalued status. As a heart attack accelerates passivity and dependency and other issues of aging for men, breast cancer accelerates the progress of women toward the double standard of aging (Bell, 1970; Sontag, 1972): not merely devalued, but devalued and dependent sooner, and desexualized as part of the devaluation. The image of women presented in Reach to Recovery material underscores the status of victim and trivializes the victimization. One is victimized not by a disease but by its cosmetic consequences: the threat of a desexualized body. The effectiveness of this process rests on the circumstances of socialization, which is facilitated by the ambiguity and anxiety that are abundant on surgical wards. The message, which does not stand up well under critical scrutiny, depends on the power of a nonconscious ideology.

Years ago, I was introduced to the power of a nonconscious ideology when I conducted a small experimental study of mothers' responses to an infant presented in pink or in blue clothing, designed as a modest test of the nature–nurture question (Will, Self, & Datan, 1976). On the one hand, proponents of the "nurture" perspective argue that differences in sex-role socialization reflect the imposition of gender roles which may or may not be appropriate for any given individual; thus mothers inflict social norms on their children before the children are able to express independent preferences. On the other hand, proponents of the "nature" perspective argue that these differences are the outcome of presocial, innate dispositional differences in female and male infants who present different cues to mothers; thus, by socializing sons and daughters differently, mothers are responding effectively and indeed with sensitivity to biologically based differences in individuals.

We tested this question by presenting a single five-month-old baby, whose dispositional cues would not vary across settings, dressed as a boy and as a girl, to mothers who were asked to interact "naturally" with the baby and were provided with a doll, a fish, and a train. If cultural norms shaped the mother's behavior, we anticipated differences in the treatment of the same baby depending on whether it was wearing pink clothing and identified as "Beth" or wearing blue clothing and identified as "Adam." If, on the other hand, the baby's needs determined the mother's response, we would expect no variation in the treatment of the baby.

It will not surprise this audience that mothers handed "Beth" the doll, held her close, touched her, comforted her if she expressed distress, and told us during debriefing that they "knew" she was a girl because she looked so feminine and soft, while "Adam" was given a train, less often cuddled or comforted if he

129

NANCY DATAN
Illness and Imagery:
Feminist Cognition,
Socialization, and
Gender Identity

expressed distress, and "looked strong" or "masculine." Mothers further asserted during debriefing that they did not believe in treating sons and daughters differently and did not treat their own sons and daughters differently in any way. Yet these mothers' behavior offers a glimpse at their children's future, which is less egalitarian than the mothers' declared attitudes: girls who will outperform boys on tests of verbal ability, boys who will show deficits in social skills as early as high school; women who will choose affiliation over achievement and pay for their choice with impoverished old age; men who will choose achievement over affiliation and pay for their choice by dying sooner.

To conclude: It has been a task of feminist psychology to expose, explore, and ultimately reject the inequities that begin in the nursery and accumulate over the life course. This chapter has explored some inequities that are part of the social response to breast cancer. It can be seen as a special case of a recent theme of *The Journal of Social Issues:* "Social Issues and Personal Life: The Search for Connections." As I learned, women with breast cancer soon discover that they are in the middle of a minefield of taboos. Feminist epistemology proves invaluable as a mine detector and has been a tool for me in guiding this effort to transform victims into survivors. If socialization is viewed as the transmission of values from one generation to the next, it may be argued that feminists are failures in socialization, and this chapter can be seen as yet one more instance of a repudiation of culture, its nonconscious ideology, and its oppressions.

Cancer is a powerful stimulus word which, thanks to a growing number of survivors, has recently begun to shed first one taboo status, that of unspeakability, and then another, that of death sentence. Breast cancer partakes of a third taboo status: it represents an assault on a symbol of sexuality (Rossi, 1986). In a review of studies of psychological research on women's responses to breast cancer, Meyerowitz et al. (1988) note: "Unfortunately, at times there has also been a tendency for authors to draw conclusions that may be founded more in stereotypes of women and their needs than in sound data." A typical statement of this stereotyped concern is expressed by Derogatis, who asserts as a hypothesis that "the fundamental female role is seriously threatened by breast cancer" (quoted by Meyerowitz et al., 1988). But as Meyerowitz, Taylor, and others have shown, it is by no means clear that cancer itself poses such a universal threat (see Meyerowitz et al., 1988; Taylor, Lichtman, & Wood, 1984; Taylor, Wood, and Lichtman, 1983).

Yet the very material intended to promote recovery assumes that breast cancer is a threat to sexual identity and imposes this assumption on women just as they are most in need of reassurance. Cancer may go into remission, but breasts do not grow back; to accept the message of Reach to Recovery is to accept mutilation as a core feature of one's postsurgical identity, and thus to accept the status of victim. And for victims the most appropriate response is grief. Survivors, by contrast, command our respect—and speaking for myself, I have done my grieving and am ready for some applause.

References

American Cancer Society (1982a). *Reach to Recovery: Helpful hints and how to's.* (Available from the American Cancer Society, 777 Third Avenue, New York, NY 10017.)

American Cancer Society (1982b). *Reach to Recovery: What is reach to recovery?* (Available from the American Cancer Society, 777 Third Avenue, New York, NY 10017.)

American Cancer Society (November 1984). *Prostheses list: 1984–1986.* (Available from the American Cancer Society, 777 Third Avenue, New York, NY 10017.)

American Society of Plastic and Reconstructive Surgeons, Incorporated (January 1982). *Breast reconstruction following mastectomy.* (Available from American Society of Plastic and Reconstructive Surgeons, Incorporated, Patient Referral Service, 233 North Michigan Avenue, Suite 1900, Chicago, IL, 60601.)

BELL, J. P. (November–December 1970). The double standard. *Trans-Action,* pp. 23–27.

BETTELHEIM, B. (1979). *Surviving and other essays.* New York: Knopf.

CLAYTON, S. D., & CROSBY, F. (Eds.) (1986). Social issues and personal life: The search for connections. *Journal of Social Issues, 42* (2), 1–221.

JANOFF-BULMAN, R., & FRIEZE, I. H. (Eds.) (1983). Reactions to victimization. *Journal of Social Issues, 39* (2), 1–227.

LEAR, M. W. (1980). *Heartsounds,* New York: Simon & Schuster.

LEOPOLD, A. (1953). *Round river,* New York: Oxford University Press.

LORDE, A. (1980a). *The cancer journals,* 2nd ed. San Francisco: Spinsters Ink.

LORDE, A. (April 1980b). After breast cancer: I am a warrior, not a victim. *Savvy,* pp. 68–69.

MEYEROWITZ, B. E., CHAIKEN, S., & CLARK, L. K. (1988). Sex roles and culture: Social and personal reactions to breast cancer. In M. Fine & A. Asch (Eds.), *Women with disabilities: Essays in psychology, culture, and politics* (pp. 72–89). Philadelphia: Temple University Press.

O'LEARY, V. (Winter 1987). Musings on the promise (and pain) of feminism. *Psychology of Women,* pp. 1, 3.

ROSEN J. L., & BIBRING, G. L. (1968). Psychological reactions of hospitalized male patients to a heart attack: Age and social-class differences. In B. L. Neugarten (Ed.), *Middle age and aging.* Chicago: University of Chicago Press.

ROSOW, I. (1974). *Socialization to old age.* Berkeley: University of California Press.

ROSSI, A. S. (1986). Sex and gender in the aging society. In A. Pifer & L. Bronte (Eds.), *Our aging society* (pp. 111–139). New York: Norton.

SONTAG, S. (1972, October). The double standard of aging. *Saturday Review,* pp. 29–38.

TAYLOR, S. E., LICHTMAN, R. R., & WOOD, J. V. (1984). Attributions, beliefs about control, and adjustment to breast cancer. *Journal of Personality and Social Psychology, 46,* 489–502.

TAYLOR, S. E., WOOD, J. V., & LICHTMAN, R. R. (1983). It could be worse: Selective evaluation as a response to victimization. *Journal of Social Issues, 39,* 19–40.

WILL, J. A., SELF, P., & DATAN, N. (1976). Maternal behavior and perceived sex of infant. *American Journal of Orthopsychiatry, 46,* 135–139.

Ynestra King

The Other Body:
Reflections on Difference, Disability,
and Identity Politics

Ynestra King is a feminist philosopher and ecofeminist. She also has a relatively minor physical disability. But how is it decided what is minor and what is not? Why are people with disabilities so often seen as *the disability, not as whole, complex human beings? King confronts tough questions about how our inability to cope with ambiguity, chance (anyone can become disabled in an instant), and dependency become projected onto people with disabilities.*

As You Read, Ask Yourself . . .

How is Ynestra King treated differently when her disability is apparent?

Why might all women with disabilities be thought to "look alike" by people who do not have disabilities?

King argues that having a disability is a fact of nature, not a social construction. Do you agree?

Disabled people rarely appear in popular culture. When they do, their disability must be a continuous preoccupation overshadowing all other areas of their character. Disabled people are disabled. That is what they "do." That is what they "are."

My own experience with a mobility impairment that is only minorly disfiguring is that one must either be a creature of the disability, or have transcended it entirely. For me, like most disabled people (and this of course depends on relative severity), neither extreme is true. It is an organic, literally embodied fact that will not change—like being a woman. While it may be possible to "do gender," one does not "do disability." But there is an organic base to both conditions that extends far into culture, and the meaning that "nature" has. Unlike being a woman, being disabled is not a socially constructed condition. It is a tragedy of nature, of a kind that will always exist. The very condition of disability provides a vantage point of a certain lived experience in the body, a lifetime of opportunity for the observation of reaction to bodily deviance, a testing ground for reactions to persons who are readily perceived as having something wrong or being different. It is fascinating, maddening, and disorienting. It defies categories of "sickness" and "health," "broken" and "whole." It is in between.

Meeting people has an overlay: I know what they notice first is that I am different. And there is the experience of the difference in another person's reaction who meets me sitting down (when the disability is not apparent), and standing up and walking (when the infirmity is obvious). It is especially noticeable when another individual is flirting and flattering, and has an abrupt change in affect when I stand up. I always make sure that I walk around in front of someone before I accept a date, just to save face for both of us. Once the other person perceives the disability, the switch on the sexual circuit breaker often pops off—the connection is broken. "Chemistry" is over. I have a lifetime of such experiences, and so does every other disabled woman I know.

White middle-class people—especially white men—in the so-called First World have the most negative reactions. And I always recognize studied politeness, the attempt to pretend that there's nothing to notice (this is the liberal response—Oh, you're black? I hadn't noticed). Then there's the do-gooder response, where the person falls all over her/himself, insisting on doing everything for you; later they hate you; it's a form of objectification. It conveys to you that that is all they see, rather like a man who can't quit talking with a woman about sex.

In the era of identity politics in feminism, disability has not only been an added cross to bear, but an added "identity" to take on—with politically correct positions, presumed instant alliances, caucuses to join, and closets to come out of. For example, I was once dragged across a room to meet someone. My friend, a very politically correct lesbian feminist, said, "She's disabled, too. I thought you'd like to meet her." Rather than argue—what would I say? "I'm not interested in other disabled people," or "This is my night off"? (The truth in that moment was like the truth of this experience in every other moment, complicated and difficult to explain)—I went along to find myself standing before someone strapped in a wheelchair she propels by blowing into a tube with a respirator permanently fastened to the back of the chair. To suggest that our relative experience of disability is something we could casually compare (as other people stand by!) demonstrates the crudity of perception about the complex nature of bodily experience.

My infirmity is partial leg paralysis. I can walk anywhere, climb stairs, drive a car, ride a horse, swim, hang-glide, fly a plane, hike in the wilderness, go to jail for my political convictions, travel alone, and operate heavy equipment. I can earn a living, shop, cook, eat as I please, dress myself, wash and iron my own clothes, clean my house. The woman in that wheelchair can do none of these fundamental things, much less the more exotic ones. On a more basic human level I can spontaneously get my clothes off if I decide to make love. Once in bed my lover and I can forget my disability. None of this is true of the woman in the wheelchair. There is no bodily human activity that does not have to be specially negotiated, none in which she is not absolutely "different." It would take a very long time, and a highly nuanced conversation, for us to be able to share experiences as if they were common. The experience of disability for the two of us was more different than my experience is from the daily experience of people who are not considered disabled. So much for disability solidarity.

With disability, one is somewhere on a continuum between total bodily dysfunction—or death—and complete physical wholeness. In some way, this probably applies to every living person. So when is it that we call a person "disabled"? When do they become "other"? There are "minor" disabilities that are nonetheless significant for a person's life. Color blindness is one example. But in our culture, color blindness is considered an inconvenience rather than a disability.

The ostracization, marginalization, and distorted response to disability are not simply issues of prejudice and denial of civil rights. They reflect attitudes toward bodily life, an unease in the human skin, an inability to cope with contingency, ambiguity, flux, finitude, and death.

Visibly disabled people (like women) in this culture are the scapegoats for resentments of the limitations of organic life. I had polio when I was seven, finishing second grade. I had excelled in everything, and rarely missed school. I had one bad conduct notation—for stomping on the boys' blocks when they wouldn't let me play with them. Although I had leg braces and crutches when I was ready to start school the next year, I wanted desperately to go back and resume as much of the same life as I could. What I was not prepared for was the response of the school system. They insisted that I was now "handicapped" and should go into what they called "special education." This was a program aimed primarily at multiply disabled children, virtually all of whom were mentally retarded as well as physically disabled. It was in a separate wing of another school, and the children were completely segregated from the "normal" children in every aspect of the school day, including lunch and recreational activities. I was fortunate enough to have educated, articulate parents and an especially aggressive mother; she went to the school board and waged a tireless campaign to allow me to come back to my old school on a trial basis—the understanding being that the school could send me to special education if things "didn't work out" in the regular classroom.

And so began my career as an "exceptional" disabled person, not like the *other* "others." And I was glad. I didn't want to be associated with those others either. Apart from the objective limitations caused by the polio, the transformation in identity—the difference in worldly reception—was terrifying and embarrassing, and it went far beyond the necessary considerations my limitations required.

My experience as "other" is much greater and more painful as a disabled person than as a woman. Maybe the most telling dimension of this knowledge is my observation of the reactions of others over the years, of how deeply afraid people are of being outside the normative appearance (which is getting narrower as capitalism exaggerates patriarchy). It is no longer enough to be thin; one must have ubiquitous muscle definition, nothing loose, flabby, or ill defined, no fuzzy boundaries. And of course, there's the importance of control. Control over aging, bodily processes, weight, fertility, muscle tone, skin quality, and movement. Disabled women, regardless of how thin, are without full bodily control.

I see disabled women fight these normative standards in different ways, but never get free of negotiating and renegotiating them. I did it by constructing my life around other values and, to the extent possible, developing erotic attachments to people who had similar values, and for whom my compensations were more than adequate. But at one point, after two disastrous but steamy liaisons

133

*YNESTRA KING
The Other Body:
Reflections on
Difference, Disability,
and Identity Politics*

with a champion athlete and a dancer (during which my friends pointed out the obvious unkind truth and predicted painful endings), I discovered the worlds I had tried to protect myself from; the disastrous attraction to "others" to complete oneself. I have seen disabled women endure unspeakably horrible relationships because they were so flattered to have such a conventionally attractive individual in tow.

And then there's the weight issue. I got fat by refusing to pay attention to my body. Now that I'm slimming down again, my old vanities and insecurities are surfacing. The battle of dieting can be especially fraught for disabled women. It is more difficult because exercising is more difficult, as is traveling around to get the proper foods, and then preparing them. But the underlying rage at the system that makes you feel as if you *are* your body (female, infirm) and that everything else is window dressing—this also undermines the requisite discipline. A tempting response is to resort to an ideal of self as bodiless essence in which the body is completely incidental and irrelevant.

The wish that the body should be irrelevant has been one of my most fervent lifelong wishes. The knowledge that it isn't is my most intense lifelong experience.

I have seen other disabled women wear intentionally provocative clothes, like the woman in a wheelchair on my bus route to work. She can barely move. She has a pretty face, and tiny legs she could not possibly walk on. Yet she wears black lace stockings and spike high heels. The other bus occupants smile condescendingly, or pretend not to notice, or whisper in appalled disbelief that this woman could represent herself as having a sexual self. That she could "flaunt" her sexual being violates the code of acceptable appearance for a disabled woman. This woman's apparel is no more far out than that of many other women on our bus—but she refuses to fold up and be a good little asexual handicapped person.

The well-intentioned liberal new campaigns around "hire the handicapped" are oppressive in related ways. The Other does not only have to demonstrate her competence on insider terms; she must be better, by way of apologizing for being different and rewarding the insiders for letting her in. And the happy handicapped person, who has had faith placed in her/him, must vindicate "the race" because the politics of tokenism assumes that there are in fact other qualifications than doing the job.

This is especially prejudicial in a recession, where there are few social services, where it is "every man for himself." Disabled people inevitably have greater expenses since assistance must often be paid for privately. In the U.S., public construction of the disabled body is that one either is fully disabled and dysfunctional/unemployable (and therefore eligible for public welfare) or totally on one's own. There is no in-between—the possibility of a little assistance, or exceptions in certain areas. Disabled people on public assistance cannot work or they will lose their benefits. (In the U.S. ideology that shapes public attitudes and public policy, one is either fully dependent or fully autonomous.) But the reality of human and organic life is that everyone is different in some way; there is no such thing as a totally autonomous individual. Yet the mythology of autonomy perpetuates in terrible ways the oppression of the disabled. It also perpetuates misogyny—and the destruction of the planet.

135

*YNESTRA KING
The Other Body:
Reflections on
Difference, Disability,
and Identity Politics*

It may be that this clear lack of autonomy—this reminder of mortal finitude and contingency and embeddedness of nature and the body—is at the root of the hatred of the disabled. On the continuum of autonomy and dependence, disabled people need help. To need help is to feel humiliated, to have failed. I think this "help" issue must be even harder for men than women. But any disabled person is always negotiating both the provisionality of autonomy and the rigidity of physical norms.

From the vantage point of disability, there are some objective and desirable aspects of autonomy. But they have to do with independence. The preferred protocol is that the attendant or friend perform the task that the disabled person needs done in the way the disabled person *asks it to be done*. Assistance from friends and family is a negotiated process, and often maddening. For that reason most disabled people prefer to live in situations where they can do all the basic functions themselves, with whatever special equipment or built-ins are required.

It's a dreadful business, this needing help. And it's more dreadful in the U.S. than in any place in the world, because our heroes are dynamic overcomers of adversity, and there is an inevitable cultural contempt for weakness.

Autonomy is on a continuum toward dependency and death. And the idea that dependency could come at any time, that one could die at any time, or be dismembered or disfigured, and still have to live (maybe even *want to live*) is unbearable in a context that understands and values autonomy in the way we moderns do.

I don't want to depict this experience of unbearability as strictly cultural. The compromising of the human body before its natural time is tragic. It forces terrible hardship on the individual to whom it occurs. But the added overlay of oppression on the disabled is intimately related to the fear of death, and the acknowledgment of our embeddedness in organic nature. We are finite, contingent, dependent creatures by our very nature; we will all eventually die. We will all experience compromises to our physical integrity. The aspiration to human wholeness is an oppressive idealism. Socially, it is deeply infantilizing.

It promotes a simplistic view of the human person, a static notion of human life that prevents the maturity and social wisdom that might allow human beings to more fully apprehend the human condition. It marginalizes the "different," those perceived as hopelessly wedded to organic existence—women and the disabled. The New Age "human potential movement"—in the name of maximizing human growth—is one of the worst offenders in obscuring the kind of human growth I am suggesting.

I too believe that the potential for human growth and creativity is infinite—but it is not groundless. The common ground for the person—the human body—is a place of shifting sand that can fail us at any time. It can change shape and properties without warning; this is an essential truth of embodied existence.

Of all the ways of becoming "other" in our society, disability is the only one that can happen to anyone, in an instant, transforming that person's life and identity forever.

The Space Crone

Ursula K. Le Guin is an acclaimed science-fiction writer and essayist. Here, she considers what it means for a woman to grow old. Le Guin imagines a world in which women grow more whole and more themselves as they age, rather than trying to conceal all signs of the passing of time.

As You Read, Ask Yourself . . .

Do you agree with Le Guin that women have lost meaning and power by imitating the life cycle of men?

What are the losses and the gains of menopause and later life for women?

What is a "crone"? Think about whether you know any crones and what lessons you might learn from them.

The menopause is probably the least glamorous topic imaginable; and this is interesting, because it is one of the very few topics to which cling some shreds and remnants of taboo. A serious mention of menopause is usually met with uneasy silence; a sneering reference to it is usually met with relieved sniggers. Both the silence and the sniggering are pretty sure indications of taboo.

Most people would consider the old phrase "change of life" a euphemism for the medical term "menopause," but I, who am now going through the change, begin to wonder if it isn't the other way round. "Change of life" is too blunt a phrase, too factual. "Menopause," with its chime-suggestion of a mere pause after which things go on as before, is reassuringly trivial.

But the change is not trivial, and I begin to wonder how many women are brave enough to carry it out whole-heartedly. They give up their reproductive capacity with more or less of a struggle, and when it's gone they think that's all there is to it. Well, at least I don't get the Curse any more, they say, and the only reason I felt so depressed sometimes was hormones. Now I'm myself again. But this is to evade the real challenge, and to lose, not only the capacity to ovulate, but the opportunity to become a Crone.

In the old days women who survived long enough to attain the menopause more often accepted the challenge. They had, after all, had practice. They had already changed their life radically once before, when they ceased to be virgins and became mature women/wives/matrons/mothers/mistresses/whores/etc. This change involved not only the physiological alterations of puberty—the shift from barren childhood to fruitful maturity—but a socially recognized alteration of being: a change of condition from the sacred to the profane.

With the secularization of virginity now complete, so that the once awesome term "virgin" is now a sneer or at best a slightly dated word for a person who hasn't copulated yet, the opportunity of gaining or regaining the dangerous/sacred condition-of-being at the Second Change has ceased to be apparent.

Virginity is now a mere preamble or waiting-room to be got out of as soon as possible; it is without significance. Old age is similarly a waiting-room, where you go after life's over and wait for cancer or a stroke. The years before and after the menstrual years are vestigial: the only meaningful condition left to women is that of fruitfulness. Curiously, this restriction of significance coincided with the development of chemicals and instruments which make fertility itself a meaningless or at least secondary characteristic of female maturity. The significance of maturity now is not the capacity to conceive but the mere ability to have sex. As this ability is shared by pubescents and by postclimacterics, the blurring of distinctions and elimination of opportunities is almost complete. There are no rites of passage, because there is no significant change. The Triple Goddess has only one face: Marilyn Monroe's, maybe. The entire life of a woman from 10 or 12 through 70 or 80 has become secular, uniform, changeless. As there is no longer any virtue in virginity, so there is no longer any meaning in menopause. It requires fanatical determination now to become a Crone.

Women have thus, by imitating the life-condition of men, surrendered a very strong position of their own. Men are afraid of virgins, but they have a cure for their own fear and the virgin's virginity: fucking. Men are afraid of crones, so afraid of them that their cure for virginity fails them; they know it won't work. Faced with the fulfilled Crone, all but the bravest men wilt and retreat, crestfallen and cockadroop.

Menopause Manor is not merely a defensive stronghold, however. It is a house or household, fully furnished with the necessities of life. In abandoning it, women have narrowed their domain and impoverished their souls. There are things the Old Woman can do, say, and think which the Woman cannot do, say, or think. The Woman has to give up more than her menstrual periods before she can do, say, or think them. She has got to change her life.

The nature of that change is now clearer than it used to be. Old age is not virginity, but a third and new condition: the virgin must be celibate, but the crone need not. There was a confusion there, which the separation of female sexuality from reproductive capacity, via modern contraceptives, has cleared up. Loss of fertility does not mean loss of desire and fulfillment. But it does entail a change, a change involving matters even more important—if I may venture a heresy—than sex.

The woman who is willing to make that change must become pregnant with herself, at last. She must bear herself, her third self, her old age, with travail and alone. Not many will help her with that birth. Certainly no male obstetrician will time her contractions, inject her with sedatives, stand ready with forceps, and neatly stitch up the torn membranes. It's hard even to find an old-fashioned mid-wife, these days. That pregnancy is long, that labor is hard. Only one is harder, and that's the final one, the one which men also must suffer and perform.

It may well be easier to die if you have already given birth to others or yourself, at least once before. This would be an argument for going through all the discomfort and embarrassment of becoming a Crone. Anyhow it seems a pity to have a built-in rite of passage and to dodge it, evade it, and pretend nothing has changed. That is to dodge and evade one's womanhood, to pretend one's like a man. Men, once initiated, never get the second chance. They never change again. That's their loss, not ours. Why borrow poverty?

Certainly the effort to remain unchanged, young, when the body gives so impressive a signal of change as the menopause, is gallant; but it is a stupid, self-sacrificial gallantry, better befitting a boy of twenty than a woman of forty-five or fifty. Let the athletes die young and laurel-crowned. Let the soldiers earn the Purple Hearts. Let women die old, white-crowned, with human hearts.

If a space ship came by from the friendly natives of the fourth planet of Altair, and the polite captain of the space ship said, "We have room for one passenger; will you spare us a single human being, so that we may converse at leisure during the long trip back to Altair, and learn from an exemplary person the nature of the race?"—I suppose what most people would want to do is provide them with a fine, bright, brave young man, highly educated and in peak physical condition. A Russian cosmonaut would be ideal (American astronauts are mostly too old). There would surely be hundreds, thousands of volunteers, just such young men, all worthy. But I would not pick any of them. Nor would I pick any of the young women who would volunteer, some out of magnanimity and intellectual courage, others out of a profound conviction that Altair couldn't possibly be any worse for a woman than Earth is.

What I would do is go down to the local Woolworth's, or the local village marketplace, and pick an old woman, over sixty, from behind the costume jewelry counter or the betel-nut booth. Her hair would not be red or blonde or lustrous dark, her skin would not be dewy fresh, she would not have the secret of eternal youth. She might, however, show you a small snapshot of her grandson, who is working in Nairobi. She is a bit vague about where Nairobi is, but extremely proud of the grandson. She has worked hard at small, unimportant jobs all her life, jobs like cooking, cleaning, bringing up kids, selling little objects of adornment or pleasure to other people. She was a virgin once a long time ago, and then a sexually potent fertile female, and then went through menopause. She has given birth several times and faced death several times—the same times. She is facing the final birth/death a little more nearly and clearly every day now. Sometimes her feet hurt something terrible. She never was educated to anything like her capacity, and that is a shameful waste and a crime against humanity, but so common a crime should not and cannot be hidden from Altair. And anyhow she's not dumb. She has a stock of sense, wit, patience, and experiential shrewdness, which the Altaireans might, or might not, perceive as wisdom. If they are wiser than we, then of course we don't know how they'd perceive it. But if they are wiser than we they may know how to perceive that inmost mind and heart which we, working on mere guess and hope, proclaim to be humane. In any case, since they are curious and kindly, let's give them the best we have to give.

The trouble is, she will be very reluctant to volunteer. "What would an old woman like me do on Altair?" she'll say. "You ought to send one of those scientist men, they can talk to those funny-looking green people. Maybe Dr. Kissinger should go. What about sending the Shaman?" It will be very hard to explain to her that we want her to go because only a person who has experienced, accepted, and acted the entire human condition—the essential quality of which is Change—can fairly represent humanity. "Me?" she'll say, just a trifle slyly. "But I never did anything."

But it won't wash. She knows, though she won't admit it, that Dr. Kissinger has not gone and will never go where she has gone, that the scientists and the shamans have not done what she has done. Into the space ship, Granny.

A Vindication of the Rights of Cunt

For as long as there has been a women's movement, language and naming have been important battlegrounds. Who has the power to decide what names will be given to women's bodies and sexuality? From "chick" and "nympho" to "ho" and "slut," men have named women in terms of their own values and desires. "Jayne Air" (a pseudonym) confronts the power to name directly when she urges young women to appropriate the word cunt *as a celebration of their own sexuality.* Cunt *is taboo, she writes, and taboo things are powerful. Just as people say admiringly of a man that he "has balls," she advocates using* cunt *to describe a woman who is bold and ready to take charge.*

As You Read, Ask Yourself . . .

What examples does "Jayne Air" give of women's self-directed used of this taboo word?

How does cunt *compare to the other words for female genitals she discusses, such as* pussy, vagina, *and* snatch?

In recent years, women have reappropriated words like girl *and* bitch; *is* cunt *going too far?*

Part of the experience of being a happening, smart . . . kind of gal involves the occasional realization that language hasn't caught up with you yet. When you're living like we do, you sometimes have to come up with your own vocabulary. Take the example of a particularly hip and innovative black girlfriend of mine who decided "def" wasn't speaking enough to her (too many overtones of gangsta rappers bitchslapping women and calling us ho's); she now has girls in the Bay Area using "deffa," a kind of feminine/feminist version of the same qualities of cool, minus the hateful crap. And while Gloria Steinem may have argued twenty years ago that "bitch" is the ultimate insult, we take it up when we feel like it, as a word that describes our femininity, our power, our PMS.

My newest favorite, like these other words, is more than mere nomenclature. It's about a mood, a lifestyle, an oppositional and in-your-face way of being at a party full of jerks, a restaurant where rude waitpeople are the rule of thumb, a concert where someone is raining on your parade, an office where your boss is too bossy, a roomful of your best girlfriends, at home alone because you feel like it. Whatever.

The word is CUNT. So many hate it. They say, "We've reappropriated 'bitch' and 'girl' but cunt is just going too far." They say, "Cunt is what really rude guys with beer bellies who hate us call us. Cunt is what nasty queens who find us disgusting call us. Cunt reduces us to—well—you know, a hole." Exactly. What I mean is, all those things are true. But they're precisely the reasons I love CUNT and find it so perfect. Cunt is taboo, and taboo things are scary and powerful. Somebody else isn't going to own that word. I figure it's so fucking dangerous, and it's so intimately about my anatomy, that it's going to be mine, too. Yes way.

But what, exactly, is cunt? What makes it lovable and good and bad? Cunt is different from bitch. Cunt is bitch's naughtier little sister. Bitch implies bitchy which implies all those "feminine" ways of getting even, like whispering behind people's backs and/or being arch instead of coming right out with it. Cunt is direct; it's unafraid to be what it is (lest we forget, cunt implies a whole messy, real thing, smells and juices and all—bitch is more sanitized). Cunt is a word that you just wouldn't say in front of your mother. Cunt is a word that can still make men suck in their breath uncomfortably and look down at the floor. It says, "There's nothing you frat boys can call me that I haven't thought of myself, before you. And I'm using it my own way, thanks so much."

Say you're in mixed company and you opine that, even though *The Specialist* was really dumb and Sylvester Stallone is an idiot, "Sharon Stone was a real cunt who almost saved that movie." Watch what happens. First of all, the women in the room are going to know you're onto something. You're obviously a feminist's feminist, cause you can admit it's fun to watch hot women in movies (maybe you don't think she's hot, but I do), and even more fun to watch them slug guys really hard in the mouth. Sure, some of your female compatriots might be taken aback. But they'll get your gist. I mean, you will have chosen your moment. You have some tact. You're one of them. The important thing here is that you're *not* a frat boy, or a guy who hates women, or whatever. In fact, you're stealing the only gynocentric term we have to say, "That woman has balls." The guys will be freaking out, but who cares? This story isn't about them.

There have been lots of divine cunts in history. I think of Catherine the Great, who used her literal cunt to great effect. Mae West was considered a cunt because she was funny and sexy but also because she insisted on directing her own movies and slept with whomever she wanted, mostly male bodybuilders many years her junior. Often a cunt is a woman you hate, but you just have to hand it to her. For example, Auden read Marianne Moore, that accomplished poet who held her own in the boys club of poets, and said of one of her works, "It's very cunty, but I like it!" That is, it has woman written all over it. That's a fundamental aspect of cunt: being a woman who doesn't apologize. Other cunts include that opera soprano what's her name who was asked to leave the Met because she said her costume was smelly and she wanted more perks and some hot tea with lemon NOW. It goes without saying that Madonna has made a career out of being a bitch who is sort of a cunt but doesn't have the guts to go all the way, while Courtney Love is too much of a cunt to care if anybody calls her a bitch. By the way, Naomi Wolf is not a cunt, although she would love to be: nobody who would wash your mouth out for saying it is a cunt. Cunt is too insouciant for that. It implies a certain devil-may-carishness about rules and etiquette.

Cunt has all the power of a magic word. There are things that make it okay for us to say cunt while men can't, or maybe it's okay for gay men who are our best girlfriends, or straight men who have passed the litmus test. Anyway, this "magic word" aspect of cunt is best illustrated by concrete example. To wit, I was once a go-go dancer in Bridgeport, and I was working at a biker bar. And in order to remain sane, it was very important that I act like a cunt, because that's really the only thing the guys in the bar would respect (never mind admire—I was just looking to get my money and get out, because some woman was giving a guy a blow job in the bathroom and it was, I admit, too scary for me). Acting like a cunt meant not making eye contact—not because I was afraid, but because I was one tough cunt. It meant going into my dressing room and reading *The New York Times* instead of socializing with the customers between sets. (Some rapist wants to buy me a Coors and assumes that this obligates me to sleep with him? Charmed. I'll stay put.) It meant holding my own and not playing the nice girl.

So I'm on stage and one of these guys says, as a little conversational gambit, "You really have an attitude, don't you?" He doesn't say it very nicely. Then he says, "You know what you are? You're a little cunt!" And he lunges at me. At which point the other dancer on the stage very coolly grabs a beer bottle and hits him over the head with it, thus taming his impulse (don't try this one at home). Luckily, he came to his senses (losing consciousness can do that to guys) and things settled down.

When I asked my savior why she did what she did, she simply stated, "He called you a cunt," and went back to doing the splits for singles. The point here is that cunt is such a powerful word, with so many associations, that if it's used incorrectly it can set you off in all your feminine, avenging fury. Now, don't you want a word like that, carefully and correctly used, at your fingertips?

I have two final things to say about why I love cunt. First of all, the thing in itself. I can never find the right word for it. Pussy is so whimsical and euphemistic and pink ("Hi! I don't really fuck!"). Vagina is so darn clinical. Beaver, too '50s and ironic. Hole, already taken. Snatch, too '70s and dumb and boycentric (like, they want to snatch it away, or what? I don't get it). I'm not advocating we all start calling it "my cunt." But sometimes it sounds better than all the other options. More in control, more girl, more "Look, you can do whatever you want but I'm going to get backstage passes to this show." Cunt is in charge, take-no-prisoners, and brazen. Like women in my favorite porn movies, who say, "I'm going to devour you with my cunt! Put it in, now!"

Finally, cunt is about being an insider. Or making somebody one of you. My girlfriends and I use it with each other when we've done something particularly admirable ("You told your boss that? You brilliant little cunt!" "You bought a pair of Betsey Johnson gold satin jeans right after I did? You cunt! Let's both wear them to my cocktail party!"). And we use it when somebody needs to be brought back down to earth, when we need to remind ourselves that some scary, powerful woman who's treated us badly better get off her fucking high horse. As in "Margaret Thatcher—the cunt!" or "Look, Jeanie, we all know that your boss is bitter and threatened by you and she's going to make your life miserable and say you're doing lousy work even though you're not, whenever she can." "You know what? You guys are right. That cunt!"

For fun and for mean, for expression and for irony, cunt is it. For me.

Celina's Commitment

Research on sexual attitudes and behavior shows that women are much less likely to masturbate than men are, although they do not have more negative attitudes toward it. Boys learn at an early age to masturbate for pleasure; many girls do not. Feminist sex educators and therapists have suggested that learning to give oneself sexual pleasure through masturbation is an important route to body self-knowledge and sexual autonomy. Yet little is known about why the gender difference in masturbation experience persists.

Celina Hex takes up this issue by singing the pleasures of the vibrator. Hex claims that women should not be denied the pleasure of solo orgasm and argues that using a vibrator makes it easier and more fun. Indeed, she says, she could no more do without her vibrator than without her answering machine.

As You Read, Ask Yourself . . .

What do you think are the reasons women are less likely than men to self-stimulate?

How does Hex characterize the sex education available to girls? Do you agree?

Is using a vibrator a good means for women to become more comfortable about claiming sexual pleasure?

Since buying my first vibrator four years ago, I have only one regret: that I didn't get one sooner. Why didn't I get one, say, when I was fifteen? Why didn't I have one during all those difficult years of college, where it could have come in so handy as a way to relax after a grueling test? Where, in fact, I could have done myself a huge favor by not going out, getting drunk, and picking up some dumb-ass frat boy in my search for sexual healing, a strategy that usually only left me, come morning, with beer breath, razor-stubble burn, and someone whose name I couldn't remember. All those nights would have been much better spent cuddling up with a cute, vibrating little pleasure device, and would have been far more sexually satisfying, as well.

When it comes to vibrators, the question should not be "Is it better than a man?" but "Is it better than your hand?" The answer to the first question is, simply, "It's different." The answer to the second is a resounding "Yes!" Listen, masturbating is fun, but sometimes you need a little jolt of electricity, so to speak. For men, that's where girlie mags, porn movies, or a good set of binoculars comes in. They save men the work of having to come up with their own fantasies. For me, the fantasy was never the hard part—it was the manual labor that could get to me at times. My little Magic Wand takes care of all that, freeing me up to focus completely on conjuring up my elaborate, perverted, and sick little sex scenarios.

Ever since I've gotten one, I've been on a mission about vibrators. "Every girl deserves a helping hand" is my motto. In fact, I think a vibrator would make the perfect bat mitzvah or sweet sixteen gift. Just think of all the orgasms a girl might otherwise miss out on. I mean, I know plenty of women who didn't have their first orgasm until they were in their twenties, but not a single man who hadn't had one by the time he was fourteen. Why is that? I don't know. Maybe boys have the advantage because they have a penis that gets hard and screams "stroke me!" at them in the middle of the night. We girls have to learn it all ourselves, and, after a few furtive attempts, well, I think I just gave up. There was nothing to see, nothing that squirted—I'm not even sure that at that age I knew that women really *could* have orgasms. And while I knew the size of my breasts down to the last centimeter (because they, at least, were getting talked about), I had no idea what a clitoris looked like, let alone what one was. That little anatomical illustration that came inside my Tampax box diagrammed my nether parts in loving detail, to make sure I didn't shove that thing up the wrong hole, but it neglected to include the clitoris. In this culture, we don't even need to practice female castration to separate a girl from her clitoris. If nobody bothers to tell her she has one, there's a good chance she may never find it.

Oh sure, I learned about the birds and the bees as a kid. I learned about how babies are made, about the whole penis-and-vagina thing. How I had ovaries and a uterus and how that little egg would come out once a month. Later, in junior high school health class, I was taught how I could keep from contracting diseases, how to avoid getting pregnant, and how to deal with the messy monthly blood, but nothing about how to find my little pleasure bud. After puberty, it seemed, all my time would be taken up just keeping my genitals safe from unwanted mishaps. Well, I'm here to say to the girls of our nation: ASK NOT WHAT YOU CAN DO FOR YOUR CUNT, BUT ASK WHAT YOUR CUNT CAN DO FOR YOU!

Of course, one of the best things it can do for you is give you orgasms.

"I'm getting these breast implants for myself" is the standard explanation given by women who are about to undergo the surgeon's knife, but I say, if you *really* want to do something for yourself, go get yourself a vibrator. If as many women bought themselves vibrators as they do breast implants, the world would be a better place. Maybe we need to start telling women that using a vibrator helps you lose weight, or that using the vibrator helps tighten your vaginal muscles, which will increase *his* pleasure. Maybe then they will be more likely to get them.

Because I'm sick of women who don't have or use vibrators responding with a sort of disdain when the subject of them comes up. They usually kind of scrunch up their noses with disgust, a response which always suggests, "Darling, I'm so sexually satisfied I don't need a vibrator." Can you *imagine* men responding in like form to the topic of porn. "You watch porno? Yo, dude! How gross!" Yeah, right. Most women don't even seem to know what vibrators actually look like or how they are used. For one thing, few people know that vibrators come in a wide variety of shapes and sizes, from small egg-shaped things to the larger ones that are sold right in your local Radio Shack as "massagers" (which is a good place to get one without embarrassment, since the men who work there don't seem to know that that's what they're used for, either). Even fewer people know that the vibrator is mostly intended for external use. Let me say it loud and clear: A vibrator is not a dildo, although some of them can be used in that way. A vibrator is just meant to be held against your clit until you explode with pleasure. Class dismissed.

To be honest, I used to be one of those women myself. I was very uncomfortable about buying my first vibrator, and I, too, thought it meant I was some kind of dried-up old spinster or something. But ever since I finally went through with it, it has become so important to me that, like my answering machine, I can no longer imagine what life was like without it. I'm mad that we women have been scared out of getting them; that they aren't more normalized in our culture. If we can talk about feminine hygiene sprays and yeast infection treatments on TV, why can't Hitachi run ads featuring a dancing little Magic Wand that promises to give "pure feminine satisfaction"? Can't Victoria's Secret have Dennis Miller or some supermodel let us in on what Victoria's Secret *really* was—that she had a supercharged vibrating love machine that never let her down?

Until then, I've got my work cut out for me. Taking my cue from the riot grrls' chant—Grrls Need Guitars!—I've come up with my own rallying cry: Vixens need Vibrators! Say amen, somebody.

PART THREE

Making Meaning

This set of stories makes up the most varied section of the book. You may find yourself wondering what connects them to each other or even what the title of the section means. We chose these readings, not for their content area, but because each represents an attempt to question what is purportedly known to be true about a fundamental category of meaning.

Our culture's certainties are conveyed to us daily. But because messages about basic cultural assumptions are rarely stated overtly, they enter our consciousness without our being aware of them. We might, therefore, accept them as our own beliefs and values without recognizing the harm they cause to ourselves and others. Sometimes, the beginning of social change is in challenging these very basic assumptions of one's culture.

Social and personal change does not have to be a solemn undertaking. The reading by an unknown author on the rape of Mr. Smith and Gloria Steinem's classic essay about what would happen if men could menstruate are witty pieces that also make important points. Both make us ask why people think feminists do not have a sense of humor. Their humor derives

from how they invert customary justifications for the way women and men are treated in our society. Ask yourself, whose definitions are considered to be legitimate? If menstruation happened to men, Steinem argues, it would be celebrated. If robbery victims were treated like rape victims, the injustice of blaming the victim would be visible for all to see.

Phyllis Teitelbaum, a specialist in standardized tests like the SAT, asks us to question the fundamental definition of ability that the tests are based on. Very few people enjoy taking the SAT, but most believe that it and other standardized tests are at least fair. Teitelbaum says that her goal is to give the reader an "Aha experience"—a sudden insight that the content and structure of these tests are arbitrary and could be quite different. What is left out of them is just as important as what is in them, because the omissions harm women and people of color. Claiming that standardized tests are androcentric, she invites us to imagine what a gynocentric test would be like.

Greta Christina questions a concept that almost everyone has used at one time or another: she asks how "having sex" should be defined. Is it defined by the act of penetration or by its meaning to the participant? Christina's friends argue it is sex if it feels like sex when you are doing it. Does this definition leave anything out? Think about how a person's memories about important events might be altered by subsequent changes in a relationship.

Michelle Fine's story is about Altamese Thomas, a young, poor, African American woman who lives in a much more destructive social environment than most of us will ever encounter. When Fine, a white feminist psychologist who is volunteering as a rape counselor, meets Altamese, who has just been raped, she is puzzled and frustrated. She tries to help, but her help does not seem effective. Altamese's perceptions about what to do after rape clash strongly with Fine's middle-class beliefs about taking control in the face of injustice. In comparing their different realities, Fine encourages us to examine how ethnic and class differences in power and powerlessness alter what it means to cope with the trauma of rape.

Mitsuye Yamada (who teaches English in a community college) writes about how racism affects women's perception of themselves. Asian Americans, she claims, are largely invisible to members of the dominant culture, who do not perceive them as feeling oppressed or angry. Asian American women are particularly influenced by the stereotype of passivity; in fact, Yamada states that they have stayed within their role so well that they have not been aware themselves that resistance was necessary or possible. Some radical feminists have argued that this kind of colonization of the oppressed individual's mind is the worst form of cultural domination.

A different kind of colonization of the mind is examined by Sherry Gorelick. As a professor of sociology and women's studies, Gorelick was exquisitely aware of the meaning of social signals elicited by her daughter as soon as she was born. These signals involved more than simple stereotypes of femininity. Her daughter was sexualized—treated like a tiny temptress—by well-meaning adults. Think about the consequences of many nonconscious encounters of the sort Gorelick describes.

While most women are encouraged—even pressured—to devote their energies to raising children, some are denied that choice. Minnie Bruce Pratt, a poet, writes about her own loss and that of another lesbian mother, Sharon Bottoms, whose children were taken from them by court decision solely because they were lesbians. Pratt's story is an example of how meaning is made by powerful social groups and used to control the less powerful. In this case, the upper-class white and (presumably) heterosexual men who hold power in the judicial system are able to define "good" motherhood—and thus to decide who is allowed to be a mother—in a way that does terrible harm to lesbian families.

We saved Kate Bornstein's and Mocha Jean Herrup's stories for last because they question the most fundamental categories of all. Bornstein has transformed herself from a heterosexual male IBM salesperson to a lesbian playwright and performance artist. Unlike most transgender individuals, however, she does not claim that she has changed from a man to a woman. Instead, she questions why we need to divide people into two and only two gender categories.

Like Bornstein, Mocha Jean Herrup calls for us to let go of the need to classify others' sex and sexuality into neat little boxes. Instead, she argues, we should accept the ambiguities of sex and gender. Herrup says that liberation is not a matter of tolerating sexual differences, but of "challenging the very forces that categorize sexuality in the first place." Cyberspace, where sex is a verbal performance independent of physical bodies, opens up the questions of "what is sexuality, and who am I?" In cyberspace environments, Herrup routinely acts out different identities, including a gay boy, a lesbian, and a heterosexual. Which—if any—is the "real" self?

The most insidious way of keeping people powerless is to colonize their minds. In these stories we have looked at the meanings of issues as varied as rape, menstruation, motherhood, cognitive ability, sexual intercourse, stereotypes applied to little girls and to women of color, and even the meaning of sex (as in male/female) and sexuality (as in gay, straight, bi or none of the above). We hope that these stories help you to better understand an early feminist maxim—the personal is political!

Anonymous

The "Rape" of Mr. Smith

This feminist classic has been circulated since the 1970s, first hand-to-hand in photo-copied form and later in print in several women's studies collections. It records a moment in history when women first began to reject men's definitions of rape and develop a woman-centered view. We don't know the identity of the original author, but we like to think that Anonymous was a woman. In any case, the article deftly shows how women were held accountable and blamed for men's violence against them. By making the crime and the victim ones that men could identify with, the author performed a powerful act of consciousness-raising.

As You Read, Ask Yourself . . .

How does the interrogation of "Mr. Smith" illustrate victim-blaming?

How does "Mr. Smith" respond to the suggestion that he caused his own misfortune?

Are women still blamed for the violence done against them by men?

The law discriminates against rape victims in a manner which would not be tolerated by victims of any other crime. In the following example, a holdup victim is asked questions similar in form to those usually asked a victim of rape.

"Mr. Smith, you were held up at gunpoint on the corner of 16th & Locust?"

"Yes."

"Did you struggle with the robber?"

"No."

"Why not?"

"He was armed."

"Then you made a conscious decision to comply with his demands rather than to resist?"

"Yes."

"Did you scream? Cry out?"

"No. I was afraid."

"I see. Have you have been held up before?"

"No."

"Have you ever given money away?"

"Yes, of course—"

"And did you do so willingly?"

"What are you getting at?"

"Well, let's put it like this, Mr. Smith. You've given away money in the past—in fact, you have quite a reputation for philanthropy. How can we be sure that you weren't *contriving* to have your money taken from you by force?"

"Listen, if I wanted—"

"Never mind. What time did this holdup take place, Mr. Smith?"

"About 11 p.m."

"You were out in the streets at 11 p.m.? Doing what?"

"Just walking."

"Just walking? You know that it's dangerous being out on the street that late at night. Weren't you aware that you could have been held up?"

"I hadn't thought about it."

"What were you wearing at the time, Mr. Smith?"

"Let's see. A suit. Yes, a suit."

"An *expensive* suit?"

"Well—yes."

"In other words, Mr. Smith, you were walking around the streets late at night in a suit that practically *advertised* the fact that you might be a good target for some easy money, isn't that so? I mean, if we didn't know better, Mr. Smith, we might even think you were *asking* for this to happen, mightn't we?"

"Look, can't we talk about the past history of the guy who *did* this to me?"

"I'm afraid not, Mr. Smith. I don't think you would want to violate his rights, now, would you?"

Naturally, the line of questioning, the innuendo, is ludicrous—as well as inadmissible as any sort of cross-examination—unless we are talking about parallel questions in a rape case. The time of night, the victim's previous history of "giving away" that which was taken by force, the clothing—all of these are held against the victim. Society's posture on rape, and the manifestation of that posture in the courts, help account for the fact that so few rapes are reported.

Gloria Steinem

If Men Could Menstruate—

Gloria Steinem, a highly respected feminist writer and a founder of Ms. Magazine, *wrote this sharp and funny fantasy. In it, she illustrates how language is used to make meaning and who has the power to determine what these meanings are to be. If men could menstruate, she speculates, it would be considered an enviable, boast-worthy, and very masculine event.*

As You Read, Ask Yourself . . .

How has women's biology been used to justify excluding women from power?

Are there other areas besides menstruation where women's biological characteristics would be more socially desirable if they were held by men?

What is more important—the biological distinction or the value society places on it?

A white minority of the world has spent centuries conning us into thinking that a white skin makes people superior—even though the only thing it really does is make them more subject to ultraviolet rays and to wrinkles. Male human beings have built whole cultures around the idea that penis-envy is "natural" to women—though having such an unprotected organ might be said to make men vulnerable, and the power to give birth makes womb-envy at least as logical.

In short, the characteristics of the powerful, whatever they may be, are thought to be better than the characteristics of the powerless—and logic has nothing to do with it.

What would happen, for instance, if suddenly, magically, men could menstruate and women could not?

The answer is clear—menstruation would become an enviable, boast-worthy, masculine event:

Men would brag about how long and how much.

Boys would mark the onset of menses, that longed-for proof of manhood, with religious ritual and stag parties.

Congress would fund a National Institute of Dysmenorrhea to help stamp out monthly discomforts.

151

Sanitary supplies would be federally funded and free. (Of course, some men would still pay for the prestige of commercial brands such as John Wayne Tampons, Muhammad Ali's Rope-a-dope Pads, Joe Namath Jock Shields—"For Those Light Bachelor Days," and Robert "Baretta" Blake Maxi-Pads.)

Military men, right-wing politicians, and religious fundamentalists would cite menstruation (*"men*-struation") as proof that only men could serve in the Army ("you have to give blood to take blood"), occupy political office ("can women be aggressive without that steadfast cycle governed by the planet Mars?"), be priests and ministers ("how could a woman give her blood for our sins?"), or rabbis ("without the monthly loss of impurities, women remain unclean").

Male radicals, left-wing politicians, and mystics, however, would insist that women are equal, just different; and that any woman could enter their ranks if only she were willing to self-inflict a major wound every month ("you *must* give blood for the revolution"), recognize the preeminence of menstrual issues, or subordinate her selfness to all men in their Cycle of Enlightenment.

Street guys would brag ("I'm a three-pad man") or answer praise from a buddy ("Man, you lookin' *good!*") by giving fives and saying, "Yeah, man, I'm on the rag!"

TV shows would treat the subject at length. ("Happy Days": Richie and Potsie try to convince Fonzie that he is still "The Fonz," though he has missed two periods in a row.) So would newspapers. (SHARK SCARE THREATENS MENSTRUATING MEN. JUDGE CITES MONTHLY STRESS IN PARDONING RAPIST.) And movies. (Newman and Redford in "Blood Brothers"!)

Men would convince women that intercourse was *more* pleasurable at "that time of the month." Lesbians would be said to fear blood and therefore life itself—though probably only because they needed a good menstruating man.

Of course, male intellectuals would offer the most moral and logical arguments. How could a woman master any discipline that demanded a sense of time, space, mathematics, or measurement, for instance, without that in-built gift for measuring the cycles of the moon and planets—and thus for measuring anything at all? In the rarefied fields of philosophy and religion, could women compensate for missing the rhythm of the universe? Or for their lack of symbolic death-and-resurrection every month?

Liberal males in every field would try to be kind: the fact that "these people" have no gift for measuring life or connecting to the universe, the liberals would explain, should be punishment enough.

And how would women be trained to react? One can imagine traditional women agreeing to all these arguments with a staunch and smiling masochism. ("The ERA would force housewives to wound themselves every month": Phyllis Schlafly. "Your husband's blood is as sacred as that of Jesus—and so sexy, too!": Marabel Morgan.) Reformers and Queen Bees would try to imitate men, and *pretend* to have a monthly cycle. All feminists would explain endlessly that men, too, needed to be liberated from the false idea of Martian aggressiveness, just as women needed to escape the bonds of menses-envy. Radical feminists would add that the oppression of the nonmenstrual was the pattern for all other oppressions. ("Vampires were our first freedom fighters!") Cultural feminists would develop a bloodless imagery in art and literature. Socialist feminists would insist that only under capitalism would men be able to monopolize menstrual blood. . . . In fact, if men could menstruate, the power justifications could probably go on forever.

If we let them.

Phyllis Teitelbaum

Feminist Theory
and Standardized Testing

Phyllis Teitelbaum, a psychologist who specializes in tests and measurement at the Educational Testing Service, examines how gender biases influence the construction of a test that affects virtually all would-be college students. You probably took SAT exams not too long ago. You may have questioned your scores, but you probably did not question whether the procedures used to test you were gender-biased. Teitelbaum charges that standardized tests are androcentric (male-centered) in structure and content. She asks us to think what a gynocentric (female-centered) test might look like.

As You Read, Ask Yourself . . .

What is the importance of each of the following: objectivity, dualistic thinking, quantitative measurement, atomistic analysis, timing for speed, and the competitive atmosphere that surrounds testing?

Did your scores on the SAT or other standardized tests affect your perception of yourself or change your plans about where to apply for college?

Could we—and should we—develop gynocentric tests?

"Tests." The very word makes people feel anxious. When the tests are standardized examinations used for admission to college, graduate schools, occupations, or professions, the anxiety level rises. Most people hate to be evaluated or graded, and the standardized format of admissions and professional tests can be particularly upsetting.

But are such examinations discriminatory? Are current standardized tests biased against women and members of minority groups? Although much research has been conducted on this question, no single conception of what it means for a test to be biased has yet emerged, and no clear answer to the question has been found.

In this essay, I will first discuss the question of sex bias in college admissions tests and summarize the consequences of the score differences between men and women on these tests. Next, I will briefly review three of the major approaches currently taken by test publishers in attempts to eliminate sex and racial/ethnic

153

bias from their standardized tests. Finally, I will present a very different approach to the question of whether and how standardized tests may discriminate against women—an analysis of such tests from the perspective of feminist theory.

My goal in applying feminist theory to testing is not merely to present an academic analysis. Rather, it is to provide you, the reader, with an "Aha" experience—a sudden insight into the arbitrariness of the current structure of things and a realization that they could be structured differently. Consider these questions: Why isn't housework counted in the GNP? Why isn't the emotional work that women do in relationships considered "labor" (Jaggar 1984)? Why must science be done in hierarchically-structured laboratories? Why can't a woman do scientific experiments in her home the way she does knitting or macramé (NWSA 1984)? Encountering these ideas in feminist theory has given me the kind of "Aha" experiences that I hope my ideas will elicit in you with respect to testing.

SEX BIAS AND COLLEGE ADMISSIONS TESTS

The issue of sex bias in standardized tests has been brought into sharp focus by a nationwide debate about the differential validity of college admissions tests—the Scholastic Aptitude Test (SAT), the Preliminary Scholastic Aptitude Test/National Merit Scholarship Qualifying Test (PSAT/NMSQT), and the American College Testing Program Assessment Exam (ACT). Phyllis Rosser (1987, 1988) has reviewed the data in this debate. I will summarize her reports here.

According to Rosser (1987:1), on average, women consistently earn higher high school and college grades than men; yet, on average, women receive lower scores than men on all three college admissions examinations. The score difference is particularly large in math; in the SAT math section in 1986 the gap was 50 points on average on a 200–800 point scale. But even in the verbal section of the SAT, where women used to perform better than men, women in 1986 scored on average 11 points lower than men. So the total score difference on the SAT in 1986 was 61 points (50 plus 11). Because women get higher grades in college than men, Rosser (1987:3) argues that the SAT does not accurately predict women's first-year college grades. According to Rosser, "If the SAT predicted equally well for both sexes, girls would score about 20 points higher than the boys, not 61 points lower."

Score differences between women and men on the PSAT/NMSQT and on the ACT are similar to those on the SAT. Rosser (1987:5–16) points out the serious consequences of these score differences:

1. College admissions—Nearly all four-year colleges and universities use SAT or ACT scores in admissions decisions, and many use cut-off scores, particularly for admission to competitive programs (Rosser 1987:4). If women's first-year grades indicate that their test scores ought to be higher than men's, then women applicants are undoubtedly being unfairly rejected in favor of less qualified male applicants.
2. College scholarships—According to Rosser (1987:8), over 750 organizations, including the National Merit Scholarship Corporation, use SAT, PSAT/NMSQT, or ACT scores in selecting scholarship recipients. In 1985–1986,

largely as a result of the PSAT/NMSQT score difference, National Merit Finalists were 64 percent male and only 36 percent female (Rosser 1987:11). The results in other scholarship programs are similar; women lose out on millions of dollars in college scholarships because of a score difference that may be invalid.

3. Entry into "gifted programs"—Rosser (1987:6–8) points out that many academic enrichment programs are offered to students who achieve high scores on the SAT, PSAT/NMSQT, or ACT. Women's lower scores result in their loss of these opportunities as well.

4. Effect on self-perceptions and college choices—There is evidence that students alter their academic self-perceptions and decide where to apply to college partly on the basis of their test scores. If the tests underpredict women's academic abilities, women may not apply to academically demanding colleges for which they are in fact qualified, and their academic self-perceptions may be set too low.

The three tests' publishers currently argue that the tests are not biased against women. The publishers have put forward several explanations for the score differences; these explanations suggest that the scores reflect true differences in women's and men's academic preparation and/or abilities. For example, some argue that women take easier courses in high school and college than men or that women receive higher grades than men because women try harder to please their teachers.

The debate over standardized college admissions tests is important for two reasons: (1) it questions whether these tests are equally valid predictors of academic success for women and for men; (2) it points out what is at stake for women if these tests are biased against them. It is not yet clear whether the score differences are due to bias and, if so, to what kind of bias. Nevertheless, the data Rosser presents on the negative consequences for women of the score differences underscore the importance of investigating whether and how standardized tests are biased against women.

SOME CURRENT APPROACHES TO ELIMINATING SEX AND RACIAL/ETHNIC BIAS IN STANDARDIZED TESTS

For over a decade before the debate about college admission tests, psychometricians and test publishers have been concerned about eliminating sex and racial/ethnic bias from standardized tests. Several approaches have been tried and currently coexist.

Judgmental systems are designed primarily to eliminate sexist and racist language from tests, to make certain that women and minorities are adequately represented in test content, and to evaluate whether some groups of test-takers have been deprived of the opportunity to learn the material in the tests (Tittle 1982). Implicit in these systems is a *content conception* of "bias"—bias is implicitly defined as the inclusion of sexist or racist content, the omission of women and minority groups, and/or the inclusion of material that some groups of test-takers have not had the opportunity to learn. In fact, there is no clear evidence that the test performance of women and minority group members is affected by the use of sexist or racist language. However, there is some anecdotal evidence that women and minority group members perform better on test material about women or minorities. In any case, for ethical and political reasons, many test publishers have established procedures for eliminating the "content" kind of sex and racial/ethnic bias. These judgmental procedures involve review of test questions by knowledgeable, trained people, often themselves women or members of minority groups, sometimes applying guidelines to identify unacceptable questions or point out inadequate representation. Test publishers who use these procedures agree that, simply on the face of it, tests should not reinforce sexism and racism, even if test performance is unaffected (Lockheed 1982). But much remains to be done in this area. For example, Selkow (1984:8–13) reports that, in the seventy-four psychological and educational tests that she studied, females were underrepresented, generally appeared in gender-stereotyped roles, and were shown in fewer different types of vocational and avocational roles than males. Moreover, many of these tests' publishers had no plans to revise the tests; and some asserted that if test-users made changes to reduce sex imbalance, such as changing names or pronouns, the tests would be invalid psychometrically because they would then be different from the versions given in validation studies.

Item bias and *differential item performance* methods of eliminating bias use a *performance conception* of bias. They determine statistically the particular test questions on which various subgroups perform poorly, compared to the majority group. Test publishers may then eliminate these questions from the test. Interestingly, judgmental and item bias/differential item performance methods do not typically identify the same test questions. For example, minority or female students may perform less well than the majority group on a question with innocuous language and content while all groups may perform equally well on a question that contains sexist language or racial stereotypes. Indeed, psychometricians have not yet been able to identify the characteristics of test questions that cause groups to perform differentially on them. Partly for this reason, item bias/differential item performance work is currently in flux. Test publishers have developed different statistics to define item bias. There is as yet no agreement on which statistic should be used to identify biased questions or on how the information should be used in test construction.

Differential validity is a type of test bias in which the test does not predict equally well for different subgroups. For example, Rosser (1987:1–3) uses this *prediction conception* of bias when she argues that college admissions tests are biased against women. Some studies of differential validity have produced contradictory results, even when studying the same test. Because of the importance of accurate prediction in making fair decisions based on test scores, research in this area is continuing.

I have no quarrel with any of these approaches. I myself am a professional test developer at Educational Testing Service (ETS), in charge of training ETS's test developers and editors to apply ETS's judgmental method. Eliminating sexist and racist language and content seems to me essential to produce a test that is fair on its face. And I am following the progress of item bias and differential validity studies with interest. From the practical perspective of the daily construction and utilization of tests, in the world as it is structured today, I believe that we need more work on these and other methods in order to create fairer, less biased tests.

STANDARDIZED TESTING
AND ANDROCENTRIC KNOWLEDGE

Most work currently being done on test bias accepts the basic underlying assumptions of standardized testing as given. What would happen if we questioned those assumptions from the perspective of feminist theory? What emerges is a radically different conception of sex bias as something inherent in the assumptions that underlie the content and format of standardized tests.

Feminist theorists have pointed out that what we have been taught to accept as standard scholarship is actually "androcentric" (that is, dominated by or emphasizing masculine interests or point of view). For example, the field called "history" has actually been the history of men; the history of women was simply left out. Similarly, "knowledge" and "science" are not universal; as currently taught, they are an androcentric form of knowing and of doing science.

The androcentric form of knowledge and science accepted in the twentieth-century United States is based on the theory of knowledge called positivism, which includes the following assumptions: scientific explanation should be reductionistic and atomistic, building up a complex entity from its simplest components; one can and should be objective (value-neutral) in scientific research (Jaggar 1983:356); and reason and emotion can be sharply distinguished (Jaggar 1985:2). This form of androcentric knowledge tends to be dualistic and dichotomous, viewing the world in terms of linked opposites: reason-emotion, rational-irrational, subject-object, nurture-nature, mind-body, universal-particular, public-private, and male-female (Jaggar 1985:2). It tends to be quantitative, and it takes the natural sciences as a model for all other academic disciplines. It contains an individualistic conception of humans as separate, isolated individuals who attain knowledge in a solitary, rather than a social, manner (Jaggar 1983:355). In addition, it includes a linear clock-and-calendar sense of time, rather than a circular sense of time (Wilshire 1985), and time is considered very important.

Standardized tests seem clearly to be based on this model of knowledge. In format, they are, as much as psychometricians can make them, positivistic, scientific, objective, value-free, dualistic, quantitative, linear-time-oriented, atomistic, and individualistic. In content, standardized tests reflect the androcentric model of knowledge by excluding everything that does not fit its definition of "knowledge" and everything that cannot be tested in a positivistic format.

First, consider the *format* of standardized tests:

1. The tests are "standardized" in an attempt to make them *objective and value-free.* Psychometricians hope that, if all test-takers receive the same test questions under the same standardized conditions and choose among the same multiple-choice answers, subjectivity and values can be excluded. But can they be? Test questions are written by subjective, value-laden human beings; questions and answer choices reflect the question-writer's upbringing

and values, despite the question-writer's attempts to eliminate them. Test-takers bring to the test very different sets of experiences and feelings, and their interpretations of questions will vary accordingly. There is no such thing as a "culture-free" test. Every test question must assume some "common knowledge," and such knowledge is "common" only within a particular subculture of the society.

2. Multiple-choice tests are *dualistic* in that they force a choice between possible answers: one is "right"; the others are "wrong." The model is dichotomous—either/or, with no gradations. But, depending on the question, a graduated model in which several answers are "partly right" may be more appropriate. If test-takers were allowed to explain why they chose a particular "wrong" answer, we might find that it was "right" in some sense, or partly right.

3. Standardized tests are relentlessly *quantitative.* Their goal is to measure a person's knowledge or skill and to sum it up in one number. (This quantification adds to the impression that standardized tests are "objective.") The single score reflects an androcentric fascination with simple quantification and precision; though psychometricians frequently state that test scores are not precise, test scores are often taken as absolute by both the public and the institutions that use the scores in decision making.

4. Tests are usually timed; thus, measurement of speed, as well as knowledge or skill, often contributes to the final score. This *linear-time-orientation* rewards speed even in subject areas where speed is not important.

5. Standardized tests are *atomistic.* Some systems of planning test content break learning down into "educational objectives" that are as narrow and concrete as possible—for example: "Can write legibly at X words per minute" (Krathwohl 1971:21). Even when such reductionistic educational objectives are not used, tests are inherently atomistic because they try to measure particular knowledge or skills separately from all other knowledge and skills.

6. Standardized tests are *individualistic* and usually competitive. A single person's performance is measured and compared, either with others' performances or with some preset standard of mastery. The ideas of "merit," of ranking, and of comparison are inherent in the testing enterprise. If there were no need or wish to compare individuals, there would be no standardized tests.

But even more important than format is *content:*

1. Standardized tests are in general designed to *test "reason" only*—the kind of knowledge that is included in the androcentric definition of knowledge. Excluded are whole areas of human achievement that contribute to success in school and work but are considered either inappropriate for testing or "untestable" from a practical point of view. Such characteristics and skills as intuition, motivation, self-understanding, conscientiousness, creativity, co-operativeness, supportiveness of others, sensitivity, nurturance, ability to create a pleasant environment, and ability to communicate verbally and nonverbally are excluded from standardized tests. By accepting and reflecting the androcentric model of knowledge, standardized tests reinforce value judgments that consider this model of knowledge more valid and important

than other ways of viewing the world. Content that is not tested is judged less valuable than that included on tests.

2. Test publishers attempt to *exclude emotion* from test content. Topics that are very controversial are avoided. Emotions that test-takers feel about the test itself are labeled "test anxiety" and considered a source of "error"; test-takers' "true scores" would be based only on reason, not emotion.

IMPLICATIONS OF THIS ANALYSIS

Is an androcentric, positivistic standardized test necessarily biased against women? The answer you will give depends on whether you believe that women test-takers have completely adopted the generally taught androcentric model of knowledge and that they are as adept in manipulating its concepts as are men. If you believe that women think the way men do, that they share men's "common knowledge," that they are as comfortable with dualistic, quantitative, timed, atomistic, competitive tests as men, and that the content excluded from the tests is no more salient to women than it is to men, then you will conclude that standardized tests are not sex-biased by virtue of their androcentric origins.

If, on the other hand, you believe as I do that women and men perceive the world differently, excel in different areas, and feel comfortable with different test formats, then you will conclude that an androcentric test is bound to be sex-biased. And you need not be a biological determinist to believe that such sex differences exist. It seems to me that the different life experiences that gender creates are sufficient explanation; growing up female is a different social and intellectual experience from growing up male (Farganis 1985:21).

As an example, focus on the testing of particular content only. Assume that, because of socialization or biology or both, women tend to excel in different areas than men. Consider, from your own reading and experience, what those different areas may be for each sex. Then construct a 2 × 2 table with "Tested" and "Not tested" along the top and with "Males tend to excel at" and "Females tend to excel at" down the left-hand side. Which cells are heavily loaded? Which cells are nearly empty? My table looks like this:

TABLE 1. Content Tested

	Tested	Not tested
Males tend to excel at	Many (eg., math, physics, chemistry)	Few (eg., aggression)
Females tend to excel at	Few (eg., reading)	Many (eg., sensitivity, supportiveness of others, oral communication, cooperativeness, creating a pleasant environment)

You may not agree with the specific examples I have chŏsen. Nevertheless, you may well find yourself agreeing that many things males in our society excel at *are* tested while many things females excel at are *not* tested. If true, this is probably a direct consequence of the androcentric format and the androcentric choice of content that shape standardized tests, and it demonstrates the sex bias inherent in tests based on an androcentric model of knowledge.

If the content and format of tests are androcentric, this might help to explain situations in which women perform worse than men on standardized tests. The task of taking a standardized test is probably harder for women than it is for men. Women who take an androcentric test may be analogous to people who learned English as a foreign language and who take a test of knowledge (economics, for example) written in English. The task of working in English probably makes the economics test harder for those who learned English as a foreign language than for the native speakers. Similarly, a woman who takes a standardized test must show mastery both of the test's subject matter and of the test's androcentric format and content, which are foreign to her. A man who takes that test has had to master the subject matter, but he probably finds the androcentric format and content familiar and congenial. Women raised in an androcentric school system must master two worlds of knowledge; men must master only one. If the man and the woman know the same amount of economics, the woman may nevertheless receive a lower score than the man because of the test's androcentric format and content. Thus, androcentric tests may not provide a fair comparison between women and men.

WHAT NOW?

It seems that the application of feminist theory leads to a sweeping condemnation of standardized tests as sex-biased. As a professional test developer, employed by a major test publisher, I find it odd to be joining testing's many critics. When I have read the attacks on testing by Ralph Nader's group (Nairn 1980), the National Teachers Association, David Owen (1985), and Phyllis Rosser (1987), my usual response has been, "Some of your criticisms may be valid, but what can you suggest that is better than our current testing methods?" Testing is easy to attack but hard to replace. I must ask myself, then, what would I put in the place of androcentric standardized tests?

One possibility would be to develop a "gynecocentric" (that is, dominated by or emphasizing feminine interests or point of view) method of testing and to include in tests the content areas currently excluded. This is a visionary, even utopian goal, but it is one worth thinking about because it may produce "Aha" experiences. Clearly, such tests would not be standardized, "objective," or competitive. Scoring, if it existed, would be holistic and qualitative, taking into account both reason and emotion on the part of both the test-taker and the scorer. Psychometrics as we now know it would not apply; no "metrics" (measurement) would be involved. But would we then have a "test" at all? Perhaps not. Perhaps a gynecocentric test is a contradiction in terms; gynecocentric methods might not provide tools that can be used for testing. Perhaps testing is intrinsically androcentric and cannot be transformed into a gynecocentric exercise.

On the other hand, it might be possible to reconceptualize testing in a gynecocentric mode, changing it into something like "unstandardized assessment" or "voluntarily requested group feedback." For example, an elementary school class wishes to know how well it has learned to interact and requests feedback from the teacher of interpersonal skills. She spends time observing the class at work and at play; then, with the class in a participatory circle, she discusses her observations and listens to class members' responses. In the workplace, instead of individual performance appraisals, there are voluntarily requested group evaluations. Colleges alter their admissions procedures to admit cooperating groups of students, rather than competing individuals. Alternatively, in a world that places less emphasis on competitive individualism than we do today, standardized tests as we currently know them might exist only for specific tasks and situations without pretending to measure general capacities (Alison Jaggar, personal communication).

For either a utopian gynecocentric form of testing to emerge or for a reduced use of conventional tests to occur, the individualistic, competitive basis of our society would have to change considerably. Testing is embedded in a culture of schooling and work that is solidly androcentric. To predict an individual's success in a college that teaches only positivistic knowledge to individuals, one needs a predictor that is at least partially individualistic and positivistic.

It seems like a cop-out to say that testing cannot change until knowledge, school, work, and society change. Certainly, tests influence knowledge somewhat when teachers and school systems "teach to the tests." And if tests began using a gynecocentric format and testing such skills as supportiveness and cooperation, tests might tend to increase the value society places on such a format and such skills. To this extent, changing standardized tests could be one way to start changing society. Nevertheless, because tests tend to reflect the social and educational system much more than they shape it, it seems likely that tests will change only after society does.

Note

I am very grateful to Alison Jaggar and the participants in her seminar, "Feminist Ways of Knowing," for their contributions to my thinking on gender issues.

References

DIAMOND, ESTHER E., and CAROL K. TITTLE. 1985. "Sex Equity in Testing." In *Handbook for Achieving Sex Equity through Education,* ed. Susan S. Klein. Baltimore: John Hopkins University Press.

FARGANIS, SONDRA. 1985. "Social Theory and Feminist Theory: The Need for Dialogue." Manuscript.

FLAUGHER, RONALD L. 1978. "The Many Definitions of Test Bias. *American Psychologist* 33:671–679.

JAGGAR, ALISON. 1977. "Political Philosophies of Women's Liberation." In *Feminism and Philosophy,* ed. Mary Vetterling-Braggin, Frederick A. Elliston, and Jane English. Totowa, N.J.: Littlefield, Adams.

_____. 1983. *Feminist Politics and Human Nature.* Totowa, N.J.: Rowman and Allenheld.

_____. 1984. "The Feminist Challenge to the Western Political Tradition." The Women's Studies Chair Inaugural Lecture, November 27, Douglass College, Rutgers University, New Brunswick, N.J.

_____. 1985. "Feeling and Knowing: Emotion in Feminist Theory." Manuscript.

KRATHWOHL, DAVID R., AND DAVID A. PAYNE. 1971. "Defining and Assessing Educational Objectives." In *Educational Measurement,* ed. Robert L. Thorndike. Washington, D.C.: American Council on Education.

LOCKHEED, MARLAINE. 1982. "Sex Bias in Aptitude and Achievement Tests Used in Higher Education." In *The Undergraduate Woman: Issues in Educational Equity,* ed. Pamela Perun. New York: Lexington Books.

NAIRN, ALLAN, AND ASSOCIATES. 1980. *The Reign of ETS: The Corporation That Makes Up Minds.* Published by Ralph Nader, Washington, D.C.

NWSA [National Women's Studies Association]. 1984. Sixth Annual Conference and Convention, June 24–28, *"Feminist Science: A Meaningful Concept?"* panel, Ruth Hubbard, Marian Lowe, Rita Arditti, Anne Woodhull, and Evelynn Hammonds. Douglass College, Rutgers University, New Brunswick, N.J.

OWEN, DAVID, 1985. *None of the Above: Behind the Myth of Scholastic Aptitude.* Boston: Houghton Mifflin.

ROSSER, PHYLLIS. 1988. "Girls, Boys, and the SAT: Can We Even the Score?" *NEA Today* (special ed.) 6, no. 6 (January): 48–53.

ROSSER, PHYLLIS, with the staff of the National Center for Fair and Open Testing. 1987. *Sex Bias in College Admissions Tests: Why Women Lose Out.* 2d ed. Cambridge, Mass.: National Center for Fair and Open Testing (FairTest).

SELKOW, PAULA. 1984. *Assessing Sex Bias in Testing: A Review of the Issues and Evaluations of 74 Psychological and Educational Tests.* Westport, Conn.: Greenwood Press.

TITTLE, CAROL K. 1982. "Use of Judgmental Methods in Item Bias Studies." In *Handbook of Methods for Detecting Test Bias,* ed. Ronald A. Berk. Baltimore: Johns Hopkins University Press.

WILSHIRE, DONNA. 1985. "Ideas presented for discussion" and "Topics for discussion." Manuscripts prepared for the "Feminist Ways of Knowing Seminar." Douglass College, Rutgers University, New Brunswick, N.J.

Greta Christina

Are We Having Sex Yet?

Greta Christina asks publicly a question that many people have probably asked them-selves in private: What counts as "having sex" with another person? She starts by sim-ply trying to tally her different sexual partners, but the situation soon gets complicated. Is "having sex" dependent on penetration, orgasm, desire, or pleasure (whose?)? Does the gender of the partner matter? Christina shows how asking one question about a ba-sic category of meaning can lead to still more, and how even the most obvious category can elude definition.

As You Read, Ask Yourself . . .

What are the limitations of defining sex as penile penetration?

How does Christina reinterpret her past behavior in the light of new experience?

How might a woman's identity be affected by the labels she assigns to her sexual activities?

When I first started having sex with other people, I used to like to count them. I wanted to keep track of how many there had been. It was a source of some kind of pride, or identity, to know how many people I'd had sex with in my lifetime. So, in my mind, Len was number one; Chris was number two; that slimy, little barbiturate addict whose name I can't remember was number three; Alan was number four; and so on. It got to the point where, when I'd start having sex with a new person for the first time, when he first entered my body (I was only hav-ing sex with men at the time), what would flash through my head wouldn't be "Oh, baby, baby, you feel so good inside me," or "What the hell am I doing with this creep?" or "This is boring." What flashed through my head was "Seven!"

Doing this had some interesting results. I'd look for patterns in the numbers. I had a theory for a while that every fourth lover turned out to be really great in bed, and I would ponder what the cosmic significance of this might be. Some-times I'd try to determine what kind of person I was by how many people I'd had sex with. At 18, I'd had sex with ten different people. Did that make me normal, repressed, a total slut, a free-spirited bohemian, or what? Not that I compared my numbers with anyone else's—I didn't. It was my own exclusive structure, a game I played in the privacy of my own head.

Then the numbers started getting a little larger, as numbers tend to do, and keeping track became more difficult. I'd remember that the last one was 17 and so this one must be 18, but then I'd start having doubts about whether I'd been keeping score accurately or not. I'd lie awake at night thinking to myself, well, there was Brad, and there was that guy on my birthday, and there was David and . . . no wait, I forgot that guy I got drunk with at the social my first week at college . . . so that's seven, eight, nine . . . and by two in the morning I'd finally have it figured out. But there was always a nagging suspicion that maybe I'd missed someone, some dreadful, tacky little scumball that I was trying to forget about having invited inside my body. And as much as I maybe wanted to forget about the sleazy little scumball, I wanted more to get that number right.

It kept getting harder, though. I began to question what counted as sex and what didn't. There was that time with Gene, for instance. I was pissed off at my boyfriend, David, for cheating on me. Gene and I were friends. I went to see him that night to gripe about David. He was very sympathetic, of course, and he gave me a back rub, and we talked and touched and confided and hugged, and then we started kissing, and then we snuggled up a little closer, and then we started fondling each other, you know, and then all heck broke loose, and we rolled around on the bed groping and rubbing and grabbing and smooching and pushing and pressing and squeezing. He never did actually did get it in. He wanted to, and I wanted to, too, but I had this thing about being faithful to my boyfriend. We never even got our clothes off. It was some night. One of the best, really. But for a long time I didn't count it as one of the times I'd had sex.

Later, months and years later, when I lay awake putting my list together, I'd start to wonder: Why doesn't Gene count? Does he not count because he never got inside? Or does he not count because I had to preserve my moral edge over David, my status as the patient, ever-faithful, cheated-on, martyred girlfriend, and if what I did with Gene counts, then I don't get to feel wounded and superior? Much later, I did end up fucking Gene and I felt a profound relief because, at last, he definitely had a number, and I knew for sure that he did in fact count.

Then I started having sex with women, and, boy, howdy, did *that* ever shoot holes in the system. I'd always made my list of sex partners by defining sex as penile-vaginal intercourse—you know, screwing. It's a pretty simple distinction, a straightforward binary system. Did it go in or didn't it? Yes or no? One or zero? On or off? Granted, it's a pretty arbitrary definition, but it's the customary one, with an ancient and respected tradition behind it, and when I was just screwing men, there was no compelling reason to question it.

But with women, well, first of all there's no penis, so right from the start the tracking system is defective. And then, there are so many ways women can have sex with each other, touching and licking and grinding and fingering and fisting—with dildos or vibrators or vegetables or whatever happens to be lying around the house, or with nothing at all except human bodies. Of course, that's true for sex between women and men as well. But between women, no one method has a centuries-old tradition of being the one that counts. Even when we do fuck each other there's no dick, so you don't get that feeling of This Is

What's Important, We Are Now Having Sex, and all that other stuff is just foreplay or afterplay. So when I started having sex with women the binary system had to go.

Which meant, of course, that my list of how many people I'd had sex with was completely trashed. In order to maintain it I would have had to go back and reconstruct the whole thing and include all those people I'd necked with and gone down on and dry-humped and played touchy-feely games with. Even the question of who filled the all-important Number One slot would have to be reevaluated. By this time I'd kind of lost interest in my list, anyway. But the crucial question remained: What counts as having sex with someone?

It was important for me to know. You have to know what qualifies as sex, because when you have sex with someone your relationship changes. Right? *Right?* It's not that sex itself has to change things all that much. But knowing you've had sex, being conscious of a sexual connection, standing around making polite conversation with someone while thinking to yourself, "I've had sex with this person," that's what changes things. Or so I believed. And if having sex with a friend can confuse or change the friendship, think how bizarre things can get when you're not sure whether you've had sex with them or not.

As I kept doing more kinds of sexual things, the line between *sex* and *not-sex* kept getting more indistinct. As I brought more into my sexual experience, things were showing up on the dividing line demanding my attention. It wasn't just that the territory I labeled *sex* was expanding. The line itself had swollen, dilated, been transformed into a vast gray region. It had become less like a border and more like a demilitarized zone.

Which is a strange place to live. Not a bad place, just strange. It feels like cognitive dissonance, only pleasant. It feels like waking up from a compelling and realistic bad dream. It feels like the way you feel when you realize that everything you know is wrong, and a bloody good thing too, because it was painful and stupid and it really screwed you up.

But, for me, living in a question naturally leads to searching for an answer. I can't simply shrug, throw up my hands, and say, "Damned if I know." So, even if it's incomplete or provisional, I do want to find some sort of definition.

I know when I'm *feeling* sexual. I'm feeling sexual if my pussy's wet, my nipples are hard, my palms are clammy, my brain is fogged, my skin is tingly and supersensitive, my butt muscles clench, my heartbeat speeds up, I have an orgasm (that's the real giveaway), and so on. But feeling sexual with someone isn't the same as having sex. Good Lord, if I called it sex every time I was attracted to someone who returned the favor, I'd be even more bewildered than I am now. Even *being* sexual with someone isn't the same as *having* sex with them.

I have friends who say, if you thought of it as sex when you were doing it, then it was. That's an interesting idea. It's certainly helped me construct a coherent sexual history without being a revisionist swine: redefining my past according to current definitions. But it just begs the question. It's fine to say that sex is whatever I think it is; but then what do I think it *is?*

Perhaps having sex with someone is the conscious, consensual, mutually acknowledged pursuit of shared sexual pleasure. Not a bad definition. If you are turning each other on and you say so and you keep doing it, then it's sex. It's broad enough to encompass a lot of sexual behavior beyond genital contact/orgasm; it's distinct enough *not* to include every instance of sexual awareness or arousal; and it contains the elements I feel are vital—acknowledgment, consent, reciprocity, and the pursuit of pleasure. But what about the situation where a person consents to sex without really enjoying it? Lots of people (myself included) have had sexual interactions that we didn't find satisfying or didn't really want and, unless they were forced on us against our will, I think most of us would still classify them as sex.

Maybe if *both* of you (or all of you) think of it as sex, then it's sex whether you're having fun or not. That clears up the problem of sex that's consented to but not wished for or enjoyed. Unfortunately, it begs the question again. Now you have to mesh different people's vague notions of what is and isn't sex and find the place where they overlap. Too messy.

How about sex as the conscious, consensual, mutually acknowledged pursuit of sexual pleasure of *at least one* of the people involved. That's better. It has all the key components, and it includes the situation where one person is doing it for a reason other than sexual pleasure—status, reassurance, money, the satisfaction and pleasure of someone they love, et cetera. But what if *neither* of you is enjoying it, if you're both doing it because you think the other one wants to? Ugh.

I'm having trouble here. Even the conventional standby—sex equals intercourse—has a serious flaw: it includes rape. If there's no consent, it ain't sex, but I feel that's about the only place in this whole quagmire where I have a grip. The longer I think about the subject, the more questions I come up with. At what point in an encounter does it *become* sexual? If an interaction that begins nonsexually turns into sex, was it sex all along? What about sex with someone who's asleep? Can you have a situation where one person is having sex and the other isn't? It seems that no matter what definition I come up with, I can think of some real-life experience that calls it into question.

For instance, a couple of years ago I attended (well, hosted) an all-girl sex party. There were only a few with whom I got seriously, physically nasty. The rest I kissed or hugged or talked dirty with or just smiled at, or watched while they did things with each other. If we'd been alone, I'd probably say that what I'd done with most of the women there didn't count as having sex. But the experience, which was hot and sweet and silly and very, very special, had been created by all of us, and although I only really got down with a few, I felt that I'd been sexual with all of the women there. Now, when I meet one of the women from that party, I always ask myself: Have we had sex?

I still don't have the answer.

Michelle Fine

Coping with Rape: Critical Perspectives on Consciousness

Michelle Fine, a white feminist psychologist, writes about her experience as a rape crisis volunteer. As a psychologist and trained counselor, she thought she knew the best means to help rape victims cope with their trauma. However, Altamese Thomas, an African American woman from an impoverished environment, challenged Fine's middle-class beliefs. In this article, Fine gives voice to her own and Thomas's competing views of reality.

As You Read, Ask Yourself . . .

What will happen to Altamese's mother and babies if she testifies about the rape?
Does Altamese have any reason to believe that the authorities will believe or help her?
Why does she decline the offer of counseling?
What did Fine learn about her belief that the best way of coping is to take control?

At 2:00 a.m. one October morning, Altamese Thomas was led out of a police car, entered the hospital in pain, smelling of alcohol. Altamese had been drinking with some friends in a poor, high crime, largely Black neighborhood in Philadelphia. She found herself in an alley, intoxicated, with pants down. She reports being gang-raped. The story unfolds, from intake nurse, the police and from Altamese herself.

I was awakened, in the small office for volunteer rape counselors, when the emergency room nurse telephoned me: "A Code-R just arrived." "Code-R" is the euphemism used to describe a woman who has been raped. I spent the remainder of the evening and some of the morning with Altamese. A twenty-four-year-old Black mother of three, two of her children have been placed by the state in foster care. From 2:00 a.m. until 7:00 a.m. we held hands as she smarted through two painful injections to ward off infection; traveled through the hospital in search of X-rays for a leg that felt (but wasn't) broken; waited for the Sex Offender Officers to arrive; watched Altamese refuse to speak with them; and returned to the X-ray room for a repeat performance—and we talked.

I introduced myself and explained my role. Interested primarily and impatiently in washing "the dirt off" and receiving necessary medical care, Altamese was unambivalent about her priorities. She did not want to prosecute, nor talk with social workers or counselors. She couldn't call upon her social supports. She just wanted to get home. For five hours, we talked. Our conversation systematically disrupted my belief that I understood anything much about the psychology of taking control in the face of injustice. Through my dialogue with Altamese, this article provides a critical analysis of the class, race and gender biases woven into the social psychological literature on coping with injustice.

THE PSYCHOLOGY OF TAKING CONTROL

When confronting life crises, injustices or tragedies, psychologists argue, people fare best by assuming control over their circumstances. Accepting responsibility for one's problems and/or solutions correlates with psychological and physical well being [1], across populations as diverse as rape survivors [2, 3], disabled adults [4], the institutionalized elderly [5, 6], unemployed men and women [7], school children with academic problems [8], even high school drop outs [9]. This article examines the assumptions which underlie present formulations of Taking-Control-Yields-Coping. Weaving relevant theory and research with excerpts from the dialogue between this rape survivor and the author, it will be argued that the prevailing coping-through-control ideologies are often limited by class, race and gender biases. Further, these models are disproportionately effective for only a small and privileged sector of society.

Psychologists have demonstrated that individuals cope most effectively with unjust or difficult circumstances by controlling their environments [10, 11]. This may involve attributing behavioral blame for the onset of bad events [12], or personal responsibility for initiating change [1]. Taking control may require participating in social programs and "getting help" [13, 14], and relying upon one's social supports [15–17].

The current Taking-Control arguments often assume that people *can* control the forces which victimize them, *should* utilize available social programs, and *will* benefit if they rely on social supports. What is not explicit is that these prescribed means of coping are likely to be ineffectual for most people [18, 19]. Persons of relatively low ascribed social power—by virtue of social class position, ethnicity, race, gender, disability or sexual preference—cannot control those forces which limit their opportunities [20]. But while it has been proposed that many then learn to be helpless [21], I maintain instead that they do assert control in ways ignored by psychologists. For many, taking control involves ignoring advice to solve one's problems individually and recognizing instead the need for collective, structural change [22]. Taking control may mean rejecting available social programs as inappropriate to one's needs [8, 23], or recognizing that one's social supports are too vulnerable to be relied upon [24]. Such acts of taking control have long been misclassified by psychologists as acts of relinquishing control.

ACCESS TO MEANS OF TAKING CONTROL: A FUNCTION OF SOCIAL POWER

MICHELLE FINE
Coping with Rape:
Critical Perspectives
on Consciousness

The control-yields-well-being proposition is empirically robust and admittedly compelling. As a psychologist interested in the social psychology of injustice, I study and support efforts which encourage people to take control of their lives. A review of this literature reveals, however, *individualistic* coping strategies, effective for persons of relatively high social power, promoted *as if* they were optimal and universal ways to cope. By establishing a hierarchy of appropriate ways to take control, this literature often 1) denies the complex circumstances many people confront, 2) *de facto* delegitimates those strategies for taking control employed by persons of relatively low social power, 3) encourages psychological and individualistic responses to injustice, which often reinforce existing power inequities [25], and 4) justifies prevailing social structures.

Advancing the position that people need to exert individual control over their lives presumes that all people are able to do so, that all people want to do so, and that to improve their life circumstances, people need to change themselves rather than social structures. Three fundamental problems with this formulation emerge.

First, if asserting individual control promotes psychological health it may be because individualism is socially reinforced in our society [26]. Positive reinforcement follows individualistic acts (e.g., "Pulling oneself up by the bootstraps") [22, 27] with social disapproval displayed for collective acts (e.g., in school these collective acts may be considered cheating; at work trouble making). The health that is associated with acts of individualistic control may therefore derive from social and ideological supports in our culture, not because individual control is inherently healthy.

Given that psychological well being stems in part from social rewards for individualism and internality, a second problem emerges with this model of coping. If unfair treatment occurs and control of that treatment is unlikely, a presumption of internality may be delusional! Externality may benefit persons whose life conditions are indeed beyond their control [28]. To nurture the much-encouraged illusion of internality in many circumstances would be unreasonable. In situations of low probability of success for redressing an injustice, attempts to redress injustice personally can breed helplessness.

It may be true that when persons of relatively high social power assert a single act of "taking control" (e.g., voice a grievance or file a complaint) they are likely to succeed. In contrast, the undocumented worker who is sexually harassed by her factory foreman might be foolish to file a grievance. "Bearing it" does not mean she has given up, but rather that she determined a solution by which she can be in control and employed. Establishing strategies to survive, when change is unlikely, needs to be recognized as acts of control.

A third problem with current control formulations is that they often decontextualize coping [29]. The presumption that psychologists can extract optimal ways to assume control over failure or adversity *across situations* reduces the complexities of the situations *ad absurdum* [18].

The strategies popular in the literature and undoubtedly effective in many cases, may benefit persons of relatively high social power (e.g., by attributing successes to stable internal factors and failures to unstable factors; taking responsibility for solutions; relying on social supports, or utilizing available social programs). As psychologists, however, we lack an understanding of how people who are systematically discriminated against and restricted to low power positions take control. We fail to understand how they determine what is controllable and what is not [30]. We dismiss control strategies that look like "giving up" but are in fact ways to survive. Even more serious, we avoid the study of those ways of taking control which systematically disrupt traditional power relations [31, 32]. Our literature legitimates existing power asymmetries.

There are two major consequences to these theoretical problems. First, control efforts enacted by low power persons are often misdiagnosed as giving up. Such attempts to take control tend to be misread as counter productive ("Why don't they do something about their work conditions if they are dissatisfied, rather than slowing down on productivity?"); distorted as self-effacing ("Even she blames herself for the rape."); diagnosed as masochistic ("She must enjoy the abuse, why else would she stay?"); classified as learned helplessness ("She always says—'I can't do anything about it.' "); or denigrated as psychological resistance ("I tried to offer help but he won't listen!") by laypersons and psychologists alike. These behaviors may indeed function as strategies of asserting control; if not resistance.

Second, the existing body of research on allegedly healthy ways of coping reproduces existing power inequities by prescribing *as optimal* those ways of coping which are effective for high power persons [33]. Social programs designed for low power persons are often organized toward coping strategies (such as individualism and reliance on social institutions) effective for high power persons. The models are deceptive for persons of low social power who depend on higher power persons, economically, socially, and/or psychologically, and have other low power persons (e.g., kin) highly dependent upon them. This precarious web of interdependencies creates conditions in which social institutions are likely to be unresponsive and individualism to be inappropriate. Many low power persons will not improve their own circumstances at expense to others, and most are unlikely to have access to standard tools of control (e.g., grievance procedures, money, or leverage with Congressional representatives). If they do, these tools are unlikely to promote the kinds of changes they need [34]. Consequently, when low power persons decide *not* to use the resources or programs offered them (e.g., "Because my mother is sick, and I have to take care of my children.") their disadvantaged circumstances may come to be viewed as deserved. The perception that they are *unwilling* to act on their own behalf provides evidence of helplessness, if not laziness. Their need to rely on high power persons is then confirmed. The power asymmetries built into these relationships are systematically justified [35].

Following, through a dialogue between the author and a woman who survived a rape, a dialogue situated in a hospital emergency room the evening of the rape, we analyze how persons of relatively low social power do assert control, and how easily a psychologist can misread these as efforts to give up.

3:00 AM   Altamese, the police will be here to speak with you. Are you interested in prosecuting? Do you want to take these guys to court?

No, I don't want to do nothin' but get over this . . . When I'm pickin' the guy out of some line, who knows who's messin' around with my momma, or my baby. Anyway nobody would believe me. [Can I wash now?]

3:30 AM   [Once the exam is over you can wash and brush your teeth. First we need to wait for the doctor for your exam.] Wouldn't your friends testify as witnesses?

Where I live, nobody's gonna testify. Not to the police. Anyway, I'm a Baptist and I know God is punishing him right now. He done bad enough and he's suffering.

4:00 AM   Maybe if we talked about the rape you would feel better.

You know, I don't remember things. When I was little lots of bad things happened to me, and I forget them. My memory's bad, I don't like to remember bad stuff. I just forget. When I was a young child, my momma told me about rape and robberies. I told her she was wrong. Those things happen in the movies, not here. When I saw such things on the streets I thought they was making a movie. Then one day a lady started bleeding, and I knew it was no movie.

4:30 AM   . . . Do you think maybe you would like to talk with a counselor, in a few days, about some of your feelings?

I've been to one of them. It just made it worse. I just kept thinking about my problems too much. You feel better when you're talking, but then you got to go back home and they're still there. No good just talking when things ain't no better.

Is there anyone you can talk to about this?

Not really. I can't tell my mother, not my brothers either. They would go out and kill the guys. My mother's boyfriend too. I don't want them going to jail 'cause of me.

She's the one who took away my kids.
If they take my baby, I would kill myself.
I ain't gonna get myself in trouble, all I got
is my baby and she already thinks I'm a
bad mother. But I love my babies and I try
hard to take care of them.

[I just don't understand why men have to
rape. Why do they have to take when
they could just ask?]

Those teachers think I'm stupid.
Sometimes they call on me and I don't
answer. When you got problems, your
mind is on the moon. He calls on you and
you don't know what he's saying. They
treat you like a dog and you act like a dog.

It ain't safe there. I live in the projects
with my baby. I can't go back there now.
It feels safer here . . . I hurt so much.

Sure. . . .

You said you sometimes meet with a
social worker. Can you talk with your
social worker?

How about one of your teachers at _____
college? Can you talk to them?

5:30 AM   Soon you will get to leave here
and go home, where you'll feel safe.

7:00 AM   Can I call you next week just to
see how you're doing?

ASSERTING RELATIONAL CONTROL

At first glance, one might say that Altamese abdicated control: She "gave up."
Unwilling to prosecute, uninterested in utilizing her social supports, she relied
on God for justice. Resistant to mental health, social service, educational and
criminal justice assistance, she rejected available options. Her coping mechanisms might be said to include denial, repression, and paranoia. She doesn't
trust her friends to testify, her family to listen, her social worker to be supportive, her teachers to understand or the police to assist. She has refused available
mechanisms of control.

And yet through our dialogue it was obvious that each of her decisions em-
bodies a significant assertion of control. Likely to be misclassified as helpless or
paranoid, she asserted strategies for taking control which insure both her well-
being and that of her kin. Altamese organized coping around relational concerns
[24]. Worried about her mother, child and siblings, she rejected options offered
to help her cope. She viewed my trust in the justice system as somewhat absurd;
my commitment to talking about the rape to friends, social workers, teachers or
family somewhat impulsive; my expectations of witnesses coming forth almost
naive, and even my role as volunteer counselor somewhat unusual.

Altamese

So, you're a nurse?

You mean you do this for fun?

. . . I don't know how you can do it all
the time.

Michelle

7:00 AM—Actually I volunteer here,
talking with women who have been raped.

I do it because I think it's important.
Do you?

Most people are denied the means to assume control over fundamentally changing their lives. Although prevailing ideology argues otherwise [36], Altamese and the millions of women who are unemployed, poor, minority and/or disabled and responsible for a network of kin, have limited options [37]. Although pursuing college, she may perhaps qualify for a low pay job some day. Given unemployment statistics, her personal style, life circumstances and lack of qualifications, her chances are slim.

The standard means of taking control promoted by counselors, policy makers and researchers, tend to be individualistic and most effective for a privileged slice of society. Trusting social institutions, maximizing interpersonal supports, and engaging in self disclosure are strategies most appropriate for middle class and affluent individuals whose interests are served by those institutions, whose social supports can multiply available resources and contacts and for whom self-disclosure may in fact lead not only to personal change, but to structural change [28, 36].

Unable to trust existing institutions, for Altamese self-disclosure would have exposed wounds unlikely to be healed. Responsible for a network of kin, Altamese could not rely on but had to protect her social supports. Resisting social institutions, withholding information and preserving emotional invulnerability emerged as her strategies for maintaining control [27]. Expecting God to prosecute, loss of memory to insure coping and fantasy to anesthetize reality, Altamese is by no means helpless.

While her social and economic circumstances are such that Altamese cannot change the basic oppressive structures which affect her, the social and psychological strategies she employs are mechanisms of control—protection for self and others [38]. An abstract pursuit of justice was not possible given her social context, commitments and concerns. She organized the realities of her life so as to manage effectively the multiple forces which *are* out to get her and her kin. Like Gilligan's concept of women's relational morality, Altamese exhibited what may be considered relational coping.

With little attention paid to relational concerns and a systematic neglect of power relations, psychologists have prescribed ways to cope as if a consensus about their utility had been established; as if there were no alternatives; as if universals could be applied across contexts, and as if these strategies were uninfluenced by our position in social and economic hierarchies. As the creators of what Foucault calls power-knowledge [33] psychologists have an obligation to expose the dialectics of psychological control and structural control, as experienced by women and men across lines of social class, ethnicity and race, levels of physical ability and disability and sexual preferences. In the absence of such knowledge psychologists impose, as healthy and universal, what may be narrow and elitist strategies for taking control.

One particular strategy, examined below, involves the prescription that persons treated unjustly or confronted by tragedy utilize available social programs. If Altamese is any indication such social programs are likely to be severely underutilized so long as they are designed top-down *for* (and not by) the persons supposedly served.

COPING WITH OPTIONS

One way to take control over adversity, supported by much psychological research (including my own), is to do something to improve one's own life circumstances; to use available options. To battered women, it may be suggested that they leave their abusive homes; to the unemployed, that they enroll for skills retraining; to the underpaid, that they learn to be assertive; to rape victims, that they "ventilate" and prosecute. Social programs have proliferated to offer individuals these services. These programs are generally designed by relatively high power individuals for persons who have what are considered personal problems. Offered as *opportunities* to improve the quality of life experienced by low power persons, these programs generally aim to correct presumed deficits [35, 39, 40]. Some disabled persons have the *opportunity* to work in sheltered workshops, often earning less than minimum wages, trained for non-marketable skills [41]. Some battered women have the *opportunity* to be sheltered in facilities which exclude women with drug or alcohol addictions, are located in unsafe neighborhoods, and limit a maximum stay of two weeks, promising an alternative to violent homes [42]. Some Black high school dropouts have the *opportunity* to earn their Graduate Equivalency Diplomas, promising greater vocational mobility, despite the fact that Black adolescent unemployment figures range from 39 percent to 44 percent for high school graduates and dropouts, respectively [43].

Efforts to fix people and not change structures, many of these options reinforce the recipient's low power position [39]. It is therefore most interesting that when such persons dismiss these options as inappropriate, ineffective or as decoys for the "real issues," these persons are often derogated [9, 23]. Individuals who reject available options, such as disabled adults who picket the Jerry Lewis Telethon claiming it to be condescending and reinforcing of the worst stereotypes, are viewed as ungrateful, unappreciative and sometimes even deserving of their circumstances [35]. The same option that appears valuable to a high power person may be critiqued as a charade by low power persons.

To demonstrate: there exists substantial evidence that high power persons do see social options (e.g., an appeal, grievance procedure, opportunity to flee) as more potentially effective than low power persons do. Experimental and survey data document that in social contexts in which an option to injustice is available, victims are more likely than nonvictims to consider their circumstances unjust, but nonvictims are more likely to rate *the option as powerful to promote change*

[44]. Victims see injustice; nonvictims see the potential for change. But, victims are *not* more likely than nonvictims to use an option to change their circumstances. Why would victims reject an opportunity to avenge injustice?

To investigate this question, victim and nonvictim responses to open-ended questions about injustice and appeals were reviewed [9]. Victims claim to be reluctant to appeal an injustice not because they do not recognize injustice, they do; not because they felt they deserved to be treated unfairly, they do not; not because they respect victimizers who commit injustice, they don't. Victims appear to be reluctant because they are in fact less likely to win an appeal, and usually have more to lose than nonvictims who would appeal. The appeal procedure in this study was designed as an *opportunity* for the victim to redress inequity, but actually offered her only a remote chance of success.

To appeal successfully, the victim or nonvictim had to convince at least one other member of a three person group that an inequity had occurred. If she appealed, a victim 1) would appear self serving, 2) could not be sure she would be supported in her appeal, 3) could, if she lost the appeal, get double confirmation that her treatment was justified, and 4) could indeed have much to lose by initiating an appeal.

In marked contrast, a nonvictim who appeals on behalf of the victim 1) would appear benevolent, 2) could be relatively sure of support from the victim, 3) could enjoy public praise for her benevolence, and 4) could gain psychologically and socially from the appeal. It is little wonder, then, that observers view options as more viable for victims than victims do themselves. It is perhaps in this role as observers that psychologists have encouraged victims' utilization of available programs and services. By not understanding how disempowering it may be to be offered an inappropriate option, while reminded that this-is-your-last-chance, even the most benevolent observer/helper can create secondary injury [45].

CONCLUSIONS

At fifteen life had taught me undeniably that surrender, in its place, was as honorable as resistance, especially if one had no choice.

—MAYA ANGELOU
I Know Why The Caged Bird Sings, 1969, Bantam Books, p. 212

As social scientists generate master strategies for taking control and promote them as universally applicable, the paradox of "therapeutic hegemony" emerges. Those individuals with the least control over the causes of their problems, much less the means for structural resolution, are prescribed psychological models for individual efficacy. As long as individual victims (or survivors) act alone to improve their circumstances, oppressive economic and social arrangements will persist. The effects of such acts of psychological control may ultimately be indistinguishable from the effects of surrender. Even acts of resistance, if initiated individualistically, ultimately buttress power differentials. Altamese's unwillingness to use the justice system, her non-reliance on kin, and her trust that God will provide or punish, do nothing for the women that these rapist(s) will attack next. Nor do they stem the wave of violence against women. What these behaviors accomplish is that they give Altamese a control strategy by which she can survive, with the remaining child, her mother, and her brothers, in a community where she can get some support. Unfortunately these behaviors also allow psychologists to continue to weave the fantasy that Altamese needs to be educated about options available to her and taught to be assertive about her needs. Psychologists can remain ever convinced that if *only* Altamese would learn to use it, the system would work to her advantage. . . .

EPILOGUE

And so as psychologists we are faced with a conceptual dilemma. Should we expand the definition of "taking control" to incorporate the lived experiences of women and men across class, race, and ethnic lines? Or, do we dispense with the concept of "taking control" totally, rejected as too narrow to be salvaged? I would argue the former. Taking control is undoubtedly a significant psychological experience; knowing that one can effect change in one's environment makes a difference. How individuals accomplish this, however, does vary by economic and social circumstance, gender and perhaps personal style. The phenomenology of individuals like Altamese needs be integrated into our conceptions of taking control in order for the concept to have meaning for those persons most likely to confront injustice, tragedy or other life crises. A feminist psychology needs to value relational coping and to contextualize, through the eyes of those women affected, the meaning of victimization and taking control. The continued assessment of "women's coping" as helplessness need be reframed.

AUTHOR'S NOTE

Encouraged by the editors of this series, I have included this note to describe methodological and ethical dilemmas faced in writing this article as a social psychologist. I also hope to persuade others, particularly clinicians interested in using this "method," to consider its inherent ethical dilemmas.

This manuscript, which reflects critical thinking about social psychological theory, was provoked by a discussion with a woman I have chosen to call Altamese. This conversation was between me, as a volunteer rape counselor (not as clinician—which I am not—nor as researcher) in an urban hospital and Altamese, an emergency room patient. The conversation took place because I work at the hospital in this capacity, not because I intended to do research on the topic of rape. The information reported does not, therefore, conform to the traditional standards of ethical practices of data collection.

The ethical dilemmas, as I see them, arise in a way not addressed by the 1983 Ethical Principles (APA): Altamese was not "informed" because at the time there was no research to be informed of; she was not "debriefed" because our only conversation took place in the course of my offering her support, not through the use of a pre-defined research instrument. Because of these factors, I remain somewhat ambivalent about the presentation of material in this article.

The problem is, simply, what to do with information gathered in a context in which research was not being conducted, in which the assumption is one of privacy, from which a publishable article evolves two years later? Three issues need to be examined: anonymity, informed consent, and assumptions about privacy.

Anonymity concerns appear to be the easiest to satisfy in both the present work and any other which utilizes a similar methodology. In the present work, names, demographics and life circumstances have been changed radically so that anonymity is well guarded. The details of the rape and reactions to it have been omitted so that no one could identify this woman—perhaps not even she herself. When information provided in any private setting is subsequently introduced in a manuscript, revealing data should be deleted, changed and/or "checked back" (if possible) for use.

Informed consent is more complicated. In this case, there was no presumption of "doing research." There would have been no reason, therefore, to request such consent. And two years later, with neither telephone nor forwarding address available, it is impossible to ascertain consent today. Of course, as someone suggested, it is possible that Altamese did sign a statement upon entering the emergency room which "OKed" the research use of relevant information, but one cannot assume this to be *INFORMED CONSENT.*

In thinking about informed consent it must be clear that 1) if a researcher is explicitly interested in gathering clinical information for research purposes all clients need to complete informed consent forms non-coercively (so that they have the option to receive services even if they do not agree to be involved in research); and 2) even if informed consent is provided, clients have the right to delete certain quotes or information from a manuscript if they feel revealed or betrayed by that section of the manuscript.

The third issue is for me the most complicated—what to do when information is provided in a context presumed to be private and confidential. Do researchers have a right to use this information for research/theoretical ends? I want to say a blanket "no" but again my own work leaves me wanting a more qualified response. A central consideration, here, is the issue of risk. In the present case, I can see no risk. Clearly, if Altamese were prosecuting these rapists, the potential risk would be enormous and publication out of the question.

This legal aspect of risk acknowledged, however, we still need to consider how we would feel if information we provided confidentially showed up in a journal article. The more explicit we can be with clients about the potential research purposes and the more we can involve clients in the importance of writing about this material (e.g., to make "public" what are experienced as "private" and "personal" problems), the less damage we will do to the trust levels between ourselves and our clients/informants; the better we will understand how clients/informants view violations of confidentiality and breaches of contracts, and presumably the better the information we will gather (perhaps too optimistic).

This article is about an encounter between two women and incorporates my impression of that encounter. I have elected to use the material, while trying to describe my ambivalent feelings about the encounter and about this article based on the encounter. In this note I have tried to reflect on the ethical dilemmas I have confronted and offer suggestions to individuals who may be interested in utilizing such a methodology systematically and intentionally:

1. Develop informed consent procedures so that all clients/potential informants are aware that information could be used for research purposes, providing services even if research consent is denied, and recognizing that introducing the topic of informed consent may systematically alter the nature of the relationship. The question needs to be asked: are there some counseling relationships in which counselors cannot simultaneously be collecting research-relevant information?

2. Beyond this safeguard, the potential risks to clients of using their information for research purposes need to be weighed, and discussed with clients.

3. Our responsibilities to people who provide us information need be respected. Researchers need to be particularly careful about abusing information provided when people assume the exchange to be private, confidential and safe.

References

1. P. Brickman, V. Rabinowitz, J. Karuza, D. Coates, E. Cohn, and L. Kidder, Models of Helping and Coping, *American Psychologist, 37*, pp. 368–384, 1982.
2. A. Burgess and L. Holstrom, Coping Behavior of the Rape Victim, *American Journal of Psychiatry, 133*, pp. 413–418, 1976.
3. R. Janoff-Bulman, Characterological versus Behavioral Self Blame: Inquiries into Depression and Rape, *Journal of Personality and Social Psychology, 37*, pp. 1798–1809, 1979.
4. R. Janoff-Bulman and C. Wortman, Attributions of Blame and Coping in the 'Real World': Severe Accident Victims React to Their Lot, *Journal of Personality and Social Psychology, 35*, pp. 351–363, 1977.
5. D. Schorr and J. Rodin, The Role of Perceived Control in Practitioner-Patient Relationships, in *Basic Processes in Helping Relationships,* T. Wills (ed.), Academic Press, New York, 1982.
6. R. Schutz, Effects of Control and Predictability on the Physical and Psychological Well Being of the Institutionalized Aged, *Journal of Personality and Social Psychology, 33*, pp. 563–573, 1976.
7. S. Cobb and S. Kasl, *Termination: The Consequences of Job Loss* (Publication #LR 77–224), Department of Health, Education and Welfare, Washington, D.C., 1977.
8. C. Dweck and B. Licht, Learned Helplessness and Intellectual Achievement, in *Human Helplessness,* J. Garber and M. Seligman (eds.), Academic Press, New York, 1980.
9. M. Fine, The Social Context and a Sense of Injustice: The Option to Challenge, *Representative Research in Social Psychology, 13*:1, pp. 15–33, 1983(a).
10. R. Janoff-Bulman and G. Marshall, Mortality, Well Being and Control: A Study of a Population of Institutionalized Aged, *Personality and Social Psychology Bulletin, 8*:4, pp. 691–698, 1982.
11. H. Lefcourt, Personality and Locus of Control, in *Human Helplessness,* J. Garber and M. Seligman (eds.), Academic Press, New York, 1980.
12. C. Peterson, S. Schwartz and M. Seligman, Self Blame and Depressive Symptoms, *Journal of Personality and Social Psychology, 41*, pp. 253–259, 1981.
13. B. DePaulo, Social Psychological Processes in Informal Help Seeking, in *Basic Processes in Helping Relationships,* T. Wills (ed.), Academic Press, New York, 1980.

14. M. Fine, When Nonvictims Derogate: Powerlessness in the Helping Professions, *Personality and Social Psychology Bulletin, 8*:4, pp. 637–643, 1982.

15. T. Antonucci and C. Depner, Social Support and Information Helping Relationships, in *Basic Processes in Helping Relationships*, T. Wills (ed.), Academic Press, New York, 1982.

16. C. Solano, P. Batten and E. Parish, Loneliness and Patterns of Self-Disclosure, *Journal of Personality and Social Psychology, 43*:3, pp. 524–531, 1982.

17. C. Swenson, Using Natural Helping Networks to Promote Competence, in *Promoting Competence in Clients*, A. N. Maluccio (ed.), Free Press, New York, 1981.

18. R. Silver and C. Wortman, Coping with Undesirable Life Events, in *Human Helplessness*, J. Garber and M. Seligman (eds.), Academic Press, New York, 1980.

19. R. Unger, Controlling Out the Obvious: Power, Status and Social Psychology, paper presented at American Psychological Association, Washington, D.C., 1982.

20. J. B. Miller, *Toward a New Psychology of Women*, Beacon Press, Boston, 1976.

21. M. Seligman, *Helplessness: On Depression, Development and Death*, W. H. Freeman, San Francisco, 1975.

22. W. Ryan, *Equality*, Pantheon Books, New York, 1981.

23. M. Fine, Perspectives on Inequity: Voices from Urban Schools, in *Applied Social Psychology Annual*, L. Brickman (ed.), *4*, Sage, Beverly Hills, 1983(b).

24. C. Gilligan, *In a Different Voice*, Harvard University Press, Cambridge, 1982.

25. E. Sampson, Cognitive Psychology as Ideology, *American Psychologist, 36*:7, pp. 730–743, 1981.

26. E. Cagan, Individualism, Collectivism, and Radical Educational Reform, *Harvard Educational Review, 48*, pp. 227–266, 1978.

27. J. Anyon, Intersections of Gender and Class: Accommodation and Resistance by Working Class and Affluent Females in Contradictory Sex-Role Ideologies, in *Gender, Class and Education*, L. Barton and S. Walker (eds.), Fatiner Press, England, 1982.

28. L. Furby, Individualist Bias in Studies of Locus of Control, in *Psychology in Social Context*, A. Buss (ed.), Irvington Publishers, New York, pp. 169–190, 1979.

29. A. Buss (ed.), *Psychology in Social Context*, Irvington Publishers, New York, 1979.

30. C. Wortman and J. Brehm, Responses to Uncontrollable Outcomes: An Integration of Reactance Theory and the Learned Helplessness Model, in *Advances in Experimental Social Psychology*, Vol. 8, L. Berkowitz (ed.), Academic Press, New York, 1975.

Invisibility Is an Unnatural Disaster: Reflections of an Asian American Woman

"It can't be helped." "There's nothing I can do about it." Resignation and passive acceptance are ways of dealing with oppression. Mitsuye Yamada describes a "psychological mind set" that convinces minorities that "we are born into a ready made world into which we must fit ourselves." However, she believes that many Asian American women fit in all too well. Passive resignation makes oppressed people invisible and their oppression seem entirely natural.

As You Read, Ask Yourself . . .

What examples of invisibility does Yamada give?

How might internalizing stereotypes about her ethnic group influence a woman's perception of the choices available to her?

Does Yamada offer ways to increase the visibility of Asian American women?

Last year for the Asian segment of the Ethnic American Literature course I was teaching, I selected a new anthology entitled *Aweeeee!* compiled by a group of outspoken Asian American writers. During the discussion of the long but thought-provoking introduction to this anthology, one of my students blurted out that she was offended by its militant tone and that as a white person she was tired of always being blamed for the oppression of all the minorities. I noticed several of her classmates' eyes nodding in tacit agreement. A discussion of the "militant" voices in some of the other writings we had read in the course ensued. Surely, I pointed out, some of these other writings have been just as, if not more, militant as the words in this introduction? Had they been offended by those also but failed to express their feelings about them? To my surprise, they said they were not offended by any of the Black American, Chicano or American Indian writings, but were hard-pressed to explain why when I asked for an explanation. A little further discussion revealed that they "understood" the anger expressed by the Black and Chicanos and they "empathized" with the frustrations and sorrow expressed by the American Indian. But the Asian Americans??

181

*Mitsuye Yamada
Invisibility Is an
Unnatural Disaster:
Reflections of an
Asian American
Woman*

Then finally, one student said it for all of them: "It made me angry. *Their* anger made *me* angry, because I didn't even know the Asian Americans felt oppressed. I didn't expect their anger."

At this time I was involved in an academic due process procedure begun as a result of a grievance I had filed the previous semester against the administrators at my college. I had filed a grievance for violation of my rights as a teacher who had worked in the district for almost eleven years. My student's remark "Their anger made me angry . . . I didn't expect their anger," explained for me the reactions of some of my own colleagues as well as the reactions of the administrators during those previous months. The grievance procedure was a time-consuming and emotionally draining process, but the basic principle was too important for me to ignore. That basic principle was that I, an individual teacher, do have certain rights which are given and my superiors cannot, should not, violate them with impunity. When this was pointed out to them, however, they responded with shocked surprise that I, of all people, would take them to task for violation of what was clearly written policy in our college district. They all seemed to exclaim, "We don't understand this; this is so uncharacteristic of her; she seemed such a nice person, so polite, so obedient, so non-trouble-making." What was even more surprising was once they were forced to acknowledge that I was determined to start the due process action, they assumed I was not doing it on my own. One of the administrators suggested someone must have pushed me into this, undoubtedly some of "those feminists" on our campus, he said wryly.

In this age when women are clearly making themselves visible on all fronts, I, an Asian American woman, am still functioning as a "front for those feminists" and therefore invisible. The realization of this sinks in slowly. Asian Americans as a whole are finally coming to claim their own, demanding that they be included in the multicultural history of our country. I like to think, in spite of my administrator's myopia, that the most stereotyped minority of them all, the Asian American woman, is just now emerging to become part of that group. It took forever. Perhaps it is important to ask ourselves why it took so long. We should ask ourselves this question just when we think we are emerging as a viable minority in the fabric of our society. I should add to my student's words, "because I didn't even know they felt oppressed," that it took this long because we Asian American women have not admitted to ourselves that we *were* oppressed. We, the visible minority that is invisible.

I say this because until a few years ago I have been an Asian American woman working among non-Asians in an educational institution where most of the decision-makers were men[*], an Asian American woman thriving under the smug illusion that I was *not* the stereotypic image of the Asian woman because I had a career teaching English in a community college. I did not think anything assertive was necessary to make my point. People who know me, I reasoned, the ones who count, know who I am and what I think. Thus, even when what I considered a veiled racist remark was made in a casual social setting. I would "let it go" because it was pointless to argue with people who didn't even know their

---

[*]It is hoped this will change now that a black woman is Chancellor of our college district.

remark was racist. I had supposed that I was practicing passive resistance while being stereotyped, but it was so passive no one noticed I was resisting; it was so much my expected role that it ultimately rendered me invisible.

My experience leads me to believe that contrary to what I thought, I had actually been contributing to my own stereotyping. Like the hero in Ralph Ellison's novel *The Invisible Man*, I had become invisible to white Americans, and it clung to me like a bad habit. Like most bad habits, this one crept up on me because I took it in minute doses like Mithradates' poison and my mind and body adapted so well to it I hardly noticed it was there.

For the past eleven years I have busied myself with the usual chores of an English teacher, a wife of a research chemist, and a mother of four rapidly growing children. I hadn't even done much to shatter this particular stereotype: the middle class woman happy to be bringing home the extra income and quietly fitting into the man's world of work. When the Asian American woman is lulled into believing that people perceive her as being different from other Asian women (the submissive, subservient, ready-to-please, easy-to-get-along-with Asian woman), she is kept comfortably content with the state of things. She becomes ineffectual in the milieu in which she moves. The seemingly apolitical middle class woman and the apolitical Asian woman constituted a double invisibility.

I had created an underground culture of survival for myself and had become in the eyes of others the person I was trying not to be. Because I was permitted to go to college, permitted to take a stab at a career or two along the way, given "free choice" to marry and have a family, given a "choice" to eventually do both, I had assumed I was more or less free, not realizing that those who are free make and take choices; they do not choose from options proffered by "those out there."

I, personally, had not "emerged" until I was almost fifty years old. Apparently through a long conditioning process, I had learned how *not* to be seen for what I am. A long history of ineffectual activities had been, I realize now, initiation rites toward my eventual invisibility. The training begins in childhood; and for women and minorities, whatever is started in childhood is continued throughout their adult lives. I first recognized just how invisible I was in my first real confrontation with my parents a few years after the outbreak of World War II.

During the early years of the war, my older brother, Mike, and I left the concentration camp in Idaho to work and study at the University of Cincinnati. My parents came to Cincinnati soon after my father's release from Internment Camp (these were POW camps to which many of the Issei* men, leaders in their communities, were sent by the FBI), and worked as domestics in the suburbs. I did not see them too often because by this time I had met and was much influenced by a pacifist who was out on a "furlough" from a conscientious objectors' camp in Trenton, North Dakota. When my parents learned about my "boy friend" they were appalled and frightened. After all, this was the period when everyone in the country was expected to be one-hundred percent behind the war effort, and the Nisei[†] boys who had volunteered for the Armed Forces were out there fighting and dying to prove how American we really were. However, during interminable arguments with my father and overheard arguments between my par-

---

*Issei—Immigrant Japanese, living in the U.S.
[†]Nisei—Second generation Japanese, born in the U.S.

183

*MITSUYE YAMADA
Invisibility Is an
Unnatural Disaster:
Reflections of an
Asian American
Woman*

ents, I was devastated to learn they were not so much concerned about my having become a pacifist, but they were more concerned about the possibility of my marrying one. They were understandably frightened (my father's prison years of course were still fresh on his mind) about repercussions on the rest of the family. In an attempt to make my father understand me, I argued that even if I didn't marry him, I'd still be a pacifist; but my father reassured me that it was "all right" for me to be a pacifist because as a Japanese national and a "girl" *it didn't make any difference to anyone.* In frustration, I remember shouting, "But can't you see, *I'm* philosophically committed to the pacifist cause," but he dismissed this with "In my college days we used to call philosophy, foolosophy," and that was the end of that. When they were finally convinced I was not going to marry "my pacifist," the subject was dropped and we never discussed it again.

As if to confirm my father's assessment of the harmlessness of my opinions, my brother Mike, an American citizen, was suddenly expelled from the University of Cincinnati while I, "an enemy alien," was permitted to stay. We assumed that his stand as a pacifist, although he was classified a 4-F because of his health, contributed to his expulsion. We were told the Air Force was conducting sensitive wartime research on campus and requested his removal, but they apparently felt my presence on campus was not as threatening.

I left Cincinnati in 1945, hoping to leave behind this and other unpleasant memories gathered there during the war years, and plunged right into the politically active atmosphere at New York University where students, many of them returning veterans, were continuously promoting one cause or other by making speeches in Washington Square, passing out petitions, or staging demonstrations. On one occasion, I tagged along with a group of students who took a train to Albany to demonstrate on the steps of the State Capitol. I think I was the only Asian in this group of predominantly Jewish students from NYU. People who passed us were amused and shouted "Go home and grow up." I suppose Governor Dewey, who refused to see us, assumed we were a group of adolescents without a cause as most college students were considered to be during those days. It appears they weren't expecting any results from our demonstration. There were no newspersons, no security persons, no police. No one tried to stop us from doing what we were doing. We simply did "our thing" and went back to our studies until next time, and my father's words were again confirmed: it made no difference to anyone, being a young student demonstrator in peacetime, 1947.

Not only the young, but those who feel powerless over their own lives know what it is like not to make a difference on anyone or anything. The poor know it only too well, and we women have known it since we were little girls. The most insidious part of this conditioning process, I realize now, was that we have been trained not to expect a response in ways that mattered. We may be listened to and responded to with placating words and gestures, but our psychological mind set has already told us time and again that we were born into a ready made world into which we must fit ourselves and that many of us do it very well.

This mind set is the result of not believing that the political and social forces affecting our lives are determined by some person, or a group of persons, probably sitting behind a desk or around a conference table.

Just recently I read an article about "the remarkable track record of success" of the Nisei in the United States. One Nisei was quoted as saying he attributed our stamina and endurance to our ancestors whose characters had been shaped, he said, by their living in a country which has been constantly besieged by all manner of natural disasters, such as earthquakes and hurricanes. He said the Nisei has inherited a steely will, a will to endure and hence, to survive.

This evolutionary explanation disturbs me, because it equates the "act of God" (i.e., natural disasters) to the "act of man" (i.e., the war, the evacuation). The former is not within our power to alter, but the latter, I should think, is. By putting the "acts of God" on par with the acts of man, we shrug off personal responsibilities.

I have, for too long a period of time accepted the opinion of others (even though they were directly affecting my life) as if they were objective events totally out of my control. Because I separated such opinions from the persons who were making them, I accepted them the way I accepted natural disasters; and I endured them as inevitable. I have tried to cope with people whose points of view alarmed me in the same way that I had adjusted to natural phenomena, such as hurricanes, which plowed into my life from time to time. I would readjust my dismantled feelings in the same way that we repaired the broken shutters after the storm. The Japanese have an all-purpose expression in their language for this attitude of resigned acceptance: "Shikataganai." "It can't be helped." "There's nothing I can do about it." It is said with the shrug of the shoulders and tone of finality, perhaps not unlike the "those-were-my-orders" tone that was used at the Nuremberg trials. With all the sociological studies that have been made about the causes of the evacuations of the Japanese Americans during World War II, we should know by now that "they" knew that the West Coast Japanese Americans would go without too much protest, and of course, "they" were right, for most of us (with the exception of those notable few), resigned to our fate, albeit bewildered and not willingly. We were not perceived by our government as responsive Americans; we were objects that happened to be standing in the path of the storm.

Perhaps this kind of acceptance is a way of coping with the "real" world. One stands against the wind for a time, and then succumbs eventually because there is no point to being stubborn against all odds. The wind will not respond to entreaties anyway, one reasons; one should have sense enough to know that. I'm not ready to accept this evolutionary reasoning. It is too rigid for me; I would like to think that my new awareness is going to make me more visible than ever, and to allow me to make some changes in the "man made disaster" I live in at the present time. Part of being visible is refusing to separate the actors from their actions, and demanding that they be responsible for them.

By now, riding along with the minorities' and women's movements, I think we are making a wedge into the main body of American life, but people are still looking right through and around us, assuming we are simply tagging along. Asian American women still remain in the background and we are heard but not really listened to. Like Musak, they think we are piped into the airwaves by someone else. We must remember that one of the most insidious ways of keeping women and minorities powerless is to let them only talk about harmless and inconsequential subjects, or let them speak freely and not listen to them with serious intent.

We need to raise our voices a little more, even as they say to us "This is so uncharacteristic of you." To finally recognize our own invisibility is to finally be on the path toward visibility. Invisibility is not a natural state for anyone.

Sherry Gorelick

The Gender Trap

It is a feminist truism that children are subjected to gender socialization from birth on-ward. A great deal of research has shown that boys and girls are treated differently and learn different social repertoires as a result. Yet even knowing those facts, the imposition of gender roles and stereotypes can take us by surprise. Sherry Gorelick writes about a "silent tyranny of everyday life": how adults project their own preoccupations about sex and heterosexuality onto the behavior of little children. Gorelick describes many inci-dents in her young daughter's life, each one seemingly trivial in itself, that add up to a disturbing picture of compulsory heterosexuality.

As You Read, Ask Yourself . . .

Do the incidents described by Gorelick sound familiar?

What does it mean when girls are sexualized by adults only when they are involved in encounters with males?

Do you agree with Gorelick that this kind of behavior devalues the bonds between females?

She was only 13 days old when we took her out for the first time, and the first encounter was a warning of those to come.

"Is girl?" our 81-year-old neighbor said in the elevator.

"Yes," we beamed.

"Congratulations. I have new great-grandson. One month old. Will be boyfriend for her."

My smile deteriorated. "Congratulations," I managed sullenly. He is old, I told myself. Old-fashioned. I have to be polite. Recognize cultural differences.

The next time we met, the conversation repeated itself verbatim. And the next. And the next. By the fourth or fifth time I lost my cool.

"She's only four weeks old, Mr. Shatgan. She doesn't need a boyfriend. She just needs to grow up!"

He seemed a bit taken aback by my anger. Perplexed, as though I were speaking in tongues. But the next time we met in the elevator, he offered the same match, and I matched it with my same impatience.

That November, she was two months old and we took her to Thanksgiving at my in-laws'. Her cousins, all boys, took great delight in playing with her, calling her by name, giving her toys, babbling at her. Billy, 4, and Jake and Peter, 11, spent much time dancing around her.

"That's good," my sister-in-law said. "She's learning to get the men dancing around her."

"Men?" I thought. "Gimme a break! They are all children. Billy is *four!*" The next year at Thanksgiving, the conversation repeated itself. Sonja Samia, my daughter, was 14 months old, and the "men" were 5 and 12. I thought to myself: "What if her cousins had been girls? The adults would have taken no notice whatsoever."

Absolutely right. Over the first couple of years of her little life, my daughter's encounters with female babies were treated by all onlooking adults as unimportant and uninteresting, or as what they really were: the meeting of two babies. Her encounters with male babies were, without exception, sexualized.

One afternoon, for example, I took her out to the park as usual. She was on top of the slide when another baby around the same age swaggered its wind-up-toy way past us. The child was dressed in a blue snowsuit with pink gloves, and my friend, a strong woman who is quite unconventional in many ways, asked the Number One All Important Question:

"Boy or girl?"

"She's a girl," the other mother smiled. "Hence the pink gloves."

"Oh," said my friend. Full stop. She turned back to me and picked up the conversation where she had left it.

Sonja Samia and the other little girl stared at each other fixedly for a long while, as children that age do, and then, as children that age do, Sonja Samia slid down the slide into my arms and the other little girl finished her cookie and toddled away.

Soon another little creature of my daughter's species staggered by, and Sonja Samia, at the top of the slide once again, fixed it in her gaze.

"It's a boy?" my friend asked the mother.

"Yes," the mother grinned, glancing at her little blue darling as the two babies stared each other down.

"Hey! Look at her!" my friend said of my daughter. "She's already got boys staring at her!"

"Sorry, he's already engaged," the mother proudly answered.

"They are babies," I said to my friend. "They are only babies!"

But it sounded like one hand clapping. No one even heard me speak. I never saw it fail: we could not be in the presence of a boy child without a match being made by some adult. The connotation, sometimes explicitly stated but most often implied, was that she would be lucky if she caught him.

Neither Sonja Samia nor the male infants could have cared less, of course. They were busy being babies. They drooled, fell down, stole cookies from each other, and poked each other's eyes, regardless of gender. It's the adults who were dreaming of lace and building porn castles in the sky.

It was not only my baby's encounters with *small* males that were sexualized by adults. They often sexualized her relationship with her father and desexualized her relationship with me.

When she was 11 months old, she took to crawling up to your face and putting her own face in it. She seemed to want to crawl down into your throat to see where the sound comes from. When she did this with me or with my female friends, everyone thought it was cute. When she did the same thing with her father, they called it French-kissing.

Once, her father was rolling around on the carpet with her, hugging and snuggling and giggling and laughing, and my friend whispered to me, "She's gonna have a powerful passion for men when she grows up."

"Why do you say that?" I asked.

"Just look at them!" she answered.

Days later, I was rolling around on the same carpet with her, hugging and snuggling and kissing and laughing. When I got up to go to the bathroom, she cried.

"She's crying for her mommy," my friends said.

They did not seem to think that she would have a powerful passion for women. At least it didn't occur to them to say so.

Her father and I cared for her equally. With the exception of breast-feeding, we did exactly the same things in the same way. We took her to day care and picked her up; we diapered her, fed her, put her to bed, played with her, snuggled her, and loved her. But when she cried for me, she was always seen as crying for her mommy, and when she cried for him, she was seen as wanting a man.

Children are erotic, so say psychologists, including feminist ones. The very *last* thing I would want to do would be to climb on a bandwagon of yet another emotional categorical imperative: women have been told too many times what we should feel, or what we do feel. So I will say only that I have experienced my daughter as very sensual, and so has her father. We are both absolutely clear, however, that we are her parents, her guardians, not her lovers.

But the world would not let him be simply her daddy. Traditional women saw miracles in his most ordinary fatherly behavior, such as when he bought socks for her. (*My* buying her socks was of course unremarkable, since I am her mother.) More modern women, those exposed to flashes of Freud and post-Freudian psychology, interpreted her father's relationship with her in quasi-romantic terms. In the eyes of the world he was either God the Father because he bought her socks, or Casanova because she loves him. He could not be simply Daddy. I, on the other hand, am merely her mother, no matter how she shows her love for me, and whether or not I buy her socks.

From the moment that we chose her name, in myriad microactions most of which are unconscious, we have been, willy-nilly, gendering our daughter. So has everyone else. (The men in my neighborhood will shadowbox with any apparently male toddler who staggers by, whether or not he is interested; they never shadowbox with female toddlers.) Yet many of the parents of boys of my acquaintance—even some feminist ones—are brand-new converts to biological determinism. Boys are more aggressive, they say. It's the testosterone. It explains so much.

So when my baby daughter tried to poke her finger in a new infant's eyes (to see how they work, I suppose), I would catch her hand and say, "No, not the eyes." When a little boy baby tried to do the same thing, his parent would catch his hand and say, "No, not the eyes," and then, more often than not, the parent would smile and say half-sheepishly, "Boys are so aggressive! No matter what I try to do . . ." But the smile was only half-sheepish because there was, I think, a thin streak of pleasure and relief. The little man had a little lion in him. The world was in order. Everything was normal.

Normal, the women's movement has shown us, is not good for women. When adults matched up my baby daughter with every passing male child, they devalued her and stereotyped her. Presumably it was only a joke. It was supposed to be cute. But it assumed that she was available and waiting, and it assumed that she would be indifferent to the specific character of the males who danced around her.

It also stereotyped sex. Adults endowed my daughter's encounters with any male creature who toddled by with a special emotional charge, as if to say, *This is important! It is about sex!* Adults regarded my baby daughter's encounters with other baby girls with inattention and indifference, even unto boredom, and in so doing they said, implicitly, "This is not important. They are only females. It is only about babies. It is not about sex."

And it is true: they *were* only babies. It was *not* about sex. But to recognize that only when the babies are of the same sex is to stereotype sex and to devalue the bonds among females. And the fact that women who are feminists also make these jokes about boys and not about girls does not lessen their effect in reinforcing sexism and compulsory heterosexuality.

These mating game stereotypes are profoundly reassuring to most people, as stereotypes always are to the people who apply them. They are perpetuated because whatever behavior fits the stereotype *fits* and whatever behavior does not fit is discarded. It becomes invisible, quickly forgotten. For if you are not the case that proves the rule, and you are not "the exception that proves the rule," then what will happen to the rule?

Better to believe—no matter how regretfully—that boys are naturally aggressive, and that every female longs for a male from when she is afloat in utero to the end of her life. So when boys act like Attila the Hun, adults nod their heads sadly and smile. They are smiling because they are relieved. Everything is in its place, in order. Better a stereotype of an oppressive order ("Boys are naturally aggressive"; "girls are easier to handle"; "every woman needs a man") than ambiguity, with its scent of unknown changes, its frightening possibilities.

How could I be so rude and ungrateful as to rail at my poor old neighbor's mating game? He was only expressing his culture—*our* culture—the harmless assumptions and gentle jokes of daily life. To criticize the mating game is to be a spoilsport, humorless, picky. To question it seems trivial, a petty violation of the normal.

I do not know what Sonja Samia will be when she is 20 years old, or 30, or 50. Will she be bisexual, lesbian, or straight, a feminist or a femme fatale?

She was, at 15 months, a very determined and self-determining little person. She would look around the room, decide what she wanted, purse her little mouth, and pursue it like a park hound stalking a squirrel. Her sureness of what she wanted and needed caused me some short-term exasperation but much long-term joy and deep-down pride. It's still the best thing about her. I aim to do everything I can to make sure that she keeps and deepens that sure sense of her own self. I am determined to encourage her to know herself as an interconnected social being, knowing and appreciating her own feelings, thoughts, and desires, whatever they may be.

As she tries to find her own path in life, however, she must pick her way through a minefield of other people's hungers, stereotypes, and fears. It is not a kid's game: it is a silent tyranny of daily life.

By the time Sonja Samia reached eight years old, her father and I had divorced. The mating game jokes among the adults have decreased temporarily, chiefly, I believe, because older girls and boys play separately. The business of rigging the mating game—and it is big business indeed—has shifted to the dreammaking machines: the idiot box and the video store.

There the Disney empire skillfully reaches through little girls' eyes, forming and fondling their fantasies. Beauty falls in love with the Beast (no matter how beastly he may be), the Little Mermaid has no female friends, and no one ever suggests that Sleeping Beauty might one day be awakened by a *princess*. That would be against all the rules. As a result, the third-grade girls now take up the mating game jokes on their own, teasing each other over who is most favored by the boys, no matter how lackluster those boys may be.

But, thankfully, theirs is also the post-Stonewall generation: Some of them have openly gay uncles or lesbian mothers. The heterosexist assumptions of the 1990s are nowhere near as suffocatingly absolute as the silence of the 1950s. There's no telling what kind of world these children, including Sonja Samia, will make when they are old enough to find their own way to love.

One Good Mother to Another

Minnie Bruce Pratt is a poet and author who lost custody of her children following a divorce because she is a lesbian. Her story illustrates the social control of meaning. What is a "good mother"? Who has the power to decide this? In Pratt's case, and for other lesbian mothers as well, a few powerful men in the judicial system were able to decide that a lesbian mother must be an unfit mother.

As You Read, Ask Yourself . . .

How are Pratt's love for and connection with her children expressed in her essay?
What were the costs to her, her family, and society of preventing her from caring for her children?
How do patriarchal social structures ensure that "heterosexuality as an institution and female subservience as a tradition" will be perpetuated?

In the *New York Times* photo, a young blonde woman sits staring, stunned. She holds up a large picture of her cherubic smiling little boy. At first this looks like a moment with which everyone sympathizes: a mother publicly grieving her child killed in a tragic accident or lost in a nightmare kidnapping. But in this photo, something jars slightly. There is no father next to the mother; her companion is a woman. The caption reads: "A Virginia court's decision to remove a child from his mother because of her lesbianism is stirring controversy. Sharon Bottoms, left, lost custody of her two-year-old son, Tyler Doustou, to her mother." At that moment, perhaps the reader's sympathy wanes or turns to animosity.

But I know her look. I've sat in that desolate place. I've had my children taken from my arms, and I've felt that my children were almost dead to me because I could not hold them or touch them.

I had two boys whom I saw emerge, bloody and beautiful, from my body. I nursed them at my breast. I bathed their perfect tiny bodies and changed their diapers. I spoonfed them babyfood spinach. I taught them how to tie their shoes. I rocked them through ear aches and bad dreams. I drove them to their first day in kindergarten.

Then, suddenly, when they were five and six, when I fell in love with another woman and left my marriage to live as a lesbian, the world looked at me and saw an unfit mother. Suddenly, my husband had legal grounds to take my children away from me and never let me see them again.

Like Bottoms, I was also a "somewhat immature and undisciplined, though loving, mother"—after all, we were both mothers at twenty-one, barely out of girlhood. Like Bottoms, I was an "irregular job holder"—finishing a Ph.D. in English literature. When I applied for teaching positions, the male interviewers would inquire, "How will you arrange child care? Are you planning to have more children? What will your husband do if we hire you?" And they never did.

But the standard for my being a "good mother" was not my parenting ability or financial stability. After all, my husband, a father at twenty-three and an unemployed graduate student, was no more mature in his role than I was in mine. No, I was considered a fit mother as long as I was married and loyal to the man who was my husband. As soon as I asserted my independence, as soon as I began a life in which I claimed the human right to form intimate social and sexual relations with whomever I chose, specifically with other women, I was seen to be a perverted, unnatural woman by my husband, my mother, the people of the town I lived in, and the legal system.

The letter from my husband's lawyer said he was seeking custody because of my "unorthodox ideas about the place of the father in the home"—my heresy consisted of disagreeing with the idea that men were superior to, and should govern, women.

Though more than fifteen years passed between my agony at losing my children and that of Sharon Bottoms, the issues remain the same. This is true despite the fact that I lost custody of my boys to my ex-husband, their biological father, while Sharon has, at least for now, lost her boy to her mother, the child's biological grandmother, who sued for custody. The reason for denying us our children was the same: simply because we were in lesbian relationships.

In the words of Judge Parsons, who ruled in Henrico County Circuit Court against Sharon: "The mother's conduct is illegal and immoral and renders her unfit to parent." Illegal because in Virginia (and more than twenty other states and the District of Columbia), sodomy—the "crime against nature" of lesbians and gay men—is still prohibited. And the 1987 U.S. Supreme Court, in *Bowers v. Hardwick*, actually stated in its majority opinion that it was maintaining the illegality of sodomy because that particular set of justices considered this kind of sex immoral, based on "traditional values."

Sharon Bottoms, as a lesbian in a committed relationship with another woman, is perceived as less fit to parent than her mother, whose live-in boyfriend for seventeen years was a man who, according to Sharon, sexually abused her twice a week during her teen years. Under the law and in the eyes of many people, Sharon's mother is more fit because she endorses heterosexuality as an institution and female subservience as a tradition, and presumably will pass these values along to her grandson. This arrangement is seen as being in the child's "best interests."

But should we not ask what kind of damage will be done to a boy if his sense of self depends on dominating another person? Should we not inquire about the immorality of teaching a child that love can only occur with state-sanctioned approval?

Much was made in the courtroom of the fact that Sharon's child calls her lover and partner "Dada." In most two-partner lesbian families, the children call one woman Mama or Mom or Mother, and the other woman some different maternal variation, or perhaps by her given name; often, these women lose custody of their children anyway. Certainly, Sharon could have been challenged for custody no matter what her child called April, Sharon's partner. But the word "Dada" evokes a truth about lesbian parenting that opponents violently condemn: Two women can raise children in a home together and challenge the very idea that gender roles, or gender expression, are irrevocably matched to biological gender.

Opponents of lesbian/gay parenting often present the "damage" to the child as a danger of him or her "becoming" gay. But this is only part of a larger fear that no matter what sexuality the child develops, the child might learn that rigid gender roles are not required. The child might learn the joy of possibility that comes when biological gender does not have to match socially mandated gender in jobs or thoughts or love.

Psychiatric specialists testified for Sharon by outlining studies that showed no noticeable difference between children reared in lesbian households and those reared in heterosexual ones. Nevertheless, Judge Parsons concurred with Sharon's mother that the child would be "mentally and physically harmed" by the lesbian relationship; he stated there was a strong possibility the boy would carry "an intolerable burden" for "the rest of his life."

Sharon can see her child on Mondays and Tuesdays but not in her own home, and not in the presence of her lover. By my divorce settlement ("And lucky to get it!" my lawyer said), I was forbidden to have the boys in my home if I shared the house with *any* person; I could take them out of their home state only if we went to be with my mother, whom my husband had threatened to call as a character witness for *him*.

To see my boys, sometimes I drove roundtrip on three-day weekends, fourteen hours nonstop there, fourteen hours nonstop back. The youngest boy wrote in his school journal how he wished he could be with me more; the oldest boy talked to me late at night, on long distance phone calls, about his depression, about how sometimes he just wanted to die.

I loved them, I called them, I saw them as much as I had time and money to do. We got through their baby years, pre-adolescence, and teens. When I finally asked the oldest, "What effect do you think my being a lesbian had on you?" he answered: "None. I think my personality was most shaped by not having you with me as a mother all those years, by having you taken away from me."

It is ironic that Sharon Bottoms's case was tried in Virginia, a state that enforced its law against racial intermarriage as late as 1967, until in *Loving v. Virginia* the U.S. Supreme Court finally declared unconstitutional all such laws. The determined political struggle of the African-American community, in the courts and in civil-rights battles in the streets, abolished a law that codified the prejudices of white Southerners.

When I fought for custody of my children in Fayetteville, North Carolina, as I struggled to live as a self-reliant woman, not dependent, not submissive, the tide of women's liberation was rising through the South. Women were beginning to challenge an economic system that uses the threat of competition between the sexes as a way to limit working people's wages, benefits, and job conditions.

Now, with cases like that of Sharon Bottoms, the gay and lesbian community is fighting to end other inhumane limits on how all of us can live and love. And now we have allies, like Sharon's ex-husband, Dennis Doustou, who asked to testify for her and who says, "Tyler means the world to her."

In 1976, when I went to a lawyer for help in my struggle for my children, he said to me, "This country is not ready for someone like you." Can we say now, in 1993, that we are ready for someone like Sharon Bottoms, just an ordinary woman, a part-time grocery clerk trying to raise a child on not enough money, but with the love and support of another woman who cares about both of them?

Let us declare, finally, that we are ready for this ordinary extraordinary woman who is saying to us, with her life, that to guarantee her right to be a lesbian and a mother is to take one more step toward liberation for *all* of us.

The Hard Part

The novel being dead, there is no point to writing made up stories. Look at the French who will not and the Americans who cannot. Look at me who ought not, if only because I exist entirely outside the usual human experience . . . outside and yet wholly relevant for I am the New Woman whose astonishing history is a poignant amalgam of vulgar dreams and knife-sharp realities (shall I ever be free of the dull lingering pain that is my peculiar glory, the price so joyously paid for being Myra Breckinridge, whom no man may possess except on her . . . my terms!).

—Gore Vidal, *MYRA BRECKINRIDGE*, 1974

Kate Bornstein, formerly a heterosexual male IBM salesperson, is now a lesbian play-wright, author, and performance artist. As a transgendered person, Bornstein uses her life story to question the idea that two sexes and two genders are natural. In these two excerpts from her book Gender Outlaw, *Bornstein shows how societal discomfort with transgendered people is used to force them into the male/female and masculine/feminine boxes. She urges us to develop more complex and subtle ways of thinking about sex and gender. For example, Bornstein informs us that when individuals make a sex change, they are told by professionals to revise their personal histories to present themselves as though they were always their present sex, and told not to associate with other trans-sexuals. How does this advice influence their view of themselves as well as the meaning of sex and gender?*

As You Read, Ask Yourself . . .

What is the difference between being labeled for what one is rather than for what one does?

Bornstein is opposed to the medicalization of the transgender condition. Why?

Television talk shows often treat transgendered people like freaks. Why are questions about the permanence of sex and gender so fascinating and so threatening?

The hard part was sorting it all out. The hard part was taking a good look at everyone else and the way they looked at the world, which was a lot different from the way *I* was looking at the world!

> *There are some transsexuals who agree with the way I look at the world, and quite a few who are really angry with me for writing this stuff. Every transsexual I know went through a gender transformation for different reasons, and there are as many truthful experiences of gender as there are people who think they have a gender.*

I know I'm not a man—about that much I'm very clear, and I've come to the conclusion that I'm probably not a woman either, at least not according to a lot of people's rules on this sort of thing. The trouble is, we're living in a world that insists we be one or the other—a world that doesn't bother to tell us exactly what one or the other *is*.

> *When I was a kid, everyone else seemed to know they were boys or girls or men or women. That's something I've never known; not then, not today. I never got to say to the grownups, "Hold on there—just what is it about me that makes you think I'm a little boy?" As a kid, I just figured I was the crazy one; I was the one who really had some serious defect.*

All my life, my non-traditional gender identity had been my biggest secret, my deepest shame. It's not that I didn't want to talk about this with someone; it's just that I never saw anything in the culture that encouraged me to talk about my feeling that I was the wrong gender. When I was growing up, people who lived cross-gendered lives were pressured into hiding deep within the darkest closets they could find. Those who came out of their closets were either studied under a microscope, ridiculed in the tabloids, or made exotic in the porn books, so it paid to hide. It paid to lie. That was probably the most painful part of it: the lying to friends and family and lovers, the pretending to be someone I wasn't. Going through a gender change is not the easiest thing in the world to do, but I went through it because I was so tired of all the lies and secrets.

> *It was a strange kind of lie. It was a lie by action—I was always acting out something that everyone assumed I was. I wonder what it would have been like if someone had come along and in a quite friendly manner had asked, "Well, young one, what do you think you are: a boy or a girl?" What would it have been like not to have been afraid of getting hit because of some wrong answer? See, "sex changes" never were an appropriate topic of conversation—not at the dining table, not in the locker room, not over a casual lunch in a crowded restaurant.*

Nowadays, I try to make it easier for people to ask questions. I tell people that I've never been hurt by an honest question, and that's true: it's a cruel opinion that hurts, not a question. But people still don't ask questions easily; maybe that has something to do with manners or etiquette. Folks seem to naturally back off from inquiring as to the nature of someone's—my—gender. It seems to need some special setting. Like in my living room, or on television, or from behind a podium at some university. It's "good manners" to say and ask nothing, and that's sad. But the children still ask.

> *Two days after my lover and I appeared on The Donahue Show, the five-year-old child of our next door neighbor came up to me and asked me, "So, are you a boy or a girl?" We'd been living next door to these folks for over two years.*
>
> *"I'm a girl who used to be a boy," I replied. She was delighted with that answer and told me I'd looked very pretty on television. I thanked her and we smiled at each other and went about our days. I love it that kids will just ask.*

Adults don't ask. Adults are afraid to ask, "What *are* you?" so we ask "What do you *do*?" . . . in hopes of getting a clue to someone's identity—gender identity seems to be an unspeakable thing in our culture, just as names are considered unspeakable in some other cultures. By the same token, we hardly ever ask outright "What kind of sex do you like?" When it comes to work, we can ask. When it comes to sex and gender, we're supposed to observe discreetly and draw our own conclusions.

Instead of asking directly, adults look in roundabout ways for answers to their questions about me and my people. Like reading transsexual and transvestite pornography which, judging by much of its content, must be written by people who have never met one of us, but who have certainly fantasized about us.

> *There's this entire wonderful underground genre of erotica. You may have seen some of the titles, they're terrific, like **He's Her Sister!** (Get it?) or **Transvestite Marriage** or **Transvestite Trap.** My personal favorites were **Captive in Lace,** and **They Made Him Love It!***

Reading those stories came in handy when I was doing phone sex for a living, because a lot of the men calling in wanted to be cross-dressed as women, or they wanted to know what it would be like to be a woman and have sex with another woman—guys want to know that sort of thing. They want to know, "what do lesbians *do* with one another." It's a sad question really: it shows how little thought they give to exactly what pleases a woman.

> *There's another whole group of people who really **like** gender ambiguity, it turns them on. I remember a group of sailors in the audience on **The Geraldo Show.** After it was announced who and what I was, they kept on looking at me, they kept on wanting something. I could*

feel their eyes traveling up and down my surgically-constructed, hormonally-enhanced woman's body. What's the pull? What is it about a sexually-blended, gender-bended body that lights those flames? I know it gets me going!

For the most part, people cautiously observe and don't ask questions, and there are plenty of opportunities in today's world to look at people like me. The talk show ratings go way up during sweeps month when they trot out the transsexuals and the cross-dressers. Then there are the drag shows and the female impersonator spectacles—even though we began them for our own entertainment and enjoyment, their widespread popularity seems to grow and grow; you've probably got one of those shows in your city, or in a nearby town. Comedy skits, like "It's Pat" (a skit based on a person whose gender is not clear) on *Saturday Night Live* are real popular. I'll have more to say about that later.

If I look past the ghettos of the drag bars and standup joints, both popular music and cinema reflect my transsexual face back to me. Glance discreetly, if you will, at some of the brightest deities in our cultural heavens. At this writing, some friends of mine are truly interested in seeing if Michael Jackson (all his other issues aside) will actually become Diana Ross. I've heard bets being placed on the gender of some of Madonna's lovers in some of her videos. And what really made *The Crying Game* the smash hit that it was? It's interesting that we can ask questions about transgender issues when there's some distance between us and the person we're asking about—we just don't ask directly.

There's a lot of writing about gender now. I keep reading the magazine articles, the newspaper columns, and the text books, pre- and post-modern. I read, watch, and listen to all the ads and commercials. You can learn a lot about gender from those commercials. I've also been watching the talk shows, listening to the call-in programs, and browsing the electronic bulletin boards. When I was very young, growing up in the 50s, I read the medical texts, devoured the tabloids, and hoarded the pornography—because I was intensely interested in me and my people. I was scared, though, shaking scared, to see what I might actually find out. But I couldn't stop reading.

See, I was a lonely, frightened little fat kid who felt there was something deeply wrong with me because I didn't feel like I was the gender I'd been assigned. I felt there was something wrong with me, something sick and twisted inside me, something very very bad about me. And everything I read backed that up.

The possibility missed by most of the texts prior to the last few years, and by virtually all the various popular media, is this: the culture may not simply be creating roles for naturally-gendered people, the culture may in fact be *creating* the gendered people. In other words, the culture may be creating gender. No one had ever hinted at that, and so, standing outside a "natural" gender, I thought I was some monster, and that it was all my fault.

In living along the borders of the gender frontier, I've come to see the gender system created by this culture as a particularly malevolent and divisive construct, made all the more dangerous by the seeming inability of the culture to *question* gender, its own creation. The studies conducted by the duly-appointed representatives of the culture were still done on the basis of observation, not conversation. I want this book to begin to reverse that trend. I want this book to be the conversation I always wanted as I was growing up, and never had the chance to have.

The time for discreet and distant observation of transgendered lives seems to be coming to an end. There's more and more evidence that transgendered folks are making a place for themselves in the culture. I'm writing this book, for example, and it's getting published because there's been a shift. Up until the last few years, all we'd be able to write *and get published* were our autobiographies, tales of women trapped in the bodies of men or men pining away in the bodies of women. Stories by and about brave people who'd lived their lives hiding deep within a false gender—and who, after much soul-searching, decided to change their gender, and spent the rest of their days hiding deep within *another* false gender. That's what we could get published about ourselves—the romantic stuff which set in stone our image as long-suffering, not the challenging stuff. And it always seemed that the people who would write *about* us either had some ax to grind or point to prove, or they'd been hurt and needed someone to blame it on. People like Janice Raymond, Catherine Millot, and Robert Stoller have ultimately perpetuated the myth that transgendered people are malevolent, mentally ill, or monsters. We got left holding the cultural bag. We ended up wearing the cultural hand-me-downs.

But there's another kind of trans(gressive)gender experience going on in this culture, and nowadays we're writing our own chronicles of these times. Our stories all tie together, our stories overlap; and you can hear lots about me in the stories of other transgendered people. My story weaves through Caroline Cossey's story. My story lies within the story of late historian Louis Sullivan. Christine Jorgensen and Renee Richards wrote chapters of my story in their autobiographies. Sandy Stone teaches her story, my story, our story in any number of her classes. Rachel Pollack paints it into her tarot cards. Christine Beatty belts it out in heavy metal and whispers it in her poetry. Melanie Phillips makes it available in on-line cyberspace. Leslie Feinberg travels back and forth across the country to make our story heard in the political arena. Loren Cameron captures it in his black-and-white stills. Kristienne Clarke brings us into her made-for-television films. David Harrison performs our story live on stage, Wednesdays through Sundays. We're all of us speaking in our own transgendered voice these days: editor and publisher JoAnn Roberts, essayist and fiction writer James Green, activist and writer Susan Stryker, publishers Dallas Denny and Davina Anne Gabriel, poet Rikki Ann Wilchins, poet and essayist Max Valerio, publisher Marissa Sheryl Lynn, playwright and composer Omewenne Grimstone, performance artist Celie Edwards—the list keeps growing. We're talking to each other in meeting rooms, through newsletters and journals, and on electronic bulletin boards. It's an exciting time, here at the beginning of a movement. It's a time when we've begun to put down the cultural baggage. We've begun sewing sequins onto our cultural hand-me-downs.

My voice on this subject is not representative of
all transgendered people. But when a minority
group has been silent for as long as we have, as
disjointed as we have been, the tendency is for
those in the majority to listen to the loud ones
when they first speak up; and to believe that we
speak for the entire group. More important than
my point of view, than any single point of view
however, is that people begin to question gender.

The voices of transgendered people are now being raised in concert with the voices of more and more people who are writing their work based on what we have to say. Suzanne Kessler, Wendy McKenna, Marjorie Garber, Jennie Livingston, Judith Butler, Wendy Chapkis, Anne Bolin, Walter Williams, Holly Devor, Pat Califia, and Shannon Bell are all asking great questions and making room for us to respond.

I've taken as much care as I could to encourage questions in this book, especially questions about my conclusions. I hope that soon after this book is published I'll have some more questions. Questions are the hard part.

Which Outlaws?

or, Who Was That Masked Man?

On the day of my birth, my grandparents gave
me a television set. In 1948, this was a new and
wonderful thing. It had a nine-inch screen em-
bedded in a cherrywood case the size of my
mother's large oven.

My parents gave over an entire room to
the television set. It was "the television room."

I've tried to figure out which questions get to the core of transgender issues—the answer to the riddle of my oddly-gendered life would probably be found in the area we question the least, and there are many areas of gender we do not question. We talk casually, for example, about *trans*-gender without ever clearly stating, and rarely if ever asking, what one gender or the other really is. We're so sure of our ability to categorize people as either men or women that we neglect to ask ourselves some very basic questions: what is a man? and what is a woman? and why do we need to be one or the other?

If we ask by what criteria a person might classify someone as being either male
or female, the answers appear to be so self-evident as to make the question triv-
ial. But consider a list of items that differentiate females from males. There are
none that always and without exception are true of only one gender.
                                        —Kessler and McKenna,
                            Gender: An Ethnomethodological Approach, 1976

Most folks would define a man by the presence of a penis or some form of a penis. Some would define a woman by the presence of a vagina or some form of a vagina. It's not that simple, though. I know several women in San Francisco who have penises. Many wonderful men in my life have vaginas. And there are quite a few people whose genitals fall somewhere between penises and vaginas. What are *they*?

Are you a man because you have an *XY* chromosome? A woman because you have *XX*? Unless you're an athlete who's been challenged in the area of gender representation, you probably haven't had a chromosome test to determine your gender. If you haven't had that test, then how do you know what gender you are, and how do you know what gender your romantic or sexual partner is? There are, in addition to the *XX* and *XY* pairs, some other commonly-occurring sets of gender chromosomes, including *XXY, XXX, YYY, XYY,* and *XO*. Does this mean there are more than two genders?

Let's keep looking. What makes a man—testosterone? What makes a woman—estrogen? If so, you could buy your gender over the counter at any pharmacy. But we're taught that there are these things called "male" and "female" hormones; and that testosterone dominates the gender hormone balance in the males of any species. Not really—female hyenas, for example, have naturally more testosterone than the males; the female clitoris resembles a very long penis—the females mount the males from the rear, and proceed to hump. While some female humans I know behave in much the same manner as the female hyena, the example demonstrates that the universal key to gender is not hormones.

Are you a woman because you can bear children? Because you bleed every month? Many women are born without this potential, and every woman ceases to possess that capability after menopause—do these women cease being women? Does a necessary hysterectomy equal a gender change?

Are you a man because you can father children? What if your sperm count is too low? What if you were exposed to nuclear radiation and were rendered sterile? Are you then a woman?

Are you a woman because your birth certificate says female? A man because your birth certificate says male? If so, how did *that* happen? A doctor looked down at your crotch at birth. A doctor decided, based on what was showing of your external genitals, that you would be one gender or another. You never had a say in that most irreversible of all pronouncements—and according to this culture as it stands today, you never *will* have a say. What if you had been born a hermaphrodite, with some combination of both genitals? A surgeon would have "fixed" you—without your consent, and possibly without the consent or even knowledge of your parents, depending on your race and economic status. You would have been fixed—fixed into a gender. It's a fairly common experience being born with different or anomalous genitals, but we don't allow hermaphrodites in modern Western medicine. We "fix" them.

But let's get back to that birth certificate. Are you female or male because of what the law says? Is law immutable? Aren't we legislating every day in order to change the laws of our state, our nation, our culture? Isn't that the name of the game when it comes to political progress? What about other laws—religious laws, for example. Religions may dictate right and proper behavior for men and women, but no religion actually lays out what is a man and what is a woman. They assume we know, that's how deep this cultural assumption runs.

I've been searching all my life for a rock-bottom definition of woman, an unquestionable sense of what is a man. I've found nothing except the fickle definitions of gender held up by groups and individuals for their own purposes.

> *Every day I watched it, that television told me what was a man and what was a woman.*
>
> *And every day I watched it, that television told me what to buy in order to be a woman.*
>
> *And everything I bought, I said to myself I am a real woman, and I never once admitted that I was transsexual. You could say I'm one inevitability of a post-modern anti-spiritualist acquisitive culture.*

A QUESTION OF PRIORITIES

I haven't found any answers. I ask every day of my life what is a man and what is a woman, and those questions beg the next: why? Why do we have to be one or the other? Why do we have to be gendered creatures at all? What keeps the bi-polar gender system in place?

I started out thinking that a theory of gender would bridge the long-standing gap between the two major genders, male and female. I'm no longer trying to do that. Some people think I want a world without gender, something bland and colorless: that's so far from how I live! I love playing with genders, and I love watching other people play with all the shades and flavors that gender can come in. I just want to question what we've been holding on to for such an awfully long time. I want to question the existence of gender, and I want to enter that question firmly into the fabric of this culture.

> *I used to watch **The Lone Ranger** on television. I loved that show. This masked guy rides into town on a white horse, does all these great and heroic deeds, everyone falls in love with him and then he leaves. He never takes off his mask, no one ever sees his face. He leaves behind a silver bullet and the memory of someone who can do no wrong. No bad rumors, no feet of clay, no cellulite. What a life! There's a self-help book in there somewhere. **Who Was That Masked Man? Learning to Overcome the Lone Ranger Syndrome.***

As I moved through the '50s and '60s, I bought into the fear and hatred that marks this culture's attitude toward the genderless and the nontraditionally gendered. People are genuinely afraid of being without a gender. I've been chewing on that fear nearly all my life like it was some old bone, and now I want to take that fear apart to see what makes it tick. Nothing in the culture has encouraged me to stay and confront that fear. Instead, the culture has kept pointing me toward one door or the other:

Girls or Boys
Men or Women
Ladies or Gentlemen
Cats or Chicks
Faggots or Dykes

I knew from age four on, that something was wrong with me being a guy, and I spent most of my life avoiding the issue of my transsexuality. I hid out in textbooks, pulp fiction, and drugs and alcohol. I numbed my mind with everything from peyote to Scientology. I buried my head in the sands of television, college, a lot of lovers, and three marriages. Because I was being raised as a male, I never got to experience what it meant to be raised female in this culture. All I had were my observations, and all I could observe and assimilate as a child were differences in clothing and manners. I remember building a catalogue of gestures, phrases, body language, and outfits in my head. I would practice all of these at night when my parents had gone to sleep. I'd wear a blanket as a dress, and I'd stand in front of my mirror being my latest crush at school—I was so ashamed of myself for that.

I was obsessed, and like most obsessed people, I was the last one to know it. The culture itself is obsessed with gender—and true to form, the culture as a whole will be the last to find out how obsessed it really has been.

WHY WE HAVEN'T ASKED QUESTIONS

I know there must have been other kids—boys and girls—going through the same remorse-filled hell that held me prisoner in front of my bedroom mirror, but we had no way of knowing that: there was no language for what we were doing. Instead, cardboard cut-out versions of us were creeping into the arts and media: in poetry, drama, dance, music, sculpture, paintings, television, cinema—in just about any art form you can think of there have been portrayals of people who are ambiguously or differently-gendered, all drawn by people who were not us, all spoken in voices that were not ours.

Dominant cultures tend to colonize and control minorities through stereotyping—it's no different with the trans-gender minority. Make us a joke and there's no risk of our anger, no fear we'll raise some unified voice in protest because we're not organized. But that's changing.

We never did fit into the cultural binary of male/female, man/woman, boy/girl. No, we are the clowns, the sex objects, or the mysteriously unattainable in any number of novels. We are the psychotics, the murderers, or the criminal geniuses who populate the movies. Audiences have rarely seen the real faces of the transgendered. They don't hear our voices, rarely read our words. For too many years, we transgendered people have been playing a hiding game, appearing in town one day, wearing a mask, and leaving when discovery was imminent. We would never tell anyone who we were, and so we were never really able to find one another. That's just now beginning to change.

> *See, when we walk into a restaurant and we see another transsexual person, we look the other way, we pretend we don't exist. There's no sly smile, no secret wink, signal, or handshake. Not yet. We still quake in solitude at the prospect of recognition, even if that solitude is in the company of our own kind.*

Silence = Death
—ACT-UP SLOGAN

SILENCE OF THE MEEK-AS-LAMBS

Simply saying "Come out, come out, wherever you are," is not going to bring the multitudes of transgendered people out into the open. Before saying that coming out is an option (and I believe it's an inevitable step, one we're all going to have to take at some time), it's necessary to get transgendered people talking with one another. The first step in coming out in the world is to come out to our own kind.

Before I dealt with my gender change, I had gold card membership in the dominant culture. To all appearances, I was a straight, white, able-bodied, middle-class male. I fought so hard against being transsexual because I heard all the teasing and jokes in the locker rooms. I saw people shudder or giggle when they'd talk about Renee Richards or Christine Jorgensen. I was all too aware of the disgust people were going through when *Playboy* published its interview with Wendy Carlos. I watched Caroline Cossey (Tula) get dragged through the mud of the press on two continents. The lesson was there time after time. Of course we were silent.

> *In the summer of 1969, I drove across Canada and the United States, living out of my Volkswagen station wagon that I'd named Mad John after my acting teacher. I was a hippie boy, hair down past my shoulders and dressed very colorfully: beads, headband, bellbottoms. I pulled into a state park in South Dakota to camp for the night. Some good ol' boys came up to my*

campsite and began the usual "Hey, girl" comments. I ignored them, and they eventually went away. Later that night, I woke up in my sleeping bag with a hand on my chest and a knife in front of my face. "Maybe we wanna fuck you, girl," is what this guy said. He brought the knife down to my face—I could feel how cold and sharp it was. "Maybe you oughta get outa here before we fuck you and beat the shit outa you." Then I was alone in the dark with only the sound of the wind in the trees. I packed up camp and left.

The following summer, I traveled across country again, this time in a VW mini-bus, but I stuck to more populated areas: I'd learned. Too many transgendered people don't get off that easy.

WHAT A TANGLED WEB WE WEAVE . . .

A less visible reason for the silence of the transgendered hinges on the fact that transsexuality in this culture is considered an illness, and an illness that can only be cured by silence.

Here's how this one works: we're taught that we are literally sick, that we have an illness that can be diagnosed and maybe cured. As a result of the medicalization of our condition, transsexuals must see therapists in order to receive the medical seal of approval required to proceed with any gender reassignment surgery. Now, once we get to the doctor, we're told we'll be cured if we become members of one gender or another. We're told not to divulge our transsexual status, except in select cases requiring intimacy. Isn't that amazing? Transsexuals presenting themselves for therapy in this culture are channeled through a system which labels them as having a disease (transsexuality) for which the therapy is to lie, hide, or otherwise remain silent.

*I was told by several counselors and a number of transgendered peers that I would need to invent a past for myself as a little girl, that I'd have to make up incidents of my girl childhood; that I'd have to say things like "When I was a little girl. . . ." I never was a little girl; I'd lied all my life to be the boy, the man that I'd known myself **not** to be. Here I was, taking a giant step toward personal integrity by entering therapy with the truth and self-acknowledgment that I was a transsexual, and I was told, "Don't **tell** anyone you're transsexual."*

Transsexuality is the only condition for which the therapy is to lie. This therapeutic lie is one reason we haven't been saying too much about ourselves and our lives and our experience of gender; we're not allowed, in therapy, the right to think of ourselves as transsexual.

> *This was where a different kind of therapy might have helped me. Perhaps if I hadn't spent so much time thinking and talking about being a woman, and perhaps if the psychiatrist who examined me had spent less time focusing on those aspects of my life which could never be changed by surgery, I would have had more opportunity to think about myself as a transsexual. It was exposure to the press that forced me to talk about my transsexuality, and it was a painful way to have to learn to do so.*
>
> —Caroline Cossey, MY STORY, 1992

Another reason for the silence of transsexuals is the mythology of the transgender subculture. Two or more transsexuals together, goes the myth, can be read more easily *as* transsexual—so they don't pass. I don't think that's it.

> *I think transsexuals keep away from each other because we threaten the hell out of one another.*

Each of us, transsexual and non-transsexual, develop a view of the world as we grow up—a view that validates our existence, gives us a reason for being, a justification for the nuttinesses that each of us might have. Most non-transsexuals have cultural norms on which to pin their world view, broadcast by magazines, television, cinema, electronic bulletin boards, and the continually growing list of communications environments.

Since transsexuals in this culture are neither fairly nor accurately represented in the media, nor championed by a community, we develop our world views in solitude. Alone, we figure out why we're in the world the way we are. The literature to date on the transgender experience does not help us to establish a truly transgender world view in concert with other transgender people, because virtually all the books and theories about gender and transsexuality to date have been written by non-transsexuals who, no matter how well-intentioned, are each trying to figure out how to make us fit into *their* world view. Transgendered people learn to explain gender to themselves from a very early age.

> *When I was ten or eleven years old, I used to play alone in the basement, way back in the corner where no one would come along to disturb me. There was an old chair there to which I attached all manner of wires and boxes and dials: it was my gender-change machine. I would sit in that chair and twist the dials, and—presto—I was off on an adventure in my mind as a little girl, usually some budding dykelet like Nancy Drew or Pippi Longstocking.*

Most transsexuals opt for the theory that there are men and women and no in-between ground: the agreed-upon gender system. That's what I did—I just knew I had to be one or the other—so, in my world view, I saw myself as a mistake: some-*thing* that needed to be fixed and then placed neatly into one of the categories.

> *There are some wonderfully subtle differences in the world views developed by individual transsexuals. Talk to a few transgendered people and see how beautifully textured the normally drab concept of gender can become.*

We bring our very personal explanations for our existence into contact with other transsexuals who have been spending *their* lives constructing their *own* reasons for existence. If, when we meet, our world views differ radically enough, we wind up threatening each other's basic understanding of the world—we threaten each other. So we'd rather not meet, we'd rather not talk. At this writing, that's starting to change. Transsexuals and other transgendered people are finally sitting down, taking stock, comparing notes—and it's the dominant culture that's coming up short. Some of us are beginning to actually like ourselves and each other for the blend we are. Many of us are beginning to express our discontent with a culture that wants us silent.

> *This Western culture of ours tends to sacrifice the full range of experience to a lower common denominator that's acceptable to more people; we end up with McDonald's instead of real food, Holiday Inns instead of homes, and* **USA Today** *instead of news and cultural analysis. And we do that with the rest of our lives.*
>
> *Our spirits are full of possibilities, yet we tie ourselves down to socially-prescribed names and categories so we're acceptable to more people. We take on identities that no one has to think about, and that's probably how we become and why we remain men and women.*

The first step in liberating ourselves from this meek-as-lambs culturally-imposed silence is for transgendered people to begin talking with each other, asking each other sincere questions, and listening intently.

MYTHS AND MYTH-CONCEPTIONS

A transgender subculture is at this writing developing, and it's subsequently giving rise to new folk tales and traditions of gender fluidity and ambiguity. For example:

> ≫ *We are the chosen people.*

> *This is the point of view of many groups, and is not the sole property of the transgendered. This point of view makes me nervous, and I usually*

disassociate myself from any group whose members proclaim some unique kinship to, or favored station with, some higher power.

≫ *We are normal men and women.*

Is there such a thing as a normal man or woman? I have this idea that there are only people who are fluidly-gendered, and that the norm is that most of these people continually struggle to maintain the illusion that they are one gender or another. So if someone goes through a gender change and then struggles to maintain a (new) rigid gender, I guess that does make them normal. That's the only way I can see the grounding to this myth.

≫ *We are better men or women than men born men or women born women, because we had to work at it.*

I don't know about this one—I think everyone has to work at being a man or a woman. Transgendered people are probably more aware of doing the work, that's all. The concept of some nebulously "better" class of people is not an idea of love and inclusion, but an idea of oppression.

≫ *We have an incurable disease.*

No, we don't.

≫ *We are trapped in the wrong body.*

I understand that many people may explain their preoperative transgendered lives in this way, but I'll bet that it's more likely an unfortunate metaphor that conveniently conforms to cultural expectations, rather than an honest reflection of our transgendered feelings. As a people, we're short on metaphors, any metaphors, and when we find one that people understand, we stop looking. It's time for transgendered people to look for new metaphors—new ways of communicating our lives to people who are traditionally gendered.

≫ *We are the most put-upon of people.*

I think this statement is sadly arrogant, and an admission of social ignorance. I heard this myth from a preoperative white, middle-class, male-to-female transsexual who is a medical doctor. I guess she hadn't heard too much about teenage African-American mothers on crack, or some other more "put-upon" people. Transsexuals get a lot of grief from nearly every level of this hierarchical culture, it's true, but it's important to maintain some perspective.

≫ *That there is a transgender community.*

Someone asked me if the transgendered community is like the lesbian/gay communities. I said no, because the lesbian/gay communities are based on who one relates to, whereas the transgendered experience is different: it's about identity—relating to oneself. It's more an inward thing. When you have people together with **those** *issues, the group dynamic is inherently very different.*
—David Harrison, IN CONVERSATION WITH THE AUTHOR, 1993

We're at the beginning stages of a transgender community, but, at this writing, there are still only small groups of people who live out different aspects of gender. I'm extremely interested in seeing what develops, taking into account Harrison's analogy of personal and group dynamics. Just now, pockets of resistance to social oppression are forming, most often in conjunction with various gay and lesbian communities.

I *have* found an underground of male-to-female gender outlaws which already has its own unspoken hierarchy, definable from whatever shoes you happen to be standing in—high heels or Reeboks.

> **Post-operative transsexuals** *(those transsexuals who've had genital surgery and live fully in the role of another gender) look down on:*
> **Pre-operative transsexuals** *(those who are living full or part time in another gender, but who've not yet had their genital surgery) who in turn look down on:*
> **Transgenders** *(people living in another gender identity, but who have little or no intention of having genital surgery) who can't abide:*
> **She-Males** *(a she-male friend of mine described herself as "tits, big hair, lots of makeup, and a dick") who snub the:*
> **Drag Queens** *(gay men who on occasion dress in varying parodies of women) who laugh about the:*
> **Out Transvestites** *(usually heterosexual men who dress as they think women dress, and who are out in the open about doing that) who pity the:*
> **Closet Cases** *(transvestites who hide their cross-dressing) who mock the post-op transsexuals.*

The female-to-male groups, as well as some working-class transgender clubs that I've been associated with, seem to be more inclusive in their membership and attendance requirements than the mostly middle-class, mostly white examples cited above, and they're also less hierarchical in both club procedure and ways of relating to one another. Very few groups exist, however, that encompass the full rainbow that is gender outlawism, and sadly, groups still divide along the lines of male-to-female and female-to-male gender outlaws.

We are all longing to go home to some place we have never been—a place, half-remembered, and half-envisioned we can only catch glimpses of from time to time. Community. Somewhere, there are people to whom we can speak with passion without having the words catch in our throats. Somewhere a circle of hands will open to receive us, eyes will light up as we enter, voices will celebrate with us whenever we come into our own power. Community means strength that joins our strength to do the work that needs to be done. Arms to hold us when we falter. A circle of healing. A circle of friends. Someplace where we can be free.

—STARHAWK, Dreaming the Dark: Magic, Sex, and Politics, 1982

*I'd like to be a member of a community some day. One of the reasons I didn't go through with my gender change for such a long time was the certain knowledge that I would be an outsider. All the categories of transgender find a common ground in that they each break one or more of the rules of gender: what we have in common is that we are gender outlaws, every one of us. To attempt to divide us into rigid categories ("You're a transvestite, and **you're** a drag queen, and **you're** a she-male, and on and on and on) is like trying to apply the laws of solids to the state of fluids: it's our fluidity that keeps us in touch with each other. It's our fluidity and the principles that attend that constant state of flux that could create an innovative and inclusive transgender community.*

I really *would* like to be a member of a community, but until there's one that's based on the principle of constant change, the membership would involve more rules, and the rules that exist around the subject of gender are not rules I want to obey.

Virtual Identity

In everyday interactions with other people, most of us would be quite uncomfortable if we were unable to tell whether we were talking with a woman or a man. Every society prescribes ways of accentuating female/male differences so that its members do not have to deal with such ambiguity very often. Means for marking gender include clothing, voice tone, speech style, hair style, body ornaments, posture, and movement. But none of these social cues is available in the new frontier of cyberspace. Instead, cyberspace environments such as MUD rooms allow people to act out any identities they want, including gay, straight, bi, female, and male. Often, it is impossible to tell whether another player is "really" what they claim to be. Indeed, when a person has many cyberspace identities, which—if any—is the "real" self?

Mocha Jean Herrup asks us to accept the ambiguities of sex and gender that are revealed in cyberspace. Herrup says that liberation is not a matter of tolerating sexual differences, but of "challenging the very forces that categorize sexuality in the first place."

As You Read, Ask Yourself . . .

If you have taken on new identities in cyberspace, how has this affected your core identity? If you have not done this, what identities would you like to try?

Some have warned that cyberspace game-playing provides easy opportunities for deceiving others. Is Herrup concerned about this?

If identity is always ambiguous and changeable, how can groups of oppressed people unite for social change?

When I came out as a lesbian at nineteen, I wasn't looking for an ambiguous support group. Filled with self-hatred and revulsion, what I really needed, sadly, was to feel normal. I needed to believe that being a lesbian was okay, and I got that affirmation not by thinking about my sexuality as anything uncertain, unstable, or ambiguous, but by thinking about my sexuality as a fixed identity with a community of people "just like me" included in the deal. I soon became an activist—joined ACTUP, then Queer Nation, and pursued an active social life. I learned to dance from a gay boy, got to "know" the women's community, and for the first time that I can remember, I enjoyed being a girl. I had an identity, and with that, a social life and a cause—the key to my power and pleasure. After years of not even being able to say the word *lesbian*, I learned to love my label.

And then things got a little queer. My lesbian identity didn't always make sense. I mean, how could I call myself a lesbian when the woman I once had a crush on continued to make my knees wobble when she turned up later as a man. Or what did it mean when my lover stroked my hair, told me I was such a good boy, and let me suck her cock? Equating my identity with my sexuality, despite all the political power and social support it brought, presented a problem when my fixed "lesbian" sexuality no longer seemed to exist. I mean, what kind of power and pleasure come from an ambiguous identity?

I started to realize that sexual liberation isn't a simple matter of asserting that a particular sexuality is okay. Liberation has to do with challenging the very forces that categorize sexuality in the first place. That is why in the last year or so I have moved from identity politics to a new domain of ambiguity. "Accept the ambiguities" has become my personal mantra. I repeat these words not to invoke their action, but to cast their spell and release the magic that comes from engagement with uncertainty.

My current desire to embrace ambiguity has a lot to do with my recent immersion in new technology. What began as an attempt to dial into an on-line women's activist network has brought an entirely new texture to my daily life. Now, I am wired. My most intimate community is an electronic one; every day I speak passionately with friends and colleagues I have never seen. I live and work—form friendships, send love letters, exchange research—in cyberspace. For me, the on-line world has become anything but virtual.

In cyberspace, a realm in which the body is not physically present, where confirmable identity markers such as anatomy and skin color are no longer visible, the fluidity of identity is thrown into high relief. Though it is possible to think about identity in this way in what we call "real life," it was in cyberspace that *I* discovered an on-line sexuality that questioned my "predilections" and asked me to rethink my identity. In this world of keystroke come-ons and ergonomically induced orgasm, I found a place to appreciate my own ambiguity.

In cyberspace, simulated environments called MUDs and MOOs provide a unique sphere for interactive communication, role-playing scenarios, and the joys of cybersex. MUDs (or Multi-User Dungeons) and MOOs (Multi-User Dungeons, Object-Oriented) can best be described as text-based role-playing games. The acronyms are really a misnomer, though, as many MUDs don't involve dungeons at all and have nothing to do with killing or winning. Rather, they are social spaces in which participants may contribute to the community by programming the database to include objects of their own design.

The two most important commands on any MUD are "say" and "emote." When you type "say," followed by the text of your speech, all participants in the "room" you are in read your words on their screens. The "emote" command works in the same way, only you type what it is you want to do. So if I am logged into a MOO as Mojo and I type "say let's head over toward that cottage" followed by "emote winks suggestively," this is what appears on people's screens:

Mojo says let's head over toward that cottage.
Mojo winks suggestively.

At which time, another player could type in a response, which might look something like this:

Paks notices the cottage in the distance and grins knowingly.

Once inside the cottage, Paks and I begin to act upon the desires we have expressed for each other. I kiss her hand, gently, and glide up her arm. With the stroke of a key, she strips slowly and seductively. As battle cries and paging requests methodically appear on screen, Paks and I roll around on the four-poster bed that appears out of mutual consent. My body gives in to this interactive, text-based arousal, and it is all I can do to keep my fingers on the keyboard. Paks unzips her pants; my tongue meets her breasts. When we finally sign off, I am astounded by the "aftersex glow" that meets me in the bathroom mirror.

In this text-based realm, participants must write the self. No longer a matter of physical attributes, identity is made intelligible through the art of self-performance. And "self" in this realm is anything but fixed; it is as multiple as the imagination, unstable and infinitely "morphable." A simple "change description" command puts identity reconfiguration at your fingertips.

To doubt the intensity of experience on a MUD is simply not to have ever been on one. I recall one of my early MUD experiences when I happened across a participant named Trance. Trance was hanging out on the Terrain of Postmodernism and I decided to teleport there directly. We struck up a conversation, "So how's the weather here on the terrain?" and shortly thereafter, teleported to Trance's own corner of the MUD, a replica of California's Bay Area.

Upon arrival, Trance and I were presented with several directional choices. I chose to go north, up to the Berkeley Hills. I may have been sitting in my shabby New York City apartment at the time, but that night I was consciously in California. It felt so nice to be outside on a cool, autumn evening, listening to Trance tell me all about growing up in Berkeley. Things were very lucid. I became chilled and hugged my sweatshirt tightly, glad that I had remembered to bring it along. Trance shivered, too, and I moved closer to this strangely familiar figure sitting next to me.

On another occasion, a friend and I decide to stretch our sexual imaginations. Both of us share a certain fascination with gay men, a curiosity I have found to occur among more and more lesbians that I know. We want to experience gay male sex, and set off for a MUD to do so. Logging on as Jamie and Mr. Benson, we travel around on another MUD, donning leather, chains, and a dog collar for me. My description reads:

A small, frail boy whose unbuttoned shirt reveals a shiny chest. His moves are tentative, and he coughs slightly as you gaze at him.

I enjoy being a helpless boy being led around by an older, stronger, demanding master. When I first log on to this unfamiliar MUD, greetings and directions buzz across my screen, causing an alphabet of chaos. I attempt to find Mr. Benson but keep getting lost in empty rooms with no obvious exits. I send out a page command. It works and I receive a message from Mr. Benson telling me that he is on his way to get his boy. I feel safe, about to be rescued from my confusion. Our cybersexplay, which takes place in an old woodshed, is an exploration of newfound needs and desires engendered by our gay male personas. The sex is about blow-jobs, erections, anal stimulation, none of which have ever been a part of my sex life before. Such acts either hadn't occurred to me or weren't anatomically conducive. But in cyberspace, I really feel like a gay man: the desire is "instinctual," the performance "natural."

My cybersex encounters aren't always an extension of a real-life erotic encounter, nor do they always fit into a gay or lesbian sensibility. When I meet Trance again (whose "real-life gender" I do not know), we decide to buy some X on Telegraph Avenue and teleport back to Trance's home, a tripper's pad complete with shaggy rug and lots of candles. We take the drug, and the words that appear on my screen tell me that things are beginning to take on a very tactile quality. Trance puts on techno-beat, and I feel the undulating rhythm, matched by the flickering disco lights that now appear. Trance has programmed a beautiful rave, and I decide then that I want Trance to be a man. I type my desires, "Mojo places a hand on your broad chest, just to see what it feels like," and he bends down and kisses my lips.

The success of this encounter with Trance inspired me to pose as "*Sassy* Chick" on the lookout for "hot guys." I love to cruise around in cyberspace wearing a tight-fitting striped T-shirt, hip-hugger jeans, and platform Pumas. I am assailed with friendly greetings and choose to answer only those whose descriptions meet my aesthetic qualifications: those who match the "Patrick Swayze type." As *Sassy* Chick, I am young and spontaneous, unaware of my own seductive powers. I love to picture myself in the arms of some big muscled, sensitive type, and it's the ones who look sweetly into my eyes that get my blood racing.

Cyberspace is different from other kinds of erotically charged mediums because it is interactive. In order to engage in cybersex, you must actively write, create, and present a self. And when this cyberspace self becomes the vehicle for real-life arousal, what you think of as your "real-life self" becomes implicated in whatever sexuality you experience on-line. Even if this cyberspace self is entirely fantastical, such as my *Sassy* Chick persona, there is always some kind of "real self" that is implicated insofar as you believe you had a role in deciding which fantasy persona to take on—which fantasy self would enable the typing self to get aroused. As the sites and sources of erotic stimulation stretch beyond the confines of your familiar sexuality, you begin to question, what is sexuality, and who am I?

From these on-line exploits, I have learned that my sexuality has much less to do with the sex of my partner and much more to do with the sex of my partner and much more to do with the art of desire itself. Cyberspace is a nonphysical realm; nothing can be seen, felt, or heard. Erotics, then, is a matter of words, not bodies. I am turned on by mere descriptions—"a well-worn leather belt," "a sharp jawline that accentuates her firm lips"—and by text that signifies actions, intentions, feelings, and physiques, not by actions, intentions, feelings, and physiques themselves. When Mr. Benson whacked me with a wooden spoon, it was not an actual spoon which got me off, but indeed, the representation of a spoon.

There has been much discussion about honesty and morality in connection with "gender passing" on-line, about the need to know people for "who they are." But had my friend Trance lied about being from the Bay Area, would there have been any cause for concern? Trance talked like someone from Berkeley, and the replica felt like the Bay Area to me. My time spent with him had a great deal of meaning to me, which simply would not be lost if Trance turned out to be what some cyberspace participants call an "identity predator."

I think that the hype about gender deceit, framed as genuine concern about being lied to, is largely about the fear of being confronted with the fact that one's sexuality is not as well-defined and unambiguous as one may have thought. There is a fear of being lulled into a "false sexuality"—of falling for someone whose "real gender" turns out to be the same as someone who considers himself or herself to be strictly heterosexual, or the opposite of someone who considers himself or herself to be homosexual. Gender play on-line, whether intentional or a matter of an inaccurate assumption, is not just a matter of crossing over from one gender to the other. Given the possibility for participants to experience very real sexual feelings that supposedly contradict one's gender, cybersex questions the very *idea* that gender and sexuality are physically grounded in the first place.

Thus, it is absurd not only to think of gender as true or false, but to think of gender at all or to assume that there exists a set of stable characteristics that are determined by one's anatomy and that in turn determine one's sexuality. Indeed, the anxiety of gender bending on-line is not simply about the fear of deception, it is also about the fear of chaos and ambiguity.

There has never been a place for ambiguity when it comes to politics. My friend Mary Beijan was not thinking about ambiguity when she became my first feminist hero by chucking a raw chicken leg into the lap of the *Playboy* representative in search of women for the "Girls of the Big 10" edition. "Here," she screamed at the rep, after going through the entire selection process. "Because it's raw meat you want, you bastard!" There was nothing ambiguous about marching in Washington to demand my right to choose, or confronting that horrible man in the shopping mall whose T-shirt rejoiced that "AIDS kills fags . . . Dead."

But when it comes to identity politics, certainty has had a frustrating, if not dooming, effect. What happens when the identity politics that bring about effective, issue-oriented struggle begin to break down? When we realize that not all women think alike, and that differences such as class and race can no longer be sutured over by the "certainty" of a common gender? That any kind of identity, no matter if it is an identity of resistance, is also a creation of boundaries? How to act when we realize that to fight AIDS we must fight homophobia, and to fight homophobia we must fight racism, and so on. We face a choice between focusing our energies on one issue or acting with the knowledge that oppression is interrelated and pursuing a more broad-based, but perhaps more indirect, approach. And (here's where it really gets difficult) how to fight those underlying power structures once we've learned that we too are *part* of those structures?

Can there be such a thing as a politics of ambiguity—a politics that recognizes we must learn how to negotiate ourselves on a terrain in which, as Cornel West articulates, everything is ungrounded, even the notion that everything is ungrounded? What would this kind of politics have to offer someone whose experience of pain and discrimination is very well grounded indeed, as mine was as a self-loathing nineteen-year-old? How does this understanding of the constructedness of identity help when, artificial or not, these identity distinctions are in fact imposed and used as a means to oppress and discriminate?

An encounter I had on an airplane with a career military officer shed unexpected light on these questions. After inquiring about the paperback she was reading, our conversation drifted into the ever-popular subject of gays in the military. I'm somewhat ambivalent about the issue: I'm against the discrimination, but not willing to devote a great deal of energy fighting for access to an institution whose activities I usually condemn. In high school, I had dreamed of being in ROTC. That was before I came out, and when I still believed in things like absolute good and evil. Despite my ideological differences, my fascination with the military was still intact, and I really enjoyed talking with the lieutenant. She told me that West Point had given her a top-notch free education and a good career. I was very impressed, and she had my respect. West Point, wow, she must be a really good athlete, too.

Then we started to talk politics. The lieutenant believed that the rigid environment necessary for an effective military would be disrupted by the presence of homosexuals. Sexual tension and sexual activities would break up the discipline, she argued. "Yeah, but how do you ever know for sure who's a homosexual?" I asked. "And anyway, all of those men and women having sex in the Gulf weren't given dishonorable discharges. If we lived in a society in which we were comfortable with all kinds of sexual relationships, would same-sex attraction still be a disruption?"

"Maybe not," she replied, "but right now, society isn't comfortable with it and so it is a disruption."

"But wasn't that the same argument for excluding black people from the military?"

As an African-American in the military herself, she thought that was an interesting point. "Yes, there is a similarity there," she acknowledged.

I said that as a white person, when I first came out, it had never occurred to me that gay people could be black too. "Isn't that weird? I mean, there I was in college and I totally equated gayness with whiteness. I guess because I had never met or seen a black person that I knew to be gay. I saw a sign up in one of the dorms for a black lesbian support group and it really took me by surprise. I wondered whether there could be more than one woman like this on campus, or whether the woman who put up the poster was just looking for a date."

The lieutenant laughed and looked startled. "You know," she said, "I completely understand what you just said. Up until this moment, gay people were always white to me too. But that makes no sense."

Somehow, during the course of this interaction, we identified with each other. Though I find myself politically at odds with the military, that didn't prevent me from admiring the lieutenant's poise and the power of her stripes. And she told me it was fascinating to talk with someone like me who had spent so much time "thinking about things." I think we could talk because, for a moment, we let go of the contours between us, the identities that had always kept us apart, and just let things be a little fuzzy.

A politics of ambiguity requires that the fronts of activism be rethought to broaden the definition of social change. Improved standards of living, freedom, liberation—these causes need not be fought for, demanded, and expressed in the form of one kind of politics. Social change is not just about the kind of political action brought about by group action. Politics is also interpersonal—about how we talk to each other and how we relate to one another when there is no group to call out our names.

There will always be a need to label—categorization is fundamental to our understanding of our world. But if we understand that such categories are dynamic ones, based not on transcendental truths but on the cultural forces of a particular place and time, then perhaps we can acquire the agility and flexibility needed to keep those categories fluid and open to future articulations.

There are differences among those we think of as the same, and similarities among those we think of as different. When we speak to each other, it is not as simple as a clash of identities. Just like on the MUD, we do in fact know each other in many ways. To embrace this complexity, to accept the ambiguity of the human experience, is to understand that what we think of as "self" and what we think of as "other" actually need one another to exist. To understand this is to look at "difference" and not judge.

Cyberspace, with its anonymity and nonphysical presence, no more masks the "truth" of identities like race or gender than visible signs like skin color and anatomy prove it. Identity, no matter how concrete the experience, is always constructed, never innate. To realize this fluidity is to understand that we are all different and the same. Accepting this ambiguity is not a political end in itself, but it may be a precondition to longstanding liberation. Accepting ambiguity can provide the agility to make sense of a chaotic world without relying on an oppressive system of static categories, and it may also provide the faith to connect.

PART FOUR

Making a Living: Women, Work, and Achievement

A powerful mythology has influenced thinking about women, work, and achievement. Success, it says, is solely a matter of individual hard work and will power; if women have not achieved as much as men, it is because too many of them lack ambition, fail to set clear career goals in advance, or let other things (such as marriage and family) interfere with getting ahead. A variation on the theme is that perhaps in the past women have been discriminated against or otherwise prevented from reaching their full potential, but today no barriers exist.

The diverse groups of women who speak about their work here tell us different stories. Perhaps the most important thread that links them is the importance of social structures in the experience of work. No achiever stands alone; her or his success takes place in a social environment that helps or hinders—usually a complex mixture of both. And the social context of women and people of color has been very different from that of white men.

But these women are far from being passive victims of social forces beyond their control. Active agency within societal constraints is ex-

pressed in each of their lives. A good place to look is in their solutions to the "balancing act." How do these women provide the money their families need, as well as take care of their own needs, while remaining primarily responsible for caring for others? How are they willing to change direction when their path is blocked?

Women's work lives have been characterized by discontinuity (movement in spurts from one goal to another), and serendipity (taking advantage of unexpected opportunities). When confronted by roadblocks, women often zigzag around them. However, for women most disadvantaged by social structures of racism and sexism, there may be little room to maneuver. The most extreme oppression in this group of stories is suffered by the *maquiladoras*, women in poor countries who work in foreign-owned factories. In Marie Racine's composite of interviews with women in a Haitian workers' cooperative, the women describe their sweatshop working conditions and their attempts to resist exploitation.

Virtually all women juggle paid work and family responsibilities, but how they do it is structured by their social class. When Marcelle

Williams began interviewing Punjabi (South Indian) women in their homes, others—husbands, grown children—kept jumping in to speak for them. Their behavior reinforced the stereotypes of Indian women as passive and dependent, yet these women handle the "double day" of paid work and family with great skill. In Shellee Colen's study of West Indian women working as housekeepers and nannies for wealthy white families, the contradictions of these two kinds of work become sharply visible. Like African American slave women before them, these women are expected to nurture the children of their employers and place them higher in importance than their own families.

More-privileged women face pressures to conform to patriarchal visions of the family, too. Women and men continue to experiment with creating nonpatriarchal family structures, in the hope that they can meet the human need for connection without perpetuating restrictive roles. Mary Crawford, a feminist and a college professor, describes her own "experiment": Can a woman and man choose to live apart, make her work equally important to his, and share parenting without wrecking their marriage and family? In her account, both wife and husband struggle with the pressure of their "deviant" choices.

Jo Ellen Brainin-Rodriguez, a psychiatrist who works with Latinas, gives a daughter's perspective on work-family issues. Because her mother was a well-known physician and feminist activist, Brainin-Rodriguez took on much responsibility for house and home from a young age. The abuse she suffered at the hands of her stepfather and her memories of her mother's endless striving to achieve deeply affected her career path and her own priorities for work and family.

Family issues are not the only complications for women's work lives. Even women who are devoting all their energy to achievement can be blocked by institutionalized sexism. Janice Yoder, a white woman, a feminist with a Ph.D., and a visiting professor at a U.S. military academy, might seem to have had all the advantages of race, class, and education. As a social psychologist, she had sophisticated analytical tools to interpret her experiences. Yet faced with an extreme version of tokenism as one of a tiny minority of women at the academy, she quickly began to suffer the diminished self-esteem, withdrawal, and depression that are the hallmarks of oppression.

Think back over the work experiences of the women in these accounts. For some, work is repetitive, boring, dangerous, and grossly underpaid. Others work long hours without medical benefits or opportunities for advancement. They experience discrimination and harassment. They work without adequate support or recognition for their family responsibilities. A common theme in all these stories is women's striving to achieve meaningful and dignified work lives despite societal constraints. By exercising power within the limits set for them, and by expanding those limits, they make their own definitions of work and accomplishment.

Marie M. B. Racine

Life in the Factory

A fixture of the global economy is the maquila *system, in which multinational corporations situate manufacturing plants in the poorest countries where they can pay extremely low wages and avoid health and safety regulations. Often, the workers in these factories are women who are desperate for money to survive and feed their families. Their ability to unionize or otherwise gain control over their working conditions is minimal.*

In this story, many voices speak. It is a composite of interviews conducted in 1998 with Haitian women of the Batay Ouvriye workers' collective, who were asked to describe what a day of work is like for them in a maquila *factory. Because of the danger of retaliation by factory owners, these women must remain anonymous. The interviews were conducted and summarized by Marie Racine.*

As You Read, Ask Yourself . . .

What basic rights do these maquiladoras *(factory workers) lack?*

What forces make it difficult for them to improve their working conditions and wages?

Can people in the U.S. do anything about the exploitation of workers in poor and less-developed countries?

We get to work at seven o'clock in the morning, and we begin to work right away. Mostly we work on sewing machines. If we are making dresses, each one of us makes a particular part of the dress, for example, the sleeve. We continue working on sleeves for a long time until there is a need to change us to another operation.

People that work on machines are called operators. Some people work as operators and other people sew by hand. Our other option is to be a person who checks the work of others, but they pay less for that! If something is not done properly, you are responsible for undoing it and correcting it, but you are paid less.

This is what you do if you are a checker: you either put a piece of tape over something that an operator has done wrong and give it back to that person to correct, or you correct it yourself.

The work of a checker is very demanding because there are many operators and they are all trying to work as fast as they can in order to meet the quota to earn 50 *goud* (US$ 3.34). You may have as many as ten operators that are putting work in front of you. You don't have time to take even two seconds to stand up. The operators are working like crazy, never looking up so they can meet their quota. Even if someone sees that she has made a mistake, she doesn't stop to correct it because if she doesn't make her quota, she will only make 36 *goud* (US$ 2.40) instead of 50 *goud* for that day. If you are a checker the pile is rising in front of you and you don't have time to look at the operator's work carefully. There may be many errors, and you are the one that is going to be called into the office.

The quota is something they have created in order to make you work more than your bodily energy really allows you to. Sometimes you are doing a job that is difficult and you are doing ten dozen. They will come and request that you do 50 dozen. But they only give you the quota when they need the extra pieces. Normally you work according to your own speed and you don't do excess work, because doing excess work is not good for you.

So, you work until about eleven thirty in the morning, and then they allow you to eat. You have to go out on the streets to find something to eat. The food they sell there is covered with dust and smoke from the road. The traffic in front of the factory is heavy. Some bosses want you to come back five minutes before your 30 minute break is over. When you go back, you start working again. You can't even go to the toilet, because they keep it closed until a quarter til one. At three thirty they ring the bell for people to stop working. You go home and that is what you have done to earn 36 *goud*. It is eight hours of work.

If you stay extra time to finish a quota, usually you have not even eaten. In the morning, you might have had one *goud's* worth of coffee and a small roll. At noon, you might have had ten *goud* worth of food—which is not enough to fill your stomach—and you may not have been able to drink any juice which costs two *goud*. If a worker doesn't eat and she tries to attain the "expert" status at work by doing high quotas, she develops an ulcer, because when the mill of your stomach is grinding and it does not find any food, it starts grinding your stomach.

When you go home, you may not have even five cents in your pocket. You go home and you just go to bed and the next morning you get up and you may not even have the money you need to take the bus, so you have to walk to work. If you find someone who can loan you five *goud*, you might have a cup of coffee or a biscuit for breakfast. They pay you every other week, and by the time you are paid, you owe everything you have earned to someone else. If you are lucky you will have enough to buy something to wear or some extra thing for that week. You are always, always in poverty.

Inside the factory, the supervisors are shouting at the workers, ordering them to work harder and harder and harder even if the worker can not do all of the work she is being asked to do. Sometimes the women are harassed sexually. Sometimes a supervisor will ask a worker to sleep with him in order to ensure her job. This may be true even if the woman is married.

When you are in a factory you are in jail. There is a security guard at the gate who opens the gate when it's time for people to go in, and then opens the door again to let you out for lunch. When you come back in he closes the gate behind you again. If there were a fire inside, many people would die.

If an accident happens at the workplace, for example, sometimes the needle punctures your finger or your hand, they don't even give the person the transportation money to go to the hospital, let alone spend money for the medical bill. When you are hurt, they just put some alcohol on the wound, and send you home. Usually there is no clinic if somebody feels ill.

Some factories have an arrangement with a doctor, but even that is another way of taking advantage of us. If you are sick and you go to one of the government doctors, he may examine you and he may order two weeks to a month of paid sick leave. But if the company has its own doctor, he will only give three days of sick leave, which may not even be paid. Or they may pay for only a day and a half. After the three days, even if you are not well, you have to go back to work because according to the doctor, you should be well after three days. If you stay home longer, when you return to work you are fired because they assume that you just stayed home for no reason. You can only get a statement from another doctor if the factory doesn't have its own doctor.

You have the hot electric light bulbs above your head and the motor of the machine heating up your feet. There is no additional space at the work station. In many places the only drinking water there is rain water collected in a barrel. Sometimes they put some salt in the water to cover up the bad taste of the rainwater or the barrel. And the conditions of the bathrooms are pitiful. Sometimes there is only one toilet for all of the employees. Often there is only a thin curtain separating you from the people outside. There is no toilet paper. They don't keep the toilets clean. There are mosquitoes and other bugs all over.

If they know that there is a possible visit from some international delegation, representatives from the US company or newspaper people, then the management might buy one five-gallon container of bottled water and put it somewhere for show.

There is also no good ventilation and there are no fans. Sometimes they keep an old broken fan around so in case a delegation comes, they can act like they use fans. The delegations come by particularly when the workers have given some information or denounced something happening there. But visitors are usually supposed to announce when they are coming, and if the management knows they are going to have some visitors, they put on a front.

When you work in a factory and start talking about organizing a union, and you try to enlist the other workers to protest the working conditions, the bosses immediately decide that they don't have any use for you. We are like slaves when we work there. We cannot defend our rights. If something doesn't go well in the workplace, we cannot say anything about it. For example, if the bosses give you an unfair quota of pieces to work on, you can't protest.

When you are working at the factory, the small amount of money that you get paid is only enough to eat at the factory. You don't make enough money to take home, let alone think about starting some savings. The 36 *goud* you receive for the day's work, you have already spent at the factory to feed yourself. You can't do anything else with it. And you have to dress, you have children to send to school, you have rent to pay. They give you 36 *goud* for an eight hour day.

We don't have a government that will speak on our behalf. The business owners get together and they tell the government what to do. We and the government are both held in the claws of the rich business owners. They discuss their own interests, but they never see the needs of the poor people.

Sometimes we go to the Ministry of Labor to complain, but the people in charge do not take our claims seriously because the bosses go and buy off the very people who are supposed to advocate for us. They are the people that know the labor code and what articles we could invoke to support our claims. The boss gives money to those people and then they turn to us and say, "Don't you know you must do what the bosses say?" You have no right to talk at all.

It's not that we don't think of strategies. Sometimes you may enter a factory to ask for work. If they are hiring, you could ask about the working conditions there and you could try to negotiate for a better wage according to your ability and stamina. But if you do it that way, they won't employ you, because they want you to work on their terms. If you look like a troublemaker, then they tell you, "Go home. You can leave. We don't need you. There are others on the streets that need the job."

Marcelle Williams

Ladies on the Line: Punjabi Cannery Workers in Central California*

Research on women's work tends to be class-biased: there are many studies of women with prestigious careers, but few of women who hold down less glamorous jobs—whose voices too often remain unheard. Marcelle Williams has helped balance the picture by interviewing South Indian immigrant women who work in a cannery production line. Here, she focuses on Mrs. Singh, who found a job despite her inability to speak English and then began to "network" to help her relatives migrate to this country. Her story is one of resilience, persistence, and taking direct action to improve her family's welfare.

As You Read, Ask Yourself . . .

What reasons does Mrs. Singh give for working in the cannery?

How do gender and ethnic discrimination affect her working conditions?

How did Mrs. Singh use covert influence strategies at work to make her job easier?

How did she use her paid work to increase her power at home?

"Well, those ladies on the lines, they have it pretty easy," Mr. Singh replied when I asked Mrs. Singh about her job as a cannery worker. Mrs. Singh's husband continued to answer for her: "And now that she has seniority, you know, she can sit around and drink tea or something like that." While I tried to talk to Mrs. Singh about her life and work at a nearby food-processing plant, she moved industriously around the kitchen, preparing snacks for her two little granddaughters and me. As a guest in their home, an old farmhouse that they had recently refurbished, I was ushered into the formal living room where I sat drinking tea with Mr. Singh, a married daughter who was visiting, and an unmarried, teen-age daughter. Although the entire family was very gracious and hospitable, whenever I asked Mrs. Singh questions about herself, the other members present frequently answered instead.

*Complete citations to all the articles referred to in this reading can be found in Asian Women United of California (1989). *Making Waves*. Boston: Beacon Press.

This situation did not occur only with this family. In fact, it happened over and over again during my interviews with Punjabi Sikh women who work in the California canning industry. Even though I requested to speak directly with the women, they were often busy in the kitchen while their family members spoke for them.[1]

At first glance my interviews seem to support previous research which stereotypes Asian Indian women as restricted to the domestic sphere of home and hearth, passive and unable to speak for themselves. In a review of the few studies of South Asian immigrant women, Pratibha Parmar states that they usually are depicted as "limited to the kitchen, the children and the religious rituals, and . . . emotionally and economically dependent upon their husbands."

However, my interviews with Punjabi cannery workers contradict the commonly held view that Indian immigrant women are economically dependent on men and do not work outside of the home. At the very least, my study documents that these women work hard *outside* as well as *inside* the home, in both the public and the private realms. Very rarely, whether at work or home, did they "sit around and drink tea." Moreover, a closer examination of my interviews shows that these women are extremely active and that their actions may speak more loudly than their apparent lack of words.

I intend to illustrate in this essay that the Punjabi women with whom I talked are anything but passive, and that they actively influence and interlink the public sphere of work and the private sphere of family. Indeed, they are often able to gain the upper hand by manipulating the stereotypic images of their supposed domesticity, passivity, and inarticulateness.[2]

THE SINGHS ARRIVE IN CALIFORNIA

In order to convey the idea that Punjabi women are active in both the workplace and the home and to show the extent to which the two realms overlap, this essay will focus on one particular woman, Mrs. Singh, her work, and her family. I met Mrs. Singh and her family during the spring of 1985, when I began interviewing Indian immigrant women who worked in the fruit and vegetable canneries of Stanislaus County in central California. Mrs. Singh knew of approximately one hundred Punjabi Sikhs who worked as seasonal laborers at a specific plant in Modesto run by Tri/Valley Growers, Inc. While I spoke with some of the women who worked at this cannery, and to women from other food processing plants, I will concentrate on Mrs. Singh since her experiences are representative, for the most part, of the larger group of Punjabi women. When her life history appears atypical, however, I will note this and provide illustrative material from other sources.

Mrs. Singh and her husband, like 30 to 40 percent of the 59,674 Asian Indians currently in California, belong to the Sikh religion, which predominates in the state of Punjab in India. Mr. Singh left the Jullundur district in the Punjab in 1971 and settled with his sister's family north of Sacramento, in the Marysville-Yuba City area, which has had a sizable Punjabi Sikh population since the early

1900s. Mrs. Singh, also born and raised in the Jullundur district where she married her husband in 1958 at the age of seventeen, followed him to America a year later with their four children.

Many scholars have traced the historical development of the Punjabi community in rural California and have commented on its inception as a bachelor group of agricultural laborers. Mr. Singh was able to immigrate because of his relationship to this earlier group through his sister. She could sponsor her brother because she had married a man whose father had entered California as a farm worker. In turn, after immigrating as Mr. Singh's wife, Mrs. Singh became a United States citizen as soon as possible so that she could sponsor the entry of her own brothers and sisters.

So, contrary to the studies of Asian Indian immigrant women that stress their dependent status and imply that they migrate only because of men, Mrs. Singh, like her sister-in-law and many other women before her, served as a vital link in the immigration cycle—men bringing over women relatives who then bring their own relatives. Unlike the usual portrayal of Asian Indian women, Mrs. Singh took an active role in migration strategies.[3]

In their search for land and new opportunities, the Singhs, like many of the Sikhs in northern California, moved southward into Stanislaus County. In 1973, Mr. and Mrs. Singh left his sister's ranch, where they had worked picking peaches and tending the orchard, and moved to Stanislaus County, which is located about sixty miles south of Sacramento near the middle of the Central Valley. They settled on the outskirts of Modesto, the largest city in the county, in the hopes of acquiring some orchard land of their own.

Although there is no official estimate of the size of the Punjabi community, the 1980 census calculates a total Asian Indian population of only 1,150 out of 293,400 people in the county. This figure may be a gross underestimation, however. Based on the Sikh temples in the area and the estimated number of families they each serve, there appear to be almost a thousand Punjabi Sikhs alone. Asian Indians other than Punjabi Sikhs reside in the county—they are primarily from the northern states, but probably every state in India is represented, as well as there being some Indians from Fiji, England, and Africa. And among them there is a fairly well-defined residential and class division. The Punjabi Sikhs tend to live in the smaller towns and more rural areas, in Turlock, Ceres, Patterson, Hughson, Denair, and Delhi; and they tend to be working-class, waged workers who also own or lease a little land. In contrast, the other Asian Indians seem to reside more often within the city of Modesto and to work in business or are professionals.[4]

Soon after they settled in Stanislaus County, the Singhs sought gainful employment. As one of the state's top ten producing agricultural counties, the county has well over three hundred food processing, packing, and distributing companies. Mr. Singh, who had been a taxi driver in India, found a year-round job as a forklift driver for a large food processing plant. Mrs. Singh worked in the fields picking various crops, sometimes along with the children of the family.

Just months after the Singhs moved into the area, Mrs. Singh found a seasonal job as an assembly line worker for Tri/Valley Growers, Inc. Fortunately Mrs. Singh was at the right place at the right time: she began working at Tri/Valley Plant 7, the world's largest "supercannery," soon after the company opened it and began expanding its holdings in Stanislaus County.

225

MARCELLE
WILLIAMS
Ladies on the Line:
Punjabi Cannery
Workers in Central
California

Since then, Tri/Valley Growers, a cooperative association of several hundred farming operations, has grown until it is now the largest fruit and vegetable processor in the state. This development is unfortunate for cannery workers at other plants, though, because Tri/Valley's growth has been related to an industry "shakedown" and merger mania that have resulted in numerous plant closures and shutdowns.[5]

WORKING AT THE CANNERY

When asked how she got her job at Tri/Valley, Mrs. Singh said that she "just went down to the [plant] office, filled out an application, and that was it." Unlike most of the other cannery workers with whom I spoke, she did not hear about, or get her job, through word-of-mouth since she was among the first Punjabis hired. Another Punjabi woman who was hired at Tri/Valley explained:

> Okay, you just talk to your friends and family about where they work, and you usually hear who is hiring. You know from talking to them if they [the companies] are any good to work for. You know, Tri/Valley is usually good to work for, and Del Monte is not so good. It used to be that if you knew the floorlady or the foreman, you could tell them that so-and-so, your brother, needs a job and he's a good worker, and he'd get on. I don't think it's like that anymore.

Through word-of-mouth communication, it is not uncommon for relatively large numbers of Indian immigrants, often related by kinship and friendship, to work together at the same plant. Of course, this kind of networking also occurs with groups other than Asian Indians and, as a result, many canneries have clusters of particular ethnic groups. One nut processing plant in Modesto, for example, has a majority of Assyrian immigrant employees; another plant has mostly Chicanos; a third has mostly "Okies." Most plants, though, like Tri/Valley's Plant 7, have a combination of several ethnic groups.

There are many Punjabi Sikhs employed by Tri/Valley Growers, but it is difficult to know the exact percentage because the company does not keep any kind of tally of their Indian immigrant employees. Based on my discussion with the workers there, I estimate that Punjabis make up about 2 percent of the work force. According to company records for 1984, over half of this labor force is Hispanic (51.26 percent), while the rest is comprised of almost 3 percent black, 5 percent "Asian" (many of whom are Southeast Asian refugees), and the remainder unspecified (presumably white).[6]

Although being 2 percent of the Tri/Valley work force may not seem numerically significant, it is socially significant in the daily lives of the Punjabi Sikhs who work there. They interact in a very close-knit social world composed of kith and kin with whom they work, at the height of the canning season, for up to ten hours a day, and with whom they may then visit afterwards. An Anglo cannery worker with whom I talked complained about the Punjabi worker's social habits:

> Yeah, they're really very clannish. You know, they sit together during breaks, and they usually manage to work together on the lines or wherever. The women are really the worst about sticking to themselves and sitting in gangs. It really

bugs me when you walk past them, and they start giggling and talking about you in their language, you know, Indian or whatever it is. I don't know, it sort of sounds like Spanish.

227

MARCELLE
WILLIAMS
Ladies on the Line:
Punjabi Cannery
Workers in Central
California

As this comment inadvertently recognizes, the social world of the Punjabi Sikh women—who make up a little more than half of all the Sikh cannery workers—may be even more closely knit because they often do not speak English fluently. Quite often the Punjabi women state explicitly that they do cannery work because English language skills are not crucial in most of the work. Mrs. Singh points out that when Tri/Valley hired her in the early 1970s, when their business was booming, the hiring personnel were not interested in whether or not she spoke English.

> I just filled out the application, and they asked me some questions. I just said "yes" to everything that they asked me; I didn't even know what they were asking. A couple of times when I said "yes," they looked at me kind of funny, so I guess I should've said "no" then. They didn't care that I didn't know the language.[7]

The Punjabi Sikh women who work at the canneries share more than a small social world and the inability to speak English fluently; they share other cultural characteristics as well. Like Mrs. Singh, most of them immigrated to California during the 1970s from either the Jullundur or Ludhiana districts of the Punjab, and since their arrival most of them have been involved in agribusiness as pickers, packers, cannery workers, and small-scale farmers. Most were hired by Tri/Valley or by other canneries during the 1970s, and consequently have ten or more years of seniority.

The vast majority of the Punjabi Sikh women who work in the cannery are middle-aged. This fact is due to immigration cycles and hiring patterns in the canning industry resulting from "boom and bust" trends since World War II. As Mrs. Singh's daughter emphasized, most of the cannery workers, including her mother, are in their forties and fifties because "only the first ladies that came over here, the very first like them, you know, they're the only ones that work there [at the cannery]. But like the children, they don't work there."

In addition to sharing similar backgrounds and characteristics, most of the Punjabi Sikh women share similar work at the canneries. Most of them work in the lower paying jobs on the assembly lines or conveyor belts in preparation and canning, two of the three departments—preparation, canning, and warehouse—at the cannery.

The preparation department is made up almost exclusively of women and consists of numerous conveyor belts that move the produce from the trucks, through a lye solution that peels it, and ultimately into machines that fill the cans. In the canning department the cans move through seamer and cook machines, which are tended by both women and men. After the cans have been filled, seamed, and cooked, they proceed to the warehouse area where almost only men work to pack, store, and later distribute the canned goods. In most of the departments, but especially in the preparation and canning departments, the work is subdivided into minute single tasks. Women on the lines, for example, grade the produce by standing alongside the belt and tossing away the unsuitable fruit, hour after hour, day after day.

Not only is work in the cannery monotonous, it is also usually uncomfortable and sometimes dangerous. The noise level is so high that it is practically impossible to carry on a conversation in many of the work areas, so workers have developed a sign language instead. The stench of the processed food is at times overpowering and causes the nausea that most line workers experience at one time or another. One woman working at a cannery summed it up: "I don't like the monotony of the belt. I hate standing all day. It's noisy; it gives me a headache. The line makes me dizzy, and sometimes I get sick." Also workers sometimes become ill because of the disorientation from working the "swing" (usually 2:00 to 1:00 P.M.) or the "graveyard" (usually 10:00 P.M. to 6:00 A.M.) shift.

Overall these conditions can be very harsh, especially during the peak part of the season—July to mid-September—when workers may put in as many as ten hours a day, with only two twelve-minute breaks and a half-hour lunch, six or seven days a week. In addition, conditions at the cannery can be dangerous. Mrs. Singh, along with most other cannery workers, recounted stories of various cannery accidents, such as the story of a woman's finger being severed by the machinery and then "canned" with the peaches.[8]

Despite the implementation of affirmative action policies, cannery work is still difficult for women because of the de facto sex segregation of the work that keeps women in the lower-paying, lower-bracket jobs in the preparation and canning departments, which are more seasonal, more monotonous, and more strictly supervised. Although there are not official distinctions made between "male" and "female" jobs or their pay scales, the job brackets—eight levels that are hierarchically ranked according to the job description and wages—are divided by sex. On the whole, men occupy the upper brackets, women the lower. As of 1984, after a decade of reform measures, women at Tri/Valley still made up 71.38 percent of the less-skilled, lower-paying, lower job brackets.

For the Punjabi women, this situation of sex discrimination is aggravated by racial or ethnic discrimination. Affirmative action measures have not changed the fact that cannery work is also ethnically segregated, with people of color occupying the lower job brackets. After working at the cannery for thirteen years, Mrs. Singh, like all of the other Punjabi women, is still a seasonal worker. She is a Bracket Five worker and, as of last year, was finally moved off the lines to a higher level job running a seamer machine. Out of all the Punjabi women working at Tri/Valley, there are only two who have been able to reach even lower-ranking supervisory positions.

Although Mrs. Singh did not complain about discrimination at the cannery, many other workers have. In another study, a Chicana testified: "Discrimination is blatant. If you're white, or know the bosses, you last maybe a week on the lines. If you're brown or a woman, you work for years and never get promoted."[9]

Given the harsh conditions at work and the discrimination that exacerbates them, why do Punjabi Sikh women continue to work in the canneries? Aside from the more obvious reasons, their previous experience in agribusiness, their language limitations, and a competitive labor market, the Punjabi women I spoke with insisted that they actively sought out cannery work because it suited their purposes: to provide more income for their families while fulfilling their domestic roles as wives and mothers.

With seasonal cannery work lasting four or five months and then unemployment benefits the remainder of the year, Punjabi women earn up to a third of the family's income and yet can also be around the house as much as possible. In a sense, they use to their own advantage the cannery management's notion that they are expendable, secondary workers, a reserve army of labor.

WORK AND THE FAMILY

The key to understanding why Punjabi women work is to know that they do not view work and the family as incompatible, dichotomized spheres. According to most Punjabi women, they gain prestige from participating in both spheres, and as it happens, these very spheres overlap anyway. As Mrs. Singh laughingly said, "My work is sort of my family, you know, with all my relatives and friends there; and, of course, my family is my work."

Nearly all the Punjabi women emphasize that they are wage workers for their families' economic benefit. I heard over and over again, "It is good for Indian ladies from good families to work here. You see, everybody works because the pay is good, and it's good for the families." Punjabi families encourage every able-bodied adult to help finance the family goal of purchasing a small plot of orchard land. The women in the families are able to aid in this endeavor by working at the canneries, and they often can secure cannery jobs for other family members too. For example, Mrs. Singh was able to refer both her brother and her husband to Tri/Valley where both took on seasonal work to supplement their year-round jobs.

It is interesting to note that the women claimed they worked at the cannery in order to contribute to the welfare of their families, thereby fulfilling their domestic obligations. Essentially, they are legitimizing their departure from traditional domesticity, by saying their entry into the workplace is for domestic reasons. While these women are undoubtedly working outside of their homes for economic reasons, they are also hoping, according to what I learned in my interviews, to change their traditional roles within the family. They use their stereotypic image of devoted domesticity to justify becoming wage earners, but at the same time actually gain more control and decision-making power within the household. Many Punjabi women told anecdotes about their increased power in the family. One woman said with great satisfaction, "Now my husband, he listens to me when I say something; when I want to buy something, I do; and when I want to go in the car, I go." Although the family as a whole usually makes the decisions about where a family member will work, Mrs. Singh showed that she could break precedent and decide herself when to quit a job:

> I worked at another plant once, and they gave me a "man's" job. It was cutting this turkey into three pieces; it [the belt] was too fast and [the work was] too hard. I was the only woman working there. I worked hard all day to show that I could do it, that I could do a "man's" job. But I quit the next day 'cause it was too hard. It was too much work, and I didn't like it.

Other Punjabi women told of using their stereotypic image as passive and inarticulate workers to avoid doing certain jobs at the cannery. For instance, since the Punjabi women cannery workers form a close-knit social group at work, they sometimes do not want to leave the lines where that group interacts the most. One woman explained: "I work very hard, but I don't want to move away from the lines, from the belt, you know, 'cause that's where my friends are. So, I don't act all gung ho when the floorlady comes by and says there's a spot for someone on the filler machines or something." Another woman who usually worked the seamer machines resisted the authority of the supervisors in this small but effective way: "When a floorlady I don't like brings over someone and tells me to train them, you know, on my machine, I act like I don't understand her. I speak Punjabi back to her and act like I don't understand English. That way I don't have to fool with them." Someone else related that sometimes when she doesn't want to do a particular job, clean-up for instance, she says, "Okay, okay," and then just stands around and chats with her friends. When the supervisor chides her, she acts as though she doesn't understand what the supervisor wants her to do and says, "No English."

These women indicated to me that they were satisfied with working at the cannery, which, after all, was better than doing farm work. They were happy at being able to contribute to their families' income and fulfill domestic duties, while simultaneously being able to change their families' expectations of them. In order to do this, the women often used the traditional stereotype of their being domestic to their advantage. In the workplace, they also sometimes manipulated the stereotypes about passivity and inarticulateness to do what they wanted versus what their supervisors told them to do. In talking about their work and family experiences, it was evident that they sometimes said little or, even more often, said what fit their stereotypic image as domestic, passive, and inarticulate women. However, these statements sometimes obscured what was really happening in their lives. The actions of the women, these Punjabi Sikh "ladies on the lines," may well speak more loudly than their words.

Shellee Colen

"With Respect and Feelings": Voices of West Indian Child Care and Domestic Workers in New York City

Despite many changes in gender roles and responsibilities over the past thirty years, women are still largely responsible for child care and housework. Some women are able to solve this dilemma by hiring other women as maids, nannies, and house cleaners. Shellee Colen argues that this work, which is "shunned by men," becomes "multiply devalued as it is passed from one woman to another along class, racial, ethnic, and migration lines." In her interviews with West Indian child-care and domestic workers in New York City, Colen gives voice to their perspective and exposes some of the contradictions of taking care of others' homes and children for pay.

As You Read, Ask Yourself . . .

What social markers do employers use to reinforce class and power differences?

What do the West Indian women want most of all from their employers?

Why are the two groups of husbands invisible in these accounts?

Are there ways in which women can support each other across lines of class and color?

I'm not looking for them to shower us down with money, with clothes, but with a little respect and feelings. You know because they want full respect from us and at the same time they want to treat us like nothing. . . . A lot of West Indians are very insulted, but we do it because we have no choice.

> —JOYCE MILLER,[1] a thirty-one-year-old Jamaican woman in Brooklyn, discussed her past experiences as a domestic and child care worker in the New York City area.

It was a situation I resented. They had hampers and stuff like that, but when they undressed, they took [off] their clothes, they just walked out of them and left them on the bathroom floor. And I'd had enough. One Monday morning, I walked in and I said I'm not picking up any clothes today. (Laughs) I decided that I'm not picking up any CLOTHES today. . . . One day I went on strike and *she (the employer) said, "Well this is what the job requires and if you're going to hold the job, it's part. . . ." I didn't do it that day but the next day I [picked them up]. . . . Her argument is that she has always picked up after her husband and that's the way he is and she accepted him like that. Since she doesn't want to pick . . . up, I'm sure she hires somebody who will pick . . . up for her.*

—MONICA COOPER, a twenty-seven-year-old former domestic worker from
Jamaica, talked about an interchange with her suburban employer.

Whether or not the employer in the second incident resembles the 1980s media image of the working woman, professional, in skirt and tie, briefcase in hand, rushing from her apartment in a gentrified New York neighborhood or that of the affluent "housewife" giving parting instructions over her shoulder about picking up the kids from school and preparing dinner as she runs to meet friends and "go shopping," most working women's experiences are very different from hers. Whatever the current media image of women who work, the world of women's work is generally low paid, dead end, and undervalued. Nowhere is this truer than private household domestic and child care work. Within a sexual division of labor that assigns child care and domestic work to all women, private household workers take over these responsibilities for some women for pay. Shunned by men, this work becomes multiply devalued as it is passed from one woman to another along class, racial, ethnic, and migration lines, within the cash nexus.[2]

In this article, ten West Indian women currently or previously employed as private household child care and domestic workers in the New York City area speak of their experiences as domestic workers, as migrants, and as mothers.[3] They tell of how and why they do domestic work, what relationships exist with their employers, and how they balance their own family and household responsibilities with wage work. At times their voices could be those of other domestic workers over the last hundred or more years.[4] Sometimes their voices resemble those of other recent women migrants to the United States who have found themselves in the service sector of the economy. At other times, they echo the experiences of other working mothers.

MIGRATION AND DOMESTIC WORK

I am their only source of support . . . I thought about how the children are getting big and I wasn't working for the greatest salary. And I was thinking that there would come a time when I could just barely support the kids. So I need to make more money. So I just thought about coming to America. Maybe I'll be able to do it there.

—JUDITH THOMAS, a Vincentian mother of four, migrated in 1980
at twenty-nine years old.

Their responsibility for themselves, their children, or other kin motivates their migration. Though all but one (who had just completed high school) were employed prior to migration, some jobs were unsteady while others offered little chance for mobility. For most, wages were inadequate. They worked a range of jobs including primary school teaching, police work, clerical and administrative assistant work in government or the private sector, factory work, postal work, higglering (petty trading), and servicing the tourist industry. Most had not done domestic work before.

Like their relatives and friends before them,[5] these West Indian women migrate to "better themselves." In New York they seek "opportunity," in employment and in education, for themselves and their children.[6] They are drawn, as well, by the availability of basic consumer goods unaffordable at home and especially important to them as mothers.

In spite of economic pressures and the expectations to migrate to "better oneself," some women, like Janet Robinson and Dawn Adams, postpone migration in order to remain with their children. Janet Robinson waitressed, did factory work and six months of domestic work that paid "just a farthing," enough "to just get the baby milk and that's it." Refusing several previous offers because she wanted to "watch my daughter grow," in 1968, at thirty years old, she accepted an offer to go to New York to do domestic work and support her twelve-year-old daughter. Dawn Adams said she "always wanted to be there to bring up my daughters. I didn't really have any thought of migrating." But after several years of teaching, nurses' training, and four years on the police force, the lack of opportunities to advance, to make better use of her talents, and to better support her mother and daughters created pressure on her to migrate in 1981 at the age of thirty-two, reluctantly leaving her children and her mother.

While to be a good mother means to leave one's children and migrate, ironically, taking care of someone else's children is often their first job in New York, especially for those without permanent residence status, the green card. Legal entrance to and residence in the United States with permanent residence status is available primarily to those sponsored by close relatives or by employers at the time of migration. Only a few in this group had this option. Most entered with visitors' visas which they overstayed, becoming undocumented. To achieve their goals, including reunion with their children, they needed green cards. To get them, they turned to employer sponsorship in child care and domestic work, the main route for West Indian women (other than marriage to a permanent resident or a citizen, or sponsorship by certain closely related permanent residents or citizens). None knew of any West Indian woman (besides registered nurses, of whom there is a shortage in New York) who had been sponsored by an employer outside of domestic work.[7]

Learning to be "Maidish"

> This is not something I thought I would ever do for a living. If somebody had said to me "You're going to clean somebody else's house to make money," I'd say, "Come off it." I had an attitude about that but then after I really thought about it, I said if this is what I have to do, I'm going to make the best until the situation changes.

Monica Cooper spoke of her domestic work experience. She did general housekeeping and took care of two children for a suburban New Jersey family in which the husband owned a health care related business and the wife did not work outside the home. She describes her responsibilities:

> Everything. Meals, cooking, everything. Everything. And at that point [1976] I was making $80 a week [laughs] for 5 1/2 days, they call it. . . . [My] day off was Sunday and I had to be back by noon on Monday. . . . I decided to do it to get my sponsorship.

After three weeks on her first job here, Marguerite Andrews, a thirty-three-[year] old former school teacher supporting four children, spoke of her adjustment. Although she had an "understanding," "good" employer, becoming a domestic worker and moving from the relative autonomy and high status of teacher to a subordinate, if not subservient, position was difficult.

> I'm not yet really adjusted to it. . . . She's not bossy or anything like that. But within myself I figure I should be more, I can't explain. . . . I don't like to use the word "maidish," but I should put myself all out to do everything. But you know this will have to take some time.

At that same time, Marguerite Andrews related an incident that took place in St. Vincent when Marguerite herself employed a domestic worker. When one of Marguerite's sons left his dirty clothes in a trail on the floor instead of placing them in the hamper, her employee refused to pick them up and wash them. Marguerite's son ordered the worker to do so, saying that she was paid to clean up after him. Although Marguerite took to heart the domestic worker's criticism of her son's manners, at that time, she shared his definition of the job. When Marguerite told me the story, she noted how her perspective on domestic work had changed and said she hoped that she would never receive such treatment. Ironically, with a change in jobs to new employers who demanded greater subservience, she has since experienced similar encounters from the subordinate position which has broadened her understanding of hierarchy from below.

Marguerite left this last job in which she had hoped to initiate sponsorship proceedings because "it is not humanly possible to stick it." Like Marguerite, others assess whether they can tolerate a particular job for the two or more years of sponsorship. Judith Thomas similarly assessed a potential sponsor job and left amicably before the procedure was begun: "I knew that the sponsor wouldn't work out with her, I couldn't last that long." Her next employers sponsored her.

Living In and the Sponsor Job

Everyone described sponsor jobs as the "worst," especially those which are live-in. Sponsored jobs on a live-in basis greatly exacerbate problems structural to domestic work. Although some employers seek to avoid exploitation and some are unaware of the impact of their behavior on the worker, many take advantage of the sponsorship situation, the workers' vulnerability, and their lack of experience with codes of behavior here. Exploitation may involve long hours, abysmal pay, a heavy work load, and particular attitudes and behaviors exhibited toward the worker.

Joyce Miller worked at her live-in sponsor job from 1977 to 1981. The couple for whom she worked, on the edges of suburban New Jersey, owned a chain of clothing stores. The wife worked part-time in the business and devoted the rest of her time to shopping for antiques, decorating, attending cooking classes, entertaining, traveling, and participating in her children's school. Joyce worked sixteen hours or more a day, was on call twenty-four hours a day, seven days a week, caring for the large house and three children for $90 a week ($110 at the time she quit). When she took a day off to see her lawyer, that day was deducted from her salary.

235

*SHELLEE COLEN
"With Respect and
Feelings": Voices
of West Indian
Child Care and
Domestic Workers in
New York City*

> The working situation there [was] a lot of work. No breaks. I work sometimes till 11 o'clock at night . . . I get up early in the morning and I get up at night to tend the baby. I wash, I cook, I clean.

As Joyce began to get "enlightened" (her words) to her own exploitation, her employer became upset.

When Dawn Adams, who was at the time undocumented, quit a short-lived suburban job, her employers threatened to report her to the Immigration and Naturalization Service. Others told of similar intimidation that plays on undocumented West Indian women's sense of vulnerability. This itself is heightened by occurrences such as INS raids at the Port Authority bus terminal on Sunday nights and Monday mornings to "catch" undocumented domestic workers returning to suburban jobs from their day off.

Workers often felt trapped in sponsor jobs with no apparent end in sight. After four years in what was supposed to be her sponsor job, Monica Cooper got "restless and very depressed." She knew that her papers had passed the labor board but that her employers had said that they would not "bend over backwards" to help with her sponsorship.

> It started one week where I would just cry. Just cry period. And I was crying constantly for this week in question and Mrs. S., she would ask me what's the matter. Because I resented them but . . . I'd wipe my eyes and I'm smiling when they're around. But this week I couldn't do it anymore. I mean they'd go out and I'm there [alone] with the kids. It was like a total disadvantage. By the time I left there I was making $100 and I was with them for 4 1/2 years . . . And this week in question, I was just crying, and crying, crying. I couldn't tell her why I was crying. She said "Is it anything we did?" But . . . it was everything. By this time I could say it's all of you. But I told her no.

Soon after this tearful week, Monica Cooper retained a different lawyer, made new arrangements for her sponsorship (by a relative), and a few months later gave notice, quit, and found clerical work. In spite of the cost in money and time, some workers do quit unsatisfactory sponsor jobs and reinitiate the process with new employers.

Judith Thomas was sponsored by a woman who owned a cafe and whose husband worked in his family's textile business. She took care of their child and maintained their three-bedroom and three-bathroom apartment (though they hired someone else to do the "heavy" cleaning once a week). She remembered this experience:

They just somehow figure because they're sponsoring you, they own you. And if they say jump, you should jump. And if they say sit, you should sit . . . when you start in at the beginning they tell you certain amount of . . . work and then as you go on they just keep on adding more and more. It was really a dedication. . . . I felt as if I wouldn't hold out. I couldn't make it. But then when I just think . . . that . . . I'd be better off staying here now and continuing, knowing that one day I'll get it all over with . . . And I think about my kids and just say regardless to what, I just have to do this. But I tell you it wasn't easy. There were some nights when I would just cry and cry and cry myself to sleep, and say, "God, how long it's going to be?"

With her green card, she has been firm about defining her job, pay, and working conditions in her current child care work for two lawyers. As she said, "I paid my dues when I wasn't legally here and I just believe that since I became legal, then every right of a legal person should be mine."

Isolation from kin, friends, and community is a painful consequence of many live-in jobs. Immersion into a foreign world aggravates the loneliness and demoralization of many new migrants. Janet Robinson said that her first employer was good, "But I was very homesick and lonely." Those in isolated suburban areas often fared the worst. Those in the city and especially those who got away on days off to their "own" community fared better. Marguerite Andrews squeezed just enough out of her paycheck to escape from her Park Avenue live-in job to a furnished room in Bedford-Stuyvesant every weekend. Joyce Miller found that the isolation of a black woman living in a white world had other consequences when people mistook her for a convict from the nearby prison when she did the shopping in town. When faced with a snowstorm on her day off, Monica Cooper paid several times her normal bus fare to "get out" of her suburban live-in job and come to New York. As she said, "There's no way on earth I'm going to have a day off and stay in there."

Speaking of a short-lived, Park Avenue, potential sponsor, live-in job, Marguerite Andrews asked,

Is slavery really abolished? There is not much difference between working in this situation and slavery. The working hours are the same, the exploitation is the same. There is no human recognition. We eat the same food, live together in the same house, but we don't mingle. I am in it but not part of it.

While a (potential) sponsor live-in job may feel like "slavery," what it resembles most closely is a form of legally sanctioned indentured servitude in which the worker performs until the green card is granted.

Despite the exploitation, several women feel gratitude toward their employers for sponsoring them. As Joyce Miller said: "That's why I give and take a lot of things. . . . A lot of things I let her get away with because I feel indebted to her." Like several others, she has maintained relations with her former employers, especially to visit the children.

In discussing the role of immigrant workers in New York, Joyce Miller said "they just want cheap labor . . . West Indians, or foreigners or what they want to call it." She indicated many ways in which undocumented workers support the U.S. economy that include providing exploited labor, retaining immigration attorneys, and purchasing food, clothing, and household items to send home regularly to kin.

237

*SHELLEE COLEN
"With Respect and
Feelings": Voices
of West Indian
Child Care and
Domestic Workers in
New York City*

Monica Cooper pinpointed racism as a major influence on immigration policy and procedure, noting the differential treatment of different immigrant groups:

> I do feel the system is set up to make it harder for black people coming here. It's . . . to a larger extent . . . people coming in from the black countries or [some of the] Third World countries . . . that sense that they have special quotas.

While not citing several political and economic factors, she compared the treatment of Korean and Haitian immigrants:

> Look at the difference [between the treatment of the Haitians and the Koreans]. You don't have to know a lot about what's going on, current events, to be able to pick that out. Black people or people from the Third world . . . [Western] hemisphere, have a harder time gaining acceptance in this country than people from the East. . . . Their papers take longer. You go through everything that says you better go home. If you can stick it out then you're the better one and you *know* that people stick it out.

In spite of "everything that says you better go home" West Indian women do "stick it out." Visions of their children and families, letters from home, support from kin and friends in New York, and the determination to meet their goals empower them to overcome obstacles in their paths. Most must travel to their home islands for the final interview, a medical examination, and the granting of the green card.[8] They visit their children and kin, and with green cards in hand, many begin their children's "papers." Legal status permits them to visit home, but worsening economic conditions, including rampant inflation, often preclude long visits or returning to live. Joyce Miller, who after several years of "doing domestic" is a bookkeeper in a Manhattan real estate office, said, "A lot of Caribbean people come here and they are surprised. . . . They are disappointed. . . . They thought the life is easier. I think it's harder here than back home. In a certain way if we could get work back home as though we get it here, we would never stay."

Some leave private household work soon after receiving their green cards. Most who remain find "better" jobs with higher salaries which they command with their legal status. Most who have been in live-in positions find their own accommodations. Some remain in domestic work while preparing for other employment through further education and leave when they find other work. Fewer remain in domestic work indefinitely with "good" employers, often in spite of further education, for a variety of reasons.[9] The majority who leave private households, work in the "pink-collar" women's jobs, especially in clerical or health care occupations.[10]

"If people only knew what we went through to be here. I try to tell them but they don't hear," lamented Shirley Green. Remembering her sponsorship experiences, Joyce Miller said,

> People don't understand how hard it is to get here. And we try to explain to them. It's terrible. And you think of all you go through. You go through all this paperwork and go through the lawyer and pay so much money and you get this blooming little piece of card, green paper. It's not even green. The day when I got I said, "This is IT?" They should have a better system than this.

RESPECT, THE ASYMMETRICAL RELATIONS
OF "DOING DOMESTIC"

I work hard. I don't mind working hard. But I want to be treated with some human affection, like a human being . . . I don't get any respect. . . . Since I came here this woman has never shown me one iota of, not even, go down to the smallest unit you can think, of human affection as a human being.
   —Marguerite Andrews DISCUSSED THE TREATMENT SHE RECEIVED ON A JOB.

While sponsored and live-in work are "the worst," carrying special meanings for the worker, they are exacerbations of problems possible structural to domestic work. Although employers exhibit a range of behaviors, even with "good employers" some problems emerge which might be considered structural to the working conditions.

Low wages, lack of benefits, lack of formal contracts, lack of job ladders, low status, limited unionization, and personalized relations situate this work at the low levels of capitalism's tertiary sector framed by the asymmetrical relations of class, race, and sex. Beyond the low pay for repetitive and exhausting work, many women have difficulties with the asymmetrical social relations of the work. Like other relations mediated by a wage, these social relations mirror the dominant/subordinate class relations of capitalism. But they do so through the additional filters of sex, race, and migration which shape them in particular ways.

Within the contemporary sexual division of labor, child care and domestic work are assigned to women as extensions of women's supposedly "natural" nurturing and caregiving. "Naturalizing" the work implies that it is unskilled and not really worth wages, trivializing it. Devalued when passed from men to women in the society at large and within the same households,[11] the work is further devalued when passed from one woman who chooses not to do it and can pay for it, to another woman who performs it in someone else's household for the wages she needs to maintain her own household. The devaluation lends particular character to the dominant/subordinate relations between employee and employer.

The asymmetrical relations are further shaped by assigning this work, and much personal service work, to racially or ethnically distinct groups (either immigrant or native born) in the context of a society suffused with ideologies about racial and ethnic superiority and inferiority. The assignment of private household, personal service work to those with low status, by virtue of gender, and racial and ethnic hierarchies, reinforces the hierarchies.[12]

Class, sex, race, and migration have shaped the asymmetrical social relations for much domestic and child care work in the United States, from the first African house slaves to the Irish immigrant "servants" of one hundred years ago and to contemporary Salvadoran, West Indian, and other workers.[13] The worker is thus categorized as "other" (as defined by the dominant white male society), increasing the separation between employer and employee as well as the potential for exploitation. Marguerite Andrews states that "The racial thing really gets me down. I'm treated this way because of race. The only difference between us [Marguerite and her employers] is race." While race may be a major difference, it does not exist apart from sex, class, and migration for West Indian women of color in creating "otherness" which reflects and reinforces the particular asymmetrical social relations of the work.

The location of domestic work in the private household further influences the social relations of the work. While the nature of housework and its status as "productive" labor has been greatly debated,[14] work located in the home is often not recognized as work and is therefore devalued. In part, this is due to an ideological construct which paralleled the movement of much productive activity out of the home into a separate workplace during the process of capitalist industrialization in the West. The ideology strictly separated the workplace and the home, linking them to a parallel ideological separation between the genders which segregated women in the home.[15] In addition, the location of this work in the private household isolates and atomizes the worker and impedes the unionization of domestic work.

In discussing the asymmetrical relations, every woman spoke most about the lack of respect shown to her by employers. What the worker experiences as lack of respect often appears to be efforts to depersonalize the very personal relations involved in the work and to dehumanize the worker in a variety of ways. On one hand are the personalized relations of the work, the worker's intimate knowledge of her employers, her responsibility for maintaining and managing the household to free its members for other activities, her possible residence in the household, and her nurturance, guidance, and care, both physical and affective, for the children. On the other hand are the wage relations of the work, and the depersonalizing, dehumanizing treatment of the worker.

> The treatment here is terrible. . . . I think the employers should treat people much better because they're cleaning up after them to make the environment clean. They're helping them out. If they can do the work themselves, they [should] stay at their house or do the work themselves. Don't treat people like that.

Joyce Miller pointed out the unacknowledged need for the employee. She spoke of how her twenty-four-hour responsibility for the children and household freed her employers but at the same time was taken for granted by them.

> She thought she had me there inevitably. She wanted me to be there forever. No one ever came there and stayed. Not because she's bad, but because of the work. The responsibility. It was a lot. She doesn't like to stay home. She had her baby [third child] and like in the space of two weeks she's gone. She's not there at day. She's not there at night.

The employer worked short part-time hours at her husband's business, "otherwise she got herself other activities. I mean hanging out with friends for the day . . . shopping. . . . They don't give me anything extra when they go on vacation [a few times a year]. Because I have the responsibility day and night." She added, "I'm not looking for them to shower us down with money, with clothes, but with a little respect and feelings. You know because they want full respect from us and at the same time they want to treat us like nothing."

At times, Joyce Miller felt taken for granted by the employers for whom she worked after getting her green card. They were a wealthy couple with an elegant co-op on the Upper East Side of Manhattan. The husband was a lawyer from a manufacturing family, while the wife, from a New York real estate family, was an aspiring magazine writer who was somewhat "spoiled" and very "untidy."

> The thing I hate, everytime I clean the house, you know that woman make a mess. She throw everything on the floor. She leave all the cabinets open, you bump your head everytime of the day. She leave all the drawers out. . . . I don't like things to be messed up. If I fix it, don't throw it down. If you use a thing, don't throw it on the floor. Put it in the hamper.

While picking up after people may be "part of the job," Janet Robinson, Dawn Adams, and others disliked finding a mess where they had just tidied up and felt frustrated when they entered the apartment they left spotless the evening before to "meet juice under the table, pieces of bread on the floor, and the child's toys everywhere."

"Like a Human Being"

> *The most important thing is to show the person that you know they are human too. Most important is how you treat them.*
>   —BEVERLY POWELL commented on employers' behavior toward the worker.

The low esteem for housework and for those who perform it was noted by some women as the "worst part." As Beverly Powell said,

> When people look down on you for cleaning up their messes, then it starts hurting. The worst thing is when they look at you as stupid, maybe not stupid, but as a damn fool. You should treat people exactly as how you want to be treated. We can't all be doctors or lawyers, someone has to clean up the dirt. I am a hard worker. I want a little consideration. If I'm paid $1,000 for work but treated like dirt, it will pay the bills, but forget it.

Like other West Indian domestic workers, Monica Cooper took pride in her housekeeping but resented her employers' distancing and denial of her as a person.

> It was like because I am the employee, because of what I'm doing, somehow I was looked down on. I was a good housekeeper. Because that's how I am. Whatever it is I do, I love to do my best. And I did my best. . . . But . . . there is a blockage in between. It's like she and I are O.K., but if a friend comes by, you feel the difference:. "Oh, now she's the housekeeper."

Whatever the relationship otherwise, it is depersonalized as it is presented beyond the household.

Clothing is one of the clearest forms of depersonalization. While for some women uniforms provide an inexpensive mode of dress that saved their own clothes for "after work," most who were asked to wear uniforms resented it. Judith Thomas "hardly ever wore the uniform because it was white" and therefore impractical for both child care and housework. She recounted a story which pinpoints a uniform's function. She accompanied her employer (a part-time grade school teacher whose husband was in business) to Miami to take care of the children. Judith said,

241

*SHELLEE COLEN
"With Respect and
Feelings": Voices
of West Indian
Child Care and
Domestic Workers in
New York City*

> She wanted me to wear the uniform. She was really prejudiced. She just wanted
> that the maid must be identified. . . . She used to go to the beach every day with
> the children. So going to the beach in the sand and sun and she would have the
> kids eat ice cream and all that sort of thing. You know what a white dress would
> look like at the beach? . . . I tell you one day when I look at myself, I was so dirty,
> . . . just like I came out from a garbage can . . . I felt real upset.

That day, noting the condition of her uniform, she asked to wear jeans and a top
and the employer agreed. The day she did, the employer's brother

> came by the beach to have lunch with [the employer]. I really believe they had
> a talk about it, because in the evening, driving back from the beach, she said,
> "Well, Judith, I said you could wear something else to the beach other than the
> uniform, and I think you will have to wear the uniform because they're very for-
> mal on this beach and they don't know who is guests from who isn't guests."

In the context of racial segregation, uniforms function to unmistakably identify
people of color as service workers, the only roles which would justify their presence in otherwise all white settings.

Food and eating are other arenas of dehumanization and depersonalization.
Some employers left food for the worker to prepare for the children but none for
the worker herself, though she might work an eight- to twelve-hour shift. One
worker was accused of consuming "too much" of a particular food, milk, which
she never drank. When one woman on a live-in job ate some pork chops which
had been in the refrigerator for several days while her wealthy corporate executive employers dined out, she was informed that several pork chops were
"missing" and that she should "find" them. With her own money, the worker replaced what she ate, and no comment was made. In other instances, the food
that is left for the women to eat is inadequate for the amount of physical labor
they perform. Janet Robinson remembered an early experience in which she was
left a lunch of cottage cheese, which seemed practically inedible to her West Indian palate. Her reaction resembles that of the Barbadian domestic in Paule
Marshall's story who exclaims, "as if anybody can scrub floor on an egg and
some cheese that don't have no taste to it."[16]

Joyce Miller spoke of the classic situation in which, as a live-in worker for
a young, wealthy family, she ate separately from the other members of the
household.

> I couldn't eat with them at the table. . . . I have to eat after they finish eating. . . .
> And then I eat in the kitchen. There are a lot of people who do that because they
> want us to know that we are not equal. That's my point of view. You are the
> housekeeper. I think the only reason why I was in their house is to clean. . . . Like
> olden days. . . . That's the part I hate. I hate that part because it's showing me a
> lot of things. You need things from me, but when it comes down to sitting at the
> table with you, you are going to show me separation there. I just don't like it.

She contrasted this experience with her former New Jersey job in which she was
underpaid but always included at the table. She said that if she went to sit by
herself, they said to her, " 'No, no, no. You've got to come right here at the table.'
. . . That was something she try to do all the time. That's one thing with her she
was great about, I never felt left out."

While spatial segregation means that some women eat in the kitchen after others, some live-in workers are denied the privacy of their own rooms. Some share a room with children. Some with their own rooms regularly take in an agitated or sleepless child in the middle of the night.

Judith Thomas spoke of the depersonalization, trivialization, and lack of respect involved in being treated like a child on a live-in job.

> It was another hard thing that as a woman, a mother, responsible for home, with a husband, and to come here to New York City and have to be living with people.... It was definitely hard for me. You know at times they would talk to you as though you were just some little piece of a girl. It was really humiliating at times.... Most of the time they wouldn't see me as that [fully adult] person.
>
> ...A couple of times I really had to tell them that. I really had to say, "Well, I want to be treated as a full adult. You know, you all must remember that there was once I had a husband and kids and had the same responsibility as you all but because people go through different stages in life, here I am now in this situation. So, you know, don't forget that. You know, remember, I was once this responsible person. And don't treat me like a child or some little girl."

In contrast, women spoke of "good employers" who are "fair," who "understand," who "have genuine human affection" and who "treated me like a human being." Besides attempting to minimize the material exploitation and disrespect on the job, some employers helped out in medical and family crises and tried to assist in the worker's education or self-development. Dawn Adams' sponsor employers, a theatrical lighting designer and her photographer husband living in Greenwich Village, was "the best person to work for." She was "willing to help" Dawn attend college by offering to continue to pay her a full-time rate though Dawn would attend classes in the morning while the child, for whom Dawn was primarily responsible, attended nursery school. Another woman who worked for this employer concurred with Dawn. Janet Robinson spoke highly of several of her employers including her current ones, two lawyers. Beverly Powell likes her current employers, involved in theater, who pay her overtime and treat her well. Those whose employers are regularly absent from the home, especially for their own full-time employment, fare the best. However, rarely did anyone speak of any employer without ambivalence. Even when airing a complaint, many workers said something like "she has her good side. Regardless of everything else, I think she's O.K." The flip side is also true. As several women said, "Nobody's perfect." Joyce Miller was often "confused" by the very friendly relations with her sponsor employer who "told [her] everything," always included her in dining and most other activities, yet paid her poorly. The basic outlines of the job include the inherent contradictions of employer/employee relations, including lack of respect, in a personalized context.

"One of the Family": Manipulation, Trust, and Distrust

The highly personalized relations of domestic work, especially that which is live-in, produce such phrases as "like one of the family." As Monica Cooper said,

They never treated me in a way that I felt like, even though I'm working for them, that I'm family. 'Cause when you're living that close to someone for 4 1/2 years, if there is no bond between you, then something has to be radically wrong. I felt that I was just used for whatever they needed.

Joyce Miller said,

whenever they want you to give your all in their favor, or anyway to feel comfortable to do what they want you to do, they use the words "we are family." That's the one I hate. "You are one of the family." That's not true. That's a password as sorry . . . if you're one of the family, don't let me eat after you. . . . They say it to make you feel O.K., but at the same time, they're not doing the right thing.

The ideology of family is used to manipulate the worker. Often used to explain why members of the *same* family should sacrifice for one another, here it is used to encourage people who are *not* family members to perform tasks or to tolerate treatment that may be exploitive. The image of family is called up to soften the edges of wage labor in personalized situations.

The image of family is most pervasive in child care. Most of the women in this group were hired primarily to care for children, which they preferred to their secondary housework responsibilities. Janet Robinson said, "I love the kids" and was echoed by many others who take pleasure in their relationships with the children. They put a great deal of thought and caring into tending the children. When the child that she took care of misbehaved, Dawn Adams said,

You know, it's not my child but I take care of her and I love her. I've been with her since she was three months old [she was then four years old]. And when she did it I was embarrassed myself.

Emotional vulnerability and exploitation are risks in child care situations, especially in conjunction with separation from one's own children. Some children received no parental discipline when they teased, hit, spit at, or were otherwise rude to the workers. When told that "Janet will clean it up," children learned to expect others to clean up after them. Several women mentioned that the parents were jealous of worker/child relationships. A jealous parent humiliated one worker by ordering her to her room when the employer's child sought comfort from the worker after being scolded by the parent. Relationships with the children often lead women to stay longer on jobs than they would otherwise; they sometimes return to visit children once they have left. The weekend after leaving a job, Beverly Powell lamented the end of a four-year relationship with the eight-year-old boy, who sometimes called her "mommy." While many women do keep in touch with the children, Beverly knew that the strained relations with the child's parents would prevent her from doing so.

I loved the kids and the kids loved me. They trusted me. . . . They could go on vacation far away and leave me with the kids and they'd call in because I was responsible enough for them to have confidence that "she's going to make them do what they're supposed to do."

Monica Cooper spoke about a major element in child care employment, trust. Beverly Powell's employers, a middle manager in a large corporation and her husband, a partner in a small import business, entrusted their son to her sole care twenty-four hours a day for five days a week at their country house each summer while they worked in Manhattan. However, the same employers who entrust their children to the worker may distrust the worker in other matters. Some women reported that the "thing she [the employer] hates most is to see me sitting down" as if the employers feared that the worker was cheating them by sitting down for a break. Though entrusting her with the care of their children for four years including while they were vacationing in the Caribbean, Monica's employers' trust vanished when she gave two-weeks notice.

> Everything was O.K. For four years I was with them and they trusted me and . . . all of a sudden . . . they couldn't find this and they couldn't find that. . . .

> Now that I'm leaving they're going to miss a [gold] chain [necklace] and they're going to miss a slip, and they're going to miss everything else.

BALANCING BABYSITTING AND BARRELS

The Responsibilities of Work and Family

> Some of them don't even talk to you. They just want to know how their kid is or how the housework is going. They never one day ask you how you're feeling or anything else. . . . They're into their own little world and their own little life and leave you out, block you out like you're just nothing. And I think that really hurts a lot. Especially when people leave five, six kids in the West Indies and come here to do housework.

Joyce Miller, above, was joined by several others who said, "They don't ask how I am." This lack of consideration and denial of the worker's human identity beyond her role as child care or domestic worker contrasts with the ideology of family, a worker's intimate involvement in the household, and being entrusted with the care of children. A failure to recognize and respect her personhood makes an impact on her life off the job as well as on it. West Indian women juggle paid child care and domestic work with "the rest of their lives" to care for their own children.

While all wage-working mothers balance work and family responsibilities with some difficulty in contemporary capitalist society, child care and household maintenance are stratified by class. The resources on which women have to draw engender different ways of handling their work and family duties. While both employer and employee may work to support their households, the wages, working conditions, and nature of kin and household responsibilities of these West Indian women mean that they have to juggle a different set of responsibilities in a different material and social context than their employers.

For example, the West Indian woman employed in domestic and child care work must stretch her wages to support herself, her children, and usually other kin as well, across town and across oceans. While wages range according to legal status, live-in or out, length of employment and individual employers, they are generally low, and do not include either medical benefits or overtime pay. Sometimes less, current gross salaries generally range between $175 and $225 a week for those with green cards. Although $300 a week was rumored to be the highest salary available in 1985, no one in this group even approached this amount. Only Judith Thomas has medical insurance paid by her employers. Several without insurance were paying off large medical bills.

With their wages, women support at least two households, in full or in part: their own in New York, and one or more composed of kin (possibly including their children) in their home country. New York housing takes the biggest bite out of their wages. Lawyers' fees, for those who hire them for their own or their children's green cards, are another major expense. Every woman sends remittances regularly. Dawn Adams was not unusual in remitting at least half of her earnings every other week to support her mother and two daughters, before her daughters joined her. Like others, she sent both money, for living expenses and her daughters' school expenses, and barrels, packages filled with food, clothing, and household goods, basic nonluxury items either unavailable or exorbitantly priced in the home country. Due to the high cost of basic items in Trinidad, Janet Robinson sends barrels every few months to her daughter and grandson. The last one contained almost $800 worth of goods including three gallons of cooking oil, forty pounds of rice, twenty pounds of detergent, flour, tea, cocoa, toothpaste, and other items. Remittances of money (including school fees for siblings and others) and goods may account for 20 to 75 percent of the domestic worker's income. Even after their children join them, West Indian women send remittances as other kin depend on them.

As Joyce Miller said, "We get paid less, they still take taxes, and at the same time we're buying the goods for the regular price. We don't get the price cheaper." Many reported working extra jobs at nights and on weekends to meet their financial responsibilities. Dawn Adams said, "You have to have your budget planned."

The lack of standardization, contracts, job security, or regular hours add to a worker's concern beyond the job. Beverly Powell was asked to change from her regular nine to six or seven, five-day shift, to take full twenty-four-hour responsibility for the eight-year-old boy from Sunday evening to Friday evening at the summer house while the parents worked in the city. She had to send her own daughter who joined her from Jamaica to live with Beverly's sister in Canada for the summer since Beverly could not be present to care for her. Her schedule became more irregular and unpredictable. For example, one Sunday morning she was requested to arrive several hours earlier than previously planned. This necessitated canceling other plans and packing up to go immediately, though on arrival she found her employers lounging with afternoon drinks, as yet unready to depart. Many women spoke about the inconsiderateness of the unpredictably shifting schedules and the impact on their lives. Dawn Adams was regularly requested to remain late just as she prepared to leave, which often interfered with her "after work" plans. Several times her employers returned very late, which, for Dawn and other women, meant later and therefore longer and more dangerous subway rides home. As she said, "It seems as if it never bothered them [that] when they were in their house, I had to be on the streets." These schedule extensions left less time in which women could accomplish their own household and kin responsibilities, be with children, other kin, or friends, or just relax. As Beverly Powell said, "No matter how well paid I am, I want a little time to myself. . . . She doesn't even think of the child that I have. And then she talks about loyalty." As different women said: "They don't think that I have my family waiting for me." "They don't think about my child." "It's O.K. for them to ask me to stay extra time because they have their family together, but what about me?"

While child care arrangements across town were difficult, those across oceans were more so. These women with young children present paid a large part of their salaries to a local babysitter, often another West Indian, who took several children into her apartment. Many women reported a variety of problems that occur in this situation. Children left at home when a mother migrates are generally kept by kin, often a mother or sister, or friends. Although the mother provides as best she can, her children may feel emotionally or materially deprived, and the situation may be stressful for her, the children, and the caretakers.

This balancing is not without its emotional costs. The pain and loneliness of leaving children was central to these women's experiences. As Dawn Adams said, "What could be harder than me leaving my kids in St. Vincent and coming here to work, not seeing them. I don't see them for about two and a half years after that last night I slept in the house with them." When Beverly Powell described getting into bed at night and wondering if her daughter had been bathed and was asleep yet, she spoke for many women who reported crying themselves to sleep many nights, missing their children and wondering about their welfare. Joyce Miller was "so very, very lonely" for her son that she said, "I think I give them [her employer's children] more because I just think of them as my own. Just 'cause I was lonely, I gave them all I have." For other women, as well, employers' children became substitutes for their own. Being torn between affluent and poor material worlds is cause for more emotional balancing. The West Indian woman may work in a world of relative wealth in which she witnesses waste "that makes your heart bleed" and go home to another with her low wages where she confronts demands from a "third world" to send goods which she cannot afford.

Determination and Resistance

In answer to the question of what gets her through, Judith Thomas replied forcefully, "I think strong will. . . . I've always had . . . a determined mind." Drawing on their strength, determination, and networks of support, these West Indian women cope with and resist the exploitation they confront on the job. Their determination to achieve their goals for themselves and their children keeps them going. It is buoyed by letters from home saying "we're praying for you" and "if it wasn't for you, we couldn't make it."

They use strategies such as defining their own tasks and airing grievances on the job. Joyce Miller answered with "my name is Joyce" when addressed or referred to as "the maid" or "the girl." Dawn Adams, tired of risking another late night subway mugging, instructed her employers to hire a separate nighttime babysitter. None of these strategies eliminates the structural problems of the work which unionization, though difficult in domestic work, would begin to address. When exploitation is intolerable, quitting is the last option.

247

*SHELLEE COLEN
"With Respect and
Feelings": Voices
of West Indian
Child Care and
Domestic Workers in
New York City*

The support, pleasure, and meaning that they derive from other parts of their lives nourishes and renews them. Women spoke of the importance of relationships with their kin and friends, education, religious beliefs, and participation in church and community activities. Their ties to children and parents are primary. They seek out and recreate networks of kin and friends to ease their adjustment, provide companionship, and share housing, information, and jobs and services. Many exchange child care and household maintenance services with a friend or relative in the same household or between households. The conversations Dawn Adams had with the other babysitters in the park are reminiscent of Paule Marshall's description of a former generation of Barbadian domestic workers talking around the table after work "to reaffirm self-worth" and "overcome the humiliations of the work day."[17] Religious beliefs and activities provide crucial meaning and support for many women. Monica Cooper, who like many others "prayed a lot," also "set up school" for herself each night with her employer's college texts. School experiences benefit others. Active participation in West Indian church and community groups in New York empower and give pleasure to many women. Their identities derive primarily from these sources and not from their work.[18]

Leaving domestic work for the pink-collar ghetto may not seem to offer much, but it holds promise for many domestic workers. When Dawn Adams' $25 raise was rescinded a few months after it was given, because her employer, though a "good person to work for," had difficulty paying it, she had had enough. She found a bank teller job with regular hours, wages, and raises, and began college study toward a business and management degree. Though she took an initial pay cut, the job provides medical and dental benefits for herself and her children, who arrived in New York five months later. Judith Thomas, who earned her certification as a nursing aide, began looking for a job with medical and dental benefits for herself and her daughters soon after their arrival. No longer "frustrated" doing housework "because of circumstance," Monica Cooper expresses the optimism of many as she prepares for a singing career and does temporary clerical work: "Now I'm doing what I want to do because that's what I choose to do. At this point in my life, I'm not settling and doing anything that I don't want to do." Few are able to avoid doing things they do not want to do, but many are pleased to leave the particular constraints and exploitation of domestic work. Their balancing act as wage-working mothers continues as they enter another world of women's work.

CONCLUSION

While much domestic work resembles activities women do in their own families for love, it is in fact embedded in capitalist wage relations. While it resembles other work for wages, private household domestic work is fraught with contradictions: between its status as wage labor and the very personalized relations involved, between the framework of the cash nexus and the intimacies of child care, between the worker's involvement in a household and the peculiar forms of exploitation, depersonalization, and dehumanization she may experience.

These West Indian women share experiences with other women as mothers, workers, and migrants. While they balance kin and work responsibilities, they do so within a strikingly stratified system of child care and household maintenance. Their domestic work experiences most resemble those of other private household workers. Their obstacles and aspirations resemble those of other female migrants. Yet the particular interaction of gender, race, class, migration, and history makes their lives distinct.

Notes

1. I have assigned pseudonyms to protect the privacy of the women whose experiences are recounted here.
2. This article is based on ongoing doctoral dissertation research. It shares much data and analysis with the forthcoming dissertation and with my article entitled "Just a Little Respect: West Indian Domestic Workers in New York City," in a collection on domestic workers in Latin America and the Caribbean edited by Elsa M. Chaney and Mary Garcia Castro which is being published in Spanish and English under the tentative title of *El Trabajo de la Cuarta Parte: Servicio Domestico en América Latina y el Caribe*.
3. This article is based on four or more interviews of two to four hours each with ten West Indian (English-speaking Caribbean) women currently or previously employed in private household child care and domestic work. The interviews and numerous other conversations with the women are part of ongoing anthropological fieldwork. These ten women range from late twenties to late forties, with most in their early to mid-thirties. All are mothers whose children reside either with them in New York or with kin or friends in their home countries. Many of them related stories of friends or acquaintances which enabled me to get a broader sense of West Indian women's experiences. In addition, interviews with immigration lawyers, Department of Labor officials, and personnel from a variety of agencies and offices which offer services to the West Indian community provided other information for this article.
4. Where "domestic work" appears alone in the text, in reference to the current research, it should be understood to mean both child care and housekeeping within the private household. Child care was the primary job responsibility of most of the women, though many, especially those who were living in, were also responsible for domestic tasks. For immigration purposes, the official designation is domestic work of which child monitoring and housekeeping are two categories.
5. Each woman interviewed has kin or friends abroad who migrated before her to England, perhaps in the peak period of the 1950s and 1960s, or to Canada and the United States, where West Indian immigration has peaked since the early to middle 1960s. Migration has been ever present in the Caribbean experience, linked to Caribbean participation in an international capitalist system. From the forced migration of Africans into slavery to the most recent migrations for wage work, Caribbean people have migrated to work. The legacy of colonialism and the persistence of multinational-influenced dependency create conditions of underdevelopment and poverty. Women experience these as unemployment, underemployment, lack of educational opportunity, limited occupational mobility, and low standards of living which pressure them to migrate. Labor needs, immigration policies, and "opportunity" influence the destination. (See D. Marshall 1982 for an historical overview of Caribbean migration. See Prescod-Roberts and Steele 1980; Foner 1978; Davison 1962; and Philpott 1973 on migration to England. See Henry 1982 for an overview of migration to Canada, and Silvera 1983 on West Indian domestic workers in Canada. See Bryce-Laporte and Mortimer 1976; Mortimer and Bryce-Laporte 1981; Dominquez 1975; and Gordon 1979 on the recent migration to the United States.)

6. Many cite their own and their children's education as motivations to migrate. Sacrificing precious nights and weekends, all but the most recent migrants have furthered their education since migrating. Some are currently studying, and others plan to resume study, especially in business and health care fields. Planning for their children's college education, unaffordable in their home countries, is central to several women's plans.

7. Domestic work has become a fairly simple path to the green card through employer sponsorship. The Immigration and Naturalization Service and the Department of Labor have several requirements, including proof of a shortage of documented workers available to work for the "prevailing wage," currently (1985) just under $200 for a 44 1/2-hour week for live-in domestic workers. Most live in as requirements favor it. Legally workers are supposed to receive at least the minimum wage throughout the sponsorship and the prevailing wage at the time the green card is granted. Because no agency actually monitors compliance with guidelines for wages and working conditions, the sponsorship situation may result in exploitation of new immigrant women.

8. Joyce Miller estimates that 15 percent of the women who return to their home islands for their final interview for their green cards find themselves in the cruel situation in which they are either detained up to several months or denied the card entirely because of improper processing of their papers or failure of their medical exam (often because of conditions such as high blood pressure).

9. Often these are older women who may confront age discrimination in the labor market. They may also have benefits through another family member.

10. Pink-collar jobs are those jobs within a sex-segregated labor market which are filled primarily by women and which are characterized by low wages, lack of unionization, little security, and few job ladders. Employed women tend to cluster in 20 out of 420 jobs as delineated by the Bureau of Labor Statistics, such as clerical, service, and sales work. (See Howe 1977 on pink-collar work).

11. See Howe 1977 on the devaluation of women's work.

12. See Spellman 1981 for a discussion of the interaction of race, gender, and somatophobia in relation to personal service work.

13. Other than rural "help" in which young women of the same class, race, and ethnicity were sent to work alongside the members of a neighboring household, sex, race, class, and migration are integral to the history of domestic work in the United States. (See Dudden 1983, Katzman 1978, Hamburger 1977, Glenn 1980, Dill 1979, Almquist 1979, Davis 1981, and others on this history.)

14. On housework, see Glazer-Malbin 1976, Gardiner 1975, Dalla Costa and James 1972, Howe 1977, Strasser 1982, and others.

15. The relegation of women to the home has another implication for the relationship between employer and employee. Though the child care and domestic workers in this group have been hired by a male and female couple, the bulk of the interaction is between the worker and the female employer who, while not performing the work herself, has been minimally assigned the management of those who do perform it.

16. P. Marshall 1983:6.

17. P. Marshall 1983:6.

18. This may derive from a "double consciousness" as well as from the "occupational multiplicity" of West Indians which Lowenthal discusses (Lowenthal 1972:141).

References Cited

ALMQUIST, E. M. 1979. *Minorities, Gender, and Work.* Lexington, Mass.: Lexington Books.
BRYCE-LAPORTE, R. S., and D. M. MORTIMER, eds. 1976. *Caribbean Immigration to the United States.* RIIES Occasional Papers 1. Washington, D.C.: Research Institute on Immigration and Ethnic Studies, Smithsonian Institution, pp. 16–43.

DALLA COSTA, M., and S. JAMES. 1972. *The Power of Women and the Subversion of the Community.* Bristol, England: Falling Wall Press.

DAVIS, A. Y. 1981. *Women, Race, and Class.* New York: Vintage.

DAVISON, R. B. 1962. *West Indian Migrants: Social and Economic Facts of Migration from the West Indies.* London: Oxford University Press.

DILL, B. T. 1979. "Across the Boundaries of Race and Class: An Exploration of the Relationship between Work and Family Among Black Female Domestic Servants." Ph.D. dissertation, New York University.

DOMINQUEZ, V. R. 1975. *From Neighbor to Stranger: The Dilemma of Caribbean Peoples in the United States.* New Haven: Antilles Research Program, Yale University.

DUDDEN, F. E. 1983. *Serving Women: Household Service in Nineteenth Century America.* Middletown, Ct.: Wesleyan University.

FONER, N. 1978. *Jamaica Farewell: Jamaican Migrants in London.* Berkeley: University of California Press.

GARDINER, J. 1975. "Women's Domestic Labor." *New Left Review* 89: 47–71.

GLAZER-MALBIN, N. 1976. "Housework: A Review Essay." *Signs* 1: 905–934.

GLENN, E. N. 1980. "The Dialectics of Wage Work: Japanese-American Women and Domestic Service, 1905–1940." *Feminist Studies* 6(3): 432–471.

GORDON, M. H. 1979. "Identification and Adaptation: A Study of Two Groups of Jamaican Immigrants in New York City." Ph.D. dissertation, CUNY Graduate Faculty in Sociology.

HAMBURGER, R. 1977. "A Stranger in the House." *Southern Exposure* 5(1):22–31.

HENRY, F. 1982. "A Note on Caribbean Migration to Canada." *Caribbean Review* 11(1): 38–41.

HOWE, L. K. 1977. *Pink Collar Workers: In the World of Women's Work.* New York: Avon.

KATZMAN, D. M. 1978. *Seven Days a Week: Women and Domestic Service in Industrializing America.* New York: Oxford University Press.

LOWENTHAL, D. 1972. *West Indian Societies.* London: Oxford University Press.

MARSHALL, D. I. 1982. "The History of Caribbean Migrations: The Case of the West Indies." *Caribbean Review* 11(1):6–9, 52–53.

MARSHALL, P. 1983. "From the Poets in the Kitchen." In *Reena and Other Stories.* Old Westbury, N.Y.: Feminist Press, pp. 3–12.

MORTIMER, D. M., and R. S. BRYCE-LAPORTE, eds. 1981. *Female Immigrants to the United States: Caribbean, Latin American, and African Experiences.* RIIES Occasional Papers 2, Washington, D.C.: Research Institute on Immigration and Ethnic Studies, Smithsonian Institution.

PHILPOTT, S. B. 1973. *West Indian Migration: The Montserrat Case.* London: Athlone Press.

PRESCOD-ROBERTS, M., and N. STEELE. 1980. *Black Women: Bringing it All Back Home.* Bristol, England: Falling Wall Press.

SILVERA, M. 1983. *Silenced.* Toronto: Williams-Wallace Publishers.

SPELLMAN, E. Y. 1981. "Theories of Race and Gender: The Erasure of Black Women." *Quest: A Feminist Quarterly* 5(4):36–62.

STRASSER, S. 1982. *Never Done: A History of American Housework.* New York: Pantheon.

Mary Crawford

Two Careers, Three Kids, and Her 2,000-Mile Commute

Women who want to have both fulfilling careers and a family still face tough choices about how to balance the two. Here, Mary Crawford, a college professor, writes about a rather drastic solution. In order to enhance her career opportunities, she moved thousands of miles away from her husband and children. Though the move was only temporary, it had effects on everyone involved.

As You Read, Ask Yourself . . .

What fears and doubts did Crawford and her husband express? What personal rewards did they find?

How did social norms make their creative life plans harder to follow?

Do you think that solutions to the work-family dilemma like this one are worth the pain and effort they involve?

A year ago I left Roger and the baby in our big old house in Iowa. Roger was busy getting ready for the semester's teaching; I was off to my new job as assistant professor of psychology at a Pennsylvania state college. Teenagers Mary Ellen and Mark, 15 and 14, earned boarding school scholarships and headed north to Minnesota. We're a tristate nuclear family, and it's a peculiar life.

I was raised in a world where married women stayed home. In all my growing-up years I remember my mother spending a night away from her children twice: when she and my father took their first vacation in 10 years and when she went to her father's funeral.

For at least some families, the world has changed since then. Still, my new life seems to make people uneasy; they don't know what sexual label to pin on me. I can't be "married," or I'd be in my husband's house where I belong. I'm not "divorced and available," but am I planning to be? After all, I am "separated." I don't think their interest has much to do with me personally; it's just that a woman's sexual availability is crucial to evaluating her as a person.

But for us, there is little ambiguity: we are still a family. The seeds of our separation were in our marriage contract:

We value the importance and integrity of our separate careers and believe that insofar as our careers contribute to our individual self-fulfillment they will strengthen our relationship. We do not consider one partner's career to be more important than the other's.

We'd finished graduate school together and solved the job problem by sharing a psychology professorship in a tiny Iowa college. For four years we'd done everything together; team-teaching classes, being mentors to our students, encouraging each other's research. We'd made time for another child, and took turns caring for him.

Eventually, the advantages of the arrangement became its disadvantages. We tired of being each other's closest colleagues. We needed to develop individual approaches to our work, without constant comparisons with each other. We each needed to pursue private career interests, and our rural isolation made branching out difficult. Paradoxically, we'd come to share too much. A little distance was in order.

Unfortunately, our unique experience didn't fit the mold of a résumé. Academic hiring committees saw only that we'd each been working part-time in a college that was both small and obscure. After two years and a number of fruitless applications, we finally agreed that whoever got an offer first would leave the other. We would allow two years for Partner B to find a job within commuting distance of Partner A. If none materialized, Partner A would return to the old shared professorship.

My worst conflicts centered around two-year-old Ben, the littlest child. The rest of us had agreed to the plan. But Ben was too small to have a voice in the decision, or anticipate the changes in his life. I never thought of taking him with me. He would be happiest in his own house, with his father's loving care.

And I had long dreamed of living alone. I was married at 18, a mother at 20, and had fantasized a life with time to work and space to breathe. I wondered who I would be without the people whose existence bracketed my life. Would I be sloppy or neat, would I run five miles every day at dawn or work and study late into the night? Would I eat junk food or serve splendid little dinners for one on the best china? Would it be miraculously easy to study without the nuisance of a family? I could not imagine what I would do with such perfect freedom.

When freedom came, it threw my world off center. I grieved for my family most terribly, especially Ben. His natural birth had been one of the great joys of my life, and the physical bond with him the strongest I have known. I thought longingly, sensuously, of his dimpled hands, sturdy legs, and innocent round belly. I wept easily, needing proof of my being. A mean-spirited word from a student or a curt remark from a colleague would do it. In a supermarket parking lot, I saw a father slap a two-year-old, and I fled to my car weak with despair.

Slowly the feelings stabilized; my sense of self began to return. And the self I discovered was very much like the person I have always been. Without my family's demands on my time I didn't magically turn into a marathon runner or a gourmet cook. Relieved of the necessity to set a good example, I remained reasonably neat and continued to eat my green beans. I accomplished the same amount of work I always had, discovering that weekends at the office are no fun. After years of feeling that the "real me" was being suppressed, I was amazed to find I'd been there all along, in the bosom of my family. I will never again be able to resent them with the old enthusiasm.

My pleasures now come from my work, my solitude, and my friends. I teach my favorite course, Psychology of Women, with a new understanding of what it means to be self-sufficient and new depth of feeling for the importance of family networks in defining our lives. I took up my research and writing again; and though I missed Roger's affirmation of my ideas, I turned to my colleagues and began to build the working relationships with other psychologists that I had missed so much in Iowa.

And I decided to enjoy my freedom—lots of dinners at the local French restaurant, all the first-run films, lazy Sundays with the *Times.* Perhaps the most exquisite pleasure—anyone who has shared living space with a family will understand—is to come home after a long day's work to a cup of tea, the mail, and the six-o'clock news in the utter peace of an apartment that is just as orderly as it was at breakfast time.

Still, there are problems. Roger and I have a feast-or-famine sex life—once a month I fly home to Iowa for three days. The distortions in our relationship are both funny and stressful. If we quarrel, we must explode-sulk-and-apologize in minutes. We haven't time for the luxury of fully developed bad moods. If we climb into bed weary, wanting just to sleep together spoon-fashion, we feel faintly guilty. This isn't what we've been fantasizing for the last month.

And then there's my relationship with Ben. On my first weekend home, I plunge into my role as Mommy. It seems to me that he is shamelessly overindulged. Nobody—even two years old and stubborn—needs three stories, six songs, four drinks of water, and a back rub before bed. I try to straighten him out, Roger and I exchange numerous sharp words, Ben cries and clings to Daddy. I realize I no longer know what it's like dealing with Ben's day-to-day needs. With a shock I see I'm behaving like the stereotype of a male absentee parent; proposing quick "cures" for his behavior and "taking charge" with demands that his live-in parent knows are unrealistic.

I realize that I am the "second parent" now, less intimately involved and less knowledgeable than Roger. Of all the changes in our lives, it is the hardest to accept. I learn to watch while Roger eases Ben through his two-year-old's struggle for autonomy, never forcing a confrontation, always respecting Ben's need to control his small world. I learn to respect Roger's need to parent in his own way.

It's easier being a parent to the teenagers. Boarding school was a great idea. They're finally in a school where the work is a challenge. They blossom. And I find myself more objective about their turmoils at a distance.

When Mark gets detention for failing to turn in assignments, I am able to see the problem as his, not mine. I point out in a friendly but detached way that if he wants to keep his scholarship he'll have to complete his assignments. If he wants advice on time-budgeting, he's welcome to write and ask. He doesn't ask, and he doesn't get detention again, either.

I can't pretend I never feel guilt. Guilt, that cradle-to-grave woman's home companion, is very much a part of my solitary life. I no sooner leave home than Ben gets sick, with chicken pox followed by complications. For a month Roger juggles his job and a child who's in pain. I am wild with worry. Selfishly I fear that Ben will connect his illness with my leaving and begin to hate me.

Late one night Roger phones and breaks down in tears of weariness and frustration. He doesn't blame me or ask me to come home. But *I know I ought to be there.* I pour it all out to a therapist friend. "Even if you were there, you couldn't 'make it all better' for Ben," she says. Her statement seems too easy an answer, but for some reason it stays in my thoughts. Exactly why does Ben "need" me? He has excellent medical care and is not in real danger. I know his father loves him as dearly as I, is at least as nurturing, and twice as patient. Do I really believe in some magical power, given to mothers, to ease the pain and make life trouble free? Perhaps it's not Ben's need I'm feeling, but my own: to be needed, and childishly, to be omnipotent.

Even now, with domestic matters under control, the guilt sometimes returns. If I were a genius, I tell myself, it would be okay. If I were the next Marie Curie or Margaret Mead, if Harvard wanted me to supervise a new research team . . . but I'm not that special, there's no justification for *my* selfishness.

There is some fundamental conflict here about *deserving* to work. And I dare say it to myself at last: *I am entitled to do work that I care about. Its value to me is at least as important as its value to the world.*

I meet many people who need to believe our experiment in living won't work. "You'll be divorced within a year" is a prediction I hear often, accompanied by a story of a couple who tried some bizarre long-distance relationship that ended in failure for the marriage. One person prophesies that Roger won't find another job within our two-year limit; the crunch will come if I refuse to give up mine. At first I'm wounded by my friends' cynicism. Don't they realize we care about each other and our marriage? I gradually see that their pessimism is too quick and too pervasive to be based on a realistic appraisal of the situation. It reflects their own needs for predictability and stability. Our experiment forces them to confront their own conflicts about risk-taking.

Our experiment *is* risky. We are beginning to stabilize; we can live this way a while longer and still be a family. But we do not do it lightly. We do it only because we need so much to have both halves of the human experience—love and work.

Jo Ellen Brainin-Rodriguez

A Daughter's Story

How do our parents' choices influence our career paths? Jo Ellen Brainin-Rodriguez grew up with a mother who went to medical school against the odds and became a women's health activist. Certainly, Brainin-Rodriguez had a positive role model, but she sometimes felt that her mother gave more to her work than to her children. Moreover, she also experienced sexual abuse from a stepfather. In this thoughtful reflection, she analyzes the many influences that led her to her present roles as wife, mother, and professional. As a psychiatrist, Brainin-Rodriguez works with Latina women who have histories of sexual abuse.

As You Read, Ask Yourself . . .

The author characterizes her mother as "driven." Would you agree?

How did sexual abuse affect Brainin-Rodriguez and how did she confront and resolve its effects?

In what ways does she want her work-family balance to be different from her mother's?

What are some other ways parents exert influence on their children's career choices?

Watching my mother become a doctor was a deterrent to my becoming a physician. I once asked her, "Why did you have to graduate first in your medical school?" My mother didn't graduate first by a slim margin; she graduated first with eight medals. It was in all the papers. She had three kids and was six months pregnant at the time, and was one of only four women in her medical-school class. What she told me was that she was so terrified she would come out last that she had to blast through. I think a lot of it has to do with her own feelings of inferiority and the fact that she had been put into slow classes when she first went to New York from Puerto Rico by people who didn't recognize her talent.

I never wanted to do anything that was as engrossing as my mother's work, but I became interested in medicine when I was doing health education in Boston, specifically work around abortion and birth control. Though I love what

I do, I am less driven than my mother to achieve professionally. I believe there are certain people in a given historical period whose actions make a huge difference in people's lives over the long term. Perhaps my mother is one of those people. I am making different choices.

I was born in New York City in December 1949. My parents had been married a little over a year. My dad was a union organizer, and shortly after I was born we moved to Lorain, Ohio, where he had work. My mother was also an organizer, but after I was born she was mostly a housewife. Within two and a half years, she had three children. The only memory I have of Lorain is of my parents arguing. When I was three and a half my mother left my father, moved with her three children back to her native Puerto Rico, and became a medical student. Her mind and her time became occupied with school, and I have memories of her studying for hours. Late at night we picked her up at the library in my stepfather's car.

As the oldest child, I became the primary baby-sitter and parent substitute. My mother married my stepfather when I was four, and my youngest brother, Daniel, was born when I was eleven. Before we had a maid, I came home from school, washed all the breakfast dishes, and then ran around making all the beds so that when my stepfather came home and started dinner, the house was tidy. I resented being held responsible for the behavior of the other kids, particularly in my teens, when my sister, only a year younger than me, had fewer responsibilities. We had a traditional division of labor in the house, despite the fact that my mother was atypical both as a student and later as a physician. My brother David never washed dishes; he mowed the lawn and washed the car—macho chores that had to be done only once a week, unlike the relentless cycle of dishwashing I was assigned.

My stepfather came from a strict, fundamentalist religious background. His father was a Methodist preacher in a little Puerto Rican town, his mother a passive matriarch adored by the family. My stepfather molested me and my sister sexually from the time I was seven until I was fourteen. Laura and I began to talk about it when we were eleven or twelve. We decided to lock the room, but my stepfather picked the lock. Finally I found the courage to stand up to him and say, "Get the hell out of this bedroom, and don't ever come here again." To my surprise, he stopped. I developed the split mind-set that a lot of abused kids have: I knew what was going on, but for many years I had a dissociative response. I saw my mother as frail and I was afraid that if we told her the truth, she would be devastated.

During my childhood I existed as if in a dreamlike state. All kinds of fears and anxieties and ambivalences arose as I began to awaken sexually. I felt conflicted and guilty. Like many, I struggled with my anger, dulling it with alcohol during my teens. For a brief time when I was thirteen I had a boyfriend, and another when I was fifteen, but I did not become sexually active until I was eighteen. In my last year of high school, I often cut class. I was secretive about what I was doing and where I was going; I frequented discos and smoked cigarettes in a sneaky kind of rebellion.

I attended the University of Puerto Rico for a year before dropping out. My mother and my stepfather were getting a divorce, and he was starting to freak out. As we became more rebellious and refused to go by the rules, I think he feared we would disclose the sexual abuse. When he offered me a ticket to New York, I took it. I had a feeling about my own power; I realized that I could make my own decisions, and as long as I didn't need my parents to provide for my food, clothing, and shelter, I could set out on my own.

Acknowledging my anger toward my mother was one of the hardest things I have ever done. The first time I said anything about how she might have protected us was in 1983, when I was pregnant with my second daughter, Tania. It took months for me just to say, in a low and gentle tone, "I really wish you had been there." In some ways I was still protecting her. It was easier for me to focus my anger on my stepfather than to confront my anger toward her. But my mother is not a fragile person. She handles conflict directly and well. Years earlier, when I finally told her what had happened, we could not have asked for a better reaction. For months she had agonized over whether Daniel should go to Puerto Rico and spend time with his father ("A boy needs his father"), and I finally snapped, "Bullshit. Let me tell you what kind of father he was." Her jaw dropped, and she burst out crying. She felt angry and betrayed. Together we pondered what the next step would be. My mother has a wonderful sense of drama, and she imagined that we might confront him like the chorus in a Greek play, singing, "I accuse you, I accuse you." Then, one by one, we'd dump buckets of paint on his head: "Brown is for the lives you've covered in shit, yellow is for your coward's eyes, green is for envy, red is for the blood on your hands." I said, "Mom, I don't think that is really practical. But it's a great image."

Finally we agreed on a plan: We would fly to Puerto Rico, join my sister and brother, and go to my stepfather's office and confront him. My mother called my stepfather and said that she wanted to meet with him one evening after work to talk about Daniel's visiting rights. The evening came, and my mother walked in first, followed by my sister, my brother, and me. My stepfather sat at his desk, and as we faced him my mother screamed, "I know what you have been doing all these years! All of Puerto Rico is going to know the filth you are!" He became fearful and grabbed her by the hair, and my brother and I grabbed him. He turned ashen. We made my stepfather sit down and try to explain himself. "Those were just fatherly caresses," he protested, but my mother said, "You don't pick locks to engage in fatherly caresses." Suddenly he wrenched himself away from us and jumped out the second-floor window. He jumped up from where he had fallen and screamed for the police. The next day we were arrested at the airport. In the end we got off, but it was expensive. My stepfather finally dropped the charges when he realized the publicity would be bad for him.

My mother is an incredible person who has left her mark on many agencies and people over the years. To me, that is all well and good, but it was her reaction to my stepfather's abuse that gave me the sense that the advocacy work she had done for children everywhere, she was willing to do for us. Going to bat for us was the most healing thing she could have done. The experience of the confrontation was very liberating for me.

On a professional level, the direction I have taken is in part a result of my experience with abuse. I am the chief psychiatrist of a unit at San Francisco General Hospital that treats general psychiatric patients. My unit specializes in the care of women and Latino patients, over eighty percent of whom have histories of abuse. I devote most of my energy in teaching to talking about abuse as an issue for patients we see. I think I am good at what I do. I have gotten to the place now where I call things the way I see them. I am polite and all that, but my style is to be direct. My mother is that way, too.

I met my husband, Stan, in a community clinic when I was a premed student. He had just finished his residency. We started living together right before I started medical school, and our daughter Amanda was born three months into my fourth year of medical school. Stan and I have been together for eighteen years. . . .

As a mother I feel I pay a lot more attention to my children than my mother did to me. I am more present; I talk to them constantly and give them my thoughts on a multitude of issues. If it were necessary to choose between my job and my kids, they would come first. I believe strongly that you can talk all you want to about politics and wax philosophical about women's rights, but if you can't give love and time and attention to your own children, it doesn't matter. Women should be able to take as much time as they want to raise children. Time off should also be available for men. However, in this country, if you don't have a lot of money, then the economic realities of raising a family often make that difficult.

My identity as a Puerto Rican and Latina is bound up with my identity as a woman. Both my identities, as a Latina and a woman, are intrinsic to the work that I do as a psychiatrist. A lot of the issues that American feminism struggles with are specific to American feminism and are not issues in the rest of the world. For that reason, I think that a lot of the female population in this country, women of color in particular, feel isolated from American feminism, with its ethnocentric, nationalistic focus. We need to make the analysis more global in perspective. For example, a big issue in American feminism is equality in the workplace. That issue is very different for women of color because they share that aspect of discrimination with their men. To me, being a feminist means being politically aware of power dynamics as they relate to gender.

I hope to continue to maintain a balance between personal satisfactions, family satisfactions, and work satisfactions. Playing the guitar and dancing recharge me for the work I do on a day-to-day basis. My work can be draining. I deal with a lot of extreme personalities in a tense environment. When I come home from work, I try to put it behind me and turn into my kids' mom, or pick up my guitar, or take a dance class. There are a lot of things I would love to do with leisure time, but I don't have as much of that now as I would like.

I am a public figure in some respects. When I go to Nicaragua, I am the representative for an organization at the academic level. But being a public figure like my mother does not interest me. I am proud of her, and I think she has contributed significantly to society, but I have missed having her present for me. She has a hard time saying no. This business of having important roles is very seductive. When she and Eddie, her current husband, were looking for a place to retire, I urged them to move to California. They debated it for a long time but finally agreed to come, since most of their grandchildren are here. But she's so busy that she rarely sees them. I told her, "I didn't invite you to California to be traipsing all over the world. I want you to be a grandmother to your grandchildren."

My mom is caring and kind-hearted, with strong morals and strong opinions. She has handed her social consciousness and her sense of justice down to us and her grandchildren. She has the ability to reflect on a thing and admit a mistake, which makes all the difference in our relationship as adults. I feel very close to her now. Standing up for us in the situation with my stepfather was an incredibly powerful model of what you can do as a human being to confront injustice for your family and the people you love. Right now my mother is as happy as she has ever been; she has found a real balance in her life. I just wish she were more present for me, which is evidence of how enduring childhood longings are.

Janice D. Yoder

An Academic Woman as a Token:
A Case Study

Janice Yoder's experience shows that even the strongest and most privileged woman can be adversely affected by social isolation, harassment, and a woman-hating environment. Situated as a "token woman" in an extremely competitive and masculinized context, Yoder began to suffer psychological deterioration. Yoder feels that her status as a psychologist, and her understanding of the sexism that was being used against her, did little to help her cope with a sustained assault of discriminatory treatment.

As You Read, Ask Yourself . . .

In this situation, was quitting her job a failure or an adaptive strategy?

How does Janice Yoder use the concepts and language of psychology to gain some distance from her pain?

Do you think that writing her own story in a psychological journal contributes to empowering herself and others?

With recent statistics continuing to document sex discrimination in academe (Stapp & Fulcher, 1983), case histories (Allport, 1942) remain an important source of information about the struggles that engage academic women. The following case history describes my experience as one of the first female civilian faculty members at a United States military academy. It is written with the following goals in mind: (a) to describe tokenism and its effects on an individual (rather than on a group) in order to illustrate its personal effects, (b) to develop hypotheses for future research, and (c) to consider some coping and change strategies to overcome the situational constraints and personal trauma of being a token. These goals seem particularly appropriate for this issue of the *Journal of Social Issues*.

JANICE D. YODER
*An Academic Woman
as a Token:
A Case Study*

Tokenism as an area of research became popular with the publication of Kanter's (1977) book, which defines tokenism as membership in a proportionally underrepresented subgroup (less than 15% of the entire group). Laws (1975), who has focused on tokenism in academia, adds richness to this definition by describing its social context. For Laws, academic women are double-deviants, first as women in a patriarchal society and secondly as seekers of accomplishments and rewards usually sought by men.

In fact, some recent research suggests that proportional underrepresentation has different consequences for women and men, and that the negative effects described by Kanter apply only to token women (Yoder & Sinnett, in press). Being underrepresented does not seem to handicap men's career development. The present paper will regard tokenism only within the context of broader societal sex role stereotypes; that is, as it relates to societal inequities for women (Richards, 1980).

Prior research on token women in business (Kanter, 1977) and the military (Yoder, Adams, & Prince, 1983) reveals three consequences of tokenism: visibility, contrast, and assimilation. Visibility arises from the salience of differences between token and dominant group members. For example, the female cadets at the academy stand out even as they march by in parades. Because of their visibility, tokens experience performance pressures, and dominants often come to resent the apparent ease with which token women get recognition. The latter may result in fears among dominant group members that women possess a "competitive edge."

Contrast refers to differences between men and women that lead to dominants' uncertainties about how to deal with tokens and the consequent isolation of tokens. Kanter (1977) describes how influential men in corporations may take their jokes and social banter from the boardroom to bars and other exclusionary places, isolating women from these informal social networks.

The uncertainties produced by contrasted differences may be resolved to some degree by encapsulating token women into stereotypic sex roles (Yoder & Adams, 1984). Kanter (1977) describes how token women come to be regarded as sex objects, mothers, pets, or iron maidens—roles that are degrading and incompatible with the fulfillment of their professional responsibilities.

BECOMING A TOKEN

In the summer of 1980 I joined the faculty of the academy as a distinguished visiting professor (VP). There were approximately 545 faculty members; of these, 97% were military officers, primarily academy graduates (56%). The overwhelming majority were men. There were 14 female military officers, and only two of the 11 civilian VPs were women—the first ever hired.

When I was interviewed for the position, my gender was important. With the newly coeducational format (female cadets were first admitted to military academies in 1976; see Durning, 1978; Stiehm, 1981; Vitters & Kinzer, 1977), the military was experiencing a gap in the number of female officers qualified to teach. Until a pool of female graduates becomes available for appointment, civilian women are regarded as a stopgap solution. An earlier longitudinal study of the integration of female cadets into the academy argued for the availability of female role models in both academic and military/tactical capacities (Adams, 1979, 1980). I was hired partly to serve that purpose.

During graduate school I had been associated with a longitudinal research project on the integration of cadet women. The opportunity for continuing and expanding my role in this research by giving me firsthand experiences with cadets' lives was of great interest. To help me further pursue this research, my position was formally described as half-time researcher/half-time teacher. One line of research I was pursuing at this time dealt with the situational consequences of tokenism for female cadets (Yoder et al., 1983). Needless to say, as a 27-year-old, single, civilian, female VP, I came to understand tokenism as both a researcher and an individual.

My life at the academy was lonely. I lived in the bachelor officers' quarters, one block from the building in which I taught. As a military base, the academy's facilities are excellent and comprehensive. One can buy a pizza, go to a movie, and get a beer all without leaving the base. One does not simply work at the academy; one lives there.

I am giving these details to show the extremes of my case. I differed from my colleagues by my civilian attire, my age, my gender, and my professional role as a researcher. The fact that I was different followed me from work to home, since these cannot be separated within the confines of a military post. I believe these exaggerated circumstances, while potentially restricting the generalizability of this case report, show the effects of tokenism more clearly than is possible in other academic settings where pressures exist in more subtle forms.

The primary resource for the present paper is a journal I kept throughout my six months at the academy. Obviously, my work on the integration of cadet women into the academy is also relevant to my case and the ideas I will present here. Finally, I kept piles of military materials—everything from the student newspaper to the historian's report, manuals, and memos, and I will refer to these where appropriate.

THE LIFE OF A TOKEN

Visibility did not produce performance pressures for me because I was not to be formally evaluated at any time during my two-year contract, and I was a VP with an admirable, albeit new, doctoral degree in the midst of a faculty mostly with master's degrees (56%). The problem of my visibility centered on perceptions of my specialness and the supposed privileges this would engender.

There was a lot of pressure for me to blend in and for me not to exploit my visibility by using my "competitive edge" over my colleagues. For example, the assignment of office space was not a simple matter. Except for the upper echelons, officers shared large rooms divided into semiprivate offices. My office was a cubicle off one of these large rooms—its small size was compensated for by a door and solid walls that assured privacy. As an added bonus, the cubicle housed a computer terminal that I used incessantly. As the semester began, I was asked to keep my door open to diminish one of the ostensible benefits of my privileged space: its privacy. Remarks about my "personal computer" encouraged me to do most of my computing at night away from the watchful eyes of my less-fortunate colleagues.

My specialness presented problems for several reasons: I had a half-time teaching load to give me time for research (in which few others engaged), many of the observations that were part of my research were conducted outside the office in the field, and I was isolated from the departmental "team."

The faculty of the academy represented success stories of military careers punctuated by a trip to graduate school and a three-year prestigious appointment to the academy. Competition and social comparisons, especially on officers' evaluations, were intense. As a civilian, I was exempt from these evaluations. Furthermore, the one salient measure of an officer's efforts was the amount of time he or she spent in the office. Shortly after my arrival, sign-out sheets were posted to keep track of officers missing during regular hours. When I spent a day in the field or stayed home to write, the perception soon developed that I was goofing off.

The primary duties of my colleagues were to teach and advise cadets. Courses were taught by teams that covered the same materials at the same time, in preparation for the same exams. The interdependency of teaching faculty encouraged "team spirit."

My differences as a civilian, a researcher, and a woman created uncertainties among my colleagues and threatened to disrupt the team. During our departmental presemester workshop, I frequently was isolated from group discussions on the grounds that I had different, and apparently irrelevant, goals. At these meetings, one subgroup dubbed itself the "Wolf Gang," used "we eat sheep!" as their motto, and howled when called upon to make group presentations. The departmental theme song chosen was "Macho Man," hardly appropriate for an academic department that included two female officers and myself. The gossip about my sexuality ranged from lesbian to heterosexually promiscuous.

This was the catch-22 of my role: Because I was different, I could not be a good team member; but, not being part of the team helped make me different and increased my isolation. I began to withdraw, reluctantly attending only mandatory events, which contributed further to my isolation.

My favorite "war stories" illustrate incidents of assimilation and role encapsulation. Specifically, I was assigned to one of two female roles: "wife" or "feminist/libber." In the former role, I was invited to a luncheon for the wives of the VPs. I learned to wear my name tag to help combat this misidentification, especially after a reception where I was presented to everyone in the reception line as the wife of the graying male VP (he wore his name tag) standing next to me. Before each introduction, I stated my name and position to deaf ears, a vigorous handshake, and a "Hello, Mrs. _____ ."

While this was mildly amusing, the effects of my second label as "feminist/libber" were not. I acquired this label by objecting to my invitation as the wife of a VP, departmental invitations open to "wives and girlfriends," being expected to bring three dishes to a pot luck dinner that I, not my wife, would cook, and sexist exam questions for our team-taught introductory psychology course: "Your new girlfriend has a habit that drives you insane. . . ." This last series of objections resulted in a suggestion book for exam questions where I could quietly record the same notes without disrupting faculty meetings. I watched as my colleagues began to get restless when I raised my hand, rolled their eyes as I spoke, and concluded by ignoring or defending. I became totally ineffectual, yet unwilling to keep quiet and thus implicitly condone these actions. My role as a deviate became predictable, unwelcome, and ignored.

Each of these processes (visibility, contrast, and role encapsulation) contributed to a downward spiral in my relations to my colleagues, especially to my department head. The ultimate result was a reevaluation of my position for the spring semester. Without discussing it with me, I was assigned a full teaching load comparable to those of my nonresearching colleagues.

This was the turning point of my short-lived adventure. Until this time, my attitudes fluctuated from acquiescence to moments of rebelliousness. I engaged in a heated discussion with the department head about my difficulties at the presemester departmental session. I insisted on going to the convention of the American Psychological Association to present a paper despite the appearance that I was being granted further privilege. It was at these meetings, among similar colleagues and mentors, that I realized that without the promise of research time my stay at the academy would not be fruitful professionally. I decided to terminate my two-year contract after completing only six months. I returned to the academy, armed with new-found self-confidence and determination, submitted my resignation, and began to search for another job.

UNDERSTANDING TOKENISM

I choose to share these particular anecdotes because they portray some of the frustrations and anxieties that come with the real-life role of a token operating in an extremely unfavorable environment. At times, they are amusing and I look forward to a time when I can humor grandchildren with my "war stories." No one event alone seems overly traumatic (see Frye, 1983). However, when you squeeze these events into six months and add the pressures of a move and a new job, separation from friends and my future husband, and my confinement to a military base, the interpersonal toll stands more clearly. Generally, these are the types of pressures that confront tokens. We ask them to go in and do a job to prove that they can do the job. The token becomes the test case, a test case doomed to suffer and often to fail. Let us hypothesize about the psychological and behavioral effects of tokenism.

Psychological Effects

I believe being a token has some measurable effect on the self-esteem of tokens. As I read my journal, I can relive the rapid decline in my self-image. On the first night, my tone was hopeful—I was filled with the adventure I was about to begin. A mere three months later I wrote the following:

> What does happen to the deviate? The deviate can convert, but short of a sex-change operation, a time machine to age me, and a personality overhaul, conversion seems out of the question for me. Be isolated? That originally was all

right with me, but that surely does not make me a team member. What can I do? Yet, the failure is placed squarely on my shoulders. "What's wrong with you?" Why can't you get along?" These questions haunt me, undermining my self-image to a point where I am reduced to crying at home alone at night . . . I feel impotent. I can't sleep, but I am never clear-headed and fully awake. I have an eye infection. Daily problems have become insurmountable difficulties. I am bored, yet I rush home to be alone. I can't work. I can't go out and have fun . . . I have become bad in my eyes; the attributions of blame have been internalized.

I engaged in a personal example of "blaming the victim" (Ryan, 1976; 1981) similar to what other researchers have found for victims of rape and sexual harassment (e.g., Janoff-Bulman, 1979; Jensen & Gutek, 1982). Like a disproportionate number of other women at the academy who left their positions early (including one of the officers in my department), I felt guilty for jeopardizing the opportunities of other women. One suggestion for future researchers is to document this turning inward and the accompanying loss of self-esteem, self-efficacy, and life satisfaction. Some of this anxiety was expressed in an eye infection; it seemed that even my body began to revolt. For fully one-half of the female cadets under the stress of basic training, anxiety is expressed physiologically in the disruption of their menstrual cycles (Vitters & Kinzer, 1977).

Behavioral Effects

My behavioral reactions fell along a continuum of withdrawal—from initially isolating myself in my apartment to eventually deciding to leave. A similar pattern is found among token women in both the military and corporate worlds. Withdrawal and attrition have important social consequences, in addition to their effects on the individual. In a movement toward social equality, tokens stand as test cases and their failures may be heralded as confirmation of the idea that they were unsuited for the position.

One approach to explaining withdrawal is person-centered, focusing on individuals as the sources of their own behavior. In contrast, situation-centered explanations focus on current environmental contingencies (Kanter, 1977; Riger & Gilligan, 1980). Women and men differ because of differences in opportunities, power, numbers, societal norms, and so on. In my particular case, a person-centered explanation for my "failure" would focus on me—my inability to blend in, my feminist values, and my emphasis on research. A situation-centered perspective, on the other hand, stresses external pressures: visibility, contrast, and assimilation that come about through the interaction of tokens and dominants. Combine these with sex-role stereotypes, and the token woman faces an aversive situation. It is not some defect in the token that causes some to withdraw; rather, it is the antagonistic and grudging *situation* that could cause anyone, male or female, to withdraw.

If the withdrawal of the token is largely the result of situational adversities, then the finding that women "fail" is a self-fulfilling prophecy (Merton, 1968). Women fail because the situation is devised, whether intentionally or inadvertently, to assure their failure. What needs to be changed is the negative situation and the individual's reaction to it. Research directed toward effective ways to change situations in order to increase the likelihood of success for both women and men is paramount.

BRINGING ABOUT CHANGE

If women are to succeed in roles that presently enlist token numbers, we must supplement effective affirmative action that facilitates *entry* into jobs with conditions that can help in *retention* and *promotion*. This is important not only for the particular individuals involved, but also because their lack of success can be used to threaten whatever standards of affirmative action currently exist (Macaulay, 1981). I have no doubt that my resignation jeopardized the opportunities of other civilian women at the academy, as I was not replaced. My work with female cadets shows that they too carry this burden. As one woman said, "anything one girl did reflected on every single girl here" (Yoder, Adams, Grove, & Priest, 1985).

Although I believe situational changes are most effective and compatible with my feminist ideology, the realities are such that tokenism often must be endured and overcome by at least one generation. For this reason, I here propose ideas for future work that concentrates on individual tokens, groups of tokens, and the situation.

Individual Tokens

When we focus on the individual, we should explore two interrelated aspects: (a) the effects of tokenism on the individual and (b) individuals' strategies for coping with and overcoming tokenism. My experiences make clear the impact of tokenism on myself: as my stress and frustration levels rose, my self-esteem plummeted. These individual consequences are well documented in other case histories (e.g., Datan, 1980; DeSole & Hoffmann, 1981; Nielsen, 1979; Weisstein, 1977). Analyses designed to explore the impact of tokenism on individuals should collect both personal (e.g., demographic, attitudinal, and personality measures) and situational (e.g., visibility, marginal peer acceptance, and role encapsulation) information in order to understand the interaction of both these sets of variables (Kulka & Colten, 1982; Sherif, 1979).

The effective coping strategies of successful, satisfied women need to be understood, and training individuals in the use of these strategies needs to be devised, implemented, and tested. Hall's (1972) descriptive study illustrates a useful starting point. Through a survey of college-educated women, Hall found that the most satisfied women used a coping strategy he labeled "structural role redefinition." This strategy involves changing externally imposed expectations: for example, negotiating an alternative set of role expectations within one's employer or family.

Tokens as a Group

Frequently women are exhorted to bond together to overcome tokenism (e.g., Kaufman, 1978). Women need to be made aware of their shared problems; effective networking is one way to accomplish this. Networks may help women validate themselves as individuals and thereby reduce the decline in self-esteem associated with tokenism. With my low self-esteem and without support, I could not break out of the downward spiral that ensued at the academy. Only leaving helped me do this. But for those who remain in the situation, effective networks may be a means by which they can cope with and change their situation.

Bonding does not occur spontaneously. In fact, tokenism itself may inhibit bonding in competitive settings (e.g., White, 1970). For example, we found that cadet women at the academy failed to sponsor incoming female cadets because the upperclass women were too burdened by their own tokenism and its consequences (Yoder et al., 1985). One of the last things these women wanted was to emphasize their gender by associating with other women.

I felt a similar discouragement with the two female military colleagues and the wives in my department at the academy. Wives did not associate with their husbands' female coworkers in much the same way Kanter (1977) describes. As for my colleagues, on one occasion the three of us sat together at a departmental meeting. This elicited comments about an exclusive "women's club" and that we were "plotting" something. Needless to say, we restricted our future interactions to less visible, nonwork settings.

Another way women are discouraged from bonding is by gossip about their sexuality. For example, a group of women bowlers at the academy was branded as lesbian. This was "validated" by their frequent hugs when one of them scored a strike. This vicious gossip seems to surround women as mentors and also in women's centers on many college campuses.

In sum, support groups may not be formed because of the situational constraints of tokenism. Institutional recognition of such groups may be limited and needs to be actively fostered over time. Additionally, women must be careful to structure support groups effectively. If a group simply touts the successes of a few superwomen, it may come to support the status quo by providing examples of success that encourage others to look inward for the source of their failures (an example of "blaming the victim"). On the other hand, the adoption of structural role redefinition by a group makes it a potential asset beyond the strivings of a lone individual with this perspective. This type of support group should be the ideal.

Situational Factors

Action research also is called for regarding situational factors: first, explore the situation and its impact, and then design, implement, and test situational changes to understand their effectiveness in bringing about desired change (see Larwood & Lockheed, 1979). However, there may be strong institutional resistance. Laws (1975) states: "Tokenism is the means by which the dominant group advertises a promise of mobility" so long as tokens do "not change the system they enter" (pp. 51–52). Tokens serve two functions for the institution: (a) they demonstrate to others that someone was good enough to make it, thereby encouraging other potential tokens to try harder (Yoder, 1983a); and (b) the presence of token group members assures the external world that the institution follows nondiscriminatory hiring practices (Laws, 1975). The effect of both of these is to reinforce the existent social structure and its apparent meritocracy (Denmark, 1980).

I believe Laws is right—dominants do not want tokens to change the system. Yet without change, tokenism and its negative effects will persist. For example, after an initial barrage of too much research directed at the first women cadets, which served to emphasize their visibility (Adams, 1979; Durning, 1978), the academy now no longer sponsors any systematic study of the current female cadets, despite persistently high attrition rates. An unstructured exit interview of most women graduates is the only remaining vestige of a once-active research program. "The woman problem is solved," I have been told. But then, why are women still referred to as "problems"?

In recognition of institutional resistance to change, research is needed not only to show the negative effects of tokenism, but also to develop realistic alternatives. These programs must include situational modifications shown to be conducive to positive organizational change. For example, our research suggests that an atmosphere of intense competition heightens the negative effects of tokenism (Yoder et al., 1984). One way to reduce this, the jigsaw technique used by Aronson and his colleagues (1978), has proven effective in newly racially integrated classrooms. Here, cooperation is necessary for the group's success, thereby making isolation and role encapsulation of tokens counterproductive.

Individual competition, however, is the hallmark of our academic system (Bowles & Gintis, 1976); changing it would be a formidable task. A more modest improvement would be to reassess standards of evaluation. At the academy, cadets are judged by criteria standardized on men. This is particularly problematic in areas involving physical prowess, an important component of each cadet's success (Rice, Yoder, Adams, Priest, & Prince, 1984). It is these biased standards that may frustrate tokens, lead to their withdrawal, and at the same time justify the current situation as being apparently nondiscriminatory (Yoder, 1983b). Women's groups can challenge these standards by calling into question the legitimacy of traditional criteria.

CONCLUSIONS

The case history method adds to the resources of feminist researchers by providing descriptive information, sharing the richness of individuals' accounts and reactions, and encouraging situational attributions (Jones & Nisbett, 1972).

People bring about change by altering both situations and their own perceptions. To do this, women's networks and feminist psychotherapists must help individuals adopt satisfying strategies, such as structural role redefinition, for working toward institutional change. Social psychologists and sociologists need to analyze existing social situations with an eye toward improvement. Kanter's (1977) and Laws's (1975) analyses are good examples. Policy-makers need to be aware of the impact of standards of evaluation, individual competition, techniques for physical training, and so on. New policies need to be devised to produce the positive qualities of all participants. Finally, social scientists need to conduct program evaluations to ensure that changes are working as projected. This system of change and feedback needs to involve all levels so that the downward spiral can be broken and progress initiated. To do this, change agents (women's networking groups, psychotherapists, social psychologists, sociologists, and policymakers) must effectively coordinate their efforts.

References

ADAMS, J. (1979). *Report of the admission of women to the U.S. military academy (Project Athena III)*. West Point, NY: United States Military Academy.

ADAMS, J. (1980). *Report of the admission of women to the U.S. military academy (Project Athena IV)*. West Point, NY: United States Military Academy.

ALLPORT, G. W. (1942). *The use of personal documents in psychological science.* New York: Social Science Research Council.

ARONSON, E., BLANEY, N., STEPHAN, C., SIKES, J., & SNAPP, M. (1978). *The jigsaw classroom.* Beverly Hills, CA: Sage.

BOWLES, S., & GINTIS, H. (1976). *Schooling in capitalist America.* New York: Basic Books, 1976.

DATAN, R. (1980). Days of our lives. *The Journal of Mind and Behavior, 1,* 63–71.

DENMARK, F. L. (1980). Psyche: From rocking the cradle to rocking the boat. *American Psychologist, 35,* 1057–1065.

DeSOLE, G., & HOFFMAN, L. (Eds.) (1981). *Rocking the boat: Academic women and academic process.* New York: Modern Language Association of America.

DURNING, K. P. (1978). *Women at the naval academy: The first year of interaction* (Report No. 78-12). San Diego, CA: Navy Personnel Research and Development Center.

FRYE, M. (1983). *The politics of reality: Essays in feminist theory.* Trumansburg, NY: Crossing Press.

HALL, D. T. (1972). A model of coping with role conflict: The role behavior of college educated women. *Administrative Science Quarterly, 17,* 471–486.

JANOFF-BULMAN, R. (1979). Characterological versus behavioral self-blame: Inquiries into depression and rape. *Journal of Personality and Social Psychology, 37,* 1798–1809.

JENSEN, I. W., & GUTEK, B. A. (1982). Attributions and assignment of responsibility in sexual harassment. *Journal of Social Issues, 38,* 121–136.

JONES, E. E., & NISBETT, R. E. (1972). The actor and the observer: Divergent perceptions of the causes of behavior. In E. E. Jones, D. Kanouse, H. H. Kelley, R. E. Nisbett, S. Valins, & B. Weiner (Eds.), *Attribution: The causes of behavior* (pp. 79–94). Morristown, NJ: General Learning Press.

KANTER, R. M. (1977). *Men and women of the corporation.* New York: Basic Books.

KAUFMAN, D. R. (1978). Associational ties in academe: Some male and female differences. *Sex Roles, 4,* 9–21.

KULKA, R. A., & COLTEN, M. E. (1982). Secondary analysis of a longitudinal study of educated women: A social psychological perspective. *Journal of Social Issues, 38,* 73–87.

LARWOOD, L., & LOCKHEED, M. (1979). Women as managers: Toward second generation research. *Sex Roles, 5,* 659–666.

LAWS, J. L. (1975). The psychology of tokenism: An analysis. *Sex Roles, 1,* 209–223.

MACAULEY, J. (1981). The failure of affirmative action for women: One university's experience. In G. DeSole & L. Hoffmann (Eds.), *Rocking the boat* (pp. 98–116). New York: Modern Language Association of America.

MERTON, R. K. (1968). *Social theory and social structure.* (rev. ed.) New York: Free Press.

NIELSEN, L. L. (1979). Sexism and self-healing in the university. *Harvard Education Review, 49,* 467–476.

RICE, R. W., YODER, J. D., ADAMS, J., PRIEST, R. F., & PRINCE, H. T. (1984). Leadership ratings for male and female military cadets. *Sex Roles, 10,* 885–902.

RICHARDS, J. R. (1980). *The skeptical feminist: A philosophical enquiry.* Boston: Routledge & Kegan Paul.

RIGER, S., & GALLIGAN, P. (1980). Women in management: An exploration of competing paradigms. *American Psychologist, 35,* 902–910.

RYAN, W. (1976). *Blaming the victim.* New York: Vintage.

RYAN, W. (1981). *Equality.* New York: Vintage.

SHERIF, C. W. (1979). What every intelligent person should know about psychology and women. In E. Snyder (Ed.), *The study of women: Enlarging perspectives of social reality* (pp. 143–188). New York: Harper & Row.

STAPP, J., & FULCHER, R. (1983). The employment of APA members: 1982. *American Psychologist, 38,* 1298–1320.

STIEHM, J. H. (1981). *Bring me men and women.* Berkeley, CA: University of California Press.

VITTERS, A. G., & KINZER, N. S. (1977). *Report of the admission of women to the U.S. military academy (Project Athena).* West Point, NY: United States Military Academy.

WEISSTEIN, N. (1977). "How can a little girl like you teach a great big class of men?" the chairman said, and the other adventures of a woman in science. In S. Ruddick & P. Daniels (Eds.). *Working it out.* New York: Pantheon.

WHITE, M. S. (1970). Psychological and social barriers to women in science. *Science, 170,* 413–416.

YODER, J. D. (1983a). *Queen bees or tokens? Person- versus situation-centered approaches to mentors.* Paper presented at the meetings of the Association for Women in Psychology. Seattle, WA.

YODER, J. D. (1983b). Another look at women in the United States Army: A comment on Woelfel's article. *Sex Roles, 9,* 285–288.

YODER, J. D., & ADAMS, J. (1984). Women entering nontraditional roles: When work demands and sex-roles conflict. *International Journal of Women's Studies, 7,* 260–272.

YODER, J. D., & SINNETT, L. M. (in press). Is it all in the numbers? A case study of tokenism. *Psychology of Women Quarterly.*

YODER, J. D., ADAMS, J., & PRINCE, H. T. (1983). The price of a token. *Journal of Political and Military Sociology, 11,* 325–337.

YODER, J. D., ADAMS, J., GROVE, S., & PRIEST, R. F. (1985). To teach is to learn: Overcoming tokenism with mentors. *Psychology of Women Quarterly, 9,* 119–131.

PART FIVE

Making a Difference

The stories gathered here illustrate the complex interaction between women as agents of change and the social forces that impinge on them. Each provides an example of a woman who resisted injustice and worked to create personal and societal change.

We begin with an "Aha experience." Ellen Neuborne, a second-generation feminist and journalist, writes about how, despite her many privileges, she came to realize that equality has not yet been achieved. She exhorts young women to become aware of how insidiously they have been programmed to remain silent and invisible in the face of injustice. Her story provides an excellent vantage point from which to examine the consequences of individual versus collective activism.

An important area of feminist activism has been challenging sexist and demeaning cultural images of women. For example, consider how older women are ignored in the mass media, patronized in interaction, and stereotyped as ineffectual, ugly, asexual, and powerless. Shevy Healey, an activist who became a lesbian and a psychotherapist relatively late in life, notes that whereas she was always proud of her various forms of "otherness" throughout her life, she found herself denying her own aging. But Healey takes a political, not just a personal, perspective on growing older, and provides a model of how to combat ageism.

Eve Ensler, a playwright and activist, received considerable media attention and reached millions of people with her play *The Vagina Monologues.* In conversation with Virginia Braun, a graduate student who does research on how women feel about their vaginas, the two women talk about why it is important for all women to develop more positive feelings about their own bodies. Claiming that our vaginas are central to our beings and our sexuality, Ensler aims her activism at helping women recognize the power and beauty of their bodies.

The mass media are a particularly potent source of stereotyped and demeaning images of women. But what can be done against such entrenched power? Tali Edut describes how she went from being "addicted" to *Seventeen* and

Cosmo as a teenager to developing a critical consciousness on the images of women they present. Edut and her friends translated their awareness into political action by founding their own non-sexist and multicultural women's magazine, *HUES*. Each of these activists, in her own way, challenges negative images of women and offers more positive, affirming alternatives.

Another major area of feminist activism has been around issues of violence against girls and women. In selections by women from the United States, El Salvador, and Guatemala, we look first at women speaking out against violence in intimate relationships, and then at resistance to state-sanctioned violence.

Abuses of power are a part of many intimate relationships. Because relationships are seen as personal and private, these negative aspects, and their connection to larger social patterns, often remain invisible. Vicki Crompton writes about the murder of her daughter Jenny, and how it made her aware of the prevalence and widespread social acceptance of male violence in U.S. culture. Crompton transcended her personal tragedy by educating others about the problem of dating violence.

In other parts of the world, civil war and the oppression of indigenous people have resulted in massive suffering for women and children. In 1981, Rufina Amaya was the only survivor of the massacre of an entire Salvadorean village by the military. Rufina escaped to a refugee camp in Honduras, and only after nine years in exile was she able to return to her country. In an interview with Marigold Best and Pamela Hussey, Amaya speaks of the spiritual and moral strength of women and the need for collective action in the face of injustice.

In "Widows Fight for Dignity and Unity," Margaret Hooks presents the story of Manuela, a Cakchiquel Indian woman whose husband and father were both "disappeared"—in all likelihood murdered by the Guatemalan army. Manuela courageously speaks for the thousands of women who have lost family members in this way: "Our suffering has helped us to understand our social situation and it encourages us to be more active in changing it. We know that if women don't do something, this killing is never going to end." She describes the collective political action of CONAVIGUA, a national action group of Guatemalan widows. In all three of these accounts about violence, connections among women are a source of empowerment. What different kinds of connections are described, and how do they enable women to support each other in challenging male violence?

All the women's activism in these stories is grounded in individual awareness of injustice. Several of the writers describe how they became aware of injustice through personal experiences. The experiences vary greatly: sexist treatment in the workplace, ageism, sexual abuse, and loss of family members to violence and warfare. However, each woman transcends her individual experiences and recognizes the need for women to work together in a common cause. These moving stories indicate that individual change is important, but collective action is even more effective. In Manuela's words, "Organization is the only way." Finally, they suggest that we cannot rest in the past successes of the women's movement. What would you say to someone who argues that problems of social inequality have largely been resolved?

Ellen Neuborne

Imagine My Surprise

Ellen Neuborne grew up in a very progressive family, with parents who are both activists. Feminism was a natural part of her life. Even so, Neuborne says, she had a few surprises waiting when she went off on her own—and the biggest surprise of all was that, despite her upbringing, she was still "programmed" to accept sexism without protest.

As You Read, Ask Yourself . . .

What examples of modern sexism does Neuborne give and how do they differ from the kinds of sexism challenged by feminists in the 1970s?

Have you ever had an experience like the ones she describes, of being silenced through sexist "programming"?

What does Neuborne want feminism to teach her and others?

Is the price she has to pay for her outspokenness worth it?

When my editor called me into his office and told me to shut the door, I was braced to argue. I made a mental note to stand my ground.

It was behind the closed door of his office that I realized I'd been programmed by the sexists.

We argued about the handling of one of my stories. He told me not to criticize him. I continued to disagree. That's when it happened.

He stood up, walked to where I was sitting. He completely filled my field of vision. He said, "Lower your voice when you speak to me."

And I did.

I still can't believe it.

This was not supposed to happen to me. I am the child of professional feminists. My father is a civil rights lawyer. My mother heads the NOW Legal Defense and Education Fund. She sues sexists for a living. I was raised on a pure, unadulterated feminist ethic.

That didn't help.

Looking back on the moment, I should have said, "Step back out of my face and we'll continue this discussion like humans."

I didn't.

I said, "Sorry."

Sorry!

I had no idea twenty-some years of feminist upbringing would fail me at that moment. Understand, it is not his actions I am criticizing; it is mine. He was a bully. But the response was my own. A man confronted me. My sexist programming kicked in. I backed off. I said, "Sorry."

I don't understand where the programming began. I had been taught that girls could do anything boys could do. Equality of the sexes was an unimpeachable truth. Before that day in the editor's office, if you'd asked me how I might handle such a confrontation, I never would have said, "I'd apologize."

I'm a good feminist. I would never apologize for having a different opinion.

But I did.

Programming. It is the subtle work of an unequal world that even the best of feminist parenting couldn't overcome. It is the force that sneaks up on us even as we think that we are getting ahead with the best of the guys. I would never have believed in its existence. But having heard it, amazingly, escape from my own mouth, I am starting to recognize its pattern.

When you are told you are causing trouble, and you regret having raised conflict, that's your programming.

When you keep silent, though you know the answer—programming.

When you do not take credit for your success, or you suggest that your part in it was really minimal—programming.

When a man tells you to lower your voice, and you do, and you apologize—programming.

The message of this programming is unrelentingly clear: Keep quiet.

I am a daughter of the movement. How did I fall for this?

I thought the battle had been won. I thought that sexism was a remote experience, like the Depression. Gloria had taken care of all that in the seventies.

Imagine my surprise.

And while I was blissfully unaware, the perpetrators were getting smarter.

What my mother taught me to look for—pats on the butt, honey, sweetie, cupcake, make me some coffee—are not the methods of choice for today's sexists. Those were just the fringes of what they were really up to. Sadly, enough of them have figured out how to mouth the words of equality while still behaving like pigs. They're harder to spot.

At my first newspaper job in Vermont, I covered my city's effort to collect food and money to help a southern town ravaged by a hurricane. I covered the story from the early fund-raising efforts right up to the day before I was to ride with the aid caravan down South. At that point I was taken off the story and it was reassigned to a male reporter. (It wasn't even his beat; he covered education.) It would be too long a drive for me, I was told. I wouldn't get enough sleep to do the story.

He may as well have said "beauty rest." But I didn't get it. At least not right away. He seemed, in voice and manner, to be concerned about me. It worked. A man got the big story. And I got to stay home. It was a classic example of a woman being kept out of a plum project "for her own good," yet while in the newsroom, hearing this explanation about sleep and long drives, I sat there nodding.

Do you think you would do better? Do you think you would recognize sexism at work immediately?

Are you sure?

Programming is a powerful thing. It makes you lazy. It makes you vulnerable. And until you can recognize that it's there, it works for the opposition. It makes you lower your voice.

It is a dangerous thing to assume that just because we were raised in a feminist era, we are safe. We are not. They are still after us.

And it is equally dangerous for our mothers to assume that because we are children of the movement, we are equipped to stand our ground. In many cases, we are unarmed.

The old battle strategies aren't enough, largely because the opposition is using new weaponry. The man in my office who made a nuisance of himself by asking me out repeatedly did so through the computer messaging system. Discreet. Subtle. No one to see him being a pig. Following me around would have been obvious. This way, he looked perfectly normal, and I constantly had to delete his overtures from my E-mail files. Mom couldn't have warned me about E-mail.

Then there is the danger from other women. Those at the top who don't mentor other women because if they made it on their own, so should subsequent generations. Women who say there is just one "woman's slot" at the top power level, and to get there you must kill off your female competition. Women who maintain a conspiracy of silence, refusing to speak up when they witness or even experience sexism, for fear of reprisals. These are dangers from within our ranks. When I went to work, I assumed other women were my allies.

Again, imagine my surprise.

I once warned a newly hired secretary that her boss had a history of discrimination against young women. She seemed intensely interested in the conversation at the time. Apparently as soon as I walked away, she repeated the entire conversation to her boss. My heart was in the right place. But my brain was not. Because, as I learned that day, sisterhood does not pay the bills. For younger women who think they do not need the feminist movement to get ahead, sisterhood is the first sentiment to fall by the wayside. In a world that looks safe, where men say all the right things and office policies have all the right words, who needs sisterhood?

We do. More than we ever have. Because they are smooth, because they are our bosses and control our careers, because they are hoping we will kill each other off so they won't have to bother. Because of all the subtle sexism that you hardly notice until it has already hit you. That is why you need the movement.

On days when you think the battle is over, the cause has been won, look around you to see what women today still face. The examples are out there.

On college campuses, there is a new game called rodeo. A man takes a woman back to his room, initiates sexual intercourse, and then a group of his friends barges in. The object of this game is for the man to keep his date pinned as long as possible.

Men are still afraid of smart women. When Ruth Bader Ginsburg was nominated to the Supreme Court, the *New York Times* described her as "a woman who handled her intelligence gracefully." The message: If you're smarter than the men around you, be sure to keep your voice down. Wouldn't want to be considered ungraceful.

A friend from high school calls to tell me he's getting married. He's found the perfect girl. She's bright, she's funny and she's willing to take his last name. That makes them less likely to get divorced, he maintains. "She's showing me she's not holding out."

In offices, women with babies are easy targets. I've seen the pattern played out over and over. One woman I know put in ten years with the company, but once she returned from maternity leave, she was marked. Every attempt to leave on time to pick up her baby at day care was chalked up as a "productivity problem." Every request to work part-time was deemed troublemaking. I sat just a few desks away. I witnessed her arguments. I heard the editors gossip when she was absent. One Monday we came into work and her desk had been cleaned out.

Another woman closer to my age also wanted to work part-time after the birth of her son. She was told that was unacceptable. She quit. There was no announcement. No good-bye party. No card for everyone in the office to sign. The week she disappeared from the office, we had a party for a man who was leaving to take a new job. We also were asked to contribute to a gift fund for another man who had already quit for a job in the Clinton administration.

But for the women with babies who were disappeared, nothing happened. And when I talked about the fact that women with babies tended to vanish, I was hauled into my boss' office for a reeducation session. He spent twenty minutes telling me what a great feminist he was and that if I ever thought differently, I should leave the company. No question about the message there: Shut up.

I used to believe that my feminist politics would make me strong. I thought strong thoughts. I held strong beliefs. I thought that would protect me. But all it did was make me aware of how badly I slipped when I lowered my voice and apologized for having a divergent opinion. For all my right thinking, I did not fight back. But I have learned something. I've learned it takes practice to be a strong feminist. It's not an instinct you can draw on at will—no matter how equality-minded your upbringing. It needs exercise. You have to think to know your own mind. You have to battle to work in today's workplace. It was nice to grow up thinking this was an equal world. But it's not.

I have learned to listen for the sound of my programming. I listen carefully for the *Sorrys*, the *You're rights*. Are they deserved? Or did I offer them up without thinking, as though I had been programmed? Have you? Are you sure?

I have changed my ways. I am louder and quicker to point out sexism when I see it. And it's amazing what you can see when you are not hiding behind the warm, fuzzy glow of past feminist victories. It does not make me popular in the office. It does not even make me popular with women. Plenty of my female colleagues would prefer I quit rocking the boat. One read a draft of this essay and suggested I change the phrase "fight back" to "stand my ground" in order to "send a better message."

But after falling for the smooth talk and after hearing programmed acquiescence spew from my mouth, I know what message I am trying to send: Raise your voice. And I am sending it as much to myself as to anyone else.

I've changed what I want from the women's movement. I used to think it was for political theory, for bigger goals that didn't include my daily life. When I was growing up, the rhetoric we heard involved the theory of equality: Were men and women really equal? Were there biological differences that made men superior? Could women overcome their stigma as "the weaker sex"? Was a woman's place really in the home?

These were ideas. Important, ground-breaking, mind-changing debates. But the feminism I was raised on was very cerebral. It forced a world full of people to change the way they think about women. I want more than their minds. I want to see them do it.

The theory of equality has been well fought for by our mothers. Now let's talk about how to talk, how to work, how to fight sexism here on the ground, in our lives. All the offices I have worked in have lovely, right-thinking policy statements. But the theory doesn't necessarily translate into action. I'm ready to take up that part of the battle.

I know that sitting on the sidelines will not get me what I want from my movement. And it is mine. Younger feminists have long felt we needed to be invited to our mothers' party. But don't be fooled into thinking that feminism is old-fashioned. The movement is ours and we need it.

I am one of the oldest of my generation, so lovingly dubbed "X" by a disdainful media. To my peers, and to the women who follow after me, I warn you that your programming is intact. Your politics may be staunchly feminist, but they will not protect you if you are passive.

Listen for the attacks. They are quiet. They are subtle.

And listen for the jerk who will tell you to lower your voice. Tell him to get used to the noise. The next generation is coming.

Shevy Healey

Confronting Ageism:
A MUST for Mental Health

Feminist activism has challenged many cultural images of women. One of the most important is stereotypes about aging and old women. Shevy Healey, a lesbian psychotherapist, writes that she had unconsciously internalized these negative images and therefore rejected and denied her own aging.

But Healey's story can also be read as a very positive one. Through coming to terms with her own aging, she realized the need for activism on behalf of older women.

As You Read, Ask Yourself . . .

What values did Shevy Healey reexamine as she grew older?

How are issues of aging intertwined with other core issues in women's lives?

Do you agree with Healey when she states that telling older women they do not look their age is not a compliment?

What are some specific examples of an activist agenda on behalf of older women?

Old age crept upon me and caught me unawares.

Like most women, I had never thought about my own growing old. When I was young I felt invincible. In my 30's I was too busy struggling through my life to think about any future. I do remember thinking longingly of "retirement" but that was because I didn't like my life very much and felt powerless to change it.

In my 40's and 50's, with my life exploding in many new directions, I felt, in my heart of hearts, that I was beating the clock. I first began my college education at age 43 and not too long thereafter got divorced after some 22 years of marriage. I continued and finished my undergraduate work while my only child was herself away at college. Deciding to go for broke, at 47 I left Southern California where I had lived most of my adult life to go to graduate school in Ohio, and at 54 I finally got a Ph.D. in clinical psychology. At 50 I made another drastic life change when I fell in love with a woman and came out as a lesbian.

With so much going on for me, I did not feel in sync with my peers and fooled myself into thinking, when I thought of age at all, that it was "a state of mind," nothing else. The experience of being out of sync was, in fact, what felt most familiar.

My mother, father, and I arrived in this country from Poland in 1923. Within six months my father died, and at age 24 my mother was left alone without any close family to raise a two year old child. I started kindergarten not knowing a word of English, and my sense of shame and alienation was more profound when my first name was arbitrarily changed by the school registrar. My own name was too "foreign" sounding; thus Sheva became Evelyn.

Although almost all immigrants were poor, we were in an especially impoverished category. At the height of the Great Depression when my mother got sick and could no longer bring home even the four dollars a week she was earning we were forced to go on county welfare to survive.

I was out of sync even as a Jewish child raised in a Jewish ghetto, for my mother was a revolutionary and an atheist. I was the only child I knew who ate bread on Pessach (Passover), and who "on principle" did not say aloud the Pledge of Allegiance to a government which hypocritically claimed to be for liberty and justice for all, while favoring the rich at the expense of the poor. At five I proudly marched with my mother, a garment worker, on my first picket line. I clearly remember running with her down an alley to escape the Philadelphia mounted police, who, with horses rearing and stomping, charged into the picket line of mostly women and children in an attempt to break the strike. By age eleven I was a seasoned Junior Pioneer leader wearing my red bandanna and marching in picket lines and May Day Parades. From the rebellious tom boy to the high school rebel, I was an "expert" in knowing what it felt like to be other than the mainstream, while at the same time having a strong sense of place and solidarity with my own political comrades.

The closest I came to being mainstream was when I finally got my Ph.D., but by then I was an "out" lesbian and feminist—both of which did not exactly clothe me in respectability.

Surely then, with all of my previous experience of otherness, I could be expected to make a relatively easy transition to the otherness experienced so acutely by old women. Absolutely not so. I continued through my 50's steadfast in my delusion that age, *my* age, was irrelevant. More and more in social circles I experienced myself as the "older" woman in the group, but coming out as a lesbian at 50 and having a wonderfully exciting decade only promoted my sense of myself as an exception. It is true that I began to fret about my outward appearance more than I ever had. The wrinkles, loose flesh, the changes in my body left me worried and split. How could my body feel so charged and sexual, my self be so full of plans and dreams and energy, while at the same time it was registering the signs of growing old? Although I never dyed my hair, by now a lovely steel gray, I did seriously consider a face lift. Only at the last minute did I acknowledge to myself that it would take more than surgery to help me resolve my internal split about my own aging.

My growing external change of status forced my growing internal discomfort to reach more conscious levels. My first intimations of what age stereotyping was all about occurred when I moved into a new community and was shocked to find myself addressed by younger people, with the ritual respect reserved for—not Mother—but Grandmother, at a time when my own grandchild had not yet been born. I began to work only part time and this meant increasing isolation from colleagues and work-related sources of respect. I found also that younger professionals who were meeting me for the first time and knew that I too was a professional assumed a respectful rather than collegial stance, while those who knew nothing about me most often ignored me completely.

My own mother and step-father, now in their early 80's, seemed to be having increasing health difficulties, but I must admit, strange as that seems to me now, I simply did not pay much attention and blithely assumed that they would go on as always, at least until some far-off future. My world changed radically and shockingly when my step-father died unexpectedly after surgery, leaving my mother alone, in failing health and total panic. Suddenly I found myself solely and increasingly responsible for my mother's care, a task which took enormous energy and struggle.

When she died some two years later at age 85, no amount of preparation helped me to experience my new position in the world, feeling orphaned at 63! I became the oldest living member of my very small family. In a way I could not foresee I was catapulted into an active awareness of my own mortality, my own vulnerability, myself as an old woman.

There ensued a series of struggles and learnings which I think are relatively typical, though at the time I thought were unique. The invisibility I experienced as an old woman felt much different from all the experiences of otherness I had ever known. Being subject to special oppression was certainly familiar enough. What was different this time, however, was how I felt inside as I experienced this oppression. Whatever fear I had experienced in being "other" throughout my life, I had always felt a core of strength and pride in who I was and what I stood for—in my poor and working class background, my Jewishness, my atheism, my foreignness, my political radicalism, my being a girl, a woman, a lesbian. Now, I was attempting to deny my otherness by denying my own aging, a denial that masked the tremendous fear I felt about being an old woman, about being "over the hill," for I had internalized the ageist stereotype that my life was all but over and I did not want it to be! Neither did I want to be part of a group stigmatized as ineffectual, useless, ugly, asexual, whining, passive, lifeless, sick, dependent, powerless—the antithesis of everything I had tried to be and make of my life.

What a dilemma: hating and dreading what being old represented, while each year becoming more clearly identifiably old. All I really wanted was to hold back the clock by some magical act of will. Truth is, I think I tried that—for a while convincing myself that if only I exercised the right way, ate the right food, lived the right kind of pure and glowing life, I would "beat" old age. I never, as yet, questioned the validity of my ageist assumptions. My fears were reinforced by watching my mother grow old and die, an old age that was full of denial and fear of the changes occurring in her body and her life, and rage at what she considered the whittling away of her self and the ending of a life that felt unfulfilled.

Looking back on that time, only now can I see how hard I was working to deny my feelings and my confusion. It was, of course, not possible to deal with a problem that I refused to identify, for I was doing what all oppressed groups try to do; I was trying to pass—to myself at least. Knowing that I felt inside a continuity with the person I always was, instead of realizing that growing old does not mean dropping off a precipice, I decided I felt "young" inside. But no matter how automatic and unconscious this universal practice of passing for younger is, it remains a deeply alienating experience. Begging the question, refusing to acknowledge my age did nothing but rob me of the core of strength I needed to sustain and guide me through this great life change, crossing the bridge between mid-life and old.

Finally, the reality of my life forced me to go beyond denial and into acknowledging and coping somehow with my unaccustomed and unwanted status of being an old woman. In the beginning of this struggle I found myself wavering between rage—at the patronizing dismissals meted out to me in many different forms, and anxiety and foreboding about my future.

Having just turned 70, I can look at my last decade and chart my progress to a rich and rewarding old age. I am able to view my own process within the context of the political, not simply the personal. This pushes me to share my experience in the hope that it can be useful to other women learning to grow up to be old. But although I think the issue has universal significance, denial about the process is so ingrained that it seems somewhat daring, even brave, to speak in detail about my own struggles to explore the dimensions of being an old woman. For the most part, neither books nor songs are written about the every day, heroic and ordinary lives of old women. Talk about being old by the old is a conversational taboo. Interestingly, only young and mid-life women feel free to speak easily and insultingly of their dread of coming into my time of life.

I owe a huge debt to Barbara Macdonald and the book she wrote with Cynthia Rich, *Look Me In The Eye—Old Women Aging and Ageism* (1991). When I read and reread this book I felt a profound and exhilarating relief. For in writing about her own life Macdonald had also named my experience and made me feel sane, less alone and less fearful. It reminds me of the excitement of discovery we women experienced in the early days of the women's movement when we learned through our consciousness raising groups as nothing else could teach us, that what was happening in our lives was not a matter of individual flaw or problem but a common experience of oppression.

So, too, has this time of my life been a sorting, testing, learning, both as I become more mindful and attentive to my own experience and as I share with other old women and learn from our common experience. Yet this ongoing process is complex and I often feel muddled and overwhelmed. When that happens, I long to find some systematic simple way, because I am that kind of a person, to categorize and define the various components of my experience.

Am I dealing, in any given instance, with the ageism, sexism, heterosexism, or anti-semitism of our society? Am I being "too" sensitive? Certainly as an old Jewish lesbian I can expect to and mostly do get treated in certain predictable ways in our oppressive mainstream culture, but my dismay is more acute when I experience the same slights, the same invisibility in my own special lesbian and feminist community. Since old women, lesbian or heterosexual, are invisible in our society, it is easy to grow used to that condition and sometimes the only clue I have that I am in the world but not part of it is an uneasy delayed reaction I have to my own invisibility. It is not always clear at first.

Or am I dealing not just with external ageism but a response that arises from my own internalized ageism, buttressed by the sexist and heterosexist models of aging I have from my mother and her generation?

Or, finally, can I trust that my response is actually coming from inside me, from my own body of life experience?

Sometimes there seems almost no area of behavior and emotion in which I can totally trust my first reaction. In almost every part of my life I am forced again and again to examine my ageist expectations, not because I necessarily want to do so from some intellectual curiosity, but because if I do not do this, false expectations and assumptions cloud and diminish my ability to actually experience my life.

I think often of the most important model I've had—my own mother and her unfulfilled old age. I have to remind myself that her life and my life have been vastly different, that the times in which we both lived, the options we had and choices we made were vastly different. I remind myself also of the research that points out that in old age there is greater heterogeneity than at any other developmental stage, which provides even less basis for the existing stereotypes about old women. Yet these cultural assumptions harden into oppressive dogmas. Ageism, primarily a woman's issue, is the extension of the sexism, heterosexism, racism, and rampant consumerism of our multi-corporate society. Old women, outliving men in greater numbers, have lost their special capacity for service to the patriarchy. They no longer function as ornaments, lovers, domestics, bearers and rearers of children, or as economic drudges in the work place. To quote Copper (1988), "The ageism which old women experience is firmly embedded in sexism, an extension of the male power to define, control values, erase, disempower and divide."

The expressions of ageism are many. A core area of my ongoing examination of my own aging is my self and my relationship to my body. This is a most complex relationship, encompassing issues of illness and wellness, fear of incapacity and actual disability, loss of independence and acceptance of interdependence, the intricate relationship of my body and appearance to my sense of self and self-esteem, my own standards and politics of beauty, and more. The interrelationship and the complexity of all of these issues make them difficult to untangle. I find comfort in reminding myself that I am not dealing with trivialities but with the core issues that we all face throughout our entire lives. The fear of aging, reaching phobic proportions among white skinned women of European background, has grave repercussions for women as they experience their own aging. My greater urgency to confront these issues is my conviction that my health, well being and life itself rest on finding my way through the swamp of the ageist myths and assumptions.

My appearance was the first indicator I could see of my own aging. The face lift that I didn't get compelled me instead to examine my assumptions about beauty and appearance. It forced me to begin specifically to confront the basic assumption underlying ageism, that youth is good, desirable, and beautiful; old age is bad, repulsive and ugly. Otherwise every time I look in the mirror I must feel contempt and aversion for how I look, or avoid looking altogether because, by patriarchal standards of beauty, I will find no beauty there. The most frequent "compliment" given to old women is "you don't look your age." Consider for a moment that what is really being said is that if you did look your age you would look ugly. There is an erosion of the self which occurs when who you are is everywhere made synonymous with unattractiveness and undesirability.

I was thrilled to read Cynthia Rich's article on Ageism and the Politics of Beauty (1988), which challenges us to look at how we arrive at our ideas about beauty and to reconsider the "mysteries of attraction." For unless we examine these "mysteries" we may well exclude, to our impoverishment, whole categories of women as attractive, particularly those who are disabled or old. Rich says, "Our task is to learn, not to look insultingly beyond these features to a soul we can celebrate, but instead to look at these bodies as parts of these souls—exciting, individual, beautiful."

My first big stretch then was to examine my own conditioned notions and reconsider more open ways to experience beauty. Most helpful to me in this process is the greater reliance I have been developing on my own senses, rather than on preconceived ideas. Skin that is old and wrinkled is soft and lovely, and as I touch my own skin and that of my lover I feel deep pleasure. Letting go more and more of my conditioning makes it possible for me to look with a clearer more loving vision at myself and the other old women around me. A shift, not yet complete, is taking place.

My relationship to my body has always been somewhat problematic. I have lived much of my life in my head and was trained, even more so than most women, to ignore my body's demands either for rest or attention. With growing psychological sophistication I talked about and regularly included in my practice as a therapist the notion of making friends with one's body. However, outside of sporadic frenzied efforts, I myself continued largely to ignore my body, and seemed to be able to do so with impunity since for the most part I was blessed with good health.

But starting in my 60's, my body no longer permits me to ignore her; she has begun to speak most loudly on her own behalf. Although I've always eaten too quickly and too much, for the first time I began to develop digestive problems. My vision, even with glasses, has become strained, and I've had laser surgery for glaucoma in both eyes. I have found that it takes me longer to recuperate, either after hard work or a transient illness, and I get downright cranky with insufficient rest. In other words, my body is showing some wear and tear after a long and arduous life. Certainly an acceptable proposition in a sane society and one that can be lived with, particularly since so many of us have paid such lip service to the need for women to attend to ourselves and our bodies with kindness and care, not only to others.

But in our culture, one of the first ageist assumptions is that to be old automatically means to be in some state of failing health and decrepitude, physical, mental, or both, and, further, to be in this state means to be valueless and a nonperson. It is no wonder, then, that women from their thirties on begin to lament their failing physical abilities, as if the standard set in the teens and 20's are the normative standards for life. My experiences with health limitations were so tied in with ageist expectations that at the first signs of what turned out to be a relatively mild condition I had a life crisis. I will not ever forget the absolutely unreasoning fear I felt the night I finally called the paramedics for what I thought was probably gas, but "given my age" could perhaps be chest pains, and signal the "beginning of the end." I'm not sorry I called the paramedics that time, or the time after. What I see in retrospect is that my fears, fed by the ageism of the medical establishment, were in large part due to my ageist expectations that my body was supposed to give out.

That incident provided me with some first-hand education about the rampant ageism of the medical establishment. I was referred from one doctor to another, experiencing a range of attitudes from the paternalistic "what do you expect at your age" to the downright incompetent in which, despite all medical information that *less* rather than *more* medication is indicated with age, I was, without diagnosis, prescribed heart medication to take for the rest of my life "just in case." Only after I became very much sicker (from the side effects of the medication) and after many expensive intrusive tests was it determined that nothing much was wrong with me that could not be controlled simply by proper diet and exercise. Of course a part of me felt foolish. But the havoc created by this series of events impressed upon me as probably nothing else would have how crucially my own welfare depends upon my confronting and challenging ageism, the ageism of the medical establishment as well as my own internalization of it. I was forced as well to learn in a new way how I must indeed listen to and attend to my body.

Medical research shows that there is no reason that most of us cannot remain in relatively good health until all but the very last stages of our life, particularly if we take proper care of our bodies. With age our bodies do demand more time and attention, and for the most part we learn to live with that greater demand. Like any other stage of life, there is a downside to old age, and I believe this is it. For all of us, young and old, our worst fear is what will happen to us in the event of chronic or severe illness in a society without adequate universal health care coverage, with a medical establishment that is racist, ageist, and sexist to the core, and with disability a social stigma. We are all haunted by the specter of being warehoused into nursing homes should we become disabled through accident or illness and unable to care for ourselves. We are taught to hate and fear disability and the disabled, and our society has tried to isolate and segregate the disabled, both young and old.

In addition, given that old age in white western European culture is thought of as a disease rather than a stage of life, it is not surprising to find that problems of living arising from greater fragility are reduced to medical problems requiring medical solutions. The medicalization of old age means that government funding gets funnelled through the medical establishment into nursing homes, vastly more expensive for the consumer and vastly more profitable for the provider than home health care.

The whole issue of possible disability raises another new area for reevaluating long held beliefs and attitudes. I have worked hard to become self-reliant and independent, and my ability to be "my own" person and do it "on my own" has been a source of pride for me. Lesbians, who do not look to men to be taken care of, place a high premium on that quality and have much difficulty in asking for help. Now, as an old woman, I am forced to reexamine the value I have placed upon personal independence at the expense of interdependence. There is much stretching to do in knowing that I am not diminished by asking for help. Should I become chronically disabled, I know I will face more critically the ongoing struggle to maintain an intact sense of myself while relying more upon others.

One thing is certain, our society makes interdependence difficult, for we live in a society segregated by race, ethnicity and age. Before I became conscious of my own ageism, I assiduously avoided anything that had to do with "old," including activities at our local Senior Center. As I began to acknowledge and accept my aging, I also began eagerly to seek out the companionship of old women, in my local neighborhood and in the lesbian community. It didn't take me long to know that the best of my learning and growth could take place here with these old women, as together we confronted the gripping issues of our lives.

Without any apparent loss of the energy and excitement of my youth, I once again became an activist, as one of the founders and organizers of the First West Coast Conference and Celebration of Old Lesbians (1987), as well as of the national Old Lesbians Organizing for Change (OLOC), which grew out of the Second West Coast Conference in San Francisco (1989). Lesbians, this time old lesbians, are once again in the forefront, on the cutting edge of the struggle for women's liberation.

We did an enormous amount of hard work to clarify our purpose and our goals as we hammered out a policy to confront the ageism within our lesbian community as well as the larger community. The uncompromising nature of our struggle was set from the start when we limited our group to old lesbians sixty and over, and when we insisted on calling ourselves OLD. The age limit exists so that old women have the opportunity to speak for ourselves, for, as an OLOC brochure (1992) says, "we are especially sensitive to those who see themselves as committed to the old, doing 'good' for the old, speaking for us. That is ageism!"

The insistence, for the first time, on 60 as an exclusive limit for belonging made 60 plus an important and empowering time in women's lives. I pointed out in my welcoming talk at the First West Coast Conference that important and painful as the problems of mid-life women may be, "to lump aging from 40 to 90+ is once again to trivialize the problems of old women—and once again to defer to younger women. We are expected to be available to nurture young and mid-life lesbians. Instead we boldly say 'No, this is our space.' We take this strong stand to affirm ourselves."

The "O" word is probably more dreaded than the "L" word. I have never yet attended a group, as either leader or participant in which the issue has not come up. Why use that word. I will never forget one group in which an old lesbian talked about how disgusting, revolting, and actually nauseating that word was. Yet we old lesbians again stood firm, accepting none of the euphemistic substitutes that came pouring in.

The OLOC brochure says that although "Old has become a term of insult and shame . . . we refuse the lie that it is shameful to be an old woman." We are neither "older" (than whom?) nor "elder," nor "senior." We name and proclaim ourselves as OLD for we no longer wish to collude in our own oppression by accommodating to language that implies in any way that old means inferior, ugly or awful. For to the degree that old women deny our own aging we cripple our ability to live. By naming ourselves old, we give up the attempt to pass. And as we break our silence, we empower ourselves and each other.

The excitement of this struggle is enormous. There were approximately 200 old lesbians attending each of the West Coast Conferences, and within a year when OLOC began to issue a Newsletter the mailing list grew to over 700 names.

Now there are clusters of old lesbians meeting in at least 14 states, with plans for some of us to caravan around the country to meet and organize additional old lesbians. There is no question that old lesbians want to network with each other and share their experiences so that they can become a force in changing the ageism of our society.

Such an exciting endeavor! I often feel astonished at how rich in exploration and discovery my life is. This is not what I expected. This self of mine, that I always characterized at its best as a seeker after truth, is still in there doing her thing! And I am surprised, for I believed the same things we were all taught about what it means to be old.

I am learning better than ever before just how political the personal is. Never has my political life been so intertwined with my personal thrust toward clarity and resolution. I believe that our work has impact, that I have impact as we old lesbians continue to organize and make ourselves visible.

As part of our active engagement with life I and my partner are constantly building our friendship circle, a community of old and new friends and comrades, based first on our own special group of old lesbians but extending intergenerationally to many women. For our community of women strengthens and sustains us.

I have always wanted to live a mindful life, and I believe that my ongoing process of checking the dimensions of my own reality keep me mindful, alert and aware.

I am bemused when I think of my many fears about growing old. I was even afraid to retire and waited an extra year because I wasn't sure that I would have either enough to do or enough money to do it with. Although money is not abundant, I am fortunate that it is an occasional rather than a chronic worry. Since we hear only the down side of growing old, I was unprepared for my life as it is now. It is different from what I expected. Not until I stopped working could I even begin to imagine the exhilarating sense of freedom which unstructured open-ended time makes possible, a delicious experience I am having for the first time in my life.

How could I expect that my old age would be so full of life and love and excitement? All the ageist cliches depict old age as a static time, and the major gerontological theories reinforce those cliches, categorizing old age as a time of disengagement, when the biological clock winds down and the spirit and psyche withdraw. I do not dispute that such characterizations may be true for some. That is not the way, however, I am experiencing my life. I am not unaware that my body is moving closer to dying, and that at the time of my actual dying, if the process is natural and not precipitated by trauma, I may indeed have a different agenda.

For now, however, my life is very much in process, full of opening new doors while looking back at old and treasured experiences. My past gives my present a richness and a backdrop for the exploration which is happening in the present. Almost every value and belief I have held is up for reexamination and reevaluation.

In speaking of my old age, I once declared with some disappointment that I have not miraculously arrived at a state of grace or of wisdom, that I am still in process. This, then, is perhaps the greatest miracle of all. That so long as there is life, there is the possibility of growth and change. Old age provides no guarantees but death. However, it does provide us with a special gift, the final challenge and the final opportunity to grow up.

References

Copper, B. (1988). *Over the hill, Reflections on ageism between women.* Freedom, CA: The Crossing Press.

Macdonald, B. & Rich, C. (1991). *Look me in the eye—old women aging and ageism.* San Francisco, CA: Spinsters Book Company.

OLOC Brochure (1992). OLOC, P.O. Box 980422, Houston, TX 77098.

Rich, C. (1988). Ageism and the politics of beauty. In Macdonald, B. & Rich, C. (1991) *Look me in the eye—old women aging and ageism* (pp. 139–146), San Francisco, CA: Spinsters Book Company.

Public Talk about 'Private Parts'

Eve Ensler is a playwright, filmmaker, and activist who has performed her one-woman play The Vagina Monologues *all over the United States as well as in Israel, Croatia, and England. Her play was developed after she interviewed more than two hundred women about their vaginas. Ensler has renamed February 14 as "V Day," or Vagina Day. Every year on this date, gala performances of* The Vagina Monologues *are staged to raise money for stopping violence against women.*

Here, Ensler talks with Virginia Braun, a graduate student who does research on how women feel about their vaginas. Claiming that our vaginas are central to our self-image, self-esteem, and sexuality, Ensler aims her activism at helping women recognize the power and beauty of their bodies.

As You Read, Ask Yourself . . .

What events in Eve Ensler's life led to her quest to "re-envision" the vagina?

Do you agree with Ensler that women are often dissociated from their bodies and their sexual desire?

Would you be willing to celebrate "V-Day"? Why or why not?

Reclaiming women's bodies is central to women's liberation. Think of feminism and the vagina, and the first image that comes to mind could well be a group of women in the 1970s, with speculum, torch and mirrors, looking at their own and other women's vaginas. Over the past 30 years, however, the vagina has attracted relatively little feminist interest. Until recently, that is. Eve Ensler, playwright, screenwriter and activist from New York, recently produced a highly successful spoken-word performance piece called *The Vagina Monologues*—a series of short monologues about the vagina, interspersed with 'vagina facts', which she developed from interviews with more than 200 women about their vaginas. Through saying the word 'vagina', through performing *The Vagina Monologues,* Ensler aims to stop 'bad things' such as rape and genital mutilation happening to women.[1] The show has received considerable media attention—both positive and critical. . . .

Ensler uses the term 'vagina' to refer not to the 'medical' vagina, but rather to the 'common-sense' vagina—all the bits 'down there'. She says, 'we haven't come up with a word that's more inclusive, that really describes the entire area and all its parts. . . . "Vulva" is a good word; it speaks more specifically, but I don't think most of us are clear what the vulva includes'.[2]

My own interest in the vagina is based on my PhD research, which looks at its social meanings, and explores what women's vaginas mean to them, particularly in terms of their identity as women. When *The Vagina Monologues* opened in London in early 1999, I saw the show. The audience was packed to overflowing, and it was an intensely moving, hilarious and thought-provoking performance. I met Ensler afterwards, and she agreed to be interviewed . . .

GINNY: One of the first things I wanted to ask you was why you started doing *The Vagina Monologues*. How did you get interested?

EVE: I always have this kind of canned response to that question, but the truth is, there are so many reasons, conscious and unconscious. On a conscious level, I was talking to a friend of mine, about menopause, and we got on to the subject of her vagina, and she said really contemptuous, revolting things about her vagina, and it shocked me. She was a feminist and a very forward-thinking kind of woman, and the contempt she had for her vagina—I couldn't put the two together. I started thinking, 'my God, this is what women think about their vaginas?' So I started to talk to other women, just casually, like friends, and I would say, 'what do you think about your vagina?' And every woman I talked to said something more amazing than the next. It just began this chain of curiosity, you know, one thing led to another.

Then there's the unconscious level. I've had a very dislocated relationship with my own vagina. Being a person who was raped very young, and abused very badly as a child, I was very, very disassociated with my own body. But I had a deep longing to get back in, to find a way back in, and you know, unconsciously, paths reveal themselves. So you start pursuing something to try to find your own path back home. So it was part accidental quest, my outrage at the treatment of the vagina and my own personal desire to be relocated in my vagina.

GINNY: And how do you see the work you're doing with *The Vagina Monologues* relating to your feminist background?

EVE: I think that if I hadn't been struggling for women's rights my whole life, and struggling for sexual liberation, and the notion of what that means, I don't know that I would have come to any of this. I think the connection between how women regard their vaginas, and how women feel, and the state of women in the world is deeply connected.

GINNY: One criticism that people might make of your work is that it is in the 1970s mould of feminism . . .

EVE: I'm not in the 1970s. I'm in the 1990s. And I couldn't have thought this way in the 1970s. I couldn't have written *The Vagina Monologues* in the 1970s, because the 1970s and 1980s had to happen for me to write them. Any person who's very upset, or outraged, or caring, or outspoken about something in the 1990s is called '1970s'—dismissed, destroyed, finished off. The 1970s was the only time women had a voice, and that voice has now been completely undermined. We're living in a time where there is very little politics any-more, and I think anybody who has any politics is called '1970s'. It's a way of erasing and reducing them.

GINNY: One thing that has struck me in relation to my own work is that over-whelmingly women don't seem to have a word that they like to talk about their genitals.[3] You say you use vagina because that's the word that people understand the whole thing to be.

EVE: It's the only word that's agreed on in a way, and that isn't derogatory. Be-cause if you think of any other words for the vagina, they're all degrading.

GINNY: Or sort of little kiddy words.

EVE: Which is degrading in an infantilized way.

GINNY: Cunt was a term feminists reclaimed, or tried to reclaim, in the 1970s, but it's still used as a term of abuse. One of your monologues is called 'Re-claiming Cunt', and you talked about how your feelings about this word had changed, and why you now use it.

EVE: I love it! It has the deliciousness, and the all-inclusiveness and the fierce-ness. Because when do men use that word? When they say 'that woman's really a cunt', what do they mean? She's smart. She has a big opinion. She doesn't go along with what they want her to do. She says no. She's difficult. She's bitchy, meaning she has an opinion. So for my money, call me a cunt. I'm very happy to accept all of those terms. I'm a cunt, I'm proud to be a cunt. And when I hear somebody say 'that woman's a cunt', I say, give me her phone number, because she's bound to be a friend.

GINNY: What sort of reactions to the show do you get from women?

EVE: It really ranges. It ranges from women who break down and can't get up because they remember being raped or incested, to a 74-year-old Irish woman who went home on 'V' day,[4] and got down with herself for the first time in her life, and looked at her vagina. Women show me their tattoos; women make me art objects, vagina objects. Women who are midwives get excited about birth; couples are blown away by remembering their child be-ing born. Lesbians feel really happy that they know vaginas as well as they do, and are seen in the piece.

GINNY: You only have one birth monologue—how did this happen?

EVE: I never had a baby, I never used my vagina for that, so it never was in my frame of reference. But suddenly I went, 'eek, there are people who have babies'.

GINNY: Somebody I spoke to felt that the birth monologue emphasized the trauma and pain of birth, rather than more positive aspects.

EVE: Most people do experience that monologue as really loving and beautiful and gorgeous, as well as being full of the trauma. I cannot tell you how many mothers have come up to me, and how many midwives, and have told me this was their *exact* experience. I have never talked to a woman who gave birth that wasn't traumatized. Everybody wants childbirth to be all pretty and nice, but I've talked to a lot of mothers, and if people have this lovely little slipping out experience, I have yet to meet them.

GINNY: One criticism that could be raised of your work, and mine,[5] is that, by only focusing on the vagina, we are fragmenting women's bodies. How would you respond to that?

291

VIRGINIA BRAUN IN
CONVERSATION
WITH EVE ENSLER
Public Talk about
'Private Parts'

EVE: That fragmentation's already *occurred*. I could be accused of objectifying the vagina, but in fact the vagina *has* been objectified. The vagina has been singled out, fragmented, so should we pretend that hasn't occurred? Or should we say, 'OK, this is a part of ourselves we have to reclaim, reconnect with, reintegrate'. Connecting with the vagina is fundamental. I think that by focusing on a piece that has been cut off we end the fragmentation, we reabsorb it back into the entire body. I can only say that I was completely fragmented when this process began, utterly fragmented, and I'm not any more.

GINNY: I read a review of *The Vagina Monologues* that raised a related criticism— it quoted a woman as saying, 'what about women's brains—surely it's the brain that's important'. How do you feel about this kind of critique?

EVE: The assumption that we will *thrive* and become successful and powerful in the workplace if we use only our brains is, in my opinion, an idiotic assumption. It's a completely sexist assumption. I think this was the way sexism really triumphed over feminism—by convincing women that the only way they would succeed was to become men, and to succeed on male terms. And women completely bought into it, I'm sorry to say. I know that when my brain's connected with my cunt I just think better. It's whole. It's more integrated. It's more, it's just more exciting. I think the corporate world insists that women separate from their sexuality, and separate from their cunt-wisdom, because corporations couldn't succeed and continue, the corporate world would tumble down, if women were fully connected with their vaginas. I am interested in the integrated brain, a brain that's working with the power, the fluids, the juice, the energy, of the vagina.

GINNY: So why do you feel it is important for women to talk about the vagina, to become consciously aware of their own?

EVE: I was raped as a little girl and the silence almost killed me, and being locked away in my own private hell almost killed me, and I think that's true for most women. The truth of the matter is, women really need to talk about their vaginas. Vaginas are very central to our beings, both physically placed in a central location, and the centre of our sexuality. And I think if we're not connected to it, it's almost like we're walking around like a car that's not connected to its motor. When you are connected, it becomes an energy, a driving force, a catalyst in our lives. It's a source of enormous wisdom, a source of complexity, and a source of strength. I see so many women who are living their lives without being connected to their vaginas.

GINNY: And do you think seeing this performance can change women, or start a change?

EVE: Yeah, I do. A lot of women have told me that coming to see this piece has changed their life. I think it just opened a relation with their vaginas that they never had. A consciousness enters, where you suddenly go 'oh my God, I've got a vagina, what a great thing'. Because most people are so disconnected from it, and so unaware of it. They're walking around with this huge gift between their legs, this huge amazing treasure that they haven't even begun to investigate, or connect with.

Personally, before I felt connected with my vagina, everything required double work because I wasn't using the central source of my energy. I was never fully sure of myself, so I was always doubting things. I was always apologetic for being here, on a fundamental level. I did everything with my head, everything was about my head, it just kind of drove me through the world. But the part of me that was outrageous, or creative, or provocative had really shut down.

GINNY: What happened when you started to connect with it?

EVE: The feeling I have now is that when I enter a room, all of me enters it. When I'm writing, I'm completely involved in it. When I'm having sex, I'm whole, I'm not disassociated. When you connect with your vagina what you're connected with is your desire. We live in a culture that is about women not having desires. And I think when you come into your vagina, to be honest, desire is imminent. It's undeniable. When women start desiring, they come into their sexuality, they come into their ambition, you know, they know what they want. Coming into your desire allows you to give yourself, but to not give your will up, or to give your needs up. You grow and you become more creative. I think most women have been taught the exact opposite. We're taught how to hold back, to shut down, to cut off, to be reserved, to not go into any given sexual situation knowing what we want, or asking for what we want, or taking what we want. And when you're able to do that sexually, I think you're able to do that in other ways too.

But most women haven't been in touch with our desire most of our lives, so it is incredibly terrifying. When I started to come into the consciousness of my vagina it was very terrifying, and part of me wanted to immediately shut it down. It's scary to feel that sexual desire. It was scary to feel that desirous all the time. It was scary to feel that *definite.* I think knowing what you desire sexually is really important. Looking at your vagina a lot. Masturbation is fundamental because it's a way of constantly checking in and opening that part of you that is trying to reveal itself. It's making your vagina *real* to yourself, so it doesn't become that abstract floating entity again. It's like grounding it. So you have to be *willing* to be a kind of warrior, to just say 'OK, I'm gonna go through this pain, but its gonna reconnect me with myself and other people'. That's the value of being connected with your vagina. It's not some narcissistic thing where you can get yourself off. It's more that when you're connected with your vagina, you are connected with the world in a fundamental way. I really see the vagina as a life-force.

GINNY: One issue you haven't addressed in *The Vagina Monologues* is the 'voluntary' genital surgery, such as labial trimming, done in the West. How do you feel about this practice?

EVE: Actually, somebody called me the other day because they're now doing laser surgery on vaginas making them tighter, and I just said 'well who does that *serve*?' Does it make sex better for the (heterosexual) *woman*? I can't see how that would make sex better for her. I mean maybe if it was tighter there would be more friction if the penis were inside, but it seems like it really serves the *man.* But this is my general attitude. I don't judge what women do because I feel like, look, we're still living in the most misogynist, oppressive, horrible times, and the majority of things that women do grow out of that. If we had moved into an era where women loved their vaginas, and were completely with themselves, and women were having all this constructive surgery, I would be highly suspicious. But we're not there yet. I mean I hate the fact that women mutilate and change their bodies at *all*. I think it's really awful that women feel *compelled* to do that, but on the other hand I don't *blame* women for doing it, because I understand the intense pressure in the culture to do it. So I think the deal is how do we change a culture so that pressure is no longer there, rather than beating women up for making those choices.

GINNY: So looking at a broader kind of social level rather than an individual level?

EVE: Exactly. I mean people say 'how do you feel about people having facelifts or breast implants?' And what I feel is look at our culture that women have to do that, that they feel better about themselves once they've done that. I'm not gonna be mad at women for buying into the most powerful, invasive, pressurizing culture in the world, that has managed to export its vision of women's bodies to almost every country. But I long for a culture where women don't feel compelled to do that.

GINNY: What, then, do you see as important work for feminism in the future?

EVE: My focus is basically on ending violence towards women. That's what I'm most concerned with. Because I think if rape, battery, incest and general mutilation were stopped, something would have shifted in the world, something major. And I think that's where we should be putting our energy. If we were to unlock the sources and reasons and whys of why women are being violated, to find a way to *stop* it, I think that we would find everything in that breath. The liberation of women, in particular their sexuality, is a huge part of that. I think one of the reasons most women close down their vaginas is because of either having been battered, raped, incested or mutilated, or had the threat of it. So to me, more than even fighting for equal *pay*, or other kinds of rights, that is fundamental. And I think that it's deeper than *anything* that's going on towards women. I think it's truly what keeps women in their place, so to speak.

I think that women have had it. They've had it with being abused, they've had it with being quiet, they've had it with bad sex, they've had it. I think they've reached a point where things have to change. That's definitely my experience, touring around the world. What I see is women hungering for community, hungering for revolution, hungering to be part of something that has meaning, hungering to work for a cause. I don't think people are happy in their little individual lives. We hunger, we crave, we need community.

293

*VIRGINIA BRAUN IN
CONVERSATION
WITH EVE ENSLER
Public Talk about
'Private Parts'*

Notes

[1]Ensler, E. (1998) *The Vagina Monologues*. New York: Villard, p. xxii.

[2]Ensler, E. (1998) *The Vagina Monologues*. New York: Villard, p. xx.

[3]For example: Braun, V. and Kitzinger, C. (1999a) ' "Snatch", "Hole", or "Honey Pot"? Semantic Categories and the Problem of Non-specificity in Female Genital Slang'. Under submission.

[4]V-day refers to 14 February, which Ensler has renamed 'V' day, or Vagina day. Annually on this day, gala performances of *The Vagina Monologues* take place to raise money for stopping violence against women.

[5]For example: Braun, V. (1999) 'Breaking a Taboo? Talking (and Laughing) about the Vagina', *Feminism & Psychology* 9(3): 367–72; Braun, V. and Kitzinger, C. (1999b) 'Telling it Straight? Dictionary Definitions of Women's Genitals, 1989–1998'. Under submission.

Tali Edut, with Dyann Logwood and Ophira Edut

HUES Magazine:
The Making of a Movement

What do teenage girls and young women learn from women's magazines? Tali Edut says that she learned not just how to choose the right shade of lipstick but also that she could never be as beautiful as the models and that she could never be complete without a man.

Many of us read women's magazines with a mixture of pleasure, guilt, and fascination. We simultaneously reject and try to achieve the ideals of femininity they portray. What are the alternatives? We could, of course, boycott (girlcott?) them. But Edut, along with her twin sister Ophira Edut, their friend Dyann Logwood, and others, decided to do something more positive and daring: to envision—and create—a magazine that promotes intelligence and self-sufficiency for women of all sizes, colors, ethnicities, and lifestyles.

As You Read, Ask Yourself . . .

How were Tali Edut and her friends affected by the white standards of beauty in women's magazines?

What did Edut learn from her experience with Sassy *magazine?*

What roadblocks were encountered when Edut and her friends attempted to publish a national edition?

What is the vision of sisterhood underlying HUES?

Hello, my name is Tali . . . and I was an addict. You see, once upon a time I had this problem. I just couldn't stop myself from subscribing to magazines for women and girls "just like me." I confess that I was a victim of the ill mainstream media; the glamorized trappings that amounted to just about every "ism" in the book. If a product was being pushed, in all its brightly colored wrapping, I was zealously tearing off the bow. Though I now publish a magazine that encourages intelligence and self-sufficiency "for women of all sizes, ethnic backgrounds, and lifestyles," it was my lifelong battle with the pressures and the standards of "successful" women's magazines that motivated me to collaborate with my girls to create *HUES* magazine.

295

*TALI EDUT, WITH
DYANN LOGWOOD
AND OPHIRA EDUT
HUES Magazine:
The Making of a
Movement*

While growing up, I learned a lot from women's magazines. I learned how to apply just the right shade of lipstick to get that "special guy" to (not) notice me. I learned that all the stretching, pulling, and lifting in the world couldn't make me pencil thin like the teenage models I was *supposed* to look like. Beauty, success, and coolness, they taught me, were reserved for an illusory circle of pale-skinned, prom-perfect ultrafemmes with tiny features and unchallenged minds. No matter how outstanding I was on my own, these glossies assured me that life was never really complete without a man by my side.

By the time I graduated from *Seventeen* into *Cosmopolitan,* I had mastered the art of picking apart my body like a twenty-piece chicken dinner. My 1970s collection of board games such as Fashion Plates and Barbie's Dream House had been shelved for a new activity—"The Mirror Game." Locked in the family's bathroom, I wasted precious teen hours staring at my reflection, wondering why I had been cursed. Everything was too big. My nose with the bump in it was a trademark of my Jewish lineage (which I hated as a result). As for my full lips, the orthodontist had pulled my mother aside to suggest we consider the option of surgically reducing them, along with my nose (my teeth were "finally perfect"). My body, which one might call Rubenesque, was all wrong to me. I wasn't gangly and long, and I didn't have a gap between my inner thighs. My round butt never sustained a comb in the back pocket as I skated around the roller rink in a tight pair of designer jeans. The only part of me I could stand were my eyes—although I would have preferred them to be a dramatic violet instead of hazel. But, I figured, since I wasn't exactly a nominee for homecoming queen, no one would really want to look in them anyway.

I was constantly comparing myself to the girls in my magazines. I would open to the article "Thinner Thighs in Thirty Days" and perform leg lifts in front of the mirror while my eyes darted between the model on the page and my reflection. As for my schoolmates, I felt every girl was prettier, cooler, sexier, and so on, than I was. Amid the Black, White, and "other" students at my working-class high school, even my upbringing in an Israeli household set me apart from my peers. I felt like a modern version of Barbra Streisand's "funny girl," the klutzy, misfit Jewess whose survival depended on a good sense of humor.

To add to the situation, I was an identical twin, so when I got sick of looking in the mirror, I shared much of my life with someone who looked, gestured, and thought a lot like the much-hated me. Family and strangers alike were forever comparing us, with no thoughts of how their unsolicited candor would make us feel. "I think Ophi is a bit thinner than Tali," people would remark. Or, "Tali has a clearer complexion than Ophi, but aren't they i-den-ti-cal?" As insecure teens, we took the comments to heart. Although we were the best of friends, we also developed a twisted support network. If one of us fretted or cried over someone's rude comparisons, the other would comfort and reassure her. But we also began picking at each other, doling out self-hatred in the form of "constructive criticism." She would suggest I pig out a little less after school, and I would rip out Stridex magazine ads for her.

At fifteen, with my family's unwavering support, Ophi and I started the "Dee-troit Diet," the first of a series of low-cal, fat-free obsessions. Although I was smart enough to pass calculus with a solid A, the equation I knew best was the one that multiplied fat grams by nine and divided that number by the calorie count. After school, Ophi and I would rush home for a couple of hours of aerobicizing with five-pound ankle weights. At the time, being thin was the only thing that mattered to me as much as getting a boyfriend. At least if my body looked more like a model's, I rationalized, maybe guys would ignore the imperfection of my face.

Like most people, I wanted to be liked and accepted. My circle of friends were cool and fun, but they weren't necessarily what you would consider popular. So at fifteen, when the tips I'd learned from "How to Snag That Perfect Boy" finally paid off, I shamefully dissed my girls, to hang with HIM (and ONLY HIM). I looked to HIM as my one-way bus ride from the reject asylum. HE was my salvation from ugliness (hey, I could get a *man*) and my ethnic cleanser (just because my name was Tali Edut didn't mean I was a "foreigner" like my parents), and he was Joe Average enough to counterbalance my artsy style. Suddenly I was double-dating, staying out until midnight, and doing all the things I'd read that a teen girl was supposed to do.

When I wasn't working out, dying my hair a brassy bottle-blond, or hanging with HIM, I was doing one of two things: studying my way into college (and the hell out of Oak Park, Michigan) or reading. Scouring the shelves, I never found, nor expected to locate, a magazine with women and girls in it who were much like me. So, after sifting through each month's delivery of *Teen* and *YM*, I would lose myself in books. I actually found books that didn't constantly remind me of how uncool I was, and they gave me something to dream about besides the prom. In retrospect, I wish I would have found Toni Morrison's *The Bluest Eye* when I was in high school. Although the character Pecola is Black and I am Jewish, I relate to her as someone who grew up feeling valueless because her appearance and ethnicity set her apart from the mainstream.

In our first year of art school at the University of Michigan, I finally reached my limit. I gained the dreaded "freshman fifteen," whereas Ophi became unnaturally thin from eating too little. Stress from late-night projects destroyed my dieting efforts. As luck would have it, I wound up with an aspiring model as a roommate, which did nothing to keep me from occasionally wolfing Pillsbury cookie dough and then sticking my finger down my throat. I had numerous failed crushes on guys whom I now would consider total losers. (My "perfect" high school boyfriend had dumped me for a sexually available local girl ten minutes before I left for school.) I had even cut down on hanging with Ophi, because I was so afraid of being called "the bigger twin." I felt alone and depressed, and I knew that something had to change.

This saga of my teen angst is not a cry for sympathetic greeting cards or a plea for a guest spot on a daytime talk show. Rather, it's an attempt to make a point about how miserable a girl's life can be when she tries to follow the manifesto of the mainstream media. I felt hopelessly inadequate when I was trying to reach a standard that for me was impossible (at least, without peroxide, colored contacts, liposuction, rhinoplasty, and enrollment in a WASP training academy). This standard wasn't just something I pulled out of a hat, either. It surrounded me—not only on billboards and in the pages of my monthly magazines, but in the minds of the majority of America's female population.

Almost every woman I knew could draft a sizable list of the things she wanted to change about herself. And I'd place bets that if there were ten items on that list, eight of them would refer to her physical characteristics. *Ummm, I'd like a slim-waist platter, along with a side of perky breasts. Oh yeah, and can you make my skin a little more . . . alabaster, please?* I now know that I could no more have gotten rid of those outer-thigh curves that one fitness-obsessed magazine writer referred to as "saddlebags," than Kate Moss could expect to runneth over the cups of my 36D bra. The point is, women shouldn't be expected to live up to any look-of-the-day other than the one we can naturally achieve through an emotionally and physically healthy lifestyle.

The saddest part about the image-obsession craze is that it keeps women so preoccupied with feeling bad about our appearances that our minds and souls become secondary. Instead of investing money in mutual funds or taking night classes, the only numbers we're interested in crunching are the ones on the scales at Jenny Craig. The struggle for self-esteem is ongoing for many women. It's undeniably easier for a woman to find outlets for self-hatred than to find ones that tell her to feel good about who she is. All she has to do is pick up a magazine. If she doesn't know that airbrushing is the only real answer to cellulite, she might believe the hype.

When we were nineteen years old, Ophi and I met Dyann Logwood. She had been sitting in the dorm room of a mutual friend when Ophi walked by, and Ophi (as she said later) was just drawn in. The two of them wound up having such an amazing conversation that they actually forgot about the guy they had each come to visit. I was introduced a couple of days later, and we soon became an inseparable trio. It was odd that we got along so well, because our backgrounds were really different. Dyann was African American, the daughter of a Pentecostal preacher. Her upbringing had been strict and somewhat conservative, in a religious sense. Although we all came from integrated schools, Dyann was among a significant population of African American students. Ophi and I were two of possibly twenty Jews in our school district, and the only Israelis. Although Jewish traditions such as holidays and seven years of Hebrew school were upheld, our family tended to be more liberal about daily life. In high school, Dyann was well known for her public speaking abilities and was nicknamed Jesse Jackson for her pro-Black speeches. Although Ophi and I were known for winning writing contests and making crazy, artistic clothes, we were more on the outside fringe. We tended to be more closeted about our Jewish heritage then, preferring to blend instead of making any grandiose political statements about ethnicity.

In spite of our differences, our friendship was both medicinal and educational. Our late-night talks over pizza and vending machine snacks were like group therapy sessions and basement political meetings. (And you wouldn't believe how good junk food tasted after years of oat bran and frozen yogurt.) It was from these talks that we gained a perspective into worlds beyond our own doorsteps.

Dyann was the first woman the two of us had ever met who didn't constantly put herself down. She wasn't afraid to take pride in the things she did well. In her mind, if you didn't believe you were "all that," no one else would, either. At sixteen, she had decided that she didn't want to go through life hating herself. She enlisted the help of a few daily affirmations, wherein she would look in the mirror and tell herself she was beautiful and strong. She swore by it as a confidence booster. That was such an odd concept for me and Ophi. We could hardly fathom looking in the mirror and saying, "You look okay, I guess." But beautiful? That was a whole new ball game. The three of us were all shaped similarly—short and thick. The difference was that in Dyann's community, being skinny was considered unattractive and "having some meat on your bones" was actually a sign of beauty. As a teen, Dyann had felt an uncomfortable urgency to sprout some curves, whereas Ophi and I had worked obsessively to diminish ours. Although Dyann had felt less impact from teen girls' magazines (the permanent absence of Black models and issues had dulled her interest), she had been unduly affected by the industry's by-product—what she referred to as "the Black Barbie syndrome." The Black woman with light skin, green eyes, and long hair (which, I learned from Dyann, is sometimes hard for Black women to grow)—essentially the Whitest-looking Black woman—was touted as the most beautiful. Whereas a lot of Jewish girls Ophi and I knew were constantly dieting, blow-drying the curl out of their hair, and occasionally spending spring break at the plastic surgeon's, Dyann was acquainted with Black women who spent hundreds of dollars getting their hair permed straight, popping colored contacts, even buying over-the-counter skin bleach.

Getting to the stage of believing she was a strong, beautiful woman wasn't easy for Dyann, though. In spite of Hollywood's portrayal of hard-core Black women who didn't take any shit, Dyann recalled regular sermons about a woman's role being to support her man at all times. She also remembered the girls at her church being commanded to "keep their legs closed." Although the women she grew up around had a strong presence, they rarely challenged the church-prescribed role of wife and mother. Similarly, although no one was directly insisting that Ophi and I become stereotypical, overbearing Jewish mothers, we always felt pressured to find that "nice Jewish boy" to make our lives complete. For all of us, growing beyond the prescribed definition of womanhood demanded a good deal of work.

While we were chowing down, we talked about a lot of things besides physical image. We'd all had interracial friendships prior to college, but they had tended to be more color-blind (you're aware of surface differences, for instance, but you choose to ignore them for fear of bringing up possibly unpleasant issues). Whether it was the self-actualizing aura of college life or the fact that we were suddenly awakening to the ills that surrounded us, the three of us couldn't seem to have a conversation that wasn't political. We talked about *everything*: How people in Dyann's classes often assumed she was there only because of affirmative action. How futile it was for Blacks and Jews to debate the significance of slavery versus the Holocaust. How sad it was that a man's influence could quash a woman's dreams. How our teachers had rarely encouraged us toward big-money careers. How hard it was to decide whether Judaism was a race or a religion. How annoying it was that our peers assumed we were sellouts or wanna-be's because we didn't hang exclusively with people inside our cultures.

From those talks a new cross-cultural guideline emerged: don't tiptoe around the issues, but also be prepared to shut up and listen. Initially we were all somewhat clueless about each other's cultures, and, I won't pretend that we

disbelieved every stereotype. (We cracked up when Dyann revealed that someone had once told her that the word *Jew* came from *jewelry*, because Jewish people owned all the jewelry stores.) It took a little while before we were able to admit that we weren't always liberal ambassadors with innate understandings of
every cultural truth and faux pas. After hanging out for a couple of weeks, we
reached a comfortable understanding that if someone said something ignorant,
another could correct her without ending the friendship, and that if someone
asked a "stupid" question, we would try to answer it without jumping down the
other's throat. Above all, we learned to listen and learn from each other's experiences. I had once believed that racism had been eradicated along with the Jim
Crow laws. Dyann's life stories helped me and Ophi see that we still had a lot of
privileges on the basis of our paler features. And, after the three of us decided
to be roommates, we saw firsthand how many apartments suddenly became
"unavailable" when Dyann walked into the rental office.

By the time we figured we knew *everything* there was to know about Black
and Jewish cultures—as if—we got the idea that our talks might be a good basis for bringing more women together across cultural "boundaries." We knew
we weren't the only three women in the world who had been affected by an era
of heroin-addicted models and Martha Stewart-like supermoms. We were especially concerned with the impact on women like ourselves, who were considered "cultural others."

While we were waiting for inspiration on the perfect way to unite all
women, I got my first behind-the-scenes look at women's magazines. I was back
at home on summer break, thumbing through my little sister's *Sassy* magazine.
At that time, *Sassy* was arguably the closest thing to a teenage feminist publication that existed. Of all the teen and women's magazines on the shelves, it was
the one publication with a voice that I could sort of relate to. The writers were
frank and opinionated, rather than prissy and NutraSweetish. So, when I arrived at the page announcing that *Sassy* was having a "Reader-Produced Issue
Contest," my interest was stirred. Essentially, *Sassy* was offering teenagers the
opportunity to "replace" its entire staff for one issue. I had always had an interest in both the media and New York City (where *Sassy* was located), so, with the
technical skill I'd gained from a couple of computer graphics classes at the University of Michigan, I decided to try for the role of art director. A few weeks later,
Neill, then the real art director of *Sassy*, phoned with the unbelievable news that
I would be taking his place for the month of August.

At *Sassy* I joined the other contest winners—a small but amazing group of
young women from all over the United States and Canada. After five minutes,
I felt my transformation from a midwestern hopeful to a cosmopolitan diva begin. We were all hyped to try out a few revolutionary ideas, as we were under
the impression that we could "recreate" this issue. I, for one, wanted to put some
of my own political awakenings into action in this mag. Unfortunately, the
reader model winners had already been instructed that to enter, they had to fit
the standard dimensions (at least 5'8" tall, size seven clothes). Still, amid the
"goth" fashion shoots (heavy black eyeliner, dyed black hair), a few of the more
political contestants and I managed to slip in a little consciousness. We included
a basic piece about feminism and an article by the Filipina reader-editor about
growing up as a "minority."

299

*TALI EDUT, WITH
DYANN LOGWOOD
AND OPHIRA EDUT
HUES Magazine:
The Making of a
Movement*

We learned our first big lesson when we chose a Black girl and a Filipina girl to model for the cover. When we met with the publishing board to discuss our potential cover design, we expected a briefing on basic concerns, such as which articles to make into headlines and the best ways to pose the models. Instead, talk turned, uh, political. We were told that if we wanted to use these two models, we also had to include a White girl in the picture. According to the publisher's supposed expertise and marketing data, a cover without a White girl would alienate a tremendous number of readers at the newsstand. The South, after all, was an important area, and they didn't want to lose any subscribers. Although the publishers never came right out and said it, the message was clear: *Sassy* was yet another magazine strictly concerned with the number of White people reading it.

Looking back, I realize that there were other tears in the fabric of *Sassy*. The hip editorial staff was constantly at odds with the number-crunching publishing board. Writers were not allowed to touch certain subjects, such as abortion and homosexuality, at the risk of losing lucrative makeup ads. The fashion department at *Sassy* was made up of beautiful and stylish women, but few had the anorexic proportions of the models they chose month after month. Gone were my notions of some insidious White man picking seven-foot girls from an uber-waif lineup. I saw firsthand how easily the status quo image of female beauty was perpetuated—and by women, at that! Here were women who actually had the power to reduce the damaging pressures on teen girls—pressures that are directly linked to eating disorders and poor esteem among girls and women; yet they were unwilling to take the risk. Their claim was that fashion companies made sample clothing in size seven only. (Perhaps at the heart of this brainwash is a group of fashion designers giddy over the yards of fabric they have saved during the thin-is-in craze.) Still, I wondered, if *Sassy* was able to use its influence to bring offbeat fashions such as combat boots to American teen girls, then how hard could it really be to rustle up a pair of pants in a size fourteen? The old *Sassy was* an "alternative," in the sense that encouraged more independence than its boy-crazy competitors, such as *Teen* and *YM*. Nonetheless, it never dethroned the Anglo beauty queen—even if she was wearing Doc Martens.

I returned from my *Sassy* summer to the University of Michigan feeling both jaded and inspired. On the one hand, I had acquired some incredible new knowledge. Not only had I peeped the inside track of the magazine industry, but I had also gained a fairly comprehensive understanding of what went into producing a national publication. On the other hand, I had learned that what goes on behind the scenes of the media is not nearly as glamorous as what's seen on the pages.

That semester, Dyann, Ophi, and I enrolled in an introductory women's studies class. Part of the curriculum included a semester-long "action project" that involved working with women's issues in some capacity. Inspiration struck while we were musing over ideas for the assignment: why not try to create our own women's magazine and distribute it on campus?

We were in unanimous agreement that we wanted this project to be not just a magazine but a movement that would bring women together across "boundaries." We envisioned a sort of sisterhood, which we defined partly in reference to our own friendship, being played out on the pages. We saw the need for greater loyalty among women. Among our peers it was often considered cooler to be "one of the guys" than "one of the girls." Sisterhood to us meant having a support network strong enough that a woman could stand up for herself without feeling crazy or alone. It also meant having a greater sense of loyalty between women, so that, for example, we would believe each other if we said we were raped, not go after our best friend's boyfriend, stand up for the girl who gets called a slut, not feel threatened by someone we think is "prettier," and so on. Beyond that, we wanted to encourage a new style of communication among women that was more direct than conflict-avoiding. The three of us were able to accept each other's differences without feeling hostile or competitive because we had an in-your-face, no-holds-barred approach to communication. We wanted to see more women talk to each other instead of about each other when dissension arose, which we felt would diminish much of the hostility that often goes on between women.

Because a conscious magazine for young women hadn't been printed to date, we didn't have a model on which to base ours. Although this made our task a little harder, it also allowed for greater creativity. Our ideas definitely diverged from the mainstream periodical selection. The publication would have to be a women's magazine of a different kind, one that would include rather than exclude. It would speak to women's intelligence, promoting self-esteem and sisterhood. It would be fun and serious, intellectual and raw at the same time. It would highlight women's experiences and direct readers to resources. It would encourage solution-oriented positivity rather than hopeless frustration. Above all, it would give women a new, real standard to look to, rather than the unattainable gloss of other women's magazines.

One of our major concerns was to provide a movement that would include women who are traditionally excluded from the mainstream—not only as participants but also as cocreators. We'd had enough of the typical women's organizations that planned their agendas with a mostly White board and then wondered why they couldn't seem to get any "women of color" to participate in their struggles. I remember feeling disgusted after the three of us attended an open planning meeting for a women's conference. Under the presumption that the meeting was going to be run democratically, we instead butted up against a "good old girls network"—a group of established self-proclaimed feminists who had a prescribed set of right and wrong answers for all women. Although the discussion participants insisted that they wanted to draw in "women of color," they were opposed to trying anything beyond setting up a special "women-of-color" booth in the waiting area and bringing in one Latina professor to speak. The meeting ended up being just another illustration of the constant marginalization of non-White women into the category of "other." (I mean, if non-White women get to be "women of color," then do White women have exclusive rights to the word "women"?) This happens so often among "well-meaning" feminist groups. They claim that they want to include all women, but they want to control quantity and the quality of women's participation.

The three of us wanted to see multiculturalism finally done right in a women's movement. It wasn't about hand-holding and singing cheesy songs. And we weren't trying to pimp "diversity" as a cover-up for token representation or do some overhyped Benetton we-are-the-world thing. Rather, we were looking for a forum wherein women of different cultures and classes could come together without losing their identities. We envisioned a successful modern women's movement in terms of the old patchwork quilt cliché. Each square would represent its own identity, but the pieces would be inextricably sewn together.

It was important to us that women of all cultures and classes be properly represented in our magazine. We agreed that a code of self-representation was the best way to handle this. If a story was to be told, we wanted it straight from the source. So, there wouldn't be any term-paper-cum-news-story on an American woman's fourth-hand experience with female circumcision; but there might be a story by a woman who had undergone the process, or there might be three women's stories. The way we figured it, the truth was best when it was undiluted by an outsider's inferred understanding. It was also important to us that we illustrate the diversity that existed within a single culture. To break down the stereotypical notion that all Asians, lesbians, single moms, and so on, think in the same way, we wanted to highlight a variety of thoughts within each community.

After much brainstorming, we decided to name our magazine *HUES,* which conveniently shaped itself into an acronym for "Hear Us Emerging Sisters." It seemed like a word that could translate into more than just the obvious multicultural innuendo. *HUES* represented to us the varying shades of womanhood. It was inclusive (rather than simply *HUE*), and, best of all, it wasn't some froufrou beauty reference like "mirabella" or "allure."

With the name decided upon, we posted flyers and E-mail across campus and soon assembled a small—but truly multicultural—group of women. The *HUES* collective—which included a bisexual Black TA, a Filipina political science major, a Nigerian-born art major from the South Bronx, a single mother attending community college, a White woman who worked with the mentally ill, a Puerto Rican–Chinese photographer, and a Jewish pre-law major—spanned an even broader range of experiences than we'd expected. Still, believe it or not, there was rarely any tension. The women who came to spend Wednesday evenings eating pizza in our living room were a lot like the three of us—openminded and willing to listen and learn. It didn't hurt that we all seemed to have good senses of humor, too. There were plenty of laughs as we sat around planning the new world order.

Before the presses rolled, the *HUES* collective took time out to assess the status of our generation of women. Would they be receptive to a new women's movement? At the time we were planning our first issue, the movie *Disclosure* (in which a male exec has an extramarital encounter with his female boss, then wins a sexual harassment case against her) was on its way to the box office, and "politically correct" was fast becoming America's favorite dirty word. The trend seemed to be toward gender neutrality rather than separatism. Not only did many women seem to fear the idea of joining together with other women, but also a lot of them saw no practical need in it. Their lives had been only covertly touched by sexism, and they were uneasy with the idea of rocking the boat.

We decided that the general attitude of our generation could be summed by the catchphrase "fear of a feminist planet." A lot of poor and non-White women associated feminism with privileged, middle-, and upper-class Whites who wanted to control their struggles and mediate their issues. In many instances the absence of non-Whites from women's groups confirmed this suspicion. Then there were the countless clueless, who still believed that pro-woman equaled anti-man. In the end, a lot of these young women wound up being feminists by default.

So, we asked ourselves, how could we package feminist ideals such as sisterhood and empowerment in a way that would speak to more than just a small segment of the female population? We started with terminology. Instead of directly calling *HUES* a feminist magazine, we subtitled it *A Woman's Guide to Power and Attitude.* We felt this allowed women to choose how they wanted to define themselves in the realm of the women's movement, be it feminist, womanist, pro-woman, or something else. Meanwhile, we focused on what we felt were the most pertinent issues. Body image, self-esteem, sisterhood, cross-cultural relations, and education topped the list. To make these issues digestible, we felt it was important to write articles in a sisterly tone and to add some humor to the lineup. It was like spoon-feeding feminism to the fearful, as opposed to ramming it down people's throats. We preferred to show through personal anecdotes rather than preach from some political pulpit. And, to keep a good balance of heavy and lighter pieces, we decided that *HUES* should highlight various facets of pop culture, from conscious fashion to music reviews to interviews with well-known women. We saw these pieces as an opportunity to give important press coverage to talented women who might be overlooked in other magazines.

Because we knew Gen-Xers were used to sensory overload, articles would have to be complemented by appealing graphics and photos. We would use models of all sizes, looks, and ethnic backgrounds throughout the entire magazine, reinforcing the idea that *HUES* represented *all* women. Unlike the "concerned" women's magazines that, for example, printed a "shocking" exposé on anorexia, only to follow with a Kate Moss fashion spread, *HUES* had to have a nonhypocritical balance between content and image.

Our aim was to make *HUES* look as well designed as any other publication on the shelves. Of course, it took a few tries to get to that point. When we finally published the first issue of *HUES* in April 1992, it was actually a half-size, black-and-white 'zine. We had raised enough money to print one thousand copies through receiving a few donations from campus groups and by throwing a few hip-hop parties around town. Articles included a piece called "Why Feminists Need Men," a piece on female rappers, and the story of a Filipina rape survivor.

The response to the premier issue was overwhelmingly positive. We got E-mail and letters from women thanking us for producing something aimed at making women feel good about themselves. Of course, there were a couple of annoying responses along the way, such as the one from a man angry about our editorial "No Justice, No Piece . . . Down with John Wayne Bobbitt." But we remained unfazed by our critics. Over the next two years, we pumped out three more issues. With each magazine we improved the quality of our contents and upgraded the "look." Our fourth issue was full size and printed on glossy paper. We added more resource-oriented articles that would connect women with helpful and proactive organizations. We finally had a good set of regular one-page columns on which to structure future issues. And, through fund raisers and the sale of ads to local businesses, we had enough money to do our first color cover and eight inside color pages.

What amazed us most was how *HUES* seemed to travel on its own. Because a lot of students brought *HUES* home from school with them, the magazine crossed state lines. We started getting calls from people across the country who loved *HUES* and wanted to subscribe. During the summer of 1994, after our fourth issue, we got a call from *Ms.* magazine, which published a one-page article about our magazine. Soon after that, the *Chicago Tribune* called. We had no idea how either publication had found *HUES,* but we realized that with our "sisters" we had created something that obviously appealed to women beyond Ann Arbor, Michigan.

At that point Ophi and I had graduated from college, and the three of us figured it was high time we took *HUES* to the next level. When we decided on our national launch in early 1995, we were pretty starry-eyed. We connected with a few national distributors who promised to shelve *HUES* in chain stores and newsstands from New York to California. We decided to complement sales with big promotional drop-offs at colleges across the country, which would also help get out the word about *HUES.* We were interested in selling ad space to companies that didn't objectify women or sensationalize culture. With the money from ad sales, we planned to make *HUES* more visible, create self-esteem workshops, and spread the message of sisterhood. Everyone—ourselves included—was *sure* that hordes of big corporations would be pouring their dollars into *HUES.* We approached companies that had advertised in other women's magazines. It seemed logical that companies would want to invest in a magazine that targeted *all* women instead of just a select handful. We boasted promising newsstand visibility, positive press write-ups, and piles of letters pouring in from women telling us that *HUES* was what they'd been waiting for all their lives.

Still, the big-money players weren't ready for us. Advertisers of universal women's products unabashedly told us that *HUES* "wasn't their audience." Even supposedly "alternative" companies such as charitable long-distance services gave us the same line. One ad agency actually told us that "ethnics don't sell." To another we were "spreading ourselves too thin with the multicultural, multisexual thing." Then we were informed that "college women don't spend enough to make them worth our ad dollars." To us, these rejections added up to one thing— society was still uncomfortable with the idea of an intelligent, self-empowered woman. Advertisers counted on women having low self-esteem in order to sell more "nighttime cellulite cream." A magazine that encouraged women to use their minds threatened the very premise many companies clung to. *What would happen if she figured out that our gym shoes aren't going to give her the body of an aerobics instructor? If she realized that our totally smudge-proof mascara won't bring her Prince Charming? Hmmm . . . let's keep her misinformed, guys.*

We also discovered that in big time publishing, a lot relies on who you know (and whether or not you are a Time, Inc., publication). Being an independently owned magazine was another strike against us. In many cases it prevented us from even getting a foot in the door. But getting rejected by everyone from Nike to Kotex was actually a blessing in disguise. It gave us an opportunity to reevaluate our goals. We had always been firm in our desire to keep *HUES* a resource for women, including women business owners. We decided to make *HUES* into an affordable network for more conscious companies to reach conscious consumers (i.e., *HUES* readers). And we had to learn a thing or two about creative financing. Although Dyann, Ophi, and I had honed the art of organizing young women into a productive unit, we had to start thinking like businesswomen as well. Dyann created a college marketing department from which college professors began ordering *HUES* for use in course curriculum, as well as an internal sales network for feminist bookstores.

We were also blessed to have families who believed in us enough to co-sign a start-up loan from a local bank. With that extra boost, along with revenues from some smaller advertisers, we launched our first national issue. It sold beautifully on the newsstand, and soon our 1-800 number was ringing with subscribers, the press, and people wanting a *HUES* woman to come speak at their conference. After that we did manage to sell a four-page ad to Levi's Jeans for Women for our second national issue, and we hoped that perhaps that would give us an edge with a few other clothing companies. Since then, we've connected with some awesome publications that share our mission, such as *New Moon: The Magazine for Girls and Their Dreams; Teen Voices;* and *Hip Mama.* In the spirit of true sisterhood, our four publications are forming an umbrella organization to support each other and share resources.

Today, Dyann, Ophi, and I are scrambling around trying to finalize the last-minute details of our eighth—and fourth national—issue, which is due to go on press in (aaaghh) only two weeks. There are articles that need to be dropped into layout, and filler columns to write and edit, not to mention that a few companies are still deciding what size ad to run. Even after five years of publishing, there is still the hectic buzz of uncertainty and instability. Still, we remain confident that *HUES* is what women need; we just may be a few years ahead of our time. In creating a publication that is not just a magazine but a movement, our goal remains to create a new standard of self-acceptance for women. And, whether or not *HUES* becomes the "femme-pire" of our dreams, we do hope the ideals—such as promoting sisterhood and including a diversity of women—will somehow translate into other women's magazines. A reporter recently asked me if I thought a magazine like *HUES* could ever move into the mainstream and be as big as, say, *Glamour.* I guess that one is up to the women of the world. For now, it still feels good to be a part of a new movement that truly includes *all* women.

A Parent's Story

Jenny Crompton's story cannot be told in her own words because her voice has been silenced. Jenny was murdered at the age of fifteen by her boyfriend, who had a long history of abusing, coercing, and stalking her. Jenny's mother, Vicki Crompton, tells Jenny's story in the hope that she may educate others about dating violence, and in memory of Jenny Crompton.

As You Read, Ask Yourself . . .

What happened when Jenny Crompton decided to break up with her boyfriend Mark?

What factors make it difficult for young teens like Jenny to avoid or prevent being the victims of dating violence?

How did Jenny's friends and the community deny the coercion she was subjected to?

What steps did Vicki Crompton take to name and speak out against dating violence after her daughter's death?

Jenny. An ordinary kid, from an ordinary family. Yet an extraordinary event changed our lives completely, and forever.

Mark. He appeared on our doorstep one evening in October 1985. I was tidying up the kitchen when I heard the doorbell ring, so I was the first one to reach the door. There he stood, a tall, blond young man, wearing blue jeans and a black leather jacket. With a charming smile, he asked, "Is Jenny home?" My first reaction was confusion. Who is this boy? Jenny had not mentioned that anyone, particularly a *boy*, was coming over. Then she came bounding down the steps, smiling, thrilled to see him. When I saw how excited Jenny was, I didn't have the heart to say no, to say that I really thought she was too young to have boys calling at the house.

That first evening, I guided them into the living room, where we all sat awkwardly, looking at each other. Jenny was far too shy to make casual conversation, and she was obviously far too taken with him. So my husband, Greg, and I kept the conversation going.

So Mark Smith came into our lives. Although Mark was very polite and answered all my questions about home and school, he was skillful at keeping the real Mark hidden. Later I would review the conversation and realize that I knew nothing about him.

For Jenny, the beginning of her relationship with Mark was a dream come true. Junior high had been an unhappy time in her life, a time when she found herself excluded. Her dream was to find acceptance in high school, to be popular and part of the crowd, and most of all, to find a boyfriend.

Her transition from girl to young woman was astounding to watch. Always a pretty child, Jenny, like so many kids, went through an awkward stage. She needed glasses at the age of ten, and with each passing year, the glasses became thicker. She also had braces on her teeth, and she grew taller, skinnier, and awkward. But by age twelve, she really started to change. First came contact lenses, which showed off her blue eyes, and she learned how to style her thick, blond hair. She developed a curvy shape and a sense of style and flair for clothes that was all her own. By the time she met Mark Smith, she was indeed a beautiful girl.

Her childhood attempts at sports were replaced by a love for dance. Through dance, she developed confidence and pride in her body. But her keen intellect was perhaps her most beautiful asset. A voracious reader since early childhood, Jenny continued that love with her studies. She was an honors student without much effort. Her talent for language was so great that by her sophomore year she was studying both French and Spanish. Her dream for her future was to utilize languages in a career, to live in Europe, to see the world.

Her interest in Mark was a bit of a mystery to me. Beyond his obvious good looks, I didn't see what the attraction could possibly be. In contrast to Jenny's love of learning, he was a poor student, uninterested in building for his future. Although my fervent hope was that he would go away to school, far away from Jenny, I was concerned enough about him to inquire about his plans after graduation now that he was in his senior year. I discovered that he had no plans. His parents had not spoken to him about his life after high school. My feeling was that he was just drifting through life. While Jenny was passionately interested in books, dance and her family, Mark's life centered on cars, his motorcycle and "riding around" with his friends. As I observed the differences between them, I knew it was just a matter of time before Jenny would tire of him and wish to be free.

Despite their age difference and lack of common interests, however, Jenny and Mark's relationship appeared to thrive. Apparently they were the talk of the school, the "perfect couple," so much "in love."

He called her daily, sometimes several times a day. They shared a locker at school and walked each other to class. They ate lunch together. He came over to our house about three nights a week. For a child of fourteen, it was pretty overwhelming. My rules were strict, but Jenny did not seem to mind. I think she knew she couldn't have handled a more intense relationship.

Some casual conversation with students employed in my office made me realize that Jenny and Mark might be discussing sex. So I said to Jenny one night in an offhand way, "Jen, if sex ever becomes an issue between the two of you, I hope you will talk to me about it first." The very next night she came to me! Without ever making eye contact, she told me she wanted to have sex with Mark and asked me to take her to a doctor for birth control pills. Horrified, I struggled to maintain my composure. I managed to stammer that I wanted to talk to some professionals first, to please wait for me to get her some help. I called every agency in the book, looking for someone who was skilled at talking to teenagers about the disadvantages of early sex. Finally I connected her with a teen from my office who felt comfortable talking about her own experiences. Jenny came home from that meeting and announced that not only was she not ready to become intimate, but that she also was going to break off her relationship with Mark completely. "I just want to be free, Mom," she told me. "I really envy my friends who don't have boyfriends." And so began the final phase of their courtship.

Mark ignored Jenny's attempts to break up. He still shared the locker, still walked her to class, still called. When she insisted that he stop, that she wanted to break up, he became more insistent, more possessive. The phone calls increased, the unannounced visits to the house more frequent. He would not move out of her locker. Because he made it so difficult, Jenny simply gave up and agreed to go back. When I questioned her, she said that she really cared for him and wasn't sure she wanted to end it. This on-again, off-again routine continued for the next several months, into the summer, until Jenny made the final break.

As Jenny increased her attempts to pull away, Mark intensified his actions to keep her locked in. He seemed to always know her plans. At first she would unwittingly tell him where she was going. Then, as she attempted to keep this information from him, he would turn to her girlfriends and find out about her activities from them. He was so skillful that, on one occasion, he showed up at a family reunion on her dad's side of the family, having been invited by Jenny's cousin with whom he had struck up a friendship. Her trips to the mall were marred by Mark's sudden appearance. Her weekly dance lessons were punctuated by his arrival, cunningly timed just a few minutes before I arrived to pick her up. The boys who expressed an interest in her were quickly squelched by a visit from Mark, who curtly told them, "She's my girl; leave her alone."

As Jenny grew more distant, he became more desperate. I realize now that he might have sat in the dark and watched our house at night. One night we decided on the spur of the moment to walk up the block for an ice cream cone. Outside our door, I noticed movement behind parked cars. Greg investigated and discovered Mark and his friend crouching behind the cars, watching our house. Another night, at midnight, I heard noises at Jenny's second-floor window. She and I looked out to see Mark standing below, throwing rocks at her window, yelling "Jenny, Jenny."

By August 1986, Jenny had had enough. Triumphantly, she called me at work one day and announced that she "had done it, really broken it off with Mark." She sounded happy, excited, relieved to be free. School would be starting in a few weeks, and Mark would not be there (he had graduated the previous spring). I never saw Mark Smith again. I thought he had gone away. The phone calls stopped. There were no more visits.

From Jenny's perspective, however, he never did go away. He just became more deceitful. She discovered that he was entering the school grounds and breaking into her locker, the same locker they had shared the year before. He would go through her things and read the notes her friends had written. She began to suspect that he was entering our home when we were gone; she told her friends that things in her room were often not as she had left them. Mark's picture, which she had put away in a drawer, kept reappearing on top of her TV. He left her threatening notes that hinted she "would not make it to homecoming" and desperate lines that said "I wish you would die." She told her friends about these things and even laughed the day of the homecoming parade, saying, "Well, I'm still in one piece." She never told me.

Friday, September 26, 1986, I woke Jenny to get her into the shower before I left for work. I hugged her and kissed her before leaving, as I always did. That morning I said "I love you, Jen," something I didn't always do. And she replied, "I love you too, Mom." We spoke briefly about the homecoming game that evening, and she asked if I could drive her to the dance or if she should ride with her friends. Then I rushed out the door. My day was uneventful. I was bored and had many things to do at home. I thought about asking my boss if I could leave work early, but I resisted the urge. I left work at my usual time and drove home thinking about the busy night ahead.

When I drove onto my street the first thing I saw were groups of neighbors standing in their yards, looking toward my house. Then I saw the ambulance, the police cars, the fire truck. I saw police officers running out of my house. I started shaking so violently that I could barely park my car. I ran out, shouting, "What is happening here?" I was stopped from entering my home and told that my daughter had been stabbed, but that "the paramedics are working on her." I watched as they carried her out on a stretcher and took her away in an ambulance. I hung onto a white and shaken Greg as he described walking into the house and finding Jenny "lying in a pool of blood." I sat in the hospital emergency room and heard them tell me that my daughter was deceased. Dead? Not Jenny. I just talked to her this morning. She is only fifteen. How can she be dead?

The days became a blur. Mark was arrested. He was tried and convicted of first-degree murder. At his trial, I learned the truth of my daughter's last months. I learned of the pressure he had put on her and his threats. I learned of the deception he forced her to participate in. I heard fourteen-year-old children describe their attempts to handle a situation adults could not handle. I saw the fear and guilt of her friends as they grappled with the thought that they could have saved her if only they had told someone what was going on. I learned that Mark had abused Jenny, slapping her and roughing her up frequently. I heard the kids say that it happens all the time at school, boyfriends hitting girlfriends, so they didn't think anything of it. I listened to a recreation of the last moments of her life: how she got off the school bus and entered our home alone to find Mark waiting for her, and how he stabbed her over sixty times with a seven-inch butcher knife, leaving her on the living room floor to be found by Greg, who came in from work carrying our one-year-old son. I heard the account of Mark's evening: how he had attended the homecoming football game with a date and how he laughed and ate and appeared very unconcerned that Jenny was dead.

Something rose up in me. Perhaps it started when I returned to work after her funeral. I realized that people expected me to carry on as if nothing had happened. They acknowledged my grief, but refused to mention the way my daughter died! I haunted the library, looking for books on the subject of teen dating violence. I remembered hearing a story, almost twenty years ago, of a young man shooting his girlfriend. Then I read of the Jennifer Levin murder in New

York City. Can it be that this is happening all over, and no one is saying anything about it? Why hadn't other mothers spoken out, tried to warn me or warn Jenny of the danger?

My involvement began slowly. I read what I could find on the subject and talked to a lot of teens. My first speech was to a church youth group, a small gathering of teens who were laughing and kidding and poking each other. As I stood at the back of the room before I was introduced, I was terrified, thinking I would never hold their attention. I started out my talk by playing a portion of the song, "The Greatest Love of All." The words are about learning how to love oneself, finding self respect. As the song had recently been popular, the kids started swaying to the music and mouthing the words. Then I turned off the player and said, "I chose that song to play for you today because of the message of the words. I also chose that song to play six months ago at the funeral of my daughter, Jenny." Total silence! For the duration of my talk, not a soul moved. As I looked at the audience I could pick out who in that crowd was being abused by her boyfriend. I saw the looks that passed between friends. I saw the down-cast eyes as I described Mark's behavior. Three years and hundreds of speeches later, I still see those things. I can pick out the ones whose lives I am describing.

On Jenny's sixteenth birthday, in an attempt to find some comfort in our grief, Greg and I attended a Parents of Murdered Children Conference. There I met two hundred parents who suffered as we did. In a group of parents who had lost a child to a boyfriend or spouse, I met Ellen Kessner, a writer who had also lost a child by murder. She asked me if she could write Jenny's story for publication. The *Redbook* article that followed (March 1988) educated thousands of parents nationwide. Suddenly teen dating violence became a household word. I was invited to appear on many TV shows. In our community, schools began including the subject in their curriculum.

Jenny is gone, a reality I must live with every day. Sometimes the grief is so overpowering that it seems I cannot survive it. But Jenny has touched so many. Her story has alerted parents and teens to the dangers of abusive relationships. She has saved many lives. And so I am able to say that she did not die in vain, that there was some purpose to her short life. It brings comfort, and it helps me go on. I'll never forget Jen. I miss her so much. I'll always love her.

Marigold Best and Pamela Hussey

Rufina Amaya:
Survivor of El Mozote

In El Salvador, 2 percent of the population owns 60 percent of the land. More than half the population lives in deep poverty, unable to meet even their basic food and health care needs. Nearly half of all children suffer from malnutrition. Starting in 1980, civil war broke out between the government and the disenfranchised poor. In twelve years of conflict, more than seventy-five thousand people died, most of them civilians murdered by government forces and death squads. More than a million Salvadoreans took refuge outside the country, returning home only in 1992 when the war officially ended. However, when this interview was conducted (1994), the lot of workers and farmers had not improved; indeed, it has continued to deteriorate since the peace agreement.

The testimony of Rufina Amaya, sole survivor of the massacre of an entire village by the military, reflects her understanding of the role of women in creating peace and community.

As You Read, Ask Yourself . . .

What is Rufina Amaya's vision of women's rights?

How does this vision mesh with her spiritual and religious beliefs?

What are the methods of organization and activism used in Amaya's community?

What message does Rufina Amaya have for women in other societies than her own?

*W*e *set out early one morning for Ciudad Segundo Montes (Segundo Montes City) in Morazán, which took its name in memory of one of the six Jesuits murdered in November 1989. It was repopulated in 1989 by 8,600 people who returned from the Colomoncagua refugee camp in Honduras, where they had spent nine years. An extraordinary degree of organization and production had been achieved in Colomoncagua—Father Segundo Montes, reporting on his first visit there, said it had turned upside down all his theories on development—and this was transported back to the barren and deserted fields and hills of Morazán, where the returned refugees began the difficult task of resettling and making a living in a country still at war.*

Rufina Amaya was the only survivor of the massacre by the military of the whole population of the village of El Mozote in 1981. The 1993 report of the Truth Commission set up under the terms of the peace accords, describes the event thus:

> *On December 10, 1981, in the hamlet of El Mozote, department of Morazán, all the men, women and children who were in that place were taken unresistingly by units of the At-lacatl battalion. After spending the night shut up in the houses, on the following day, December 11, they were deliberately and systematically executed, by groups. First the men were tortured and executed, then the women were executed, and finally the children, in the places where they were shut up. The number of identified victims exceeded 200. The figure increases if the unidentified victims are taken into account.*

The entire edition of The New Yorker *of December 6, 1993, was devoted to an article by Mark Danner, "The Massacre at El Mozote." It describes the meeting with Rufina of some members of the Argentine team investigating the slaughter:*

> *At the black road, the Argentines turned left, as they did each evening, heading down to Gotera, but this time they stopped in front of a small house—a hut, really, made of scrap wood and sheet metal and set among banana trees some 15 yards from the road. Getting out of the car, they climbed through the barbed wire and called out, and soon there appeared at the door a middle-aged woman, heavyset, with high cheekbones, strong features, and a powerful air of dignity.*

When the Argentines told her of the skulls they had found that day—25 of them, all but two the skulls of children—Rufina said: "Didn't I tell you? All you could hear was that enormous screaming.'"

Rufina got away to the refugee camp in Colomoncagua, Honduras, and now lives in Ciudad Segundo Montes. We sat with her in her hut and heard her reflections on life after the war, while her small daughter carefully brushed and braided her mother's hair.

RUFINA AMAYA: At this moment we women need to have spiritual and moral strength to face up to all the problems of our situation in every country. Because this is happening in all countries: women have always been devalued in every aspect and that is not right. As women we have to recover our values, our rights and our dignity in order to be equal to men, to have the same strength, and for men to recognize that. We are all human and we all have to be equal. God did not make some of us more and some of us less. Here, we women in the church are always working with women's groups, which we call Congregations of Christian Mothers for Peace, on behalf of the pastoral team of Morazán and also of San Salvador. And this makes us think and reflect on some Bible readings where it is clear that women were the bravest. They went to look in the tomb. They were brave enough to go there when the men did not have enough courage. So why should we stand by and see women's human rights being violated in all sorts of ways?

Now that we women have managed to speak out a little bit about the role of women, we think that what the constitutions of El Salvador and other countries say about women having equal rights is real. We don't mean that we ought to have more than the men, no, never, but we ought to have a dialogue. The first thing for us in defending our rights is to know how to defend them and how to respect them. Because, if we can defend our rights through dialogue, we won't fight, we'll begin to talk, to reflect as women and with our husbands, what will be the best future for our children, for our family.

The truth is that the best health, the best life, the best future is to live in peace with our family. If we can begin to overcome the problems in the home and live together as a Christian family, then we'll be able to live together as a community and give our children a Christian education which serves as an example. The Catholic church recognizes that men have been valued above women. The church's concern is that there should be love for all. This God we truly love and who loves us all should be a light for a family and for a people. If we don't really believe that we are all human beings and have that living faith in our hearts, perhaps we won't be able to live in peace. Because peace will come when we all realize that we are brothers and sisters, children of the same God.

The Word of God which we take into our hearts, the living faith in God, is the greatest treasure we can have. No one can take that away and, really, that is what is needed in our people. Some of us believe, others don't. Some think only of power and money and whoever has them gives the orders. And that is a mistake—to feel that if he's got money then he has a lot of power and wants to be greater than God. There is nobody greater than God. The big mistake people make is about money. If someone has enough money he no longer cares if his brother or sister is in the street or another brother or sister has fallen down, he doesn't help him up. Why? Because he has what he needs to live and the life of others doesn't matter to him. And the important thing is to love your brother or sister as yourself. That is the commandment of the Word of God. We may have everything, but if we don't see our brother or sister, we are losing the best thing.

It is pitiful to see that a country like yours which is so rich and developed still has people living on the streets with nowhere to sleep. It is painful because in a developed country the responsibility lies with the government to look after the people, if the government is humane. El Salvador is not a developed country, it is a poor country. But economic resources have been badly used. That's why there is so much poverty and that's what caused the war, because there has been bad distribution of the riches of the country. El Salvador could produce enough for everyone, but the distribution has been manipulated by the rich.

PAMELA: Do you think the Salvadoran people feel deceived because things have not changed much since the end of the conflict?

RUFINA: There is a lot of concern. For the majority of the poor the concern is to see changes after so much suffering—yet we are pretty much the same as before. Government policy has hardly changed, nor has the economic situation. There are poor people still living in places where it is really not possible to live. We have come out of a war and so much suffering and loss of loved ones and we see that we still cannot have a true and just peace in our country because the accords which were made are not complied with. The demand of all the citizens of El Salvador now is that the accords be fulfilled so that peace will last.

MARIGOLD: Can you tell us more about the organization of women?

RUFINA: In Segundo Montes the organization of women is quite strong. There are two groupings: the Congregations of Mothers for Peace and the Association of Women, although it is often the same women in both. The Congregations are purely Christian. We have monthly assemblies, sometimes of 60 to 80 women. When we get out good advance publicity we get more.

PAMELA: Is awareness of women's rights growing?

RUFINA: Yes. We've always explained our rights to the large number of women who come to the Congregations of Mothers and in our pastoral work. Many women are beginning to understand and to demand that their dignity be respected, because if we don't talk about the rights of women and the dignity of women, we ourselves are violating women's rights.

MARIGOLD: Can everyone here in Segundo Montes earn a living?

RUFINA: No. Only a few have jobs. The majority are wondering how to live, with their little plots, growing a few basic things. Some go outside the community to work as laborers, for example, because there are not enough jobs in Segundo Montes.

My job is social work. It has no salary. We live with a little allowance that they give as an encouragement—not a salary, just a minimum for expenses such as transport and an occasional meal. But it is not a salary like the other workers get. My commitment has always been to God. In Honduras I organized the Congregation of Mothers, and my commitment has always been to the Word of God. I can't stop that just because they don't give me a salary, and while I can I shall keep up the effort to work with the mothers.

MARIGOLD: Have you any hope for the future?

RUFINA: Yes, my hope is that now that we are here in peace, the country will remain at peace. We have faith and hope that we shall live better, even if it is only that minimum of us who are working. And I have hope for the future of my daughter too, God willing, if we have peace.

PAMELA: Have you any message for us to take home with us?

RUFINA: The message I would give to the women of your country is to tell them to carry on, to recover their rights as human beings, that the rights of all human beings are equal. Men must understand that we all have the same rights and the same duties in all countries. We must struggle for respect for the rights and dignity of women, but if we want our rights respected, we ourselves must respect the rights of others. That is how one builds, by respecting and loving and by being respected and loved. That is what is needed at this moment in order for us to become examples among our people and not stay with our arms crossed.

We have to study, we have to read the Bible and look for what spaces are available for women in the Bible, beginning above all with our mother, the most holy Mary. She was the mother of Christ. What were the steps Mary took on behalf of her son? She was a committed woman, who saw her son and who struggled, and she too was converted. We women must keep that as an example so that we can convert ourselves like Mary. She didn't betray Jesus, she didn't betray God. We too must be a fortress because we are human beings and although we are weak, God will help us in our weakness and protect us. That is what I would say.

Margaret Hooks in conversation with "Manuela"

Widows Fight for Dignity and Unity

The indigenous (Mayan Indian) people of Guatemala are the majority of the population, but they have been kept impoverished and silenced by some of the ladino *(European-descent) minority. Guatemalan indigenous women have struggled against tremendous odds—lack of literacy, inability to speak the language of the power elite, and the need to focus on basic economic survival. Moreover, their country has been engaged in a protracted civil war and military dictatorship.*

Despite these odds, indigenous Guatemalan women have formed a nascent women's movement within the past two decades and are becoming increasingly visible as leaders. One of the most influential of their political action groups is CONAVIGUA, the National Coordinating Committee of Guatemalan Widows, which was founded in 1988. The women of CONAVIGUA, whose husbands were murdered by the Guatemalan Army, are transforming the grief and rage of their personal tragedies into political activism.

The speaker in this interview (conducted by Margaret Hooks) is Manuela, a Cakchiquel Indian woman who is a member of CONAVIGUA's executive committee. She is in her early thirties and has two young children. Her husband was "disappeared" in 1985.

As You Read, Ask Yourself...

How was Manuela able to obtain an education?

How was her family affected by the war?

What are CONAVIGUA's goals as expressed by Manuela?

What are the methods of organization and activism used in CONAVIGUA?

When I was seven years old I started work so that I'd be able to go to primary school. I earned five cents a day looking after little children. A school note book cost three cents at the time, so I was able to afford it. Then our parish priest noticed that I got on well with people and invited me to take part in the Christian courses he gave. I learned that God wants peace for his people, that He doesn't want you to think only of yourself, but to take into account the situation of others. I began to understand a lot of things.

When I was about 18 I was the leader of a youth group. After the earthquake, when many houses collapsed and many people died, we got together with lots of other groups. Little by little I became involved in organizing cooperatives and Christian groups. One of these was a group seeking to build a local hospital to benefit the whole community. While working on this project I obtained a scholarship to do a nursing course in Cobán. However, some people who were collaborating with the army didn't believe that I was leaving to study. They thought I had gone to join the guerrillas. This caused a lot of problems. In 1980 the army started looking for me and my situation became difficult. Still, with my parents' encouragement I carried on with my work. Then the army took over the village and built a military base. They started picking up a lot of the community leaders—catechists, cooperatives and youth group leaders. So I had to leave my village and go to the capital.

At the end of 1982, I heard that the army had gone to my home, and when they couldn't find me or my brothers and sisters they took my father away. He was 58 at the time, and involved only in church work. This upset me deeply because he'd never done anybody any wrong.

Eight days later, the army raided the house again and took away my sister. During the raid, the army officer told my mother not to worry about my father any more because he was "at peace." "Be content," he said, "he's not in pain any more. He didn't suffer much."

WIDOWHOOD

I met my husband here in the city, through my work. He was also a leader, a *campesino* leader. We were in the same situation, we had both had to leave our villages and come to the capital. I was very lonely at the time, I'd broken off all communication with my family, for their safety and mine. He was company for me, and I felt a little bit safer. At least the affection I no longer had from my family, I now felt with him. But we were only together for two years. I don't really know what happened to him. On May 24, 1985 he left for work and he never came back, so he is "disappeared." At the end of 1987, I was told he was being held at the Chimaltenango military base, but I was too afraid to do anything. I knew that it was the army that had taken him, but I was frightened because so many people have been abducted who never reappear. I can't really believe that he could still be alive, although I still hope that he is and that one day he'll come back. But I know the reality of my country.

I have two children, one is five years old and the other is six. As they are still very small I've never properly explained to them about their father. The older boy knows. He was only two at the time, but he went everywhere with his father and he can't get it out of his mind: "My daddy left me, all of a sudden he went away." Through [overhearing] my conversations with other women he has come to realize that his father is "disappeared." I've told him that I don't know if he will come back or not. "Who has got him? What happened?," he asks. I tell him that I simply don't know. Now the children fear that we won't be able to stay together. "Daddy went away without telling us where," they say. "He 'disappeared,' so might you." This is the lot of the woman whose husband is "disappeared." Thousands of us suffer in this way. Nevertheless, our suffering has helped us to understand our social situation and it encourages us to be more active in changing it. We know that if women don't do something, this killing is never going to end.

317

MARGARET HOOKS
IN CONVERSATION
WITH "MANUELA"
Widows Fight for
Dignity and Unity

LEARNING TO DEFEND OURSELVES

I became involved in CONAVIGUA when I was invited to attend one of its meetings. Like many women, as I became conscious of our situation I gradually lost my fear. The truth is that people are traumatized by all these "disappearances," by so much suffering and waiting. It took me nearly two years to shake off my trauma and to see our other needs: poverty, unemployment, and lack of food for the children. So many widows have these problems.

Now I am working full time for CONAVIGUA. As the organization grows, a great deal of time and effort is required. Especially since only a few of us can read and write, so we have to contribute more.

More than 5,000 women belong to CONAVIGUA. Virtually all of us are Indians and we suffer enormous discrimination. The Indian woman is usually the one who retains most vestiges of Mayan culture, evident in her clothing and in the way she speaks. Her Spanish is not so good and she cannot express herself well, so she is the one who suffers more.

CONAVIGUA's biggest problem at the moment is that we don't have the funds for training, in literacy for example. One of our principal goals is for women to gain the skills necessary for us to be integrated into the social and political life of the country. For hundreds of years, Indian women have hardly participated at all because we have been dominated by men. A lack of education has also limited our integration into society. Because of poverty we have been brought up to work, rather than to go to school. As soon as we were able we had to learn how to weave, to clean the house, to take the animals to pasture and to look for work in the countryside. We have been very isolated within our communities. But now we want indigenous women to become part of society and to participate in its development.

There are ignorant and macho men in the villages who say that women have no right to get organized because we are only women. They look upon women solely as objects. When women start to get involved and go to meetings we have been able to defend ourselves against sexual abuse, and that's what a lot of men don't like. Many *compañeros,* however, are aware of the situation—mainly catechists and community leaders who are interested in the development of the community—and they support the work of CONAVIGUA. They know that it is the most important vehicle of expression for indigenous women.

HOW WE ORGANIZE

CONAVIGUA committees are formed at various levels: hamlet, village, town and department. There is no restriction on age. Everything depends on the women's willingness and desire to defend herself. Our main objective is to defend our rights and dignity, and also to achieve unity among women—especially among widows. Being organized is the only way women can demand our rights. It is the only way our voice can be heard. Nobody takes any notice of you on an individual basis.

Our meetings are generally for women only. Although, when we are in meetings with men—in union meetings, for example, where men are the majority—we don't feel inferior, or cheated. We always give our opinions wherever we can.

Many of our committees have been harassed by the army and women have had their lives threatened, because the military doesn't want us to be organized. Because we are widows, we are at the heart of this country's suffering. The army sees us as an enormous scar left behind by all the violence.

There are more than 45,000 widows in Guatemala and the military is afraid of what might happen if we were all to become organized. From our point of view, they are the ones responsible for there being so many widows. Although big landowners are also to blame, because many Indian women's husbands became ill and died due to overwork on the *fincas*. Nonetheless, the vast majority of the women in CONAVIGUA are widows as a result of the violence.

We are now beginning to communicate with a group of *ladina* women here in the city. We are aware that poverty affects them equally. It is the system that has divided us. We know that *ladina* women are also discriminated against, especially those in the squatter settlements, and we want to strengthen our contact with them. Indian women, however, are more vulnerable to discrimination. In the countryside the military have no respect for us. Not only are we subjected to sexual abuse, but we are also obliged to cook the soldiers' food and wash their clothes. There have also been a lot of rapes and many young girls and older women have become pregnant as a result. For widows, this has meant more children without a father. Some women have been raped by the same soldiers who killed their husbands! Because of their situation many of these women opted for abortion. A lot have had the children but then given them away . . .

This was most common between 1981 and '82, when women had to go to the military bases and work for the soldiers. Matters began to change when the first women's groups formed and women decided that there needed to be an organization that would defend them—especially the widows, who were most subject to abuse since they didn't have husbands to protect them. It was only when the military started to force married women to work for them and their husbands objected, that the men of the community started to support the widows.

ORGANIZATION IS THE ONLY WAY

Through CONAVIGUA we hope that we women will learn to stand up for ourselves, to improve ourselves and to create a better future for our children. We don't want to leave them with the legacy of the past. Many children were witness to the massacres and saw the deaths of their fathers and mothers. Many lost both parents.

The least we hope to achieve is for women to realize that their participation is worthwhile. In CONAVIGUA we have learned to care for each other and to understand our suffering. Before, women didn't talk about our suffering. We were closed up inside ourselves and our homes, and we didn't want to know about what had happened to anyone else. Now we have learnt to share our experiences and suffering, and as a result we have come to understand each other and our particular problem as widows better. For example, I talk to the other women in the organization about feeling a need for affection. I feel this most when my children ask me where their daddy is and when he is coming back. It is not so much the need for a man, that's the least of it, but there are times when you feel lonely, when you need someone to talk to . . .

Although I have fears for my children because of my work, I feel that I have something to contribute to CONAVIGUA and that children should learn about what their mothers go through. They also need to understand that organization is the only way.

319

MARGARET HOOKS
IN CONVERSATION
WITH "MANUELA"
Widows Fight for
Dignity and Unity

Afterword

By now you have read many women's stories. We hope you have discovered that women are not all alike. Their stories differ, depending on so-called objective factors such as sexual orientation, age, ethnicity, and social class circumstances. These are beginning to be explored by social and developmental psychologists (especially those interested in a multicultural perspective). But personal history is also transformed by the meaning of such categories for each woman. Think about what it means to be a lesbian mother, a black intellectual, or an old activist when these labels have contradictory meanings in our society.

How do self-definitions influence a woman's behavior? This question is especially important when the self appears to contradict what the social system says a woman ought to be. How can a woman's sense of self—her individual identity—be represented by psychology? As feminist psychologists, we wrestle to reconcile individual subjectivity and group data. We are especially concerned with the question of the place of the individual's story in psychology.

Although these questions have not yet been answered, we believe that the individual life story contributes to psychology in a number of ways. We will summarize a few ideas we have thought about and invite you to provide some of your own.

First, we believe these stories are important because they can be used to disrupt the idea that psychology has created universal laws of behavior. They suggest that groups of women are no more alike or different than are women and men. They argue that psychology must move beyond its traditional laboratory context if it truly wants to understand human beings. We believe that psychology must also look at how meaning is constructed and conveyed.

The value of these stories does not depend, however, on whether they are "true." All stories, including our own, are both "true" and "untrue" at the same time. They enrich more official histories by filling us in on the conscious meaning of events in women's everyday lives. But, they also show us how a woman's experience of her own life can be changed and reinterpreted depending on later circumstances.

Second, many of these stories tell us about how women change as they come to understand the power of social categorization. Rejecting the categories set out for them in advance, the women who speak in this volume have taken for themselves the "power to name" by claiming the right to describe—and reinterpret—their own experience. Some of them also speak for other girls and women who might not have had a voice without their help. Their stories tell us that naming is a privilege of individuals as well as society and that it is never too late to rename.

Third, these stories tell us that differences among women need not be a source of divisiveness. Telling each other our stories can become a source of community—one that has become lost as society has become more technical and urbanized. We ask you to continue your experiences with this book by asking others around you for their stories. Listen to personal histories from both closely related women such as your mother or grandmothers and women who are very different from yourself.

We hope you have enjoyed these personal histories and feel that you have gotten to know many of the women who have narrated them. A few of these women were famous in their own time and have been forgotten. Others are un-likely to be known by anyone except their relatives and friends. They teach us that every woman does not and cannot deal with her reality in the same way, and they force us to be careful in making judgments about the "best" way to cope. Many of them do, however, suggest that communal strategies may be more useful than individualistic ones.

Finally, these stories help us to ask, Where do we go from here? Stories are important because they validate other women's struggles and because they have important lessons to teach each of us. The future is not necessarily an im-provement on the past, and all change is not necessarily progress. These stories warn us that if we forget our histories we may be doomed to repeat them.

Credits

Part One

p. 5: Laurel Furumoto, Mary Whiton Calkins (1863–1930): Fourteenth president of the American Psychological Association, *Journal of the History of the Behavioral Sciences, 15,* 1979 pp. 346–356. Copyright © 1979. Reprinted by permission of the author.

p. 17: Source: Mary Crawford, from *Ms. Magazine,* August 1981, pp. 86–89. Copyright © 1981. Reprinted by permission of the author.

p. 22: From WOMEN CREATING LIVES: IDENTITIES, RESILIENCE, AND RESISTANCE by CAROL FRANZ and ABIGAIL STEWART. Copyright © 1994 by Westview Press. Reprinted by permission of Westview Press, a member of Perseus Books, L.L.C.

p. 45: Noemi Alindogan-Medina, "Women's Studies: A Struggle for a Better Life," is reprinted by permission of The Feminist Press at The City University of New York from Changing Lives: Life of Asian Pioneers in Women's Studies, edited by the Committee on Women's Studies in Asia (New York: The Feminist Press at The City University of New York, 1995). Copyright © 1994 by Committee on Women's Studies in Asia.

p. 58: "A Question of Class" by Dorothy Allison, from *Skin: Talking About Sex, Class & Literature.* Copyright © 1994 by Dorothy Allison. Reprinted with permission of Firebrand Books, Ithaca, New York.

p. 73: Reprinted with the permission of Simon & Schuster and Phoebe Eng from WARRIOR LESSONS: AN ASIAN AMERICAN WOMAN'S JOURNEY INTO POWER by Phoebe Eng. Copyright © 1999 by Phoebe Eng. All rights reserved.

Part Two

p. 83: From Judith Ortiz Cofer, *From a Latin Deli,* 1993. Reprinted by permission of the University of Georgia Press.

p. 91: "When I Was Growing Up," by Nellie Wong from *This Bridge Called My Back: Writings by Radical Women of Color.* Copyright © 1983 by Cherrie Moraga & Gloria Anzaldua. Used with permission of the author and Kitchen Table: Women of Color Press, P.O. Box 908, Latham, NY 12110.

Part Four

Part Five